Continuous Delivery Pipelines

How to Write Better Software Faster

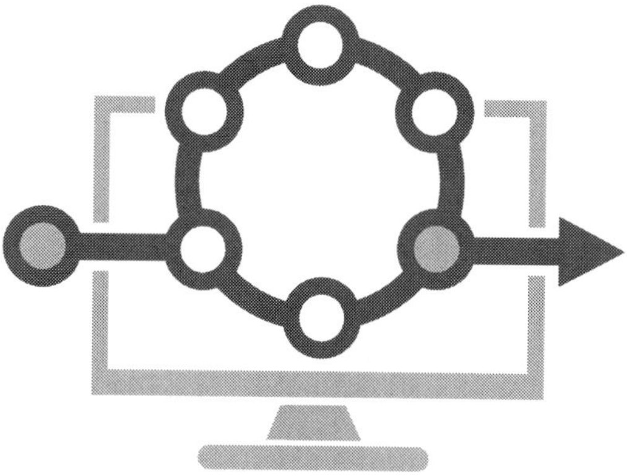

By Dave Farley

Author: Dave Farley

Published 1 February 2021

This book is dedicated to my wife Kate, who helped to create it in both small and big ways.

Contents

Preface

This book is intended as a practical description and guide to the idea of the Continuous Delivery Deployment Pipeline: specifically how to create Deployment Pipelines, what to consider while creating them, and how to use them to their best advantage to support software development.

While writing my book "Continuous Delivery" I coined the term "Deployment Pipeline" to describe the automated practice that supports CD. The CD Deployment Pipeline encompasses all of the steps necessary to create something releasable, and then, finally, to deploy that change into production. The automation of these steps makes this process repeatable and reliable and dramatically more efficient than more conventional approaches.

This book is a guide to help you to get started on your first Deployment Pipeline, or to help you to improve and further develop your existing Pipelines. This book is a close companion to my training course "Anatomy of a Deployment Pipeline" in which we explore the information in this book in some depth.

The first section, "Deployment Pipeline Foundations", describes the principles of Continuous Delivery and Deployment Pipelines in general and how to think about them to best effect. It describes several ideas that underpin the Continuous Delivery approach, and ideas for the basis for the rest of this book. It moves on to describe some practical steps that I believe represent the best approach to getting your Deployment Pipeline started, what to focus on and in what order to create things.

Section two, "Deployment Pipeline Anatomy", describes each of the principal, essential, stages of a Deployment Pipeline in some detail, and offers guidance and advice on the construction of effective implementations of each stage. In this section we also cover several common, though optional, stages that may be worth considering, depending on your business and the nature of your software: looking at ideas like Testing Performance, Security and other "Non-Functional" requirements.

The last section, "Whole Pipeline Considerations" examines some broader, cross-cutting ideas that inform the use and creation of effective Pipeline: looking at ideas like "Infrastructure as Code" and "Continuous Compliance".

This is not intended as a replacement for my other book "Continuous Delivery", which is a much more authoritative exploration of Continuous Delivery in general, and of Deployment Pipelines specifically. Rather, this is a condensed, practical guide to getting an effective Deployment Pipeline up and running.

This book was written in collaboration with my wife, Kate Farley. Kate and I worked on this together, which helped to keep us both a bit more sane, during COVID19 lockdown. Our intent in writing this book is for it to act as a useful practical guide to making changes, it is intended to be short, and to the point.

Part One

Deployment Pipeline Foundations

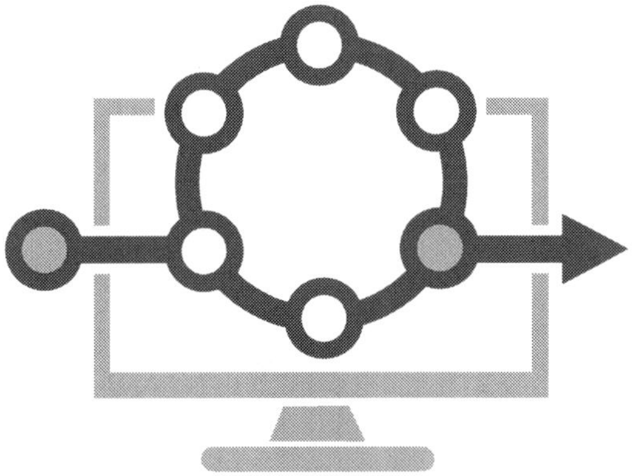

Chapter 1

Introduction to Continuous Delivery

Continuous Delivery emerged in the early 2000s, building on the techniques of Continuous Integration, and was popularised by mine and Jez's award-winning 2010 book "Continuous Delivery: Reliable Software Releases Through Build, Test, and Deployment Automation".

The term **Continuous Delivery** is taken from the first principle of the Agile Manifesto (2001), which states:

> *"Our highest priority is to satisfy the customer through early and continuous delivery of valuable software"*

What is Continuous Delivery?

Continuous Delivery is the best way of developing software that we currently know of. It is the *state of the art* for software development, enabling its practitioners to deliver *Better Software Faster*. Teams that practise Continuous Delivery develop higher quality software, more efficiently, and have more fun while doing so. Businesses that employ Continuous Delivery have better staff retention, are more successful, and make more money.

We have research to back up these claims. Data from "The State of DevOps Reports" quantify the profound impact of Continuous Delivery on the effectiveness and efficiency of software development.

For example:

44% more time spent on new features

50% higher market cap growth over 3 years

8000x faster deployment lead time

50% less time spent fixing security defects

50% lower change-failure rate

21% less time spent on unplanned work and rework

It's little wonder then, that some of the biggest, most successful software businesses on the planet practise Continuous Delivery. Companies like Amazon, Google, Netflix, Tesla, Paypal, and many more.

Continuous Delivery is an holistic approach. Continuous Delivery encompasses all aspects of software development and is an holistic approach, which I define as:

> *"going from idea to valuable, working software in the hands of users."*

Continuous Delivery focuses on optimising the *whole* of that span and is therefore not only a technical discipline: it also requires optimal organisational structure and performance; and, an appropriate culture and ways of working. It includes the ideas of DevOps, collaboration and teamwork - where teams are empowered to make decisions and share responsibility for their code.

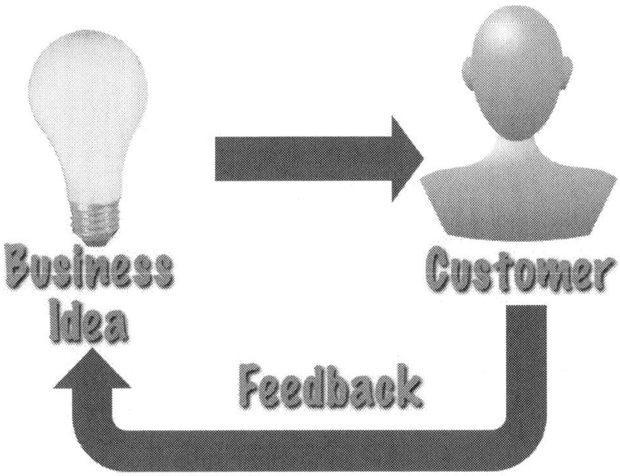

FIGURE 1.1 - IDEA TO WORKING SOFTWARE

Continuous Delivery is achieved by working so that our software is always in a releasable state.

> *Why is this fundamental idea so valuable to the development of quality software?*

This way of working is the antithesis of traditional software development, where whole products, or systems, are developed over weeks and months, often with different elements being written by different teams, and brought together for a major release exercise: only then are defects and integration issues discovered, involving lots of rework, stress, delays, the abandonment of features, and disappointed customers.

Instead, through Continuous Delivery, we work in small steps, testing each tiny piece of new code as we proceed: incrementally building up more comprehensive changes from these many small steps. Our aim is to commit each of these small steps as we make them, committing changes multiple times per day: all the time maintaining our software in a releasable state with each tiny change. This fast, dynamic, creative process means that we can make progress every day, avoid the problems of major releases, and have software that is always in a releasable state.

By working in small steps and making tiny changes frequently, we reduce the risk of complex interactions, compound errors and lengthy delays caused by rework.

There is only one definition of "done" - not partial or proxy measures suggested by other disciplines. The change is complete when it is delivered into the hands of its users.

Continuous Delivery means working iteratively.

The development of quality software involves:

- Analysing the problem, or opportunity
- Designing a solution to the problem
- Writing code and tests
- Deploying software into production
- Getting feedback so we know that the software solves the problem, and meets the customers' requirements

Unlike traditional development methods, in Continuous Delivery we don't have separate processes for: design, development, testing and release. We do these things in parallel, iteratively, all the time.

Continuous Delivery optimises for learning.

Developing software is a creative process, where tools and techniques can be applied with expertise, to realise ideas and create new and better ways of doing things. To learn what works, we must risk failure, and the safest way of doing that is to proceed with small *experiments* where we evaluate ideas and can discriminate between good and bad ideas; good and bad implementation.

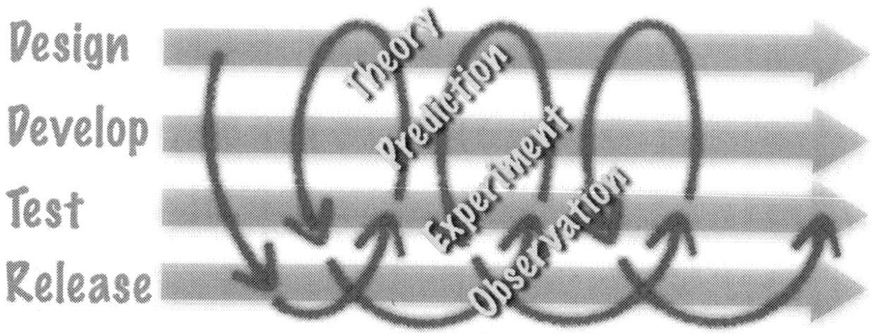

FIGURE 1.2 - FEEDBACK DRIVEN, EXPERIMENTAL PROCESS

Continuous Delivery gets us fast and frequent feedback from our customers and our tests, to enable us to learn and improve. We monitor and measure, and collect data, so that we can make evidence-based decisions. Accurate measurement requires *controlling the variables*, and version control, so our data is reliable and repeatable. We build in feedback loops throughout the software development process, as summarised in this diagram:

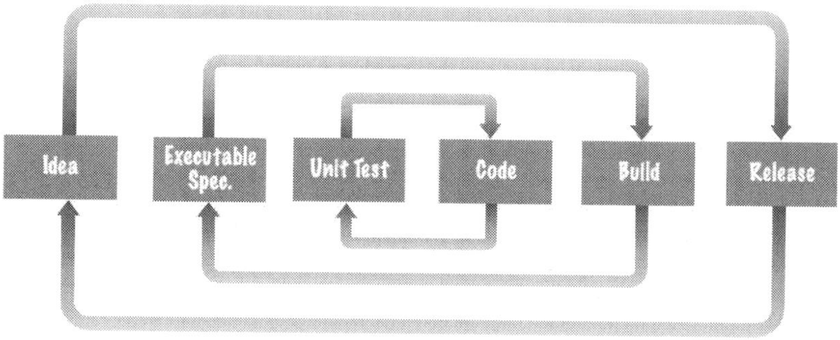

FIGURE 1.3 - COMMON FEEDBACK LOOPS

Continuous Delivery is achieved through automation.
We look for ways to automate everything we can: testing and validating our changes, using computers for what they are good at, i.e repeatability and reliability; and freeing up developers' time to utilise their creative, problem-solving skills.

Continuous Delivery is an engineering discipline.

I define **Software Engineering** as:

> *"the application of an empirical, scientific approach to finding efficient solutions to practical problems in software."*

We *build quality in* through continuous evaluation of our software to give the developer a high level of confidence that their code is good. One passing test, or series of positive tests, is not enough to tell us that our code is good. But just one *failing* test tells us the our code is not good enough. We follow the scientific principle of *falsifiability* and test our code in order to reject it. If one test fails we will reject that **Release Candidate** and revert to the previous version of the system.

We use a **Deployment Pipeline** to organise all steps required to go from *idea to releasable software* and we automate as much of our development process as we can, to ensure that we produce software repeatably and reliably.

A great place to start with Continuous Delivery is to measure the **Lead Time** i.e how long it takes for new code to complete its transit through the Deployment Pipeline. We can then identify opportunities to reduce the Lead Time, and so speed up the delivery of software to customers. *(Chapter 18 includes some advice on "Improving Lead Time".)*

Continuous Delivery is a *Lean* approach.
We aim to get the maximum output for the least amount of work, by applying agile and lean principles.

We use a Deployment Pipeline to organise our development activities efficiently, and focus on reducing the Lead Time by reducing waste, duplication, overheads, handovers, delays, complex organisational structures and anything that is not directly helping to develop quality software.

Continuous Delivery is not a fixed procedure, or set of tools that can be installed and followed. It is an approach for continuous learning: continuous improvement. We can get initial gains quite quickly, by: building a Deployment Pipeline; focusing on reducing Lead Time; and introducing automation and measures. But then we refine and speed up, and experiment and make mistakes, and learn and improve, over time. We make tiny changes to our code: ensuring that it is always in a releasable state.

> *The best Continuous Delivery practitioners release small software changes into production* thousands *of time a day, and measure their Lead Time in* minutes*!*

Three Key Ideas

Continuous Delivery is founded upon three key ideas:

- The reliable, repeatable production of high quality software.
- The application of scientific principles, experimentation, feedback and learning.
- The Deployment Pipeline as a mechanism to organise and automate the development process.

Seven Essential Techniques

To become proficient in Continuous Delivery we must practise the following:

- Reduce the Cycle Time
- Automate Nearly Everything
- Control the Variables
- Work in Small Steps
- Make Evidence-based Decisions
- Work in Small Empowered Teams
- Apply Lean & Agile Principles

The practical application, of these seven techniques, to a Deployment Pipeline, are described throughout this book. If you are not yet familiar with these Continuous Delivery fundamentals, and would like to be more confident in applying them, you can learn and practise Continuous Delivery techniques through my "Better Software Faster" training course[1]. And go on to study the "Anatomy of a Deployment Pipeline" course[2].

1 Find out more about this course here: https://bit.ly/CDBSWF

2 Find out more about this course here: http://bit.ly/anatomyDP

Chapter 2

What is a Deployment Pipeline?

Continuous Delivery is about getting from idea to valuable software in the hands of its users, repeatably and reliably. The **Deployment Pipeline** is a *machine* that helps us do that, by organising our software development work, to go from **Commit** to **Releasable Outcome** as quickly and efficiently as possible, repeatably and reliably.

The idea of the **Deployment Pipeline** was developed on one of the largest agile projects of the day, carried out by software consultancy *ThoughtWorks* in the early 2000s. It was first publicly described in a talk I gave to a GOTO conference in London, and is described in detail in the *"Continuous Delivery"* book I wrote with Jez Humble.

> *But why did we call it a Deployment Pipeline, when it is about so much more than "deployment"?*

Because when we were developing these ideas, I was reminded of 'instruction pipelining' in *intel processors*. This is a parallel processing approach, and a **Deployment Pipeline** is the same thing. In a processor the evaluation of a condition, the outcome if the condition is true, and the outcome if false, are all carried out in parallel. The Deployment Pipeline is organised to achieve something similar: once the fast technical Commit Stage tests have passed, the developer moves on to new work. Meanwhile the Pipeline continues, in parallel, to evaluate the change the developer committed through the Acceptance Stages. So we can gain from doing the slower, Acceptance work, in parallel with new development work. *(I go on to explain how we achieve this later in Part Two of the book.)*

Scope and Purpose

In the Deployment Pipeline we control the variables, version control our code and systems, and organise our experiments, tests, feedback and release into production. When new code has completed its transit through the Deployment Pipeline, there is no more work to do and the software can be safely released into Production.

The Deployment Pipeline defines releasability and is the only route to production. It therefore includes any and all steps that are necessary for new software to be releasable, i.e: all unit tests, acceptance tests, validation, integration, version control, sign-offs and any other tests or requirements to achieve releasability. When the work of the Deployment Pipeline is complete, we will know that the software is sufficiently fast, scalable, secure, and resilient, and does what our users want it to do.

The objectives of the Deployment Pipeline are to:

- Discard Release Candidates on any failing test, and so reject changes that are not fit for production.
- Carry out all necessary testing on all Release Candidates, so that there is no more work to do.
- Complete this cycle multiple times a day, so that we gain timely, valuable insight into the quality of our work.
- Generate a Releasable Outcome on successful completion, so that our software is ready to be delivered into the hands of its users.

The correct scope of a Deployment Pipeline is an independently deployable unit and therefore could be:

- an individual microservice
- a whole system
- a module, or sub-System (maybe)

We should not be building a separate Pipeline for each team, or architectural layer, or separate Pipelines for the build, test and deploy steps in our process.

The Deployment Pipeline is NOT:

- only an automated build, test and deploy workflow
- a series of separate Pipelines for build, test and deployment
- just a collection of tools and processes
- for proving that new software is good

A Deployment Pipeline is a falsification mechanism, where we can fix, and learn from, failed tests quickly. It is not a tool to prove that our software is good. Rather, it is a mechanism based on the scientific principle of challenging our hypotheses, i.e: testing new code to see if it fails. Even if just one test fails, we know our code is not good enough and is therefore not fit for production.

The Deployment Pipeline optimises our ability to go from Commit to Releasable Outcome as quickly as possible, without taking unnecessary risks. We aim for a balance between our desire for instant feedback, and the need for comprehensive, definitive results. Our aim is for fast feedback, multiple times-per-day, and a high level of confidence that we can safely release our changes. These ideas are somewhat in tension, fast feedback vs high levels of confidence, and so we must optimise for both to hit the 'sweet-spot'.

The Deployment Pipeline is organised to carry out fast, technical testing first. This provides early, quality feedback and a high level of confidence that this code is *releasable*, before we move onto acceptance and other tests. These may take more time, and can be run in parallel with developers starting new work - as long as the developers keep their eyes on their changes to ensure that their code passes through the remainder of the Pipeline safely.

The Deployment Pipeline is a platform where we can test ideas and make changes safely. The Pipeline enables the collection of test results, and produces data about Lead-Time, Stability and Throughput, which can all be used to make evidence-based decisions.

The Deployment Pipeline supports development teams in producing high-quality software, and requires their commitment to this *scientific* way of thinking and adoption of these effective behaviours, in order to realise the considerable benefits of Continuous Delivery.

Key Stages of a Deployment Pipeline

The *simplest* version of a Deployment Pipeline includes these four stages:

1. **Commit Stage** - Developers commit new code and undertake fast, lightweight, technical tests to get fast feedback (aim for < 5mins) and a high level of confidence that the code does what they think it should.
2. **Artifact Repository** - A successful output from the Commit Stage is a Release Candidate that is saved (and version controlled) in the Artifact Repository.

3. **Acceptance Test Stage** - User-centred testing of Release Candidates: in life-like scenarios and a production-like environment, to evaluate the code from the users' perspective.
4. **Ability to Deploy into Production** - If a Release Candidate successfully passes all steps of the Deployment Pipeline we are ready, confident, to deploy it.

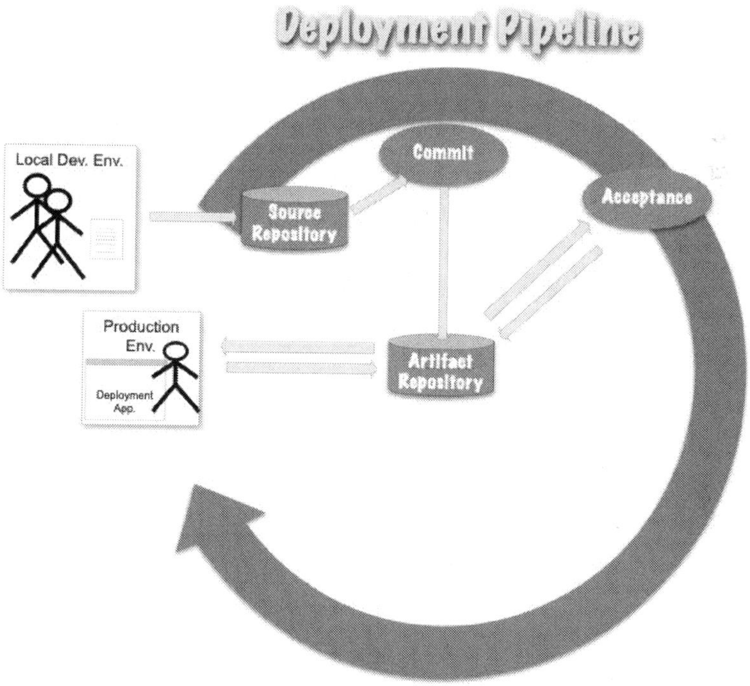

FIGURE 2.1 - SIMPLE DEPLOYMENT PIPELINE

Key Practices for a Deployment Pipeline

Version Control

Our aim is to ensure that every bit and byte that we deploy into production is the one that we intend. So we will take Version Control very seriously and apply it to everything: code, dependencies, configuration, infrastructure - EVERYTHING!

Automation

We automate everything we can in the Deployment Pipeline so that development activities are repeatable, reliable and carried out efficiently, often in parallel, with consistent results.

Automation is not just for the code and the tests. Automation should extend to: the build and deployment infrastructure; monitoring and measurement of the software and how it is developed; and, data and data structures, too.

Testing

We include in the Deployment Pipeline, any and all tests that are necessary to determine the **releasability** of our software. This includes:

- Fast, technical Commit Stage tests
- In-depth Acceptance Tests
- Other tests e.g: Performance, Scalability, Resilience, Security, etc.

Test Driven Development (TDD) - Writing tests first, before we write the code, makes the development process overall more efficient, and faster, because we spend less time fixing bugs. TDD encourages good design. We build quality in by testing throughout the software development process to identify, and remedy, any problems early.

Manual Testing - Manual testing is costly, low quality, and not a good use of human creative skills when used for regression testing. In Continuous Delivery, we eliminate manual regression testing. Manual testing, though, is useful for exploratory tests and to assess the usability of our software from the perspective of an external user.

(We expand further on TDD, Automation and Version Control in Chapters 4 - 6.)

Working Efficiently

A goal of the Deployment Pipeline is to go from Commit to Releasable Outcome several times per day.

To achieve this short Lead Time means working efficiently and removing waste from the software development process. We include only the *essential* steps necessary to release software into production, and carry out each necessary step only *once.*

By getting fast feedback from unit tests, the developer can move onto other work when the tests have passed, and work in parallel with further evaluations, like acceptance tests.

By completing the whole cycle in an hour, or less, we gain several chances to find, and fix any problems that we find, within the same day. This means that we have a much better chance of keeping all of our tests passing, and keeping our software in a releasable state, and that means that we can deliver new software quickly.

Small, Autonomous Teams

Continuous Delivery teams work collaboratively, sharing responsibility for their development process. They do not divide up the responsibilities for designing code, writing code, testing code and deploying systems into production, and they do not 'throw changes over a wall' to the next person in the process.

Instead, these tasks, and responsibilities, are shared by the whole team, who support one another with the skills that they have. This is sometimes referred to as "DevOps", and we see it as an essential component of our ability to deliver continuously.

To achieve this, the team will need to be multi-skilled, autonomous, empowered and small. Small teams are more efficient and productive in a creative, experimental, learning work environment: communications can flow more easily, and they can move and adapt more quickly.

The Deployment Pipeline empowers the development team by giving them the visibility and control necessary to produce high-quality code that they can be proud of.

A Lean Machine

The Deployment Pipeline applies scientifically rational, engineering principles, and a *Lean* approach to software development.

At its simplest, producing software entails only four things:

- Requirements
- Code
- Testing
- Deployment

By including ALL of these into the Deployment Pipeline, we can optimise for efficiency and utilise the Deployment Pipeline to realise our core Continuous Delivery practices, i.e:

- The Pipeline produces data and enables the measurement of test results, Lead Time, Stability and Throughput, which we can use to make evidence-based decisions.
- Focussing on Lead Time, and getting efficient feedback, allows us to deliver fast.
- We build quality in by testing throughout the process to identify and remedy any problems early.
- We eliminate waste by including only the essential steps necessary to release software into production, and by doing each step only once.
- We optimise for the whole system, by including any and all tests and steps in the Pipeline that are necessary for the software to be releasable. At that point there is no more work to do.
- We amplify learning by getting measurable feedback on every change we make.
- We empower the team by giving them the visibility and control necessary so that they can be responsible for the design, quality, testing and deployment of their code.

Conclusion

The Deployment Pipeline is the ONLY route to production: all new code, and all changes to existing code, will be tested, audited, traced and recorded through the Pipeline.

> *Imagine building, from scratch, a comprehensive Deployment Pipeline that includes EVERYTHING needed for for some future vision of our system!*

But that is not where we start. The next chapter describes how we start to build a Deployment Pipeline - simply, iteratively, in small steps.

Chapter 3

How to Build a Deployment Pipeline

This chapter comprises a **step-by-step** guide to putting together a Deployment Pipeline. This approach is recommended for:

- people/organisations that have plenty of experience and want to improve the speed and efficiency of their Deployment Pipelines,
- people/organisations who have never built, or used, a Deployment Pipeline before,
- use as a checklist, to review an existing Deployment Pipeline and identify any gaps, or challenges, which the advice in later chapters may help to address.

We do not start to build a Deployment Pipeline by working out a complex plan to build all the steps, tests and processes necessary for some future vision of the complete system. We follow the principles of Continuous Delivery: working iteratively, in small steps.

Initially we just need the four essential components of the Deployment Pipeline:

1. Commit Stage
2. Artifact Repository
3. Acceptance Stage, and
4. Ability to Deploy into Production

and we start with a simple use-case.

Getting Started

We start simply: by building, or selecting, a **Walking Skeleton** - a tiny implementation of the system that performs a small end-to-end function, and building just enough Pipeline to support it.

We take a really simple **Use Case**, or story, which involves the bare bones of our system, and implement the Deployment Pipeline for this simple example.

We build this minimum example app, and use its construction to guide the creation of the simplest Deployment Pipeline, that will serve our needs and help us establish how we will work in future - TDD, acceptance tests, auto-deployment - Continuous Delivery!

It is best to start with a team-centred approach to building the Deployment Pipeline, by collectively agreeing the starting case and the tools and techniques to employ. Working as a team, pulls in different ideas and expertise, and ensures that developers understand what is expected of them and how their behaviours impact on colleagues and the rest of the development process.

Imagine a simple system, a Web UI, some Logic and some Storage.

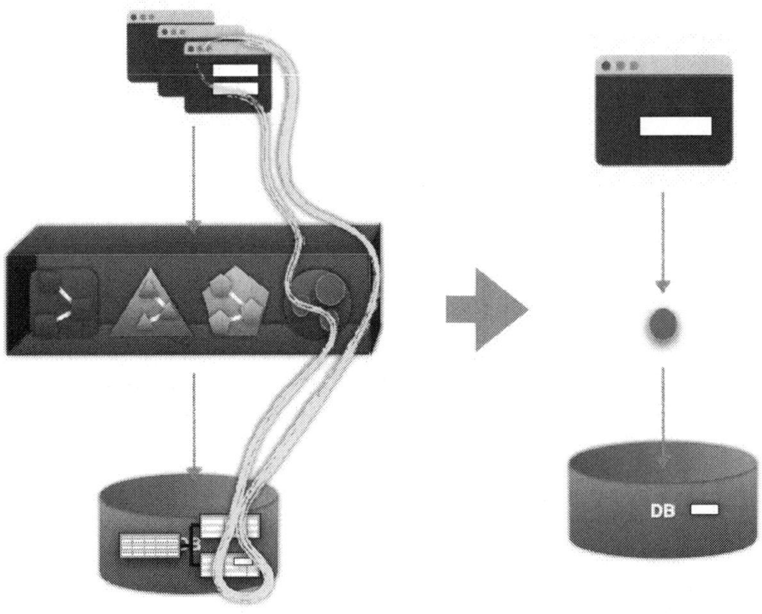

FIGURE 3.1 - 'WALKING SKELETON' EXAMPLE

- Set up the Version Control System (VCS)
- Keep everything in one Repository (for now)
- Decide how to test the UI code (e.g Jasmine, Jest, Cypress, Puppeteer…)
- Write some tests and commit them together with the code.

Create a Commit Stage

Next, we decide how to run the initial fast, technical tests, and establish some simple conventions so that whenever new UI tests are added, they will be found and run.

- Pick a Build Management System
  (e.g: Semaphore, CircleCI, Armoury, Jenkins, TeamCity...)
- Configure the BMS and hook it up to the VCS.
- Get the BMS running the UI tests on every Commit.

Then, we decide how to test the logic. Maybe it will be different tech, so we will pick a testing tool, and establish folder-naming conventions, etc. We will configure the BMS to pick these changes up too, and to run the unit tests for the logic.

Create an Artifact Repository

We select a packaging approach (.Net Assembly, .EXE, Docker Image...) and change the Commit Stage to generate a *deployable thing*. This is our **Release Candidate**

We give each Release Candidate a unique ID - this can be a simple sequence number, or the ID generated by the Artifact Repository.

Change the Commit Stage so that the Release Candidate is stored in an **Artifact Repository** when all tests pass. This doesn't need to be complex - it just needs to be able to identify the newest Release Candidate at this stage (some disk space and a few shell scripts are enough).

Create an Acceptance Stage

We start by writing an **Acceptance Test** that describes the desired behaviour of our system, *before* we write the code. We write these tests as **Executable Specifications** that focus only on WHAT the system/ code should do; and say nothing about HOW it does it.

(There is more advice about writing Acceptance Tests in Chapter 10.)

In order to run the Acceptance Test in the Deployment Pipeline, we need to automate the deployment of the new, simple, app.

- Write some scripts to initialise the database (DB) so it is ready to use by the app: a clean installation from scratch.
- Commit these changes too, to the same repository.
- Automate the configuration of the Acceptance Test environment.
- The DB deploy scripts will form part of the deploy scripts, to get the DB ready for use.

In the BMS, setup a separate process to run the Acceptance Stage, so that every time Acceptance Tests finish, the process checks for a new Release Candidate that has passed all the Commit tests. If no such Candidate is found, check (poll) every few minutes for new work to do. New work for the Acceptance Stage is a new Release Candidate that hasn't run through acceptance yet. This is better than scheduling the acceptance run after every successful Release Candidate, because it avoids creating an ever-growing backlog of work. The Acceptance Stage jumps ahead to the newest Release Candidate on each run.

When the Acceptance Stage finds a new Release Candidate, automate the deployment of the candidate into the Acceptance Test Environment. Deployment should finish when the app is up and running and ready for use - build something simple that can check that. Once the app is ready for use, run the Acceptance Test.

Create simple reports from the BMS, for the results of all tests, that make it obvious when tests pass or fail. Start with simple reports - they can be refined later. Remember, **any test failing, anywhere, means we kill that Release Candidate!**

When the Acceptance Stage finishes, there should be a record of the success, or failure, of the Release Candidate. Set up somewhere to store these results using the Release Candidate ID from the Artifact Repository as a Key - for these results and for any other information collected.

Create a Simple Version of Production

Continuous Delivery means working so that the software is *always in a releasable state*, so that we can decide when and how to deploy into production. **Continuous Deployment** is when we deploy the changes automatically into Production once all steps in the Pipeline have passed.

We need to decide which is the appropriate production release approach for our system - Manual or Automated?

- Write a simple process to seek Release Candidates that have passed all tests.
- Deploy the **newest** Release Candidate.
- Create a simple Web UI for manual releases, **or**
- Create a process (maybe in the BMS) for automated deployments.

We use the same mechanism that was created to deploy Release Candidates into the Acceptance Test Environment, to now deploy the Release Candidate **Into Production.**

We now have a working Deployment Pipeline!

Next Steps

We have put the Source Repository, Artifact Repository and Automated Testing in place. We have established a fake (but life-like) Production Environment to complete the Deployment Pipeline. And we have established some ground rules for how we work as a team.

This may have taken a couple of weeks, and can feel like a lot of work and a significant up-front investment of time, but once up and running, the Deployment Pipeline will accelerate, along with the team's expertise and productivity. And we will begin to reap the benefits of the initial investment.

Now we have the simple Deployment Pipeline in place, the next story will only need more tests and new code!

Over time, we can add more checks and more sophistication to the Deployment Pipeline. One of the important next steps is to automate and version-control the Pipeline, so that we can make changes to it safely and build it up progressively. *(See "Defining Releasability", Chapter 15.)*

We can add other tests and whatever else is necessary to determine the releasability of the code, e.g security, performance, resilience, compliance, data-migration, etc., depending on the nature and complexity of the software being developed. These topics are explored later in Part Two. But first, we will look at three Continuous Delivery practices that are essential to the effective running of a Deployment Pipeline, i.e:

- Test Driven Development
- Automation
- Version Control

Chapter 4

Test Driven Development

Test Driven Development (TDD) is an important idea for Continuous Delivery Deployment Pipelines, because it encourages an iterative way of working, an incremental approach to design, and helps us to write **Better Software Faster.**

What is TDD?

Code is fragile and tiny mistakes (the sort of *off by one*, or *reversed conditionals*, errors that programmers make all the time) can cause major defects, or catastrophic failure in software. Most production failures are caused by these trivial programming errors, which could be readily exposed by simple statement coverage testing. We want to check, early in the development process, whether our code does what we think it should.

TDD is actually more about design than it is about testing - driving the development of software by writing the test before we write the code, which has many benefits for the quality of our code and the efficiency of its production.

TDD is an error detection protocol, which gives us a *dual path verification* that our coding actions match our intent. In some ways this is analogous to the accountancy practice of *double-entry bookkeeping*, in which there are two different types of entry for every financial transaction. In TDD, the **test** describes the behaviour of the code one way; the **code** describes it in another way. They meet when we make an assertion in the test.

TDD is often associated with the mantra - Red, Green, Refactor

First write a test, or *specification*, for the intended behaviour of the code.

> **RED** - Check the test by running it and seeing it fail, *before* writing the code.
>
> **GREEN** - Make the smallest possible changes to the code to get from a failing test to a passing test.
>
> **REFACTOR** - When the test passes, work in small steps to improve the code to make it more general, readable and simpler.

TDD is not about test coverage. We don't try to write lots of tests before starting to code: that is not TDD. Instead we write the simplest test that we can think of, and see it fail. We write just enough code to make it pass and then refactor the code and the test to make them great. Then, we add the next test.

A high level of test coverage is not a useful goal in itself, but may be a side-benefit of a comprehensive approach to TDD. We don't chase coverage: our goal is to drive changes to the code from tests.

TDD is a talent amplifier which improves the skills of the developer and the quality of the code they write. It is worth investing the time and effort to learn these techniques. *(There are many on-line resources to help[3].)*

Test First

Test Driven Development is based on the idea of writing the test *before* writing the code. This may initially seem backwards, but is in fact the best approach, for the following reasons:

- We can test the test, by running it and seeing it fail. If the test passes before we have written the code, we know there's a problem with the test!
- It forces design of the code from the public API, so encourages design-by-contract.
- There is a looser coupling between test and code, so tests are more robust as the code changes, and so are more likely to continue to work.
- It encourages design for testability: testable code has the same properties as high-quality code.
- Overall, the development process is significantly more efficient and faster, because less time is spent on rework and fixing bugs.

The advantages of the **Test First** approach, in terms of the quality, efficiency and cost of production, are such that we must resist the temptation, or any organisational pressure, to 'hurry up' and write the code first! - This is counter-productive.

3 Check out my videos: https://youtu.be/llaUBH5oayw and https://youtu.be/fSvQNG7Rz-8 and the Cyber Dojo site: https://cyber-dojo.org

Test All the Time

TDD is the best way to create the fast, efficient, tests that we can run in minutes as part of the Commit Stage. But it is not limited to unit testing, or to just the Commit Stage, and should be applied *throughout* the Deployment Pipeline.

We carry out technical, unit tests at the Commit Stage. We also carry out other checks to increase our level of confidence in our code - such as tests to assert any coding standards, or to catch common errors. These developer-centred tests check that the code does what the developer expects it to.

We then carry out acceptance testing, from a user perspective. Acceptance tests should be carried out in life-like scenarios and in a production-like environment.

Then we do any and all other tests we need to achieve the releasability of our software. This varies according to the nature and complexity of our software, but can include tests for:

- System and Component Performance
- Resilience
- Scalability
- Security, Compliance, and Regulatory Checks
- Data Migration

Although we try and automate everything, manual testing is good for exploratory testing; testing the usability of the system; or, testing 'crazy cases' to see what might break our code.

When we have feedback that ALL our tests have passed, and we can't think of anything else to test, the Release Candidate has successfully transited through all the stages of the Deployment Pipeline: there is no more work to do, and we are free to release the change into production.

The Impact of Test-First on Design

In Continuous Delivery, we optimise our design and development approach for **testability**. Working to ensure that our code is more *testable* improves the quality of our design.

When we begin with a test, we would be daft if we didn't make it easy to write and capture the intent of the code simply. This means that we apply a gentle pressure on ourselves to make our code easier to test.

The characteristics of testable code are:

- Simple, efficient, and easy to read and maintain
- More modular, more loosely coupled, and with better separation of concerns
- Higher-cohesion and better abstraction
- The code works!

These attributes of testability are also the attributes of high-quality software. Code with these attributes is more flexible, more readable, and more compartmentalised: insulating change in one part of the code from other areas, making it not only easier to change, but also safer to change.

Using 'Testability' to Improve Design

This is an important idea for our ability to engineer better outcomes for our software.

There are few techniques that help us to design better software, but Test Driven Development is one. In fact, TDD is less about testing and much more about good design.

In order to create software that is easily *testable* we need software that we can interact with, and that allows us to capture the results of those interactions, so that we can match them in the assertions in our tests.

If the tests are difficult to set up, this suggests that the code may be too complex and difficult to debug. By driving our development from tests, we are very strongly incentivised, in a practical way, to create **testable code**. As we have described, the properties of *testable code* are also the hallmarks of well-designed software. So TDD helps to steer us towards better, higher-quality, design.

This is significantly as a result of TDD forcing us to apply *Dependency Inversion* so that we can inject test-time components with which we can capture, and fake, those interactions that we want to test.

TDD is about evolving our solutions and designs as a series of small steps and so is fundamental to our ability to continuously deliver high-quality changes.

Chapter 5

Automate Nearly Everything

Automation - An Essential Component of Continuous Delivery

Automation is the key to writing *Better Software Faster*, and is the engine that drives an effective Deployment Pipeline. Through *Automation* we can speed up our software development activities, carry out multiple processes in parallel, and reduce the risks of human error.

Manual processes are costly and not easily repeatable. Manual testing is often repetitive, low quality and not a good use of a human being's creative skills (with the exception of exploratory testing).

We aim to automate any and all repeatable processes that don't require human ingenuity. We automate everything we can in the Deployment Pipeline so that our development activities are repeatable, reliable and carried out efficiently, and with consistent results.

Automation allows us to make mistakes and recover quickly from them. And not just for the code and the tests: Automation should extend to the build and deployment infrastructure, and data and data structures too.

Test Automation

Through automation of our tests we can get high quality, fast, measurable feedback, with auditable records of the tests that we run, and their results. We aim to automate the fast, technical tests in the Commit Stage, and the more complex, user-centred acceptance tests, as well as any other tests that determine the releasability of our software, later in the Pipeline (such as: performance, scalability, resilience, security, etc). By incorporating, and automating, all these evaluations within the Deployment Pipeline, we create a more reliable and repeatable development process, which is more resilient, robust, secure and scalable.

Rather than wasting valuable human skills to carry out regression testing, we can write detailed 'scripts' for automated tests for the machines to implement.

We will automate:

- the configuration of the test environments
- the deployment of the Release Candidates into the test environments
- control of the test execution, and
- the tests themselves

so that our tests are reproducible and produce reliable results.

Build and Deployment Automation

Builds should be efficient and deterministic. We automate the build processes so that they run quickly and produce a repeatable outcome, i.e: if the same build is run, on the same code, it will produce identical outcomes every time.

Whether we prefer a manual or automated production release for our system, we use the same tools, procedures and technologies throughout the Deployment Pipeline: the same automated mechanisms are used to deploy into develop or test environments, that we use to deploy into Production.

This consistent, highly automated approach means that, by the time we get to Production, everything has been tested together multiple times, and we have a high level of confidence that everything will work. We know that the deployment works because we have already configured the environment, and deployed and tested this version of the Release Candidate many times.

We automate the deployment no matter how complex, or how simple. We make deployment a single, push button, act.

Automate Data Migration

The simplest approach to data migration is to apply it as an automated, integral part of deployment, so that every time the system is deployed, the migration will run.

Automation ensures we can migrate data efficiently and effectively when we upgrade software and deploy our software changes. We will automate our tests to validate data, with respect to data migration. There should be NO manual intervention in the configuration and deployment of data.

Automate Monitoring and Reporting

The Deployment Pipeline automates the collation of results from all tests, to provide rapid, quantifiable feedback on our evaluations. Some automated tests can be run periodically, at weekends, without extending people's working hours. Automation is essential if our system is required to deliver on a massive scale, to a fine degree of precision - when measures may need to be accurate to micro- or nano- seconds.

The Deployment Pipeline offers a way of consistently and automatically gathering useful information about our software and how it is developed. Through automated monitoring, we can set well-defined success criteria, and clear pass/fail thresholds, and automate reporting throughout the Deployment Pipeline. In particular, we want to automatically collect data on Throughput and Stability (*see "Measuring Success" Chapter 18*).

We automate tests and measures, to consistently produce data points over time, track trends, and identify where to investigate further. The automated collation of this data can be used to create simple, instantaneous, dashboards to share with the team.

The Deployment Pipeline can automate the generation of Release Notes, to produce detailed documentation of every behaviour of the system, and automatically create an audit trail - a complete history of every change that we have made to our system.

Infrastructure Automation

To be deterministic, we automate the provisioning and the updating of our infrastructure to reduce variance and achieve repeatability and reliability. We want to know that we have built our software from components that have not been compromised, so we adopt automated dependency management to check that the dependencies we use have not been corrupted. We aim to eliminate human write access to production systems.

Benefits of Automation

We automate everything we can in the Deployment Pipeline so that:

- Our development activities are repeatable, reliable and carried out efficiently, with consistent results.
- We can migrate data efficiently and effectively when we upgrade software.
- We can deploy our software changes in all environments.
- We get high quality, fast, measurable feedback from our tests, and a high level of confidence that our code is good, before we deploy into production.
- We can run tests in parallel and repeatedly, and always get consistent results.
- Progress is visible, with auditable records of all changes, the tests and the results.
- We reduce the risk from human error.
- We can efficiently use the same mechanisms for deploy into develop or test environments that we use to deploy into production.
- We can include everything in the Deployment Pipeline that we need to get the software into production, and there is no more work to do.
- We can proactively determine when our system has problems without waiting for users to find bugs.
- We can offer frequent releases into production, and get user feedback on our new features and products.

Tips for Automation

- Work in Small Steps
- Control the Variables
- Identify what activities in the Deployment Pipeline do not require human ingenuity
- What Automation could replace human intervention?
- How could Automation support human decision-making?
- Make changes incrementally and measure the impact
- Version control everything

Chapter 6

Version Control

Control the Variables

As Software Engineers, we would like every bit and byte of our code in use, to be precisely what we meant it to be when we wrote it. But there are so many things that can affect our code in production, that we must do everything we can to limit the impact of these influences: in other words **Control the Variables** and adopt pervasive **Version Control.**

What to Version Control?

The **Source Repository** is probably what we first think of first when it comes to **Version Control**. But to be able to repeatably and reliably deliver quality software quickly into the hands of its users, we need to Version Control EVERY aspect of our systems and processes:

- source code
- environment configuration
- dependencies
- software infrastructure

- databases
- web-servers
- languages
- operating systems
- network configuration

and even the Deployment Pipelines themselves!

Reproducible Systems

> *Imagine what it would take to be able to successfully deploy any version of the system from any point in its history?*

Our Version Control should be good enough that our systems can be easily and consistently reproduced, and are therefore disposable.

> *Consider what needs to be in place to be in control of everything necessary to reproduce the software in a new production environment?*

To be deterministic, we automate the provisioning of our infrastructure to reduce variance and achieve repeatability and reliability.

At the Commit Stage of the Deployment Pipeline, any new code or change is a potential Release Candidate. We give each Release Candidate a unique ID and we test and deploy this precise set of bits and bytes, using the same technologies that we will use in Production, so that we get consistent, repeatable and reliable results.

The Route to Production

As the ONLY route to Production, EVERY change flows through the Deployment Pipeline. We always make all changes to code, production and configuration, via Version Control. The Deployment Pipeline validates and records every change, test and outcome, so that, for every bit of new code, we have a record of:

- which version of the language was used
- which version of the operating system
- which tests were run
- how the production environment was configured

and so on...

Branching

Continuous Integration was invented as an antidote to the complexities caused by **Branching**.

Branching is about hiding information: dividing up the work, and working on it independently, in ways that team members cannot see each others' work. Branching comes with the risk that one person's work may be incompatible with the changes of their team-mates.

We want to limit this divergence and aim for only one interesting version of the system - the current one.

We achieve this by working:

- to make small changes to Trunk/Master and continuously evaluate them,
- to share information so that changes are transparent, and developers can see if their code works with everyone else's on the team,
- so that when developers make a correct change, everyone else has that same version, almost instantaneously, and
- so that our software is always in a releasable state, and any of these small changes to Trunk/Master may be deployed into production.

My ideal-world **Branching Strategy** is:

> *"Don't Branch!"*

If branches exist at all, they should be *tiny*, *few* in number, and *short-lived*, i.e: merged *at least once per day*. When we are working well, we will merge every 10, or 15 minutes, to get fast feedback on our changes and optimise the Deployment Pipeline to be efficient and thorough.

Recent **DevOps Research & Assessment** reports found that merging frequently is a reliable predictor of higher Throughput, Stability and overall software performance.

Part Two

Deployment Pipeline Anatomy

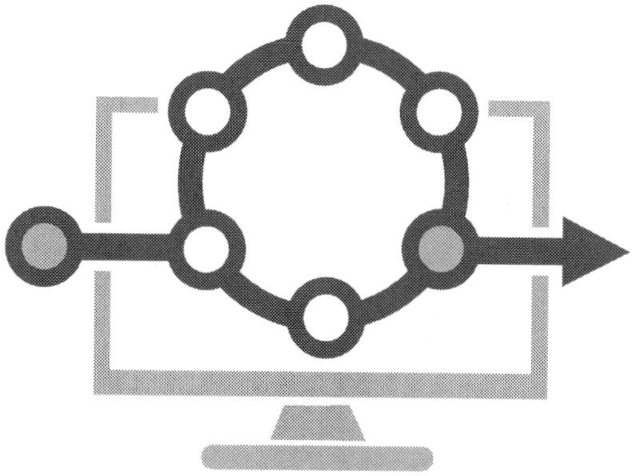

Chapter 7

The Development Environment

Paving the Way for the Deployment Pipeline

It may be tempting to overlook the **Development Environment**, or make assumptions that what we need is already in place, but it is here where we can set things up for greater success and to make things so much easier later on.

We should take some time to establish a Development Environment that has:

- **Quality Tooling** - to enable fast and efficient feedback, so we can learn quickly.
- **Good Connectivity** - network access and information resources so developers can explore ideas and find effective solutions.
- **A Simple Setup** - so that a new team member has the necessary hardware, OS, access permissions, correct language, access to source control, VCS, etc.

- **Team Relationships** - agree ways of working (e.g Pairing) so that all members of the team can quickly become effective and make a contribution to the code.

The Development Environment should provide the ability to:

- Run Any Test, ideally locally.
- Deploy the Whole System, ideally locally.
- Locally Modify Configuration of the deployed system to enable experiments, simulations and tailoring to different circumstances.

Once we have made suitable arrangements for our Development Environment, we can progress into the **Commit Cycle** of the Deployment Pipeline, which includes: the **Source Repository** and the **Artifact Repository**, and which contains many of the technical components of Continuous Delivery.

Chapter 8

The Commit Cycle

The Gateway to the Deployment Pipeline

The **Commit Stage** is where we get fast, efficient feedback on any changes, so that the developer gets a high level of confidence that the code does what they expect it to. The output of a successful Commit Stage is a **Release Candidate**

The goal of the Commit Stage is to achieve a high level of confidence that our changes are good enough to proceed, and to achieve that confidence as quickly as we can.

The common steps of a Commit Stage are:

1. Compile the Code
2. Run Unit Tests
3. Static Analysis
4. Build Installers

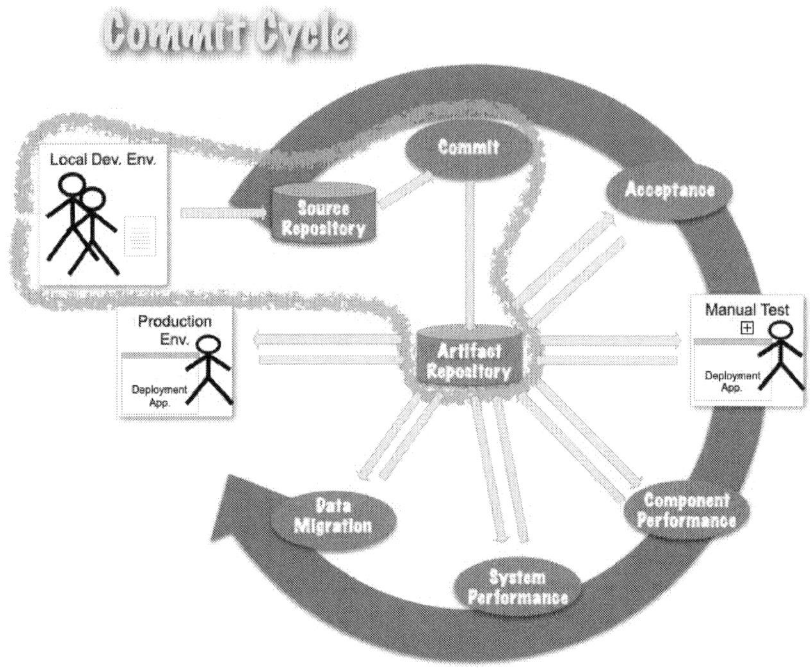

FIGURE 8.1 - THE COMMIT CYCLE

Commit Stage Tests

The Commit Stage is where we do the fast unit and technical tests, best suited to getting results in a few minutes, and we leave other more complex and comprehensive tests to later in the Deployment Pipeline.

The recommended approach to writing and testing new code at the Commit Stage (and throughout the Deployment Pipeline) is **Test Driven Development**. *(See more about TDD in Chapter 4.)*

In addition, we will add tests that are designed to catch the most obvious, common errors that we can think of. We will then proceed to gradually add to our suite of Commit Stage tests, as we learn from failures further along the Pipeline - writing tests for those common failures that we can catch sooner in the Commit Stage.

The vast majority (99%) of Commit Stage tests will be **Unit Tests** - ideally the fruits of TDD. But there are other valuable tests that should be included, to evaluate the system architecture, or quality of the code:

- analysis to check whether our coding standards are met
- LINT-style, and Checkstyle evaluations
- checks on data migration
- compiler warnings,

and so on...

The following diagram, has been gently modified from the original by Brian Marik[4] and and shows how different types of tests can be categorised into:

- tests that "support programming" vs those that "critique the product" and
- tests that are "business facing" vs those that are more "technically focused".

Commit Stage tests are *technically focused* and intended to *support programming.*

4 Brian Marik's test quadrant is described in more detail here https://bit.ly/34UNSso

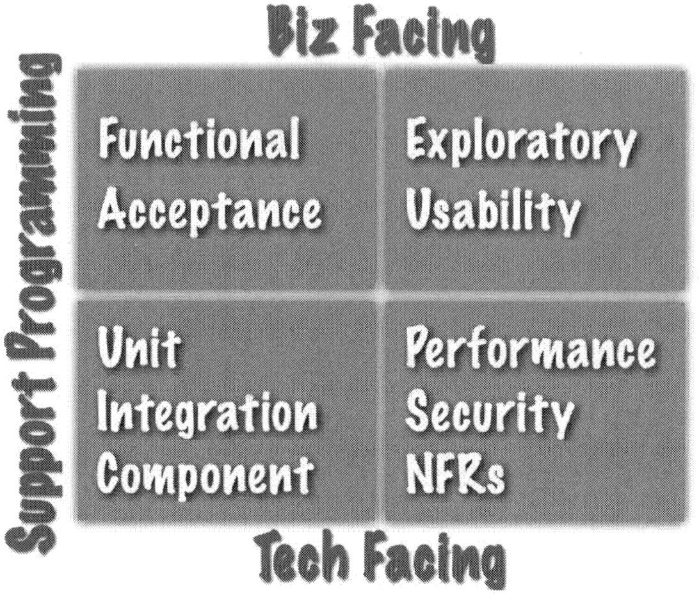

FIGURE 8.2 - BRIAN MARIK'S TEST QUADRANT

We can use the Commit Stage as a tool to support our decision-making, by writing simple tests that are designed to fail, to alert us to events where we need to stop and think carefully about how best to proceed.

Feedback in Five Minutes

My first **Rule of Thumb** is that

> *Commit Stage tests should provide quality feedback to the developer within 5 minutes.*

This is a practical manifestation of the *compromise* between wanting instant results and needing reliable results. 5 minutes is about the maximum amount of time for developers to wait and watch to see if their tests pass, and be ready to quickly correct, or revert the code, if any of the tests fail. Any longer than 5 minutes and developers are likely to move on, or not pay full attention.

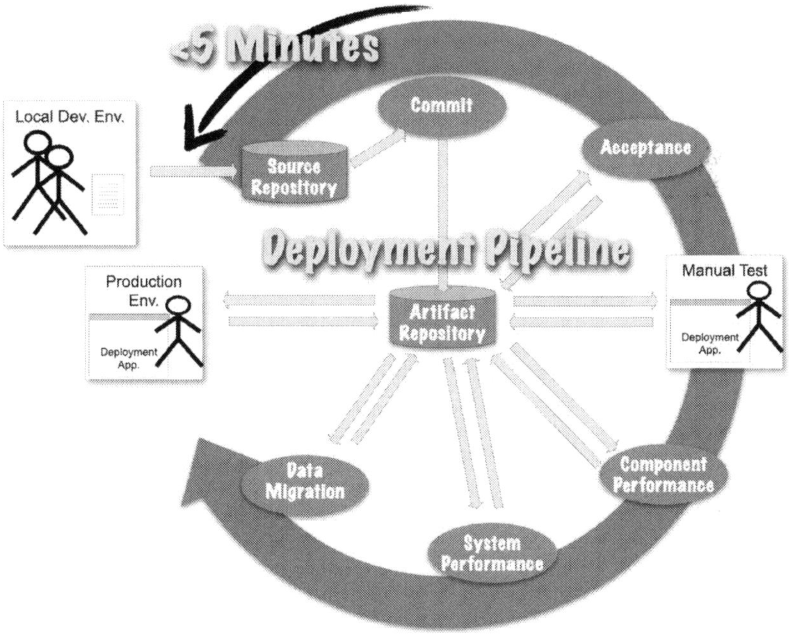

FIGURE 8.3 - FEEDBACK IN FIVE MINUTES

The Commit Stage is complete when all the technical, developer-centred tests pass. Now the developer has a high level (>80%) confidence that their code does what they expect it to. We package the results of a successful Commit Stage to create a **Release Candidate**. This should be the code that will be deployed into production, if it makes it that far.

To get results from our tests in under 5 minutes, we need to optimise for precision and efficiency. So we will avoid network access, disk access, database access and starting up the application - all of which introduce complexity and delays.

When working well, the developer will be committing changes every 10-15 minutes. To achieve that level of productivity, to get fast feedback in under 5 minutes, and be able to quickly revert and correct any defects, means working on small pieces of code and working in small steps.

Working in Small Steps

Working in Small Steps is one of the foundational principles of Continuous Delivery, and enables us to adopt an incremental and iterative approach to design and implementation.

- Making small, simple, frequent changes to our software is less risky than making big, complicated, infrequent changes.
- Simpler changes are easier to understand and easier to revert if necessary.
- Smaller steps mean smaller mistakes, faster feedback and the opportunity to learn and improve more quickly.
- Smaller steps can be completed more quickly and help us to achieve our Continuous Delivery goal of our software always being in a releasable state.

This incremental way of working starts before the Commit Stage. When defining requirements:

- Capture tiny increments from the perspective of the user,
- Break down large requirements into smaller pieces,
- Ensure requirements describe WHAT the software will do and not HOW it does it.

Don't try and include all features and changes in one Commit.

If a problem or feature is too big, break it down into smaller pieces.

Build features and releases from multiple Commits, to evolve products gradually, with frequent user feedback.

Work so that each Commit is safe, tested and ready to deploy into production, even when the feature, to which the Commit adds, is not yet ready for use.

Aim to commit at least once per day, and work so that every Commit can be released into Production - Continuous Integration.

Continuous Integration

Continuous Integration (CI) is critical to the Commit Stage of the Continuous Delivery Deployment Pipeline.

CI is not just a technical discipline. These techniques are an effective way to build collaborative teams and one of the few, foundational principles that transcend any tools and contribute to the development of better quality software.

There are two approaches to CI: Human; or, pre-Commit/Gated CI.

> **Human CI** - is primarily about ways of working, team disciplines and behaviours.
>
> **Pre-Commit, or Gated CI** - uses tools to support these disciplines and automate many of the processes.

Both approaches require the CI mindset.

Continuous means at least very often! So we aim to commit at least once per day, to get the best feedback on our changes and optimise the Deployment Pipeline to be fast, efficient and thorough.

Before committing a change, the developer should *run tests locally on their code*, to avoid stalling the Deployment Pipeline because of minor errors. Once the developer commits their change, they wait and watch to see if it passes the Commit Stage tests. These tests have been designed to give fast feedback, so this is only about a 5 minute wait. The person who wrote the code is the person most likely to spot any problems, understand them and fix them quickly, and so prevent any hold-ups for the rest of the team.

If we commit a change that causes a test to fail, then, here comes another **Rule of Thumb**...

Allow 10 minutes to commit a fix or revert the change.

Usually, if we work in small steps, any change is simple and so unlikely to hide complex problems. This means we should be able to identify and remedy any defect quickly. If the problem is not understood, or will take too long to fix, then we revert the change, to give ourselves time to think, and so remove blockages from the Pipeline.

If the code passes the Commit Stage tests, the developer can *move onto new useful work*, while the Deployment Pipeline continues to evaluate the code and carry out other automated steps. However, it remains the developers' responsibility to continue to monitor the progress of their code through the rest of the Pipeline. They are interested in the outcomes of the acceptance tests, performance tests, security tests, and so on. If any test fails, at any stage in the Pipeline, the software is no longer in a releasable state, and it is the responsibility of the developers who committed the change, that caused the problem, to make the correction.

E-mail notifications are too slow, and too easy to ignore, so *information radiators* or *instant alerts* are better ways to notify the team about build fails. They also help to recognise, incentivise and support the CI disciplines.

Our top priority is to keep our software in a releasable state. The Deployment Pipeline defines *releasability*, so if a test fails, our software is no longer releasable! We need to keep the route to production unblocked.

Therefore, **if a team-mate has introduced a failure, and left, revert their change.**

Pipeline failures are a top priority for the team, to keep the path to production clear. If it is not clear who is responsible for a failure, the people whose changes *could* have caused a failure agree between them who will fix it.

These same behaviours and responsibilities also apply to Pre-Commit, or Gated, CI. This approach is slightly different in that we first commit a change to the Commit Stage, not the VCS. Only if these Commit Stage checks pass, do we merge the change with the VCS. In this way, we have a high level of confidence that the VCS is in a good, clean state.

Gated CI means more infrastructure to build, and a risk of merge failure post-commit, but this approach can help embed ways of working and support teams that are new to CI.

Generating Release Candidates

The rest of the Deployment Pipeline is focussed on deploying and testing **Release Candidates** - the outputs of a successful Commit Stage.

The job of the rest of the Deployment Pipeline is evaluating these candidates for their suitability for release.

If all the tests in the Commit Stage pass, then we generate a Release Candidate - a *deployable thing*, the unit of software that will end up in Production, should the Release Candidate make it that far.

If the aim is to deploy a .EXE into production, we create the .EXE here. If we deploy Docker Images, we generate them now. Whatever the deployable target is for the software, that is what we aim to create at the successful conclusion of the Commit Stage.

Our objective is to minimise work and to control the variables. Generating our Release Candidate *now*, when we have the bytes to hand to make it, minimises work. Deploying and testing the exact sequence of bytes that we aim to deploy into production ensures that our test results are, at least, testing the right code.

Summary

- Commit Stage tests should provide quality feedback to the developer in under 5 minutes.
- If a test fails, we allow 10 minutes to commit a fix or revert the change.
- If a team-mate introduces a failure, and is not around to fix the problem, we revert their change.
- If the code passes the Commit Stage tests, the developer moves onto new useful work.
- We work in small steps and aim to commit at least once per day.
- Package the results of a successful Commit Stage to create a Release Candidate.
- Release Candidates are stored in the **Artifact Repository.**

Chapter 9

The Artifact Repository

The Heart of the Deployment Pipeline

The **Artifact Repository** is the logical home for all Release Candidates, and where we store, permanently, all the Release Candidates that make it into Production.

Scope and Purpose

The job of the Artifact Repository is to **Version Control** our Release Candidates. There are excellent commercial and open source tools for this (such as *Artifactory*), but at its simplest, an Artifact Repository only requires the following elements:

- An allocated **Folder**
- **Shell Scripts** to coordinate the behaviours we want
- A protocol for **Directories**, based on file names and time stamps, and
- An **Index File** as a map to identify required versions.

(Build-time dependencies are not essential, but are often included in commercial and open source tools.)

The Artifact Repository is the cache of Release Candidates. The **Deployable Units** of software that are produced from a successful Commit Stage are assembled and packaged into Release Candidates and stored in the Artifact Repository.

The Artifact Repository is the *version of truth*. The Release Candidates stored here are the exact bits and bytes that we intend to deploy into production. If our software configuration management was perfect in all respects, we would be able to recreate, precisely, a Release Candidate from the version control sources and build systems.

However, this level of precision is difficult to achieve and so the Artifact Repository acts as a reliable store of truth that we can depend on.

We will store successful outputs in the form that they will be deployed into the rest of the Deployment Pipeline - the test environment and into production. We separate out any environment-specific configuration from the Release Candidate. Modern container systems (such as *Docker*) make this easier. We use the same deployment mechanisms wherever we deploy. We do not create target-specific builds, or target-specific Release Candidates.

When working well, we may produce Release Candidates every 10-15 minutes - that is a LOT of binary data, so we need to manage our data storage effectively.

Storage Management

If we complete Commit Stage tests in under 5 minutes, and our Lead Time (a complete transit through the Deployment Pipeline) is under an hour, we may produce 10 or more Release Candidates for every Acceptance Cycle.

But we only need to progress the *newest* Release Candidate and we can discard any earlier, or failing, versions from the Artifact Repository. (We will keep the history and meta-data though, as this is useful information.)

Each Release Candidate will be assigned a unique ID - this is best done as a simple sequence number, so we can easily identify which, of several possible versions, is the newest. We can now use this ID as a key, to all of the information that we hold about the Release Candidate, and reckon things like *"How many changes have been made between Release Candidates?"*

Semantic versioning may be useful for other purposes, but we use sequence numbers as IDs for Release Candidates, and treat semantic version numbers as a *display name* (in *addition* to the unique ID) as a way to communicate to users what the Release Candidate means.

We should aim to perform a periodic purge to discard any Release Candidates that don't make it into production.

We should also aim to permanently store ALL Release Candidates that do make it into production, in the Artifact Repository.

Next Steps

We now shift from the Commit Cycle's technical focus (determining whether our software does what the developers expect it to do) and creation of a deployable **Release Candidate**, and move on to evaluating the code from the users' perspective. We move into the **Acceptance Cycle**.

If the aim of the Commit Cycle is to achieve about 80% confidence that our Release Candidates are releasable, through the Acceptance Cycle we will carry out further evaluations to determine releasability and achieve a sufficient level of confidence to allow us to deploy our changes into Production. Our aim is that, when the Pipeline completes, we are happy to deploy without the need for any additional work.

From now on we evaluate deployed *Release Candidates.*

Chapter 10

The Acceptance Stage

Confidence to Release

The transition from the **Commit Cycle** to the **Acceptance Cycle** represents a shift from a technical, developer-centred focus, to considering whether our code does what the *users* of the software want it to do. We carry out evaluations from the *perspective of the external users of the system*, until we achieve enough confidence that we are ready to release.

Aims of the Acceptance Stage

- To evaluate our changes from an external user perspective
- To test in life-like scenarios
- To evaluate in production-like test environments
- To eliminate the need for manual regression testing
- To achieve a sufficient level of confidence that our software is functionally ready for production

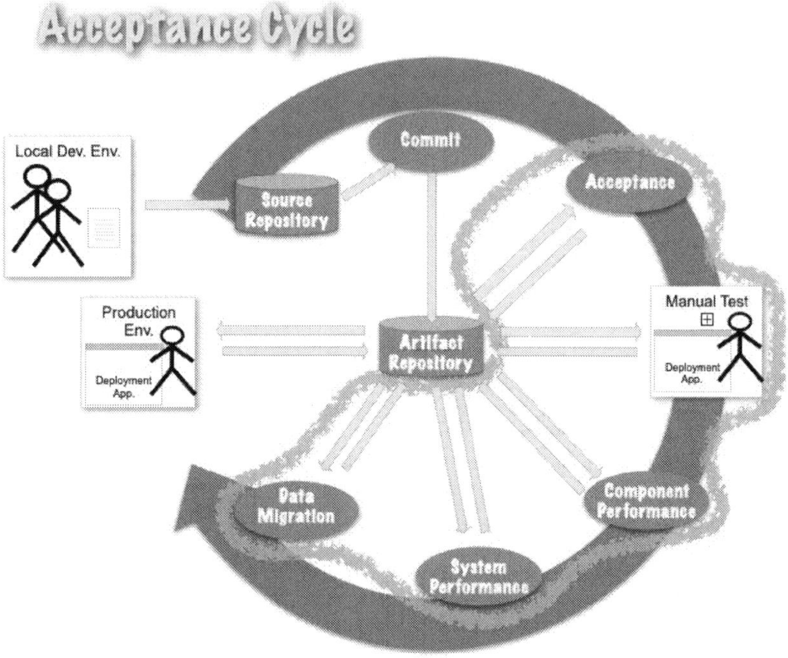

FIGURE 10.1 - THE ACCEPTANCE CYCLE

Don't confuse the **Acceptance Stage** with User Acceptance Testing, which involves a human sign-off informed by customer feedback.

In Continuous Delivery we include automated Acceptance Tests in our Deployment Pipeline, and aim to completely eliminate the need for manual regression testing. *(See more on Manual Testing in Chapter 11.)*

Steps in Running Acceptance Tests

Before we start testing, we need to first deploy the Release Candidate so that it is ready for use. Here are the common steps implemented in an **Acceptance Test Stage**

1. Configure the environment, ready for the Release Candidate.
2. Deploy the Release Candidate.
3. Carry out a *smoke test*, or *health check* to ensure that the Release Candidate is up and running, ready for use.
4. Run **Acceptance Tests**

We follow these steps and start from the same point for every deployment of our system, through the Acceptance Cycle, until the Release Candidate makes it into Production.

What are Acceptance Tests?

Effective Acceptance Tests:

- Are written from the perspective of an external user of the system
- Evaluate the system in life-like scenarios
- Are evaluated in production-like test environments
- Interact with the System Under Test (SUT) through public interfaces (no back-door access for tests)
- Focus only on WHAT the system does, not HOW it does it
- Are part of a systemic, strategic approach to testing and Continuous Delivery

How to Write Acceptance Tests[5]

The most effective way to create an Acceptance Test is to write an **Executable Specification**, that describes the desired behaviour of the new piece of software, *before* we write any code. Acceptance Tests focus only on **what** the system/code should do; and say nothing about **how** it does it. So we start each test with the word **"should"**. All tests should be written from the *user perspective* (NB the user of the code may be another programmer, or interested third-party, not just an end-user of the software.)

We do this for every change that we intend to make. These specifications guide the development process: we work to fulfil these Executable Specifications as we carry out lower level, TDD testing until the specification is met.

We make the scenarios that these tests capture *atomic*, and don't share test-data between test cases. Each test-case starts from the assumption of a running, functioning system, but one that contains *no data.*

The Acceptance Tests are *business facing,* i.e written from the perspective of external consumers of the system. Acceptance Tests are designed to *support programming* and guide the development of code to meet the users' need. *(See Figure 8.2, in Chapter 8.)*

These functional, whole-system tests are difficult to get right. It helps to consciously work to separate concerns in our testing, to allow the system under test to change, without invalidating the tests that evaluate its behaviour.

---

5 You can watch my video for further guidance here: https://youtu.be/JDD5EEJgpHU)

The Four-Layer Approach

I recommend adopting a four layer architecture to Acceptance Test infrastructure so that the system can change, without invalidating the test cases.

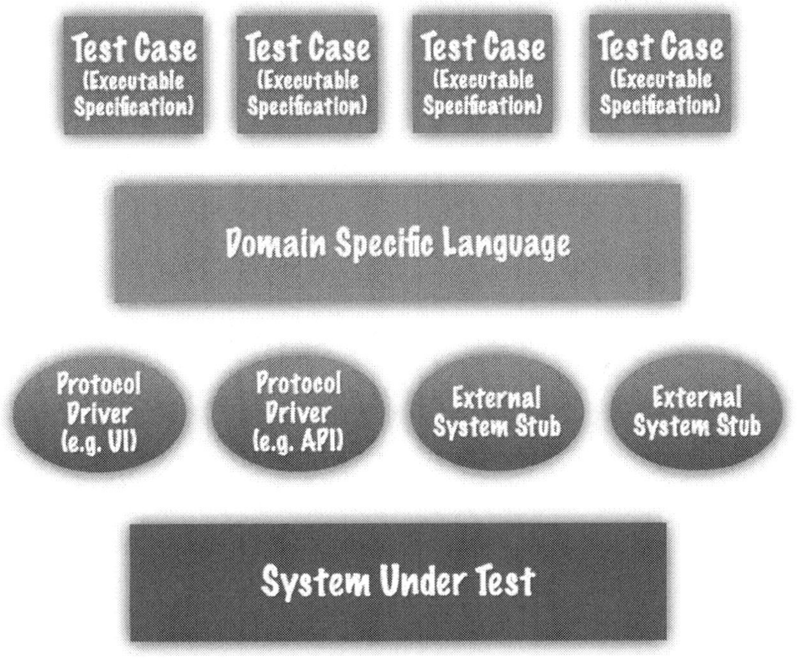

FIGURE 10.2 - FOUR LAYER ACCEPTANCE TESTING APPROACH

Executable Specifications

We capture WHAT we expect the software to do, and not HOW it should do it. For example, we say things like "*placeAnOrder*" or "*payByCreditCard*", and not things like "*fill in this field*" or "*click this button*". We adopt the language of the problem domain. The Executable Specifications should be readable by a non-technical person who understands the problem domain.

Domain Specific Language (DSL)

This layer supports the easy creation of Executable Specifications. This layer enables consistency, re-use and efficiency in the creation of Acceptance Test Cases (Exec Specs). It provides functions like "*placeAnOrder*" which Exec Specs can call on.

We aim to grow the DSL pragmatically, i.e: create two or three simple test-cases that exercise the most common / valuable behaviour of the system, and create the infrastructure that allows these tests to execute, and to pass.

Protocol Drivers

Protocol Drivers sit between the DSL and System Under Test (SUT) and translate from the high level language of the problem domain (e.g "*placeAnOrder*") to the language of the system, using more detailed concepts like *"navigate to this URL"*.

We isolate all knowledge of how to communicate with the system here. Protocol Drivers encode real interactions with the SUT and are the only part of the test infrastructure that understand *how* the system works.

System Under Test (SUT)

We deploy the system using the same tools and techniques as we will use to deploy it in Production. It is important to delineate the SUT from systems that other people are responsible for, in particular, third-party dependencies. We fake all its external dependencies, so we can thoroughly test to the boundaries of the system that we are responsible for.

Imagine throwing the SUT away and replacing it with something completely different, that achieves the same goals - the Acceptance Tests should still make sense.

> *Imagine testing buying a book on Amazon.*
> *Could the tests work just as well for a robot shopping for books in a physical store?*

This four-layer approach takes discipline and time to adopt, but can result in enormous savings in time, and improvements in quality.

Automating the Acceptance Stage

We aim to eliminate the need for manual regression testing, and automate any and all repeatable processes, in the Deployment Pipeline. Manual processes are slow, unreliable and expensive. There is a role for Manual Testing *(see Chapter 11)*, and we should use human beings where they can have the best effect - in creative processes and in qualitative assessments. We use our computers to carry out routine, repeatable tasks. They are much more efficient and reliable than we are, for that kind of work.

As well as testing the code, we can test the configuration and deployment.

By using the same (or as close as possible) mechanisms, tools and techniques to deploy into test environments, as we will use when we get to Production, we can get a high level of confidence that everything will work together. By the time we get to Production, everything has been tested together multiple times, we have reduced the likelihood of 'unpleasant surprises', and we have a high level of confidence that everything will work.

Acceptance Tests can act as a kind of *whole system super-integration* test. If we assemble all the components that represent a deployable unit of software and evaluate them together, if the Acceptance Tests pass, we know that they are configured appropriately, work together and can be deployed successfully.

Scaling Up

Acceptance Tests take time and can be expensive. We need enough tests to spot unexpected problems, but we don't, usually, have unlimited resources. We can design the test infrastructure to run multiple tests in parallel, within available resources, having regard to which tests take the longest amount of time.

We can use *sampling* strategies, and grow the number and complexity of Acceptance Tests as the software grows. In this way, we achieve test coverage as required to determine the releasability of the software, and not as a goal in itself.

The aim should be to allow developers to add any test that they need, but also for developers to care enough to think about the cost, in time, of each test. Again we have the trade-off between thoroughness and speed. Both matter, but 'slow and thorough' is as bad as 'fast and sketchy'!

Tips for Writing Acceptance Tests

- Incorporate Acceptance Tests into the development process from the start.
- Create an Executable Specification for the desired behaviour of each new piece of software before starting on the code.
- Think of the least technical person who understands the problem-domain, reading the Acceptance Tests. The tests should make sense to that person.
- Create a new Acceptance Test for every Acceptance Criteria for every User Story.
- Make it easy to identify Acceptance Tests and differentiate them from other sorts of tests.
- Automate control of test environments, and Control the Variables, so the tests are reproducible.
- Make it easy for development teams to run Acceptance Tests and get results, by automating deployment to the test environment and automating control of test execution.
- Automate the collection of results, so developers can easily get the answer to the question "*Has this Release Candidate passed Acceptance Testing?*".
- Don't chase test coverage as a goal - good coverage comes as a side-effect of good practice, but makes a poor target.
- Leave room to scale up the number and complexity of Acceptance Tests, as the software grows in complexity.

Chapter 11

Manual Testing

The Role of Manual Testing

We previously stated that one of the aims of the Acceptance Stage is:

"*To eliminate the need for manual regression testing.*"

However there IS a valuable role for **Manual Testing**. It is just that manual *regression* testing is slow, unreliable and expensive, and not a good use of human skills.

In striving for more accuracy and repeatability from Manual Testing, organisations often resort to writing increasingly detailed scripts for the testers to follow. Following these scripts is boring and demotivating.

A better solution is, instead, to write the detailed 'scripts' or automated tests for the machines to implement. We can use our computers to carry out routine, repeatable tasks more reliably and quickly, and free up people to fulfil the more valuable, more appropriate role of *exploratory* testing.

This plays to human strengths - like 'fuzzy pattern matching'. We want people to evaluate the software and make a subjective assessment of how easy and enjoyable it is to use, and to spot 'silly' mistakes early on.

Until now, we have talked about automating everything we can in the Deployment Pipeline. How can we also facilitate exploratory testing and allow people to 'play' with the new software?

Our highly automated approach, in which we use the same deployment mechanisms throughout the Pipeline, facilitates deployment flexibility. We only make Release Candidates that have passed acceptance testing available for Manual Testing.

This means that we don't waste a valuable human's time evaluating software that is not fit for production. We know that the software works and fulfils its functional needs from our automated testing, and so we want humans to look for other things.

At this point we are left with only 2 decisions to make:

> *Which version of the Release Candidate should I run?* and
> *Where do I want to run it?*

By providing tools to support this, we make the choice a self-service one, and so offer increased flexibility to our Manual Testers.

Because we use the same deployment mechanisms throughout the Deployment Pipeline, we can reuse the tools, procedures and technologies that we used in preparing for acceptance testing. We follow the same simple steps:

Ensure the Release Candidate is ready for testing, and the correct version of the Release Candidate and dependencies, is in place.

1. Configure the environment, ready for the Release Candidate.
2. Deploy the Release Candidate.

3. Carry out a *smoke test*, or *health check* to ensure that the Release Candidate is up and running, ready for use.
4. Start **Manual Testing**

Manual Testing is not a *release gate*. It is not the final step in the software development process.

When to Add Manual Testing

Manual Testing is not an essential component of every Deployment Pipeline. For many types of software it is unnecessary: automated testing can do a better job.

However, it is useful for software with a significant UI component, where a broader assessment of the *usability* of a system is helpful.

The primary characteristic of Manual Testing in Continuous Delivery is really that Manual Tests are one-off explorations of the system. They are subjective impressions of the system, not a thorough, rigorous, examination.

Although my usual diagrammatic representation of a Deployment Pipeline shows Manual Testing within the same cycle as all other steps and processes, it can't work this way in reality. The Manual Testers cannot work to the same timescales as automated acceptance testing, they are too slow.

It may be better to think about Manual Testing being off to one side, running in parallel with the developers' work, in a more collaborative, *agile*, way of working. Manual Testers can explore each small Commit and give helpful feedback to the developers as development proceeds.

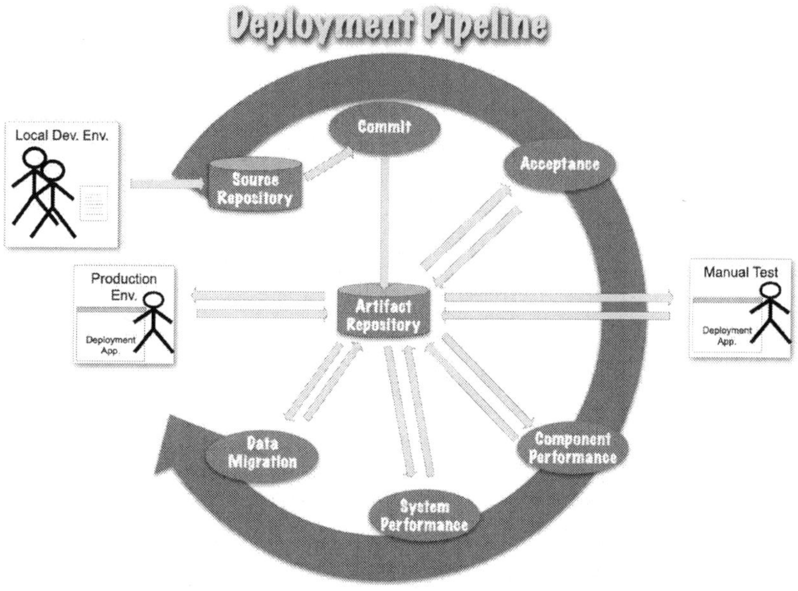

FIGURE 11.1 - MANUAL TESTING IN PARALLEL

Chapter 12

Performance Testing

Evaluating the Performance of our System

We now have a simple working Deployment Pipeline that evaluates any change to our code to check whether it does what the developer expects it to - **Commit Stage** tests, and whether the new code does what an external user of the system wants it to do - **Acceptance Tests**. But there are other steps and tests that we may need to incorporate into our Deployment Pipeline, to complete what constitutes *releasability* for our system.

One of the next steps to add into the Pipeline is an evaluation of the whether the **Performance** of the system is fast enough and reliable enough.

Performance Tests typically cover:

Usability: How slow is the system from the users' point of view? Is it annoying to use?

Throughput: How much stuff can our system process?

Latency: How long does it take to get results back?

Soak-Testing: Long-running tests to find out if protracted use causes any unforeseen problems.

Pass/Fail Performance Tests

Our range of **Performance Tests** is likely to produce large quantities of interesting data. To avoid drowning in tables and graphs, we need to clarify *what* is being measured, and define what level of performance is *good enough* (or not!) to create **Pass/Fail Thresholds**.

Graphs are useful as a feedback mechanism, to identify trends close to threshold, which might indicate when we are heading towards a test failure and thus prompt us to make pre-emptive improvements.

In general, our aim is to establish **Pass/Fail Tests** for all Performance Tests. We do not want to simply collect piles of performance data and leave this for human interpretation. This kind of data collection certainly has a role and can give useful insight, but for our Deployment Pipeline we want simple, well-defined success criteria.

The most sensible measures to achieve a Pass/Fail Test are **Throughput** and **Latency**. We capture these measurements, and establish threshold values that make sense in the context of our testing. *(See more on "Measuring Success" in Chapter 18.)*

It is important to allow room for variance in the tests, because there will be some. We start by establishing sensible theoretical limits for Latency and Throughput and set these in the tests. Then, if the tests fail too often at these thresholds, we analyse what is going on to see if the problem is with the performance of the system, or the variability in the results. If the former, we need to either: fix the system; or, lower our expectations. If the latter, we need to work to better **control the variables**!

Testing Usability

If the performance of our system is not a business goal or driver in its own right, then **Usability**, i.e: the users' experience, may be the most important aspect of performance for us to consider.

Our **Usability Tests** should evaluate feedback about the performance of our system under normal patterns of use. We can organise this by using our DSL to define scenarios from the user perspective, and measure run times for a likely mix of scenarios. We can then set reasonable *pass/fail criteria* for our tests.

This can be scaled up, by adding more scenarios, or different combinations of scenarios, and running scenarios in parallel, to *stress* the system and identify where there are risks of failure. These can challenge, and may refine, our *pass/fail thresholds*.

The degree of precision required for Usability Tests is at the level experienced by the user - typically hundreds of milliseconds. If the success of our system is dependent upon performance down to micro- or nano-seconds, then we need to take more control to achieve greater precision, and critically, repeatability, of measurement. *(See "High-Performance, Low-Latency Systems" below.)*

Component-Based Performance Testing

> *Which* components *of our system are likely to be performance critical?*

These can be evaluated separately, in isolation from the whole system, with distinct *pass/fail criteria* for each component. This gives us much stronger control over the variables, and so these tests are more reliable and repeatable. We can measure the performance of each component in production, or analyse their performance characteristics, and identify potential constraints or load, which will help us define *pass/fail criteria.*

These tests can be a good prompt to stop and think about our next course of action. If the test fails we can choose to:

- revert the change,
- redesign the code to improve performance, or
- change the test threshold.

System-Level Performance Testing

Usability and Component-based tests involve defining likely scenarios, and understanding our most performance critical components. **System-Level Performance Testing** complements this by evaluating the *whole* system, using a mix of use cases, looking for *unexpected* problems. We can:

- either record inputs from production,
- or create a realistic, but simplified, simulation of normal patterns of use.

This allows us to replay, or simulate, different scenarios and measure their performance. Even at this level we can adopt threshold values which help us to establish *pass/fail criteria.* We can run a series of *stress-tests*, by progressively ramping-up load and thereby establishing a *reasonable worst case scenario* to identify usable, sensible, maximum and minimum thresholds for our tests.

High-Performance, Low-Latency Systems

If our system is required to deliver on a massive scale, to a fine degree of precision, then our measures may need to be accurate to micro- or nano- seconds. In these circumstances, **Automation** of performance monitoring in production, and **Controlling the Variables**, are essential. We run simulations, and compare actual performance in operation, with the simulations, tests and thresholds, to check their accuracy and use this feedback to verify the Performance Test model, adjusting as necessary.

Long-Running Tests

Long-running tests, also known as **Soak Tests** should not be used to define *releasability*. They may run for days, or weeks, and do not fit within our Deployment Pipeline timescales. They do not help us to ensure that our software is always in a releasable state. So we need to ask:

> *Do these tests perform a useful function? Or are they some kind of comfort blanket?*
>
> *Can we reduce, or eliminate them entirely?*

Soak Tests are often used as a 'safety net' to protect against inadequate testing elsewhere in our development process. If this is the case, then the best strategy is to fix the cause of the problem, not react to the symptoms.

> *How we can improve the quality and reliability of our Commit Stage and Acceptance Stage tests?*
>
> *If these long-running, Soak Tests are providing useful information, how can we get these answers sooner?*

Time is one dimension in our measurements: the precision with which we measure is another. We can often eliminate the need for Soak Tests by increasing the accuracy of our measurements rather than increasing the duration of our tests.

Long-running tests are often used to spot *resource leaks*. In which case do they really define *releasability*? We might still be able to eliminate them if we can increase the precision of tests within the Deployment Pipeline.

Control the Variables

Performance Tests can be big and complex, and there may be different types of test running concurrently, so it is important to **Control the Variables** in order to get reliable, repeatable results. So, we should explore:

- *What external factors are most likely to influence the system under test? Can we isolate or fake these?*
- *Is there scope for doing more Component-level testing?*
- *Could we run the Performance Tests on a separate, dedicated, network?*
- *Are we using the same hardware and configuration for Performance Testing as we have in Production?*

Chapter 13

Testing Non-Functional Requirements

What are Non-Functional Requirements?

Although something of an *oxymoron*, **Non-Functional Requirements** is the widely used term for technical requirements of the system, such as: scalability, resilience, fault-tolerance, security, disaster recovery, and others. These are behaviours which impact on the users, and, if they constitute releasability of the software, they should be evaluated as part of the Deployment Pipeline.

Scalability

To test the scalability of our software, we can re-use the same environment we established for performance testing. We can identify periods of greatest load from the record of the system in operation, and scale-up 5x, 10x, even 100x load, to measure signs of stress and identify failure thresholds.

This should be automated and can be run periodically, e.g: at weekends. There is no need to evaluate every Commit in this way.

Resilience

We should treat fault tolerance, resilience and disaster recovery as requirements of our system, and, as such, write user stories and create automated tests for these scenarios, which we can run in the Deployment Pipeline.

For this approach, we selectively fail different parts of our system during the course of a test. We can also test for these behaviours in production - **Chaos Engineering**.

> *A well-known example of this is at Netflix, where the software is designed to be resilient under stress and failures are intentionally introduced, in production, to measure the impact on the system and its resilience in response.*

A test strategy which combines both test and evaluation in production provides excellent assurance of the robustness of the system.

Regulation and Compliance

If we know what compliance and regulatory standards our software is required to meet, we can create automated tests to evaluate whether any change we make results in a failure to meet these requirements.

(Chapter 17 contains lots more information about Regulation and Compliance.)

Provenance

We want to know that we have built our software from components that have not been compromised. We should establish a secure store of common dependencies from known sources, and adopt automated dependency management to check that the dependencies we use have not been corrupted. We should aim to eliminate human write access to production systems.

Audit and Traceability

The Deployment Pipeline is the perfect place to create an **audit trail** - a complete history of every change. If we connect the Commit with the requirements management system (e.g by tagging the Commit with the ID of the story, or reason for change) we get an end-to-end record of every change:

- who made the Commit
- what tests were run
- the results of the tests
- the environments used
- which Commits made it into Production
- which did not and why...

This is a fantastic resource for proving compliance and fulfilling the expectations of regulators.

Security Testing

Security is highly likely to be a criterion for *releasability* of our software, and as such, we must test for security requirements within the Deployment Pipeline, and not treat this as an add-on, or separate gate-keeping exercise.

We write tests for any required security behaviours, and test for them in the Commit Stage by scanning for common causes of security problems. We can also automate common penetration tests.

Team Responsibility

These, sometimes highly technical, security and regulatory requirements may need to involve specialists, but they are *everyone's responsibility* within the team. The specialists are best employed to advise the writing of stories and Executable Specifications, and coach and advise developers in test thresholds for their code, but they should not act as 'gate-keepers'.

Conclusion

By incorporating, and automating, all these evaluations within the Deployment Pipeline, we create a more reliable and repeatable development process, which is more resilient, robust and secure.

Chapter 14

Testing Data and Data Migration

Continuous Delivery and Data

Continuous Delivery is not just about code. The **Data** that our systems produce and rely upon must be able to change too, if we hope to be able to learn and to grow our systems over time. If the Data can change, then we must manage that change.

Changes to Data can be thought of in two parts:

1. Changes to the Data Structure - that defines how we interpret the data, and
2. Changes to the values that the Data represents - the records that our software generates and works on.

These are related: if we allow structure to change, then we must think about how to handle Data Migration of the values held in those structures.

We will explore here three aspects of Continuous Delivery and Data:

3. Data & Data Migration
4. Testing Data Migration
5. Data Management

Data Migration

The simplest approach to **Data Migration** is to apply it at deployment - **Deployment-Time Migration**. We make Data Migration an automated, integral part of deployment, so that every time we deploy the system, wherever we deploy it, the migration will run. There may be little or no data to migrate in an acceptance test environment, but we will run Data Migration anyway.

Data Migration Testing Stage

The most important phase of testing for Data Migration is to unit-test the migration scripts themselves. We use fake data and run these tests as part of the Commit Stage to gain fast feedback on the quality of the changes.

It may also help to increase confidence in complex Data Migrations that run at deployment time, by rehearsing them before release. For this we create a **Data Migration Test Stage** in the Deployment Pipeline. This stage will check migrations with data sets that are representative of our production system.

To prepare the environment ready for Data Migration Tests, we follow the same four-step process as we have for other test stages, i.e:

1. Configure Environment
2. Deploy Release Candidate
3. Smoke Test / Health Check
4. Run **Data Migration Tests**

An Approach to Data Migration Testing:

- **Clone** current Production Data - automate the cloning and run scripts in the Production Environment on the cloned version
- **Anonymise** the Production Data (if necessary)
- **Copy** the anonymised Production Data across to the test systems to use as the basis for migration testing
- **Deploy** the Release Candidate
- **Run** simple smoke tests on post-migration major use cases

This type of testing may be helpful to build confidence in Data Migration, but in reality may have limited value if testing elsewhere is robust and effective.

Data Management

The usual **Continuous Delivery** principles apply to management of data in the Deployment Pipeline, i.e:

- Make changes in small steps
- Test everything to make sure the changes are safe

- Design to support change
- Automate as much as possible, and
- Version everything

Our *approach* to all this can make it easy, or hard, to accomplish these things. It is usually helpful to start from the perspective of **Data in Production**: to get data structures correct, we may need to make changes to the records and evolve the structure of those records. It is much easier to evolve the structure if we make *additive* changes. Deletions lose information and so can make it impossible to step back a version.

Our aim, as ever, is to be repeatable and reliable and so this will involve **version control** of everything that might change the data, i.e: DDL scripts, migration scripts, delta scripts, etc.

Recommended Techniques for Managing Data Schema Change

- Employ NO manual intervention in the configuration and deployment of data.
- Automate tests to validate data, with respect to Data Migration.
- Use *Database Refactoring* techniques. (The book "Refactoring Databases" by Scott Ambler, describes these in detail.)
- Version schemas with monotonically increasing sequence numbers: each change in structure ticks the sequence.
- Record every small change in a delta script identified by that sequence number.
- Store the desired version of the schema, along with the application.
- Store the current version of the schema along with the data.

Maintain a record, committed along with the application, of which version of the data it needs to work. The simplest way to do this, is to keep the specification of the version of the data store in the same VCS as the application, and commit them together. This minimises any problems of dependency management.

As the Data Structure evolves, the data stored will need to migrate so that it is still usable. Create a delta script for each small change. Script the change in structure, and then also script any migrations that are necessary to 'move' the data from the previous version to this new current one. Use the schema sequence number as the ID of the script.

An Example of Data Schema Change:

Current DB schema version 5. Our system holds a record of the current version of the schema - "5".

We need to change it, so we change the schema by creating a Delta Script which defines the change in structure and how to migrate any already existing records at version 5 to the new version - version 6. We call the delta script something like "Delta-6".

We change our app so that it can work with 'Version 6' and change its record of the schema that it needs to "6". We commit all of these changes *together* to our VCS, and everything should work!

Delta Scripts

Delta Scripts are the instructions that describe the change to the **Data Schema**, and instructions for how to migrate the data from the previous version of the schema. Every change made to the structure or content of the database should be implemented as one of these Delta Scripts.

We test the *behaviour* of the migration scripts - to check that the script migrates the data in the way that we intended it to. We don't necessarily test the data itself. We store the tests and tests results in the same VCS along with the system that uses it.

The objective of these tests is NOT to test that a database ends up in a particular state, but to validate that the migration does what we think it does. So these tests are best done with fake data and fake cases.

At the point that we want to deploy the system, we read the current version from the data store. Deployment tools examine the new Release Candidate and read the version that it expects. If these two versions differ, we play, in sequence, the Delta Scripts required to migrate the data from one version to another.

We can also add Delta Scripts to undo changes - to step back to the previous version, this allows our migration tools to migrate from any version to any version.

Limits of Deployment-Time Migration

At the point when the system is deployed, the deployment tools will apply the appropriate deltas, rolling forwards or backwards to the target version.

There may be some Data Migrations that take too long to perform at Deployment Time. For these sorts of migration, consider using **Run-Time Data Migration** strategies instead. Here are a few examples (but the detail is beyond the scope of this book):

- **Lazy Migrator** - Migrate old records when they are accessed.
- **Lazy Reader** - Interpret old records and present them as new to the system on demand.
- **Down-Time Migrator** - Search for old records to migrate when the system is otherwise idle.

Testing and Test Data

There are three categories of **Test Data**:

1. **Transactional** - data that is generated by the system as part of its normal operation.
2. **Reference** - mostly read-only, look-up data that is used to configure the system (usually lists of something useful).
3. **Configuration** - data that defines the behaviour of the system.

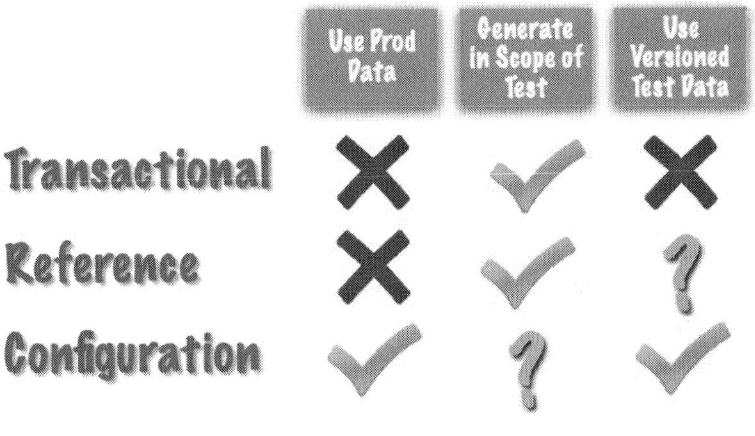

FIGURE 14.1 - TEST DATA MATRIX

Production Data is big and unwieldy, and is therefore not well-suited to testing Transactional, or Reference Data.

Wholly Synthetic Data should be used for testing transactional scenarios in application, so that we can better target the behaviours that we want of our system.

Synthetic Data is also recommended for testing Reference Data, although versioned test data may sometimes be appropriate.

For Configuration testing, it is recommended to use Production Data in order to evaluate production configuration changes.

Conclusion

So, now we know that the Release Candidate:

- does what the developers think it should do,
- does what the users want it to do,
- is nice to use,
- is fast enough,
- meets non-functional requirements, and
- works with the users' data.

> *What else is there to think about before we are ready to* ***Release Into Production?***

Chapter 15

Release Into Production

Defining Releasability

The Deployment Pipeline is the only route to Production. We therefore need to include any and all steps that are necessary for new software to be **releasable**, i.e: everything that we need to do to know that the software is sufficiently fast, scalable, secure, and resilient, fulfils its purpose and does what our users want it to do.

So, once we have built a simple Deployment Pipeline, for the simple version of our system,

> *What other steps should be added to define releasability?*
>
> *And which should be done first?*

This will vary from product to product, and from organisation to organisation. So there is no simple checklist to work through, but here are some things to think about when growing a Deployment Pipeline to support the development of new software:

- The range of different *users* of the system and their different types of requirements.
- What performance, technical, or compliance standards can be assessed against *pass/fail thresholds* within the Pipeline?

- The full range of possible tests: units tests, acceptance tests, exploratory tests: tests for security, component performance, resilience, stability, data migration, etc.
- Can we improve version control?
- The addition of monitoring points and measures required for evaluations and impact analysis.
- What documentation is required by auditors, regulators, or other third parties?
- Any integrations, or dependencies?
- What validations, approvals and sign-offs are required?
- Processes that are currently carried out outside, that should be moved into the Pipeline.
- What manual processes can be automated within the Pipeline?
- Any *waste* activities, that do not directly contribute to releasability, that can be eliminated from the development process.
- What else can be done within the team, rather than separate input from others?

And anything else that *must* be done so that, when new code has completed its transit through the Pipeline, there is no more work to do and it is safe to release **Into Production.**

The aim is to maximise the work that the automation does, while aiming to minimise human intervention. Where human decision-making is required for one of these things, consider supplementing it with automation so that a person is presented with only the information that they need to make the decision, and the tools to record their decision, and so allow the Pipeline to continue in its progress as efficiently as possible.

Remember, we don't need to do everything at once. We take an iterative, incremental approach, so the most important questions is:

> *What are the essential steps needed to support the development of the next feature of the system?*

Following a Lean approach will help:

> *What is the Current Status?*
>
> *What is the Objective?*
>
> *What is the Next Step?*
>
> *How will we Know if we have Succeeded?*

The Production Environment

This is the final stage of our Deployment Pipeline. We have done everything that we can think of to evaluate our Release Candidate, so that we have assurance that it is as safe, as it can be, to be pushed **Into Production**.

Unlike conventional approaches to software development, when we apply Continuous Delivery techniques, **Release into Production** is NOT a fraught, nervous event where leave is cancelled, people are on-call and we feel certain that something will go wrong and we'll spend long hours in the coming days and weeks fixing the problems. We know that the deployment works because we have already configured the environment, deployed this version of the Release Candidate many times, and carried out smoke tests / health checks so that we know it is up and running and ready for use.

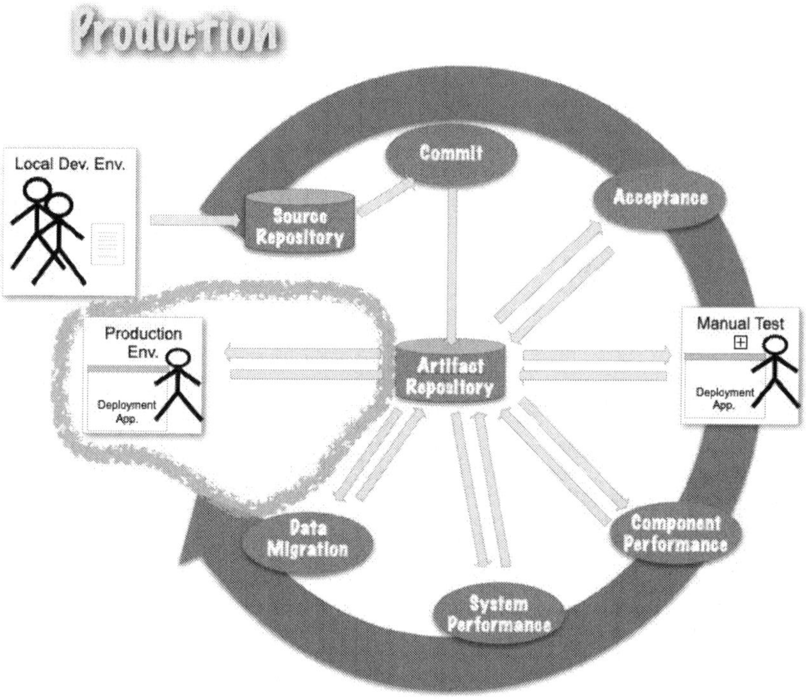

FIGURE 15.1 - INTO PRODUCTION

There is always the chance that we may get *unexpected* problems though - there may be things that we have missed, simply because we didn't think of them. So the Production phase is yet another opportunity to learn.

When to Release[6]?

In **Continuous Delivery**, we work so that our *software is always in a releasable state*. We are free to make a business decision about *when* it makes most sense to deploy - depending on the nature of the product, any risk or safety considerations, the impact on the customers, etc.

Continuous Deployment, on the other hand, means that the *deployment is automated*, so, as soon as the Deployment Pipeline determines that our Release Candidate is good, it is automatically deployed into Production.

Release Strategies

In an ideal world, we would be able to switch from the old version of the software, to the new version, without any interruption of service. In the real world though, we want to manage this transition. Here are some of the common approaches:

Blue/Green Deployment

We work with two different versions of the system: we update one while the other is in operation, and switch over when we are ready to deploy.

Rolling Transition

Both the old and new versions are live, and we gradually migrate traffic to the new system, until the old system is no longer used.

---

6 There is further information in my video on Release Strategies: https://youtu.be/mBzDPRgue6s

Canary Release

We start by deploying into low risk: low volume environments and, once assured that the changes are safe, we progressively deploy into more and higher risk environments.

> *Netflix uses a combination of these strategies and deploys new features to locations around the world where it is the middle of the night and usage is at its lowest. This is monitored as usage increases through the day, so deployment can be stopped if there is a problem, before prime-time usage.*

A/B tests

We deploy two different versions of the system, monitor both, and compare the impact in Production, on customers, and for the business.

Feedback from Production

To learn about our software we want to monitor feedback from our Production systems. We can monitor:

> **Technical Information** - such as: memory usage, disk usage, CPU usage, queue depth, error logs, and performance measures.
>
> **Functional Information** - which is about: the *business performance* of the system, data on user journeys, A/B testing, and other business metrics.

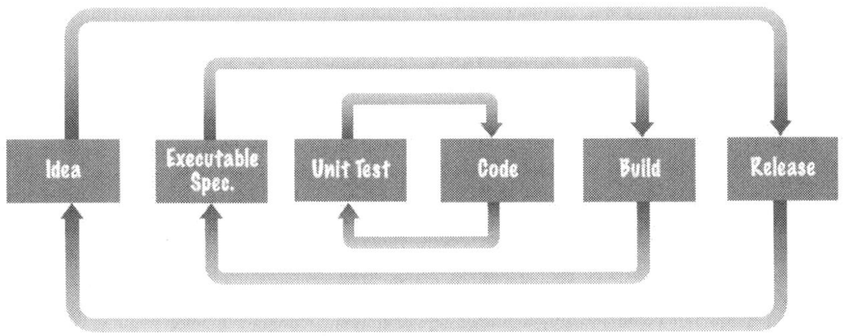

FIGURE 15.1 - COMMON FEEDBACK CYCLES IN CONTINUOUS DELIVERY

In Production

> *Our changes are now out there in Production.*
> *So what else is there to do?*

We continue to learn. We gather information to inform business decisions. We get feedback to understand what our customers make of our software.

The Deployment Pipeline automates the collation of data, to provide rapid, quantifiable feedback and this should continue once we are in Production.

Immediately following the release into Production, we may use smoke tests to validate that everything is ready for us. The acceptance test DSL is a great tool for this.

If we are releasing frequently, we can reduce work by auto-generating **Release Notes**, to describe the changes that we are releasing.

We can include **Authorisations** within the Deployment Pipeline, to give us an audit record of who performed what actions.

We might also monitor:

- who is using the system, and how they are using it
- what is the impact of the change we made
- is the new feature being used, enjoyed, and by whom
- what are the business benefits

(There is more on business metrics and success measures in Chapter 18.)

Conclusion

Continuous Delivery has many benefits for development teams, in respect of their efficiency, productivity, quality of code and job satisfaction. Here, at the end of the Deployment Pipeline, we can really appreciate the other benefits to the business:

- We are able to be experimental, to try out different versions of our system, discover what our customers make of our software and what they prefer.
- We can release new features to our customers fast, frequently and safely, to be the best in our market.
- The Deployment Pipeline is the primary tool for **Digital Disruption.**

Part Three

Whole Pipeline Considerations

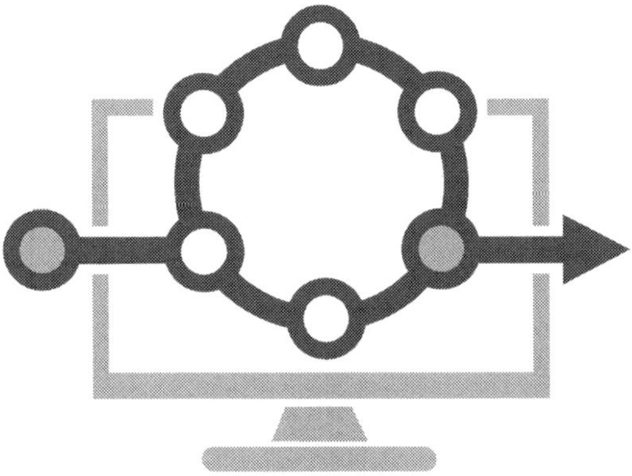

Chapter 16

Infrastructure As Code

To achieve the goals of *repeatability and reliability* that we seek for Continuous Delivery, we must **Control the Variables**. One of the key variables is the **infrastructure** that supports the software systems that we build.

What is Infrastructure As Code?

Infrastructure As Code is the use of software techniques to configuration-manage the infrastructure, and applies to:

- the operating systems
- programming languages
- libraries
- scripts
- schemas
- messaging infrastructure
- web-servers
- network switch configuration
- relational database management systems
- data migration

… and everything and anything that allows us to accurately reproduce the system as a whole.

This infrastructure is a *dependency* of the system, which we control through **Automation**, of both the provisioning and the updating of the infrastructure, and by using effective **Version Control**.

We want to know that every bit and byte in production is the one that we intend, and is reproducible. The best way to do this is to ensure that every change to our infrastructure flows through the Deployment Pipeline.

Infrastructure Configuration Management

There are three broad strategies for **Infrastructure Configuration Management:**

1. Ad-Hoc, or Manual Admin
2. Configuration Synchronisation
3. Immutable Infrastructure

Ad-Hoc, or Manual Admin

This is a common approach, in which the environment is configured by means of an admin console, but is a *terrible idea!* This approach is low-quality, unreliable and inconsistent, prone to human error, and each server is slightly different. The configurations generated by this approach are sometimes referred to as *snowflakes*, because each server is unique and unrepeatable.

Please don't do this!

Configuration Synchronisation

This involves creating a model of the configuration that is reproduced for each deployed environment. We have a declarative definition of what the infrastructure should look like and a *central model* which is version controlled. This means we can easily scale-up and make changes to many servers simply and consistently. The model is testable and we can evaluate each step in any change to the configuration. But this approach does not handle deletions well, and requires good team discipline for it to work reliably.

This approach works best when **no manual write access** to the servers is permitted - so there is no *configuration drift* caused by people tinkering with the servers.

Immutable Infrastructure

This is a powerful approach in which we recreate the infrastructure from a script every time we deploy. We therefore get exactly what we defined, any changes are testable, and the configuration is readily scalable. Any manual changes will be overwritten the next time the system is deployed. The downside of this approach is that it can take time to provision the system for every deployment.

Recommended Principles

Whichever Infrastructure Configuration Strategy is chosen, there are some common principles to look for in the system:

- Easily reproducible
- Disposable

- Consistent
- Repeatable
- Freedom to change and refine

Recommended Practices

- Use definition files. Make the infrastructure *soft*. Create a script that can be version controlled.
- Script everything so that systems are *self-documenting*, repeatable and auditable.
- Version control everything.
- Continuously test systems and processes.
- Make changes in small steps.
- Keep services continuously available.
- Prefer *unattended execution* - push button to trigger the deployment and configuration of everything, without manual intervention at stages.

For further reading on this subject, I recommend the excellent book "Infrastructure As Code" by Kief Morris.

Infrastructure As Code and the Cloud

Infrastructure As Code is NOT a Cloud technique. It pre-dates the emergence of the Cloud, which has made the management of the configuration of massive systems much easier. For Cloud-based systems, **Immutable Infrastructure** is recommended to enable elastic scalability, just-in-time provisioning and dynamic configuration of systems.

Chapter 17

Regulation and Compliance

There is a common mis-perception that Continuous Delivery is not achievable in large bureaucratic and regulated organisations. This is not borne out by the evidence.

DevOps Research & Assessment (DORA) collate and analyse information from thousands of software organisations, of all sizes and types, to produce annual "State of DevOps" reports. Their research consistently finds that **there is *no* correlation between poor performing organisations and their size, bureaucracy and their regulation**. Rather, conversely, that if these organisations apply Continuous Delivery techniques, they are able to achieve high measures for software and team performance.

Responding to Regulatory Requirements

Different industries and services experience different levels of regulation according to understood levels of risk. The regulatory requirements are intended to protect consumers from careless mistakes, or deliberate wrong-doing, and to make producers accountable for their actions.

Many organisations' approach to reducing risk and striving for safety in their software development process is to exert additional controls, such as:

- an external approval process, often requiring manual sign-off by senior personnel,
- increasing the number and level of 'authorisation gates',
- a risk averse approach to change - preferring to stick with what has worked in the past.

Despite the prevalence of these types of responses to risk, the evidence is that they do not work, and are in fact *counter-productive* because they:

- reduce the frequency of releases,
- make each release bigger and more complex,
- are therefore more likely to introduce mistakes and so compromise stability,
- slow down innovation, making it difficult to improve and respond to the business environment,
- therefore damage the financial strength of the organisation and its ability to invest
  the resources needed to effectively manage risk,
- constrain teams and encourage a culture of following a process, rather than one of experimentation and learning to find new ways to deliver better outcomes,
- consume effort in the increased scrutiny and reporting burden, which detracts from the time available to develop new features for customers,
- create a negative tension between the push of these sorts of controls and the pull of getting things done, which can result in people finding ways to avoid or subvert the compliance regime.

The **DORA report** states that:

> "*We found that external approvals were negatively correlated with lead-time, deployment frequency and restore time, and had no correlation with change failure rate.*
>
> *In short, approval by an external body (such as a manager or Change Approval Board) simply doesn't work to increase the stability of production systems…*
>
> *However, it certainly slows things down. It is in fact worse than having no change approval process at all.*"

By contrast, the application of Continuous Delivery techniques, reduces risk by making change in small steps: making every change easier to continuously evaluate, and quicker to revert and fix any problem, without major disruption. By working so that our software is always in a releasable state, we reduce the chances of any major failure.

Techniques that Facilitate Regulatory Compliance

I led the development of one of the world's highest performance financial trading systems, at the London Multi-Asset Exchange (LMAX) - a Start-Up operating in a heavily regulated industry, overseen by the Financial Conduct Authority (FCA). We adopted Continuous Delivery from day one and built a Deployment Pipeline, for *all* the software produced by the company, that met FCA reporting and regulatory requirements.

Regulatory Compliance at LMAX

- All changes (to the code, tests, infrastructure...) flow through the Deployment Pipeline.
- Effective Version Control.
- Pairing[7] - in code, operations and deployment, as part of an agreed regulatory regime.
- Machine-generated Audit Trail - which contains a complete record of all changes, versions, actions and who performed them.
- Test cases created to assert regulatory and security requirements.
- Immutable Infrastructure approach to infrastructure configuration management.

(Read more about the LMAX Deployment Pipeline in Chapter 19.)

What Can Go Wrong?

In 2012 Knight Capital went bankrupt in 45 minutes. This trading company mis-traded $2.5 billion in a single day. At the end of the trading day, after manually correcting $2 billion in trades, they were left owing $440 million.

The US Securities & Exchange Commission (SEC) Report into the Knight Capital bankruptcy, suggests some lessons we can learn.

---

7 Pairing is a cultural and technical practice in which two programmers work together to learn and improve the quality and efficiency of their software development. You can find out more here: https://youtu.be/aItVJprLYkg

Weaknesses in Knight Capital's development approach:

- Manual organisation of releases.
- Manual changes to multiple servers.
- No review of the deployment by a second technician[8].

> "*During the deployment of the new code, ... one of Knight's technicians did not copy the new code to one of the eight servers... and no-one at Knight realised that the Power Peg code had not been removed from the eighth server, nor the new RLP added*"
>
> **SEC Report, 2012**

This is an illustration of why an Ad Hoc / Manual Admin approach to infrastructure configuration management is a *terrible idea! (See "Infrastructure as Code - Chapter 16.)* It is prone to human error: it is too easy to miss something that might have disastrous consequences.

The Deployment Pipeline as a Tool for Compliance

The Deployment Pipeline is an excellent tool for managing compliance, meeting regulatory requirements and providing assurance of the reliability and repeatability of our processes.

The Deployment Pipeline should be the *only* route to Production: no additional steps, external authorisation processes, or security checks.

8 We recommend Pairing with its inherently contemporaneous reviews, in preference to a separate, later review by a "second technician" (as suggested by the SEC Report).

Everything flows through the Deployment Pipeline and in this way we can easily collate the entire history of each Release Candidate as it makes its way into Production.

If we treat auditors and regulators as *users* of the system, we can write stories that capture their requirements and use the Deployment Pipeline to generate the information they need in an appropriate reporting format.

If our multi-disciplinary, team approach to development involves audit, we can understand what the auditors learn about our processes, and involve them in making improvements.

The Deployment Pipeline can automate the generation of Release Notes, and produce detailed documentation of every behaviour of the system

Continuous Compliance

> *Still think that Continuous Delivery cannot be practised in regulated environments?*

I think the opposite is true! Continuous Delivery is the best way to get assurance of Regulatory Compliance!

Chapter 18

Measuring Success

Making Evidence-Based Decisions

There is no instant route to Continuous Delivery: it takes work. We make progress incrementally and iteratively. We take small steps and measure our progress - producing data so that we can make **Evidenced-Based Decisions** about how we can continuously improve, so that we can produce the best possible software in the most efficient way.

One of the *essential* ideas of **Continuous Delivery** is that we use information to inform business decisions, and not rely on guesswork, previous experience, or ideology.

The Deployment Pipeline offers a way of consistently and automatically gathering useful information about our software and how it is developed. We could measure: the number and type of tests, test results, changes made, time taken, load, usage, failure rate, business metrics, energy usage..... The potential for gathering data is so great, that we need to be really clear about what it is that we'd like to know, so that we put the appropriate measures and monitoring arrangements in place. Simple quantitative measures - like how many changes have been made, or how many lines of code have been written, do not tell us anything particularly useful.

If our aim is to write **Better Software Faster**, then the three most *useful* measures are:

1. Purpose
2. Quality
3. Efficiency

At first, these may look like imponderables, but we have some robust measures that we can use to quantify these attributes.

Purpose

We want to know that our software delivers something useful, and of value, to its users. The Deployment Pipeline enables us to try out ideas, make changes quickly and deliver new features frequently, and get feedback in production.

Measures of purpose will always be contextual: what is important to measure depends on the nature of the business.
The following business metrics, in production, can often help us determine what our customers make of our software:

- **Acquisition**: the number of people who visit the service
- **Activation**: the number of people who have a good initial experience
- **Retention**: the number of people who come back for more
- **Revenue**: the number of people who subscribe, or make a purchase
- **Referral**: the number of people who recommend the service to other people

These are sometimes known as Pirate Metrics - AARRR!

Quality

We can determine the quality of our work, by measuring **Stability** - a combination of:

- **Change Failure Rate** - we monitor, at various points throughout the Deployment Pipeline, how often we introduce a defect in the different parts of our process, and
- **Failure Recovery Time** - we measure the amount of time when our software is *not in a releasable state*, i.e: the time it takes to remedy the problem.

Efficiency

Throughput is a measure of the efficiency with which we produce new software, and can be measured as:

- **Frequency** - how often we can release changes into Production,
- **Lead Time** - how long it takes to go from Commit to a releasable outcome.

Throughput and Stability

These are the four metrics that we monitor throughout the Deployment Pipeline to gauge our Throughput and Stability, and are easy to automate:

1. Change Failure Rate
2. Failure Recovery Time
3. Frequency
4. Lead Time

We do not selectively choose between these measures - all four together create the value. After all, being fast but failing frequently, or being extremely stable and very slow, are not good outcomes.

DevOps Research & Assessment (DORA) collates and analyses information from thousands of software organisations, of all sizes and types, to produce an annual "State of DevOps" report. Year on year, they have identified a strong correlation between high measures of **Throughput** and **Stability**, and **High-Performing Teams**. These reports also show that high-performance is achieved by striving for better Throughput AND Stability, not one at the expense of the other. By working towards improving Stability, we also improve Throughput, and vice versa. There is a *virtuous circle* effect.

The Continuous Delivery techniques of making frequent, small changes, and automation, and the practices of **Continuous Integration** and **Trunk-based Development** are *proven* ways to achieve high measures of Stability and Throughput. These are not marginal benefits. The highest performing teams are *thousands* of times faster, and they produce a small fraction of the change failures, than the poorest performers.

The DORA reports also show that organisations that deploy very frequently into production are more commercially successful i.e: they are more likely to exceed productivity, market share and profitability expectations. By measuring Stability and Throughput through the Deployment Pipeline, we can incrementally improve, not only the quality and efficiency of our software, but the performance and success of our business.

There is therefore a clear case to invest in getting better at Throughput and Stability, but we need to know:

Where should we invest our time and efforts?

New tools? Stand-up meetings? A radical architecture change?

We want to make **Evidence-Based Decisions**, based on data not *dogma*.

We build into our Deployment Pipeline the ability to measure the impact on Throughput and Stability for *any change we make*: to the code, the infrastructure, our development approach, even the team behaviours. We want to know if any given change to technology, or organisation, has a positive effect, a negative effect, or no real affect at all! Which changes are worth making?

We automate this measurement, in order to consistently and reliably produce these data points over time. We can then track trends, and look at averages and peak variations, so we can identify where to investigate to better understand the reasons for an improving, or deteriorating, position.

For more on this topic, I recommend these books:"Accelerate", by Nicole Fosgren, Jez Humble, Gene Kim; and "Measuring Continuous Delivery", by Steve Smith

The automated collation of this data can be used to create simple dashboards to share with the team. The team can then understand how well they are currently doing, what they could improve, what actions they may take, and measure the impact of their changes. They may want to set objectives: what might be an acceptable, or aspirational failure rate? or time to recover? They are empowered to experiment with changes, understand their progress and make informed decisions.

Calculating Lead Time

Speed is essential, because there is an opportunity cost associated with not delivering software. If it takes months to deliver new features to customers, we are likely to get beaten in the market place by our competition. We want to measure **Lead Time** and make small steps to continuously improve and get faster.

It should be straightforward to identify each stage in our development process, and include monitoring points in the Deployment Pipeline to measure how long each stage takes, and what the Lead Time is overall. Understanding how long it takes to complete each of the steps to get from *idea to valuable software in the hands of the users*, gives us insight into where we can speed things up, remove blockages and overcome delays.

If we can speed up our Lead Time, we will gain faster feedback on the quality of our work, and gain better feedback on the quality of our products. The act of working to reduce Lead Time encourages us to adopt leaner, more effective practices as we get closer to being able to achieve a *releasable outcome multiple times per day*: or even being able to release new features in minutes! rather than in days or weeks.

Improving Lead Time

To achieve the goal of transiting each Commit through the Deployment Pipeline in under an hour, means working efficiently: including only the *essential* steps necessary to release software into production, and by doing each step only once. There may be opportunities to make *big* improvements early on, potentially reducing Lead Time by 50% or more, by tackling wasteful, and slow activities.

My Rule of Thumb Timescales

Aim to:

- Complete Commit Stage tests in **under 5 minutes** - to get fast, efficient, quality feedback and a high-level of confidence that changes are releasable.
- When a test fails, allow **about 10 minutes** to identify and commit a fix, or revert the change - so that there are no further hold-ups to the Pipeline while working through more complex problems.
- Complete acceptance tests and all other checks and steps through the Deployment Pipeline in **under an hour** - to give several chances to find and fix any problems in the same day, and ensure that the software is always in a releasable state.

Suggested Steps to Improve Lead Time

1. Summarise the development process: identifying all the tests and steps included in each stage of the Deployment Pipeline.
2. Measure (or estimate) how long each step and stage takes. Add monitoring at key stages to improve the quality and reliability of these measures.
3. Think about:
   - What is the purpose of each step? Why are we doing this?
   - What must be done before new code can be released?
   - How are teams organised? How is work allocated? How do teams communicate and collaborate?
4. Identify where there is potential to:
   - Speed up the slowest steps in the Pipeline: complete steps more quickly, or remove them completely if they don't add value.
   - Eliminate waste - reduce, or remove actions that are not essential to the releasability of the software. Do everything that you must do, once and only once.

- Prevent or reduce delays between steps - look for things held in a backlog queue; or subject to approval by another body
- Do more within the team, without waiting for input from others.
- Undertake evaluations in parallel.
- And of course, automate as much of the process as possible.

5. Prioritise and make incremental improvements over time. There is no need to do everything at once. In fact, the Continuous Delivery way is to work in small steps, measure the impact of the changes, and work gradually towards the objective.

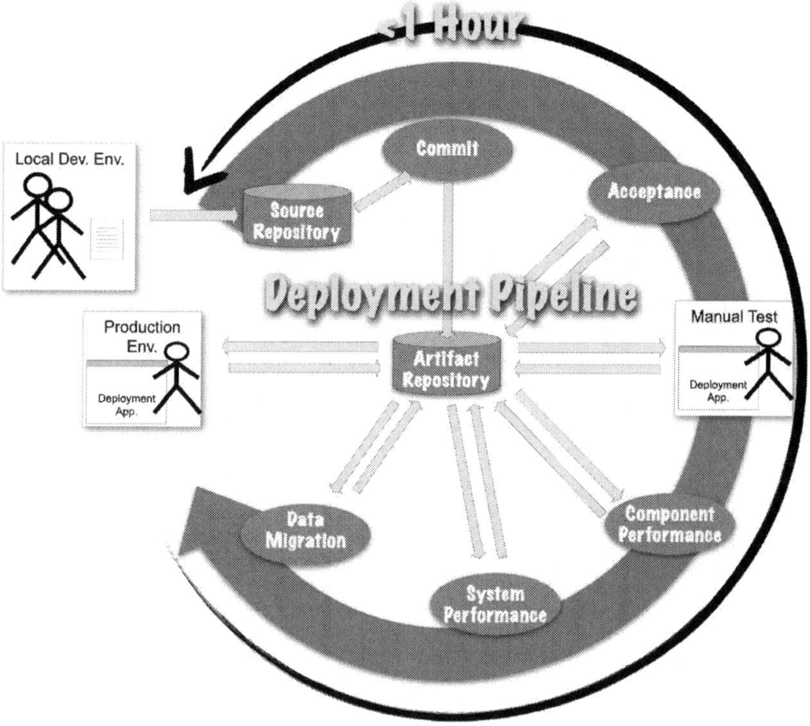

FIGURE 18.1 - COMPLETE CYCLE IN UNDER ONE HOUR

Follow a Lean Approach

Ask/answer the following questions:

What is our Current Status?

What is the Objective?

What is the Next Step?

How will we Know if we have Succeeded?

Chapter 19

The LMAX Case Study

This Case Study takes a look at how the **London Multi-Asset Exchange - LMAX** built, and used, their Deployment Pipeline, applying the same approach and techniques described in this book: and what we can take away from this experience to help us build our next Deployment Pipeline.

About LMAX

LMAX's original goal was to provide a world-class financial trading system, and make it available to any institution, or trader with a few pounds, on the internet. The system therefore needed to fulfil an unusual combination of requirements, i.e:

> i) extremely high-performance, with microsecond response times, to meet the needs of trading institutions, and
>
> ii) flexible scalability, to meet the needs of a web-facing, public trading venue.

LMAX operate in a heavily regulated sector, and needed to get FCA (Financial Conduct Authority) approval to some of their innovative approaches. So regulatory compliance, as well as high-performance and scalability, were guiding tenets of the system from the outset.

I joined LMAX as Head of Software Development, when it was a Start-Up, so we had the advantage of starting with a blank-sheet and adopting Continuous Delivery from day one. We began work on the system by getting the Deployment Pipeline in place.

We started simply: building a bare-bones Pipeline, in just 2-3 weeks, to support the development of the first couple of features of the system.

Over the next 5 years, we added to, and evolved, the Deployment Pipeline to fit the needs at the time. The Pipeline became more sophisticated as the software grew into a complex, high-performance, financial exchange which handles £billions of other people's money every day.

Scope and Scale

The scope of the LMAX Deployment Pipeline was *all* the software that the company produces: the whole enterprise system for the company. There was a development team of about 30 people in all roles, committing and evaluating changes within the same Deployment Pipeline.

The Pipeline gave a definitive statement on releasability: all steps and tests that are necessary for the development of the software were incorporated into the Pipeline - there were no additional external reviews, steps, or sign-offs.

The Deployment Pipeline grew with the software to handle nearly 100,000 tests, process 1.3x the daily data-volume of Twitter, commonly transact £100 billion in assets each day, and archive over 1TB of data every week.

The Pipeline integrated with 20 to 30 external third-party systems, of various kinds and functions: from providing APIs for external trading, to complex integrations with clearing houses and customer verification systems.

Every change, on any part of the system, was automatically regulatory compliant because the production of all the FCA documentation and audit requirements were built into the Deployment Pipeline.

Design, Tools and Techniques

The system was built in Java. The first version of the Deployment Pipeline was a mix of build and shell scripts, using ThoughtWorks' open source "Cruise Control" build management system (BMS) initially. This was later migrated to Jenkins.

In fact most, if not all, tools and parts of the system were migrated at some time. We used the technology that seemed most appropriate at the time, and changed and evolved implementations and choices as the system grew and changed, and we learned more about what was required and what worked.

This kind of thinking was not limited to the Deployment Pipeline. The system as a whole was modular, and architected in a way that allowed changes to be made as our understanding grew, and to change course when mistakes were made.

At one point the development team swapped out the RDBMS system that was used for the primary Data Warehouse and replaced it with an open source alternative. Because of the modular design of the system and the power of the Deployment Pipeline, this whole exercise took less than a day.

This demonstrates that design, approach, patterns and techniques matter much more than the specific tech!

The tools and the team may change over time, but the upfront investment in creating a resilient and flexible Deployment Pipeline has many benefits long into the future, as recently commented on by developers currently working on the LMAX system:

"*The LMAX codebase is by far the nicest commercial codebase I have ever worked with. It has retained its flexibility after all these years...Also the test coverage we have is unparalleled.*"

"*It's not just coverage: the LMAX codebase is one where I could legitimately answer the question "***why is this line of code the way it is***?" By breaking that code and just looking at the test failures.*"

We created many of our own tools and technologies - innovating a custom-built architecture for ultra-fast messaging and a multi data-centre fail-over. The team tested the system using Test Driven Development (TDD) techniques throughout the Deployment Pipeline, and by incremental release into production, to validate changes as the system grew in capability.

LMAX automated nearly all decision-making: only leaving complex, human decisions in place where they added real value.

Everything was version controlled, and systems and whole environments could be recreated from scratch. So Infrastructure as Code, automated infrastructure management and deployment automation were the norm.

We adopted Pair Programming to ensure the quality of the software and to spread expertise throughout the team. The programming pairs organised their work around testing: starting with a new story and writing at least one acceptance test for each acceptance criteria, for every new feature.

A Domain Specific Language (DSL) was developed to write acceptance tests in a way that described the behaviour of the system, without describing how the system actually worked. In this way, the tests were loosely coupled with the system under test, meaning that the system could change, but the tests remained valid.

LMAX applied Continuous Integration techniques. The developers committed regularly, every few minutes: working on Trunk, to get the clearest picture that their changes worked with changes made by other members of the team.

The Commit Stage in 4 Minutes

When the developers were ready to Commit, they tagged the Commit with a message including the ID of the story, or bug, that they were working on. This allowed Commits in the Version Control System (VCS) to be linked to the stories and bugs in the requirements management system. This provided a complete set of information that described the progress of any change. Meaning that we could automate things like Release Notes and audit records, which could tell the history of every change to the system.

The Commit Stage was configured to build the system, compile all new code together, and run the tests. If all tests passed, a Release Candidate was created ready for deployment. The Commit Stage comprised 35 - 40,000 unit tests, a few hundred analysis tests (such as asserting coding standards) and a few hundred data migration tests. All this was completed in just 4 minutes.

Achieving this level of testing and speed of feedback involved significant work to optimise processes, using techniques like running parts of the build and many of the tests in parallel.

This evaluation gave the developers a high-level of confidence that the code did what they expected it to, and if all tests passed, they could move onto new work. If any test failed, then the problem was revealed to the development team very quickly. The system failed fast! This meant that we could act immediately to fix the problem, or revert the change. Fixing any Pipeline failure was a priority for the team, so we could ensure that the software was always maintained in a releasable state, and this took precedence over other activities.

If all tests passed, the Commit Stage packaged the software, generating deployable components of the system - mostly JAR files. These Release Candidates then progressed to be evaluated through the Acceptance Cycle of the Deployment Pipeline.

The Acceptance Stage in 40 Minutes

The objective of the Acceptance Stage of a Deployment Pipeline is to check whether the software does what the users want it to. Acceptance tests are written from the perspective of the users.

At LMAX, we defined "users" as:

- Traders
- Third-party systems
- The Financial Conduct Authority
- System Administrators, and
- Other programmers, testing the public trading API.

By incorporating these perspectives and evaluations into the Deployment Pipeline, we could ensure that any change to the system automatically met regulatory and user requirements, and integrated with external systems.

The team wrote new acceptance tests for every success criteria, for each new feature, of a constantly growing system. The Acceptance Stage grew to include 15 - 20,000 whole system tests. The team very rarely needed to delete any acceptance tests.

LMAX invested significantly in the ability to scale-up to ensure that our Pipeline could deliver feedback on the results of acceptance tests in under 1 hour, even in the face continual growth in the number of acceptance tests. We built an acceptance test grid of some 40 - 50 servers, which dynamically allocated test cases to servers as they became free.

With a focus on speed, efficiency and optimisation, the Pipeline enabled all necessary evaluations to be completed in under 40 minutes. In this time, maybe 10 Release Candidates had been generated by the Commit Stage. So, when the Acceptance Stage was next free, the *newest* Release Candidate was deployed. This meant that changes were *batched up*, avoiding the potential problem of a backlog of work being generated by the Commit Stage, which would have meant that the slower Acceptance Stage would never catch-up.

Tests and code were committed together, with acceptance tests for new features marked as "in development". These were not run in the Pipeline until the code was ready, and likely to pass. This avoided cluttering the Deployment Pipeline with failing tests that were still *work in progress*.

Once the acceptance tests were written, the developers practised fine-grained TDD: testing and refactoring to grow and refine the software, Commit by Commit, piece by piece, until the specification was met and the acceptance tests pass.

A Decision on Releasability in 57 Minutes

Our Deployment Pipeline was the *only route to production*, and we therefore included any and all steps that were necessary for new software to be releasable. So, in addition to the technical unit tests and user-focussed acceptance tests, we also included:

- Static Analysis for Code Quality
- Security Features
- Fail-Over Scenarios
- Admin Scenarios
- Time Travel Tests
- Manual Exploratory Tests
- Performance Tests
- Scalability and Resilience Evaluations
- Data Migration Tests
- Compliance and Regulatory Requirements
- Tactical Tests to Fail Fast for Common Errors

Manual Tests

Automated testing removed the need for manual regression testing, but manual exploratory testing evaluated the *usability* of the system.

We created a simple UI, which showed the Manual Testers a list of Release Candidates that had passed acceptance testing, so they didn't waste time on work that might not pass automated testing.

Manual test environments were configured using the same systems and tools as used in all other environments (including Production).

The Manual Testers could choose from a list of available test environments, select any Release Candidate, and *'click go'* to run their choice of exploratory evaluations to assess the quality of the system from a subjective point of view.

Performance Tests

LMAX carried out two-stage Performance Testing:

- **Component Level** - which tested parts of the system thought to be performance critical, in isolation. These tests were implemented as *pass/fail* tests based on threshold values for acceptable levels of Throughput and Latency.
- **System Level** - evaluated the behaviour of the whole system, via a controlled replay of a life-like mix of scenarios.

LMAX implemented system-level performance testing by recording the inputs to the system during a period of high-demand. We then instrumented this recording so that it could be, computationally, scaled-up, and ran these tests at 5x normal load.

Scalability & Resilience

Scalability testing was carried out periodically. Once a month we used scalable system-level tests to ramp-up load, 5x, 10x, 20x and so on, until the system showed signs of stress. This was automated, and scalability runs were carried out over a weekend when the system performance environment wasn't needed for development.

Data Migration

In addition to data-migration unit tests run in the Commit Stage, further checks were included in the Pipeline to ensure that data migration could be carried out in the appropriate time-scale for our release process.

The LMAX Deployment Pipeline included everything necessary to get a definitive answer on releasability: checking all technical and user requirements, for any change to any part of the the system, in under 57 minutes. After carrying out all these steps and checks, there was no more work to do, and the Release Candidate was ready to go into Production.

Into Production

LMAX practises Continuous Delivery, not Continuous Deployment. Changes were not automatically released once they had successfully transited the Pipeline. The *newest* Release Candidate, that the Pipeline had determined to be good, was released at a weekend - when the markets are closed.

Smoke tests and health checks were run to confirm that the system was live and ready for use, using the same DSL that we had used for acceptance testing.

The same configuration and configuration management tools were used for production deployment, as had been used throughout the Deployment Pipeline.

Using the same configuration and mechanisms is not only more efficient, but also means that the specific configuration, and the tools and techniques that established it, have been tested and shown to work many times during the transit of the Release Candidate through the

Pipeline. So we were confident that there was little risk of failure in the move to production.

Release into Production usually took between 5 and 10 minutes, including data migration.

> *It was 13 months and 5 days before a bug was noticed by a user.*

If you want to learn more about the LMAX system, you may like to read this article that I contributed to, by Martin Fowler - https://martinfowler.com/articles/lmax.html

Take-Aways

Here are some of the practices and techniques that we used, and learned from, at LMAX, that could be applied to other Deployment Pipelines:

- Don't get hung up on the tech! Choose tools that are appropriate at the time and be prepared to change them when you need to. Design, approach, patterns and techniques matter much more, and last much longer, than specific technologies.
- A modular approach to design makes it easier to change out technologies.
- Automate everything you can to improve speed, version control, consistency, repeatability and reliability.
- Assign a unique ID to each Commit and Release Candidate, so that your Pipeline can generate a complete record of every change.
- The unique ID should make it clear which Release Candidate is the newest so that the Pipeline does not waste time on older out-

dated versions, or create a backlog. Sequence numbers work well for this.

- Make it a shared team priority to fix Pipeline failures before starting new work - to keep the Pipeline moving, and maintain the software in a releasable state.
- Focus on the slowest parts of the process and experiment with ways to speed up. Put measures in place to assess the impact of any changes and improvements.
- Look for processes that can be run in parallel to speed up each step and get fast feedback from testing.
- Think about the range of different types of "users" of your system, and reflect their requirements in Pipeline tests and processes, to avoid adding checks and approvals outside the Pipeline.
- Include every test and step necessary to get a definitive answer on releasability for your software - this will vary project by project.
- Mark work-in-progress acceptance tests as "in development", so you don't clutter the Pipeline with failing tests.
- Don't waste the Manual Testers' time on regression testing (which should be automated) or evaluating work which has not yet passed automated testing.
- Use the same configuration and mechanisms for automated testing, manual testing and production. This is more efficient, because you create these things once, and you get to test configuration changes and deployment in the Pipeline - so you know it works by the time you release your software.
- Grow the Pipeline incrementally. Start simply: add sophistication as you learn and your system grows. Follow a Lean approach.

Chapter 20

The Role of the Deployment Pipeline

Continuous Delivery is the most effective way that we know of to develop high-quality software efficiently. It is about more than only Deployment Pipelines. My preferred way to express this is that we are optimising the software development process from "Idea" to "Valuable software in the hands of our users". We measure success in this optimisation based on the speed and quality of the feedback that we can gain.

We use the goal of aiming for fast, high-quality feedback as a kind of forcing-function to steer us to improve our software development activities.

If we succeed, we end up with a continuous flow of ideas. To maintain this continuous flow requires many changes to how we think about, and undertake, our work. Many of these changes are outside the scope of the Deployment Pipeline and so outside the scope of this book. However, the Deployment Pipeline sits at the heart of this problem.

It allows us to pull together a number of issues that, otherwise, are problems on our route to fast feedback. This gives us much more visibility and control of those problems, and so opportunities to fix them.

To do well at Continuous Delivery you need more than only a great Deployment Pipeline, but a great Deployment Pipeline will significantly help you on that journey, and you really won't be doing well at Continuous Delivery without one.

The Deployment Pipeline is an organising mechanism around which we can build an effective, efficient, high-quality development approach.

I hope that you have enjoyed this book, and found the ideas in it helpful.

Appendices

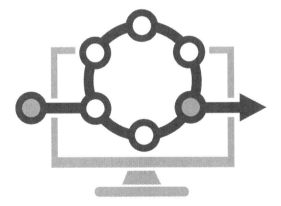

More Information

Continuous Delivery is sometimes misperceived as being all about deployment automation. Deployment Pipelines are often seen as being another name for a build-script. This book, clearly, does not take that view.

The Deployment Pipeline is an organising idea, an engineering tool that can help us structure our work and make us more efficient, more effective AND more creative.

This is an engineering discipline for creating better software faster, and as such is a very big topic.

This book is a beginning, you can learn more from the following resources:

The Continuous Delivery Book

If you would like to learn more about the ideas of Continuous Delivery, my book, "**Continuous Delivery - Reliable Software Releases Through Build, Test and Deployment Automation**", published by Addison Wesley, is widely seen as the definitive work on this topic.

You can find it here: *https://amzn.to/2WxRYmx*

The Continuous Delivery YouTube Channel

I run a YouTube Channel where I publish videos every week, Wednesdays at 7pm UK time, on the topics related to Software Development and Software Engineering, supporting and building on the ideas of Continuous Delivery and DevOps.

You can find it here: *https://bit.ly/CDonYT*

Continuous Delivery Training

My company has created an online school, with CD, DevOps and Software Engineering training courses, on the adoption and application of Continuous Delivery concepts to software development.

You can learn more about our training courses here: *https://bit.ly/DFTraining*

This book is an ideal accompaniment to our "**Anatomy of a Deployment Pipeline**" training course. You can find more on that course here: *http://bit.ly/anatomyDP*

Further Reading

Finally, there are several other books that are mentioned throughout this book. Here are links to those, and a few more that I can recommend.

Continuous Delivery: Reliable Software Releases through Build, Test, and Deployment Automation, by me and Jez Humble
https://amzn.to/2WxRYmx

Specification By Example, by Gojko Adzic
https://amzn.to/2TlfYaH

Growing Object Oriented Software Guided by Tests, by Nat Price & Steve Freeman
https://amzn.to/2Lt3jho

Test Driven Development: By Example (The Addison-Wesley Signature Series), by Kent Beck
https://amzn.to/2NcqgGh

Release It!, by Michael Nygard
https://amzn.to/38zrlNu

Refactoring Databases: Evolutionary Database Design, by Scott Ambler & Pramod Sadalage
https://amzn.to/36BjHrT

Infrastructure As Code, by Kief Morris
https://amzn.to/3ppZXxJ

Accelerate, The Science of Lean Software and DevOps, by Nicole Fosgren, Jez Humble & Gene Kim
https://amzn.to/2YYf5Z8

Measuring Continuous Delivery, by Steve Smith
https://leanpub.com/measuringcontinuousdelivery

The LMAX Architecture, by Martin Fowler
https://martinfowler.com/articles/lmax.html

Please note that some of these are 'affiliate links', and so, if you buy through these links, I will get a small commission, at no additional cost to you.

About the Author

Dave Farley is a pioneer of Continuous Delivery, thought-leader and expert practitioner in CD, DevOps, TDD and software development in general.

Dave has been a programmer, software engineer and systems architect for many years, from the early days of modern computing, taking those fundamental principles of how computers and software work, and shaping ground-breaking, innovative approaches that have changed how we approach modern software development. Dave has challenged conventional thinking and lead teams to build world class software.

Dave is co-author of the Jolt-award winning book - "Continuous Delivery: Reliable Software Releases through Build, Test, and Deployment Automation", and a popular conference speaker on Software Engineering. He built one of the world's fastest financial exchanges, is a pioneer of BDD, an author of the Reactive Manifesto, and a winner of the Duke award for open source software with the LMAX Disruptor.

Dave is passionate about helping development teams around the world improve the design, quality and reliability of their software, by sharing his expertise through his Continuous Delivery consultancy, YouTube channel, training courses and books.

Thank You for Buying My Book

Thank you for buying my book. I hope that you enjoy it and, more importantly, find it helpful.

If you do, and you'd like to see more from me, you can:

Follow me on Twitter @davefarley77

Watch my YouTube videos: http://bit.ly/CDonYT

Checkout my training courses: http://course.cd.training

Buy my other book, "Continuous Delivery: Reliable Software Releases through Build, Test, and Deployment Automation": https://amzn.to/2WxRYmx

Join my mail-list and get updates on everything above as well as regular, useful content: http://bit.ly/CD-List

STORM SURGE

To Dr. David Scharf—
Every good wish to a
great physician, as well
as a colleague on the
L.A. County Sheriff's Dept.
Hope you enjoy the book.
Bill

William Neil Martin
10/22/01

STORM SURGE

William Neil Martin

10250-MART

Library of Congress Number: 2001118418

ISBN #:	Hardcover	1-4010-1046-6
	Softcover	1-4010-1045-8

This book was printed in the United States of America.

To order additional copies of this book, contact:
Xlibris Corporation
1-888-7-XLIBRIS
www.Xlibris.com
Orders@Xlibris.com

This book is dedicated to my wife, Marie, with all my love. Without her daily support in every aspect of our lives Storm Surge would not have been attempted, much less completed.

ONE

Los Angeles, California (Sheriff's Jurisdiction)
Sunday
July 6, 1969

THE LOS ANGELES County deputy sheriff recognized the unmarked car when it was still a block away. So could any child over the age of seven, especially in a ghetto community adjacent to the city of Los Angeles. What was there not to recognize? A '68 Plymouth four-door sedan, pea green in color with black-wall tires.

The most telling giveaway, though, were the vehicle's two male occupants, one black and one white, each wearing a white shirt and tie.

They had to be cops.

As the car approached, the deputy stepped off the curb and removed a rope from the barricade that had been set up to deny public parking access in front of the crime scene.

The Plymouth pulled to the curb and stopped. The black man emerged from the passenger side and extended his hand in greeting to the deputy.

"Hello, Jim," he said as they shook hands.

"Sergeant Flowers. It's good to see you again."

The driver had gotten out of the car and walked around to the curb, where the other two were standing.

"Jim, I'd like you to meet my partner, Sergeant Archie Penner. Arch, this is Jim Thurman. Jim and I worked together at Lennox Station."

The middle-aged redheaded sergeant and the young blond deputy shook hands, and Sergeant Flowers silently noted how both men stood out like sore thumbs in this predominantly black neighborhood.

"Actually, Sergeant Flowers and I didn't exactly work together," Thurman said. "He was a detective sergeant and I was a patrol deputy. Heck, I don't think I was off training more'n a few months when he transferred to Homicide."

"Who are you working with these days?" Flowers asked.

"Jerry Parker," Thurman replied. "He's guarding the entrance to the apartment."

Flowers glanced toward the building nearest them. It was a standard two-story apartment complex, the length of which ran perpendicular to the street. A sidewalk ran along the side of the structure, providing access to each of the half dozen downstairs apartments. The faded pink stucco exterior was badly in need of a fresh coat of paint. Even the late afternoon sunlight could not brighten the building's dingy appearance.

Flowers looked at Penner. "Well, I guess we better go have a look."

"It isn't pretty," Thurman said. "Triple homicide. The place looks like a cyclone went through it."

"Does it look like it might've been a residential robbery?" Penner asked.

"Not that we can tell. The TV and stereo are still there, and I saw a twenty dollar bill on the nightstand, near the male victim." Thurman thought for a moment. "No, it looks to me like the only intention was murder."

"Upstairs or down?" Flowers asked.

"Downstairs. Apartment number two."

"Do you have everybody rolling? Crime lab? Coroner?" Flowers asked, then regretted it as soon as the words were spoken.

"Of course," Thurman replied, a little hurt that he would be questioned about such a routine matter.

"Sorry, Jim. I should have known better." Flowers didn't bother to mention how often deputies tended to forget such "routine " matters.

As Flowers and Penner walked toward the building Thurman called after them. "It's easy to find the right apartment. It'll be the one the deputy is standing in front of."

Flowers looked back and saw the grin on Thurman's face. "Thanks a lot." He returned the grin, knowing the exchange was made to show there were no hard feelings.

They walked through an open wrought iron gate adjacent to the building and along the sidewalk the short distance to apartment number two. A black uniformed deputy sheriff stood in front of the entrance. He was talking to another black man. At six feet three inches, the deputy towered over the shorter man, in spite of the huge Afro that formed a dome four inches above his scalp.

"Afternoon, Jerry," Flowers said as he and Penner approached the deputy.

"Garland!" The deputy exclaimed with a smile. At thirty-one, he and Flowers were the same age, and had been casual friends since 1958, when they both entered the academy.

Flowers introduced Penner, then Jerry Parker introduced the man with the Afro.

"This is Tyrone Adams. He's the informant."

"Nice to meet you, Mr. Adams," Flowers said. "Would you mind telling us what led you to call the Sheriff's Department?"

"Cause they's dead people in there"

Flowers suppressed a smile. Penner and Parker glanced at each other and made no attempt to suppress theirs.

"Are you the one who discovered the crime?" Flowers asked.

"Yeah."

"How did you happen to be here, and how did you get into the apartment? Are you a family member?"

"Oh, no. We ain't related. But me an' Walter, he's the dead man, we brothers."

"One of the victims is your brother? I thought you said you weren't related."

"We ain't."

"He means they're friends," Parker said. "You know, brothers of the skin, so to speak." He shook his head in feigned disappointment. "Garland, you've been downtown too long. You're out of touch with the ghetto."

"I guess I must be," Flowers said, then returned his attention to the informant. "Sorry, Mr. Adams. Let's try again. How did you happen to be here?"

"Well, me an' Walter was supposed to meet down at Leo's at noon to shoot some pool."

"Leo's is a beer bar and pool hall several blocks from here," Parker offered.

Adams continued, as if there had been no interruption in his narrative. "But he didn't show up. That ain't like Walter to be late. He usually gets to Leo's before I do. He's a great pool player. Makes a lot of money on them tables."

"Is there a chance he might have hustled the wrong person?" Penner asked.

Adams looked hurt. "Walter don't hustle. He just shoots good pool."

"No offense," Penner said. "Please continue."

"So, by one-thirty he still ain't showed. Now I'm startin' to get worried. I couldn't call cause his phone wasn't workin'. So I decided to walk over here.

"When I got here I knocked but they weren't no answer. But he musta been home cause his car was parked out back. So I looked in that window over there." He pointed to the double-paned sliding glass window which set about six feet to the right of the door. "That's his and Maureen's bedroom. The shade was up a couple inches, the way it is now, and I peeked in. I couldn't see much, but what I did see was enough. A leg was hangin' over the side of the bed. It was Maureen's. I could tell on account of it was white and didn't have no hair on it."

This time Flowers, Penner and Parker each fought to suppress a smile.

"I tapped on the glass and yelled out Walter's name. Then I yelled out Maureen's. I knew she was there cause her leg was there. But she didn't budge.

"I ran to the manager's apartment. She lives right there in number one. I told her something was bad wrong over in Walter's apartment. So she let me use her phone to call the sheriffs."

"Did you go inside at all today?" Flowers asked.

"No sir! I waited till the police got here. After they went in, Deputy Parker here, he come out and told me what all he saw." Adams paused and for a moment Flowers thought he might break down and cry. But he composed himself and added, "Walter . . . Maureen . . ." He could not hold back a sob. "And little Georgetta."

"Little Georgetta? How old is Georgetta?" Flowers asked.

Adams thought for a moment. "I think she's twelve. Ten or twelve."

For a fleeting moment Flowers thought of his own three-year-old daughter, but he forced the thought from his mind. He had learned that it was not healthy to personalize the tragedies of others.

"Why?" Adams asked. His shock was beginning to turn to grief. "Why did this have to happen?"

"I don't know," Flowers said. "But we intend to find out." Flowers and Penner then walked past Parker and entered the apartment.

THE LIVING ROOM was just as Deputy Thurman had described it. A flower vase had been thrown across the room, leaving water stains on the wall and broken glass on the soiled carpet. The cheap coffee table had also been thrown, or kicked, across the room and lay on its side in a corner. The sofa had been overturned and was lying upside down in the center of the room.

"Your friend Jim was right," Penner said. "It does look like a cyclone came through here."

"Yep," Flowers said as he gazed around the room. "The storm came in, wreaked havoc, killed some people, then left."

"You'd think that all the noise would've gotten the attention of the neighbors," Penner said.

"Not in this neighborhood," Flowers said. "Folks aren't anxious to stick their noses in things that are no concern to them. It could get them killed."

Penner sighed. "Yeah, I know."

Archie Penner was highly respected as an investigator and was well aware of how things were in the street. Ten years older than Flowers, he had nine years departmental seniority on the younger man, eight years seniority as a sergeant and six years seniority in the Homicide Bureau. He had been both mentor and partner to Flowers since the younger man's transfer into the elite investigations unit.

Penner followed Flowers into the hallway, then turned right and entered the master bedroom. A king size bed occupied most of the space in the room. On the side nearest the investigators the body of a black man who appeared to be in his early thirties lay on his left side. The covers had been kicked away from him, probably during the struggle, and he was clothed only in a pair of boxer shorts. His head, resting on a pillow, was tilted backward and slightly upward at an awkward angle. The eyes were closed but the mouth was open. It was obvious to Flowers that the man's neck was broken.

On the far side of the bed the body of a white woman, dressed in a threadbare pink negligee, lay on her back. Her left leg dangled from the side of the bed. She appeared to be in her late twenties. Her eyes were wide open and her tongue protruded slightly from her mouth. The marks on her neck indicated that she had been strangled. Her pillow lay on the floor at the foot of the bed.

Other than the bed, two small nightstands and a large dresser were the only pieces of furniture in the room. The top of the dresser was bare, but on the floor at one end were numerous feminine items such as hairpins and various lotions, as if the items had been swept from the dresser top. There was little else in the room to ransack.

Penner went to the head of the bed on the far side and bent over the woman for a closer inspection of her neck.

"I've come across a lot a strangulation cases over the years," he said. "But I do believe these are the most severe marks I've ever seen." After a pause he added, "Whoever did this had very powerful hands."

Flowers, who had been exploring the contents of a wallet that he had picked up from the nightstand near the male victim, looked briefly at the woman's neck. He set the wallet back on the stand, then leaned over for a closer look at the man's injuries. He put a hand behind the victim's neck and rubbed, as if massaging it.

"I see what you mean," he said, shaking his head. "Despite the rigor, it feels as if everything inside this man's neck has been detached."

Now came the part that Flowers dreaded. He let Penner lead the way as they crossed the hallway and entered the smaller bedroom. This was one aspect of the job that he hated, and he knew that, as long as he lived he would never get accustomed to viewing the remains of a murdered child.

But the scene was not what they expected. The room was neat and tidy, and nothing appeared to be out of place. The body of the child lay on her back. She was covered to the chest with a sheet and a flower-printed bedspread. Her arms were outside the covers with the hands folded, one across the other, as if in repose.

Flowers stared at the child's pretty face. Her eyes and mouth were closed. Her complexion was a light brown. Her hair was also brown, with a reddish tint to it. It was quite apparent that she was of racially mixed blood. Had she been allowed to grow up, he thought, she would have developed into a very attractive woman.

Penner lifted the covers and made a cursory examination of the body, then replaced the bedspread and sheet. "No marks or bruises. No sign of injury whatsoever."

"She was smothered to death," Flowers said as he continued to stare at the child's face.

"Smothered? You sure?"

"Well, I'm not a medical examiner, but I'm ninety percent sure an autopsy will prove she was smothered."

"How do you think he did it? Assuming it was a he. If it was the same person who killed the other two, he certainly didn't use his hands. With his brute strength, he would've left marks on her face."

"Remember the pillow that was lying on the floor in the other room?"

"Yes."

"My guess is that he took that pillow from under the woman's head, brought it in here, and I hope to God it was while the child was asleep, put it over her face and smothered her. He then returned the pillow to the other room."

"Assuming your theory is correct, why do you suppose he went to all that trouble?" Penner asked.

"Now that's a question I can't answer."

THE CRIMINALIST ARRIVED from the crime lab just as Flowers and Penner stepped from the child's bedroom. He was accompanied by the print deputy and a photographer. Flowers briefed them on the crime and walked them through the apartment. They were all experts on the collection and preservation of evidence, and Flowers knew better than to point out specific areas on which to focus. He was confident they would do a thorough job.

As soon as Penner and Flowers were called to handle this case it was agreed that Flowers would be the lead investigator. Penner was already investigating a rather complicated homicide. It, therefore, fell on Flowers to handle the details of this case.

While the crime lab was doing its job inside the apartment, the two detectives went to each apartment in the complex to get statements from the occupants. Most of them were either not at home or refused to answer the knock on the door. Those who did respond had nothing to contribute. No one heard or saw anything.

By the time Flowers and Penner were finished interviewing the tenants, the deputy coroner had arrived and was taking charge of the victims' remains.

In front of the apartment building a television news crew had set up its video equipment and was attempting to get a statement from Deputy Thurman. Flowers knew he could trust Thurman to keep them from getting past the wrought iron gate. By Los Angeles standards this was not a major news event. Ghetto murders were quite common. Whether or not it would even be broadcast depended upon the latest events related to Vietnam, civil unrest, or other acts of protest that dominated the airwaves. The activity, of course, drew a crowd of onlookers; mainly pedestrians who had been walking along the street and were attracted by the news cameras, as well as the two coroners' wagons that were double-parked in front of the apartment building.

After the bodies had been taken away and the crime lab had completed its collection of evidence, the apartment was secured. Flowers gave a brief, generic statement to the news reporter, then he and Penner departed.

When they were seated in the car and Penner was starting the engine, he asked, "Well, what do you think?"

"About what, the news interview or the crime?"

"The crime. Who cares about the news interview?"

"I don't know," Flowers said. "But I think we can rule out robbery. I checked the victim's wallet. It had several tens and twenties in it, and there was a twenty dollar bill lying on the nightstand in plain sight."

Flowers fell silent as Penner turned the wheel of the Plymouth and merged into traffic. Then he said, "I suggest we pay a visit to Leo's. Who knows, maybe the guy ticked off some sore loser during a game of pool."

"Could be," Penner said. He thought for a moment, then added, "Have you considered the possibility that it might have been racially motivated?"

"You mean some bigot who couldn't stand the idea of a white woman shacking up with a black man?"

"Yeah, something like that."

"It crossed my mind. But if that's what it was, why the fuss over the little girl? Why would a racist be so sensitive toward a child of mixed blood? It doesn't make sense."

"Yep, It's a puzzler." Penner smiled. "I'm just glad it's *your* puzzler."

"Thanks a lot," Flowers said, then added, "There are a few things that I'm fairly certain about."

"Like what?"

"Barring any proof to the contrary, I'd say that our suspect is a male and that he acted alone. Judging from the positions of their bodies, my guess is that he killed the man and woman at virtually the same time.

"Of necessity he would've had to kill the man first, because the man would've offered the most resistance. Had the struggle been prolonged, the woman would have awakened and jumped out of bed. As it was, she barely had time to get one leg off before she was attacked . . . after the killer had broken the man's neck.

"Of course, the whole thing had to have happened very quickly, or it would have awakened the little girl."

"How do you know the girl wasn't awakened?" Penner asked.

Flowers sighed. "I don't know. I guess it's just wishful thinking."

"What makes you think he acted alone? Why couldn't the man and woman have been murdered simultaneously by two different people? As far as that goes, the child might have been killed by a third person."

"I don't think so. This has all the earmarks of an act of personal rage. It's hard to find conspirators in such a crime." After a pause, Flowers added, "Of course, you might very well be right. We can't rule out any possibility. I'm going on nothing more than a hunch.

I just hope we get a fingerprint, a witness, or something. I'll take any break that comes our way."

As it turned out there were no fingerprints, and an exhaustive search for witnesses proved futile. It would take two weeks and another multiple homicide before Flowers got his break.

TWO

Friday
July 18, 1969

WITHIN TWO DAYS of his release from state prison B. C. Jones found employment. He was hired as a swamper on a trash truck. His employer was Bert's Disposal Company. Collecting trash was not exactly the most desirable way to make a living, but all things considered, it was the best job that Jones could hope to find.

He was a powerfully built man of twenty-six. At six feet six inches he weighed 280 pounds, and none of it was fat. He had been big and naturally strong all of his life, and after six years of lifting weights at Soledad Prison his chest and arms had become massive. His days had been spent in the exercise yard and his nights had been spent brooding alone in his cell.

B. C. Jones was a mulatto, the product of a white mother and a black father. His skin was light brown, with several dark brown blotches on his forehead and cheeks. They were too large to be freckles and too flat to be moles. His features were those of a black man. His short, thick hair was a yellowish brown.

He could not remember a day in his life when he felt that he belonged to any race. He was neither black nor white. As far as B. C. Jones was concerned he would always be an outsider.

MOST OF BERT'S disposal business was in the southwestern section of the county, in the small urban communities just outside the city limits of Los Angeles. On Fridays the route of the trash collection truck to which Jones was assigned was in Lawndale, one such community whose population consisted primarily of the working class.

Jones stood on a step at the rear of the disposal truck and held on to a hand rail as the large, odorous vehicle made its way along a narrow residential street. The modest stucco houses on both sides appeared to have been designed by the same architect. Twenty years earlier these had been the dream homes of war veterans anxious to take advantage of the G.I. Bill. But time and neglect had taken their toll. The littered streets, drab-colored houses and yards without grass bespoke of residences not owned by their occupants and of landlords who lived far away.

The truck slowed and pulled to the right curb. Jones stepped off and sauntered toward a large battered metal oil drum that served as a trash container. It had been placed adjacent to a driveway that ran alongside a small house that lent faded evidence that it had once been painted green. At the end of the driveway a pickup truck was parked in front of a detached garage. The truck was facing the street and the hood was up. A man was leaning over the fender, apparently working on the engine. He was shirtless, and his white skin glistened in the bright sunlight. On the ground nearby a portable radio was blaring at full volume, and the entire neighborhood could hear the Rolling Stones lamenting their failure to get any satisfaction.

Jones had learned that he could get more accomplished if he concentrated only on the chore at hand. At the moment his chore was to collect the trash, and not watch the white man work on his truck.

Then, as he was lifting the large can, the side door of the house opened and a young black woman stepped outside onto the driveway, and Jones could no longer concentrate on his chore. The woman was holding a screaming infant, and he could tell, even from twenty feet away, that the baby was of mixed blood. He did not move as he held the fifty-five gallon drum filled with trash the way others might hold a sack of groceries. He stood at the curb and stared at the white man and the black woman . . . and the crying baby that had no race.

"Robert," the woman said, "I need you to go down to the store and get the baby some formula."

The man under the hood made no reply and the woman spoke more loudly. "Robert, I need you to . . ."

"I heard you!" The man shouted as he backed away from the truck and stood erect and faced her. He was tall and thin, with long, brown, stringy hair. "Can't you see I'm up to my arm pits in grease? I ain't goin' nowhere!"

"But he's hungry, Robert."

"Then you go to the store. I'm busy."

The woman went back into the house. Just as the man was about to return to his work on the truck he noticed the trash collector staring at him.

"What're you lookin' at?" He asked. There was a defiant snarl in his tone.

Jones continued to stand and stare. He thought no more of the man's defiance than he would a yapping Chihuahua.

The man was surly by nature and, under different circumstances, might have walked out to the street and challenged the trash collector. But as he looked more closely at this giant who held the oil drum like it was an oatmeal box, he thought better of it.

Rafael Luna sat in the driver's seat of the disposal truck and watched his swamper in the rear view mirror. Jones was just standing there, holding the trash can. It was apparent that something had gotten his attention.

Luna did not care for B. C. Jones. The man was big and ugly, and about as dumb as an adobe brick. But worst of all, he was slow. They should have been at the dump by now, emptying their load and finishing up for the week. But Jones was holding them up. He was wasting time back there. Luna wanted to get out, walk to the back of the truck and yell at Jones, but he was afraid the big dufus might rip his head off. Instead, he lightly tapped on the horn.

The sound of the horn caused Jones to return his attention to the chore at hand. Moving to the rear of the vehicle he lifted the heavy trash container high enough to dump its contents into the hold of the disposal truck. He then set the can on the curb where he had found it. The truck was already beginning to move when he stepped onto the swamper's foothold.

The thin man with long stringy hair waited until the trash collector was out of hearing, then he loudly issued a string of profanities. When he decided that the truck was far enough down the street, the man sauntered to the curb. He cursed the big ugly trash man once more, then raised his hand in a dramatic gesture and extended his middle finger.

THREE

Sunday
July 20, 1969

AT TWO A.M. B.C. Jones was wide-awake. He lay on his back and stared at the ceiling, his feet extended past the foot of the tiny twin bed. He had slept fitfully since turning in at ten P.M. He could not get that skinny white man and that black whore out of his thoughts. But most of all he could not erase the image of the little baby. He hated to think of it growing up in this ugly world.

These thoughts had been with him since Friday, and throughout Saturday they had been his constant companions. Even as he tried to sleep they were there, as if functioning independently in his head. Gradually the thoughts evolved into a voice that dominated his will. A dozen times Jones tried to force himself to sleep, and a dozen times the voice awakened him with its terrible plan.

At 2:15 Jones gave in to the entity in his head that was now stronger than his will to resist. He succumbed to it just as he had two weeks earlier when he went to that apartment building and kept that young girl from having to live a life of revulsion and shame. He remembered the girl with a touch of sadness. She was such a pretty thing. Then he thought of her parents and how he had punished them, and he thought of how satisfied he had felt afterward.

Pulling his legs to the side of the bed, he raised himself to a sitting position and rubbed his hands over his face. A moment later he stood up and fumbled in the dark for his clothes.

B.C. JONES HAD lived in the modest apartment since his release from prison four months earlier. It was conveniently located near a Safeway supermarket and a Thrifty Drugs, and within six blocks of a MacDonald's. Around the corner was a rundown movie theater that ran second-run movies at discount prices. Bert's Disposal was a mile away.

Though his apartment was small and poorly furnished, B.C. liked it because he could walk to all the places that were important to him. Aside from public transportation, walking was his only means of getting around, for he had never learned to drive. His daddy had tried to teach him shortly after B.C.'s sixteenth birthday. But after one lesson he gave up and announced that B.C. was too stupid to drive. He had better stick to walking. B.C. never made any further effort to learn, for he had no intention of going out of his way to have someone else remind him of his stupidity.

B.C. had no friends. The only person in the neighborhood to whom he spoke was his landlady, who lived in the apartment building. But Jones was quiet and always paid his rent on time, so she really had little to say to him. Besides, there was something about him that frightened her, so she took the rent money from him once a month and tried to avoid him the rest of the time.

With his first paycheck B.C. put a TV set on layaway and three weeks later he made the final payment and was able to bring it home. He spent most of his leisure time eating chocolate-covered cupcakes and watching cartoons on his new TV. Occasionally he would go to the local movie theater. He especially liked animated features and westerns.

IT WAS A seven-mile walk to his destination, but Jones gave no thought to the distance. He liked the cool air on his face in the early hours before dawn. The streets were deserted. The bars had been closed for over an hour, and the drunks were either at home or in jail. There weren't even any police cars roaming the streets. A feeling of excitement rushed through him as he put one foot in front of the other and moved ever closer to that skinny man's run-down house in Lawndale.

BREAKING INTO THE house was not a difficult task. The screen door, after years of being kicked open and slammed shut, had long since fallen apart, and now remained permanently open, hanging loosely on its hinges. The cheap lock on the hollow wooden door was not designed to keep out serious intruders. Jones' only concern was the noise he might make.

He gripped the doorknob in his right hand, then placed his massive right shoulder against the door and gave a sudden, powerful push. The flimsy lock could not withstand the force, and it gave way with little resistance.

Jones quickly backed away and moved to the side of the house. He waited a full five minutes in the shadows and listened. When he was convinced that the sound had not awakened anyone, he returned to the front door, hesitated a few seconds, then stepped inside. It took only a moment to become accustomed to the interior darkness and detect the outlines of furniture. Then he moved slowly across the living room, careful not to step on any unseen objects lying about.

He found the hallway and turned left, toward the front bedroom. Adults like to sleep in the front of the house, he thought, and put the kids in the back. So this is probably their room.

A nearby street light provided sufficient illumination for him to make out the couple asleep on the double bed. They lay on opposite sides, near the edge, with their backs to each other.

Jones stood at the foot of the bed and stared for a moment. The voice inside him was filling his head with thoughts of passionate hate. He hated the man for being so mean and he hated the woman for being with him. But mostly he hated them both for bringing an innocent baby into a world that would treat it with contempt.

He moved to the right side of the bed where the man slept. In one fluid motion he cupped his right hand under the man's neck and the heel of his left hand on the man's forehead. Jones lifted the head six inches and turned it so that it was facing up. This placed the head at an oblique angle to the body. The man's eyes opened and a startled expression appeared on his face. Jones pushed hard on the forehead. A cry from the man was stifled by a loud crack at the base of his neck.

The woman stirred, then rolled onto her back. Jones lifted his knee over the body of the man and placed it in the center of the bed, then leaned over and grabbed the woman's neck with his left hand. He pressed down hard with his thumb and index finger on either side of her throat, then squeezed inward. The woman's eyes opened wide and she made a brief gurgling sound as her tongue extended and her eyes bulged. She struggled for several seconds, then her body went limp.

He pulled himself up and off the bed. He stood over the man for a moment, then nudged him. Satisfied that the longhaired skinny white trash was dead, he turned away to leave. Just as he was walking out of the room, he remembered something. He went to the woman's side of the bed and took the pillow from under her head. It had to be the mother's pillow. Jones could not stand the thought of the man's pillow touching the baby's face.

A minute later he returned to the master bedroom and threw the pillow onto the bed. He stared angrily at the two corpses before turning to go. As he was walking out of the room he passed a chest of drawers. With one hand he reached behind it and pulled it over. It fell forward, strewing a dozen knick-knacks onto the floor. The top portion of the chest fell against the foot of the bed and the drawers opened, spilling socks and underwear.

Jones moved into the living room and was about to walk out of the house when he saw a large framed photograph on top of the console TV. It was a portrait of the white man, the black woman and the baby.

He was suddenly filled with renewed rage. He grabbed the picture frame and twisted it in his powerful hands until it broke. Shattered glass fell to the floor. He removed the photograph, then threw the mangled frame across the room, where it hit a mirror above the fireplace. He ripped the photo into several pieces and let them fall to the floor like confetti.

Jones pulled the large TV over on its face. He grabbed a nearby floor lamp and threw it, but the electric cord, which was plugged into the wall, slowed its momentum and it fell abruptly onto the worn and dirty carpet in the center of the room.

He stepped out of the house and closed the door behind him. He glanced around to see if the noise had aroused the neighbors. A dog barked in the distance, otherwise the neighborhood was quiet.

Jones left the house and walked at a leisurely pace toward his apartment. He had gone less than a mile when the anger began to subside. By the time he had walked two miles the voice inside him had quieted and he began to be filled with a sense of satisfaction, the same as he had felt two weeks earlier.

He could see the dawn beginning to break over in the east. By the time he arrived at his apartment it was fully light, but it was Sunday morning and the streets were still deserted.

Entering the apartment, he went straight to his bed and collapsed. He was exhausted and overcome with a sensuous pleasure. He soon fell into a deep sleep. He would sleep soundly throughout the day and all night, and would awaken early Monday morning, rested and temporarily fulfilled.

FOUR

Sunday
July 20, 1969

IT HAD BEEN one of the best birthdays Garland Flowers could remember, even if he did have to make the arrangements himself. It began at ten A.M., when he drove to Hacienda Heights and picked up his wife, Rochelle, and their three-year-old daughter, Danielle. Garland and Rochelle had been separated for six months, though neither had made any attempt to file for divorce.

They had brunch at the International House of Pancakes, then Garland drove them to the zoo, where they spent the remainder of the day. From there they went to his apartment in Torrance and barbecued hamburgers on his eight-foot-square private patio. Afterward they had cake and ice cream, then Danielle promptly fell asleep.

After tucking the child into his bed, Garland returned to the living room and turned on the TV. He and Rochelle then snuggled on the sofa and awaited the live broadcast of man's first landing on the moon.

Rochelle had balked at first, reminding him that tomorrow was a work day and they both had to get up early. Garland pointed out that the moon landing was an historic event of epic proportions, perhaps the greatest milestone of the twentieth century. Witnessing it was an occasion to be shared with loved ones. With feigned resignation she gave in. Though she was both impressed and amused by his argument, the fact was that it had been a wonderful day, and she was reluctant to see it come to an end.

As Garland watched Walter Cronkite explaining to the TV audience what it could expect to see in the coming hour, Rochelle stared tenderly at her husband. If only there had been more days like this, she thought, things might have been different.

GARLAND FLOWERS MET Rochelle Bullock in 1962 while attending Harbor Jr. College. He was already a four-year veteran of the L.A. County Sheriff's Department and was taking classes part-time, majoring in Police Science. Rochelle was a full-time student. Her major was Business Administration.

They dated for almost two years before getting married in June 1964. They moved into an apartment in Long Beach. By this time Rochelle had graduated from Harbor College and was now enrolled at Long Beach State. Garland was assigned to an evening patrol unit at Lennox Station, in one of the busiest patrol areas of the county.

In the first three years of their marriage it seemed that nothing could go wrong for either of them. In January 1965, Rochelle graduated from Long Beach State and was hired by Sears as a management trainee. This was regarded as quite an achievement for a black woman in the mid-sixties.

In February an opening came up in the Lennox Station Detective Bureau and several detectives recommended Garland for the job. He was a hard working patrol deputy and was well known on the streets. His list of informants was more extensive than that of any of his peers, and so was his record of high quality arrests. No one was surprised when he was selected for the detective assignment.

So he traded his tan and green uniform for a brand new suit from Sears, purchased by Rochelle at a ten-percent employee discount. This type of suit, either dark blue, dark brown or charcoal gray, along with a white shirt, conservative tie and wing-tip shoes, would become his mode of attire, even after the rest of the world began to go crazy with bright multicolored polyester shirts and burgundy trousers that flared at the bottom.

A year earlier Garland had passed the sergeant's test with a score high enough to place him on the list of candidates eligible for promotion. He knew that he would eventually get promoted, but did not know when. As it happened, his name came up less than two months after his transfer to the Detective Bureau, and he was concerned that he would be transferred to another unit of assignment, which was the general policy with newly promoted sergeants.

His lieutenant, who did not want to lose his new investigator, appealed to the area inspector, who, in turn, took Flowers' case to the division chief. On April 4, 1965, Garland Flowers was promoted to sergeant and was allowed to remain in the Detective Bureau.

On December 19, 1965 Danielle was born, and their apartment suddenly seemed to shrink. Two months later they purchased a house in Hacienda Heights, a middle-class community on the eastside of the county. Shortly afterward Rochelle went back to work at Sears, where she was a division manager in the ladies' ready-to-wear department.

Life was good.

In the three years that he was assigned to the Lennox Detective Bureau Garland's reputation as an investigator continued to grow, but he never forgot his roots in patrol. Whenever a patrol deputy made an exceptionally good arrest or went out of his way to develop leads, Garland never failed to write a glowing commendation to the deputy's supervisor, praising the deputy's performance. Garland could often be seen having coffee with patrol crews, laughing and joking with them. He was well-liked by the deputies, and they frequently provided him with valuable leads and other information. This assistance from patrol proved vital on numerous occasions in solving all sorts of cases.

There was nothing phony about Garland's association with the patrol deputies. He sincerely liked being around them. But he also knew a simple truth, and that was that a little praise never hurt anyone. Most cops felt that their efforts were never appreciated, and a simple compliment went a long way toward motivating one to take that extra step in completing a task properly. Everyone profited by it.

Garland's excellent investigative skills caught the attention of Captain John Gilford, of Homicide Bureau. In 1968 an opening came up in that bureau and Captain Gilford requested Sergeant Flowers for the job. His talent and experience were enough to qualify him, and the fact that he was black didn't hurt matters either. The country was caught up in civil unrest. Racial disturbances had been ongoing since the Watts Riot three years earlier.

Garland's transfer to Homicide Bureau took effect on April 7, 1968. Three days earlier Dr. Martin Luther King, Jr. was assassinated in Memphis, Tennessee. Though not intended as such, it was a sound political move to transfer a black man to such an elite position at that particular time.

He was placed under the mentorship of Sgt. Archie Penner, and they liked each other from the start. Penner had a great sense of humor, and got along well with his fellow detectives. He was also regarded as an excellent investigator and, on occasion, had been assigned high profile cases. He enjoyed a high level of credibility among his peers, and this worked out well for Garland. Penner's endorsement of him guaranteed his acceptance throughout the Bureau.

One of the first things that Flowers learned was that homicide investigators had no life of their own. They were subject to call twenty-four hours a day. They had to go where the leads took them. He found himself working twelve to sixteen hours a day, seven days a week, until the case was closed. Of course, no one had the luxury of handling just one case at a time. Each investigator usually had at least a half dozen that he was handling simultaneously. Homicides were rampant, and days off to be spent with the family were few and far between.

After a while it began to put a strain on their marriage. Garland was so preoccupied with his job that he didn't notice at first.

Then Rochelle started to complain. Instead of listening to her, he became annoyed, saying that she didn't understand. This was his job, and she would just have to learn to live with it.

She did try to live with it, but the longer he worked Homicide the more cases he was assigned and the more deeply involved he became. If anything, he was spending even more time away from home. Her concern was more than the fact that he was gone much of the time. She was also frightened for him. He was spending that time out on the streets, in bad areas, hunting down murder suspects. Every time the phone rang for him in the middle of the night she became frightened. Then he would get up, get dressed and leave, and she would spend the rest of the night lying in bed, wide awake and filled with apprehension.

In January 1969 she left him, taking Danielle with her. She had no desire to seek a divorce, but she felt that she had to get away. This way, at least, if he were called away in the middle of the night, she wouldn't know about it.

Soon after she left, Garland moved into the apartment in Torrance, so that Rochelle could move back into the house.

NEIL ARMSTRONG STEPPED off the lunar landing module and became the first human in the history of the world to set foot on the surface of the moon. The black and white image on the television screen was only moderately clear, but Garland and Rochelle held each other and were awed by what they saw.

"That's one small step for man, one giant leap for mankind."

Armstrong had barely finished uttering these words when the phone rang. Rochelle jerked slightly and Garland could feel her fingers dig involuntarily into his arm.

Please God, not tonight, he prayed silently. Garland avoided making eye contact with Rochelle as he leaned toward an end table and picked up the phone receiver.

"Hello."

"Sergeant Flowers?"

"Yeah."

"This is Deputy Carlson."

"Hello, Carlson. They got you stuck in the barrel tonight, huh?"

"Yeah, I got the duty on moon landing night. Say, I hate to tell you this, but it looks like you're gonna be called out."

"It's not my turn in the call-out rotation," Flowers objected.

"I know, but it looks like this is one you're going to end up handling anyway."

"How's that?"

"You remember the triple homicide you got a couple weeks ago? The mixed couple and their daughter?"

"How could I forget?"

"Exactly. Well, we got another one. Same M.O. in every respect, except this time it's a white man, black woman and a baby boy."

"Where?"

"It happened in Lawndale."

Flowers found a pencil and scratch pad as the deputy gave him the address. He breathed a sigh of disgust and said. "Ok, I'm rolling. But I have at least a ninety minute e.t.a."

"Thanks, Sarge," the deputy said, then added, "By the way, I'm sorry I had to call you."

"Yeah, me too," Flowers said, then returned the phone to its cradle.

Before he could turn back to her, Rochelle had quietly gotten up and was walking toward the bedroom. A moment later she returned, holding the sleeping Danielle in her arms.

"You will have time to take us home, won't you?" She asked.

"Of course."

He turned off the television, then went to the bedroom to get his wallet, badge, weapon and car keys. When he returned he found Rochelle sitting on the edge of the sofa, holding their daughter and slowly rocking her back and forth. Her sob was barely audible, but it was sufficient to cause a pang of guilt to rush through him like the blade of a cold steel knife.

FIVE

Tuesday
July 22, 1969

THE HALL OF JUSTICE was, perhaps, the most imposing structure in the Los Angeles Civic Center. It was fifteen stories high and took up an entire city block, between Broadway and Spring Streets. Its front entrance was on Temple Avenue. The slate gray stone exterior gave it the appearance of having been constructed of solid granite. It was located diagonally across the street from the Los Angeles City Hall. Both buildings were dedicated in 1926, though the Hall of Justice gave one the impression that it was much older.

The Hall, as its occupants referred to it, was the headquarters of the Los Angeles County Sheriff's Department. The Sheriff and his numerous administrative minions took up the first few floors. On the sixth floor was the Detective Division headquarters.

Sgt. Garland Flowers stepped off the elevator, turned left and walked slowly through the wide corridor toward the offices of Homicide Bureau, which took up the entire northeast portion of the building's sixth floor. He was tired, and visits to the medical examiner's morgue tended to put him in a depressed mood. The fact that witnessing autopsies was a routine part of a homicide investigator's job did not mean that he had to enjoy it.

He had spent every waking moment since the phone call on Sunday night trying to dig up even the smallest clue as to the identity of this multiple murder suspect. The count was now six victims and zero clues. A search for witnesses had proved futile. But this was not surprising, since the medical examiner had placed the times of death between 4:45 and 5:00 o'clock Sunday morning. Of course the neighbors heard nothing, despite the fact that a door had been broken in and furniture had been thrown about.

The latest male victim was such a jerk that the neighbors avoided him. The woman was ok, and it was a shame about the baby, but the man's demise was no loss to anyone.

Archie Penner was waiting for him when Flowers entered the large office area of the Bureau. He was halfway to his desk when Penner met him with a broad smile on his face.

"What're you so happy about?" Flowers asked.

Penner ignored the question. "How'd the autopsy go?"

"Just as we suspected. The causes of death were exactly the same as in the other case." Flowers arrived at his desk and flopped into the chair. "I'll tell you, Arch, I've never seen two cases whose M.O.'s were so similar." He paused long enough to breathe a deep sigh. "One thing's for sure. If we solve one crime, we'll solve the other, because there's no doubt in my mind whatsoever that the Lawndale murders and the Lennox murders were committed by the same person."

Penner placed his posterior on a corner of Flowers' desk and smiled down at him. "A short while ago I got a call from the crime lab. Looks like we might have a make on the suspect."

Flowers sat up in his chair, forgetting the exhaustion from two days of almost no sleep. "What'd they find?"

"A thumb print," Penner said. "Remember the broken glass from the picture frame in the living room? Well, apparently our boy got careless and left a nice print for us when he decided to tear up the photo."

"You said we had a make. Who does the print belong to?"

"A parolee by the name of B.C. Jones."

"How long's he been out?"

"Four months."

"What was he in for?" Flowers asked.

"Voluntary manslaughter. We're still waiting for his rap sheet from Sacramento."

"If he's on parole, let's get in touch with his parole officer. He should be able to tell us everything we need to know about this guy."

"My thought exactly," Penner said. "Why don't you try to locate the P.O. and I'll accumulate the crime scene photos and reports, then we'll go brief the captain."

CAPTAIN JOHN GILFORD took a final drag on his Lucky Strike before extinguishing it in the half-full ashtray on his desk. He was a heavy-set man with a balding head and a deep voice. In his mid-fifties, he looked every year of it. He was five years away from a forced retirement, and if he could spend his remaining years in Homicide, he would retire a happy man.

Gilford had been a detective since the 1940's, a time when a trench coat and felt hat were part of a plain-clothes cop's everyday attire. Even in these waning years of his career, he still looked as if he had just stepped from the pages of a Raymond Chandler novel.

Sergeants Penner and Flowers, and their supervisor, Lieutenant Joe Skinner, sat across the desk from Captain Gilford and waited for him to light his thirtieth cigarette of the day.

"We should all thank Teddy Kennedy for taking the heat off of us," Gilford said as he exhaled smoke through his nose. "If it weren't for that little incident on Chappaquiddick Island last week, the press would be in *our* hair instead of his. As it is, we'd better show some progress on these cases. Six murders in two weeks, involving two racially mixed families, is just a little too much for the news hounds to ignore."

"It looks like we might have a break in the case," Lt. Skinner said.

"What kind of break?"

"A thumb print." Skinner looked at Flowers. "Garland, since it's your case, why don't you give the boss an update?"

"The print comes back to an ex-con by the name of B.C. Jones," Flowers began.

"What does B.C. stand for?" Gilford asked.

"Nothing. Apparently he doesn't have a first name. Just initials. He's been out of prison since March. It wasn't hard to locate his parole officer, and I just spent a half hour on the phone with him." Flowers paused long enough to glance at Skinner and Penner. "From what the P.O. told me I'd bet my next paycheck that Jones is our boy."

"And what did the P.O. tell you?"

"Well, after he finished his tirade about the lunacy of the California Adult Authority and how they should have their heads examined for granting Jones a parole, he gave me some background information.

"B.C. Jones was born in L.A. in 1943, so that'd make him, what, twenty-six now? His father was black and his mother was white, which gives us at least some kind of tie-in with the murder victims.

"Jones wasn't exactly the sharpest kid on the block. In fact, he has a rather low IQ. He was always a couple grades below his age group, and, naturally the other kids weren't allowed to have anything to do with him. The fact that he was big for his age didn't help matters either. He dropped out of school when he was sixteen. He never finished the eighth grade, and he reads at about a fourth grade level.

"Apparently his father was a brutal man, and while Jones was growing up the old man beat him fairly regularly with a razor strop."

"What about the mother?" Skinner asked. "What kind of role did she play in all this?"

"From what the P.O. could gather, the mother was a weakling. I guess she just stood by and watched. Probably afraid that, if she tried to interfere, she'd get a piece of the razor strop herself. She died while Jones was in prison, so the P.O. never got a chance to interview her.

"Anyway, B.C. grew up to be a big boy. By the time he was eighteen he was six-five, and would grow another inch before he was through. He weighed 250 pounds and was strong as a bull.

"Shortly after he turned nineteen, he was at home one day, watching TV. The old man yelled at him to turn the volume down. B.C. ignored him, so out came the razor strop." Flowers grinned slightly. "It was the last time the old man used that strop. In fact it was the last time he did anything, because B.C. choked him to death. Just like two of our victims were choked to death.

"Jones was arrested for murder. But when the mother gave a statement as to the beatings that went on in the house, the D.A. was concerned they might make a strong case for self-defense. So he agreed to reduce the charge to voluntary manslaughter if Jones would plead guilty.

"He would've gotten out in three years, but apparently he had trouble getting along with his fellow inmates. Apparently someone made fun of his mixed blood and Jones almost killed him. So they tacked a few more years on. He spent a total of six years behind bars, and he spent most of that time lifting weights. The P.O. says that Jones is now six-six and weighs over 280 pounds, and is certainly powerful enough to kill a grown man with his bare hands."

No one spoke for several seconds as Captain Gilford pondered the information that Flowers had given him. "What do you think, Arch?" he said at last.

"I agree with Garland. His mixed blood gives us a racial connection, though we still don't know what his motive was. His physical size gives him the ability to commit the crimes with his bare hands, which fits in with the Medical Examiner's findings. And, of course, the thumbprint places him at the scene . . . at least at the scene of the Lawndale murders."

"There's one other thing I forgot to mention," Flowers said. "The P.O. said that Jones works as a trash collector for a company called Bert's Disposal, which has a contract with the city of Lawndale. We'll be checking with them to see if Jones was assigned to a truck in the vicinity of our victims' residence. Our concern is that if we go snooping around there before we're ready to arrest him, we may scare him off."

"I think you've got enough now," Gilford said. "I suggest you get an arrest warrant, then go pop him. Afterward you can obtain statements from his place of employment." After a pause, he asked, "Do you have anything else to run by me?"

"No," Flowers and Penner both replied.

"Then I suggest you get busy. You have a lot of work to do. Can you obtain a photo of him?"

"The P.O. has a recent photo in his file. But he gave us a pretty thorough description that we can go on for now," Flowers said.

" Are you sure you'll be able to recognize him?"

Flowers and Penner looked at each other, then Penner said, "Captain, aside from our suspect's gargantuan size, he's a light skinned black man with dark blond hair and big freckles on his face. He sort of stands out in a crowd."

Captain Gilford suppressed a grin as he pressed the butt of his cigarette into the ashtray and reached into his shirt pocket in search of Lucky Strike number thirty-one. "Joe, I need you to stay here. We have a few more cases to discuss. As for you two wise guys, you can go."

SIX

Tuesday
July 22, 1969

IT WAS LATE afternoon by the time Flowers and Penner obtained the arrest warrant. The deputy district attorney at first had been reluctant to draw it up, citing an insufficiency of evidence, but this was typical of the D.A.'s office. If the case was not absolutely airtight they tended to hesitate in issuing warrants. But this particular deputy D.A. was well acquainted with the two homicide investigators and he respected their judgment, and was eventually persuaded to draw up the warrant.

While they waited for the warrant to be issued, Flowers suggested to Penner that they call the parole officer and invite him to accompany them to Jones' residence. Since the P.O. knew the suspect it might help matters if he were present. Besides, it would be nice to have another person available in case Jones resisted. Penner thought it was a good idea and Flowers made the call.

An hour later, with Penner sitting on the passenger side, Flowers turned their unmarked Plymouth sedan onto Century Boulevard from Western Avenue and proceeded east until he arrived at a Chevron station. He pulled to the rear of the station and parked between a phone booth and a dull gray '67 Chevrolet sedan that was unmistakably a government vehicle.

"That's gotta be him," Penner said as he opened the passenger door.

"Yeah," Flowers replied. "Only a civil service employee would drive a car that ugly in this part of town."

As they emerged from their car a black man with an Afro hairstyle and dark glasses stepped from the driver's side of the Chevrolet. He wore a pink shirt open at the neck and dark gray trousers with a distinctive flare at the bottom.

"Sergeant Flowers?" The man asked as he walked toward them.

"That'd be me," Flowers said. "Garland Flowers."

"I'm Horace Blackburn. It's nice to be able to put a face to a voice."

"This is my partner, Archie Penner," Flowers said as they exchanged handshakes.

Flowers was relieved to discover that the parole officer was well over six feet tall with a muscular build. Flowers himself was a half inch over six feet and weighed 183 pounds. Penner was the smallest of the three, at five-ten and 150 pounds. If Jones decided to put up a fight, the combined efforts of all three of them just might be enough to restrain him long enough to get handcuffs on him.

"Say, Horace," Penner began, "Why is it that you guys from State Parole get to wear casual threads while us county peons are stuck wearing these monkey suits?"

Blackburn grinned. "Beats me. I guess they figure we parole officers have to relate to our clients."

"Oh, that's right. I forgot," Penner said teasingly. "By the time you guys get them, they've all been rehabilitated."

Blackburn's grin faded. "Yeah . . . rehabilitated. Like our friend Jones was rehabilitated."

"Speaking of Mr. Jones," Flowers said. "Why don't we go see if we can change his residence to the L.A. County Jail?"

"Good idea," Blackburn said, his smile returning. "Why don't you fellows follow me? He lives about a half a mile east of here, over in Watts."

CENTURY BOULEVARD WAS alive with late afternoon traffic. Pedestrians were beginning to patronize the numerous eating establishments that occupied both sides of the boulevard. The food outlets offered such cuisine as fish and chips, fried chicken, hamburgers and soul food. Occasionally a vacant lot where a building had once stood, or a boarded-up structure badly damaged by fire, stood out as a reminder of the riots that devastated this part of the city four years earlier.

Flowers and Penner followed Blackburn for several blocks along Century Boulevard, then they turned north, onto a street that was just wide enough for two lanes of traffic and the cars that were parked along each curb. The neighborhood into which they entered was a blend of commercial establishments, run-down single family residences and small apartment buildings. Among the businesses were an auto parts store, a radiator repair shop and a used battery outlet. The street and sidewalk were littered with discarded cans, glass bottles and paper. The narrow parkway between the street and sidewalk was mostly dirt, with occasional patches of bunch grass. Countless bits of broken glass were ground into the hard-packed earth. The surroundings were typical of any ghetto neighborhood in any city in the country.

Blackburn pulled to the right side of the street and parked adjacent to the curb in front of a two-story apartment building. Flowers parked the Plymouth behind the Chevrolet.

The two homicide investigators joined the parole officer on the sidewalk, then Blackburn led the way to apartment number one, where the landlady resided. He knocked on the door, then they waited a full minute before it was opened.

She was an elderly black woman with silvery gray hair. Her upper lip had deep vertical lines that were indicative of a heavy smoker, and the lower lip sunk into a mouth that was void of teeth.

"Hello, Mrs. Thomas," Blackburn greeted.

"Hello, Mr. Blackburn," she said. There was a look of concern on her face. "Is anything wrong? Is Mr. Jones in trouble?"

"We'd just like to talk to him. Do you know if he's home?"

"You mean you ain't checked his apartment?" She asked with a hint of suspicion.

"Uh, no," Blackburn said. "We just thought you might want us to check with you before going into the complex." He knew the landlady wasn't buying his flimsy story, but he didn't want to tell her that, for safety reasons, it was best if they knew for sure whether or not he was in the apartment before they approached it.

"He was here earlier, but he stepped out a little while ago," she said. "I expect he went to the store, like he usually does at this time. He should be back shortly."

"Would you mind if we waited in his apartment?" Blackburn asked.

Mrs. Thomas shrugged. "If that's what you want to do." She was well aware that she had no choice. She knew that Horace Blackburn was her tenant's parole officer, and he had a legal right to inspect a parolee's residence at any reasonable hour of the day.

She disappeared into her apartment, then returned a moment later with a small ring of keys. She led the way up a flight of metal stairs and along a catwalk toward the rear of the building.

B.C. JONES WALKED up the street from Century Boulevard. He carried a brown paper bag with a Safeway logo on it. Inside the bag were a package of bologna, a loaf of bread and two boxes of chocolate cup cakes. This was to be his evening meal.

He was walking past the radiator shop when the two cars, parked in front of the apartment building, caught his attention. Jones immediately recognized the Chevrolet as belonging to his parole officer, and there was no mistaking the Plymouth. It was an unmarked police car.

Jones moved slowly toward the front of the cars, where he had a clear view of his apartment, then froze in his tracks. Mrs. Thomas was letting two black men and a white man into his apartment. One of the black men was Mr. Blackburn. The other two looked like cops.

A passerby gave him a wary look as Jones asked aloud, "They must know it was me. How did they find out?"

Cradling the bag in one arm as if it were a football, he turned and ran toward Century Boulevard. Turning east, he ran past the Safeway market and the Thrifty Drugs before slowing to a fast walk. He came upon a half dozen people standing at a bus stop just as an RTD bus pulled to the curb. He joined the group and stepped into the bus, having no idea as to its destination.

FLOWERS GAZED AROUND the apartment's living room. The furnishings were Spartan to say the least. Against one wall was a green vinyl easy chair with cotton stuffing bulging from several cracks on its back and arms. Adjacent to the chair was a cheap end table, the finish of which was a blond veneer marred by scratches and stains. Against the wall directly opposite the chair was a new twenty-one-inch black-and-white TV. It rested precariously on a flimsy TV tray. A rabbit-ear antenna formed a v-shape above the set.

"The only thing that belongs to Mr. Jones is the TV," the landlady said smugly. "I furnished everything else, including the refrigerator and his bed.

"Oh, yes," she added, "the easy chair also belongs to him. He liked it so much I gave it to him."

"That was good of you," Blackburn said in a patronizing tone. He stole a glance at Flowers, who rolled his eyes upward and wondered silently how much extra she gouged Jones in rent for such generosity.

In the bedroom was a narrow twin bed. Across from the bed was an old chest of drawers containing underwear, socks and about a dozen comic books. The bathroom was stocked with the barest essentials.

The kitchen was moderately clean, with a few dirty dishes in the sink. In the cupboard were cans of chili, pork and beans, chicken gumbo soup and Spam. The only items in the refrigerator were a bottle of cold water, a small jar of Miracle Whip and a bottle of ketchup.

It took only a few minutes to thoroughly search the modestly furnished apartment. Flowers wasn't exactly sure what he was looking

10250-MART

for. He just wanted something . . . a photograph . . . a note . . . anything that would link Jones to the murder victims, especially the victims of the first crime. So far, the only thing he had to tie Jones to that crime was the modus operandi; that is, the means and method by which the crimes were perpetrated. The two crimes were so similar that any reasonable person would conclude that both were committed by the same person. Tangible proof would certainly make the case more airtight, and therefore satisfy the D.A. Unfortunately, no such evidence was to be obtained from B.C. Jones' apartment.

They waited a full hour before the investigators realized they were wasting their time. Mrs. Thomas, who had remained with them, not so much to protect her tenant's interest as to satisfy her intrusive nature, insisted that something was wrong. Mr. Jones was never away this long when he went grocery shopping.

Leaving the landlady to lock up, Flowers, Penner and Blackburn returned to the sidewalk beside their parked cars.

"Well, Garland," Penner began. "This is your case. What do you suggest we do now?"

"First of all, since this is L.A.P.D.'s jurisdiction, we need to notify them to let'em know what's going on. Then I think we need to borrow an undercover unit from Fugitive Detail to stake out the place in case he comes back."

Flowers paused, then added, "Off hand I'd say we were burned. I suspect that, while we were in the apartment, he came up, saw these two cars and . . . ."

"And any self-respecting ex-con knows an unmarked car when he sees it," Penner finished.

"Exactly," Flowers said. "I think he made us, then split."

Blackburn shook his head. "I'm sorry. It's my fault. I should have known better. I know for sure that he knows my car. Hell, he's even ridden in it."

"Don't take all the blame," Flowers said. "Arch and I are the cops. We're the ones who should have known better." He took in a deep breath and exhaled an audible sigh. "I think it's safe to say we all blew it."

SEVEN

Phoenix, Arizona
Wednesday
July 23, 1969

B.C. JONES HAD never been out of the state of California. Yet here he was in a Greyhound Bus depot in Phoenix, Arizona. He was frightened, not of anything physical, but of the unknown. When he ran away after seeing the cops entering his apartment the previous day he had given in to a basic survival instinct. He would run as far as he had to run to keep from going back to that cell at Soledad. Now he was stranded in a strange town in another state and he did not know what his next move would be.

It had been a long night for Jones and he was tired. After boarding the RTD bus on Century Boulevard he had ridden it as far as the Los Angeles Civic Center. He got off near the City Hall and walked a few blocks. He envisioned all the cops in L.A. searching for him, and they seemed to be on every street corner in the city, so he boarded another bus. It took him to El Monte; a suburban community located about ten miles east of downtown L.A.

Except for six years in the pen, Jones had spent his entire life in Los Angeles, yet he had never been east of Atlantic Boulevard. He had heard of El Monte in TV commercials, or at least he had heard of El Monte Legion Stadium. It was a place where teenagers went to dance and listen to live rock and roll bands. In El Monte he caught another bus that took him to West Covina. He changed buses again and ventured as far as Pomona.

It was late evening when he wandered into the Greyhound Bus terminal in Pomona. The first thing he heard upon entering was a voice over the public address system announcing the departure of a bus in fifteen minutes for Phoenix. On a sudden impulse, as well as a need within him to put distance between him and the police in L.A., Jones decided to take that bus.

He proceeded to the ticket counter and asked how much it would cost to go to Phoenix. When the agent told him, Jones reached into his pocket, removed a wad of cash, and purchased a ticket.

B.C. Jones had no concept of banking. Checking and savings accounts were completely foreign to him. And if there was one thing he learned in prison it was that the only way to protect your money was to take it with you wherever you went. If you left it in your cell it would be gone when you returned. For six years this was deeply ingrained in him, and after his release from prison Jones continued the practice of keeping his money with him at all times.

He lived well within his means, for he was a frugal spender. Jones himself did not know how much money was in his pocket, but it was at least a few hundred dollars.

At seven A.M. it must have been a slow part of the day in the Phoenix bus terminal, for Jones sat alone among the rows of cushioned straight-back chairs. Passengers came and went, and employees busily performed whatever tasks they were assigned, but Jones was the only one seated. He was still clutching the Safeway grocery bag. Its contents were intact, except for one of the boxes of chocolate covered cupcakes, which he had devoured somewhere between Pomona and Phoenix.

Jones was beginning to feel irritable from lack of sleep. He wished that he were in bed in his apartment. Then reality began to set in as he realized that he would probably never see his apartment again. What would happen to his brand new TV set? He briefly considered the possibility of his landlady, Mrs. Thomas, holding it for him, but as a clear picture of Mrs. Thomas came into focus he knew that she would just keep it for herself. He began to feel depressed as fatigue and disappointment crept over him. But the worst part was in not knowing where to go or what to do next.

A middle-aged black woman moved in his direction from the ticket counter. She carried a small suitcase, and was about to take a seat two chairs away from Jones when she glanced his way. Something about the way this strange man stared back at her caused the woman to change her mind and move to another row of seats.

Jones stared hard at the woman. She was heavy-set. Her hair was beginning to gray, giving it a naturally bluish tint. She reminded him of someone, but he couldn't place her.

There had never been many women in Jones' life. Aside from Mrs. Thomas, the only other woman he had met since getting out of prison was Mrs. Phelps, who worked in the office at Bert's Disposal. But the woman in the bus depot didn't remind him of either Mrs. Thomas or Mrs. Phelps. Then, of course, there had been his mama, but the woman definitely didn't remind him of her. She was skinny and white. This woman was black and fat.

B.C. Jones frowned as the image of his mother came to mind, and the unpleasant memories associated with her. As he tried to force these thoughts out of his head a sudden recognition came to him.

Auntie Doreen!

The woman reminded him of his Auntie Doreen. A sense of warmth seeped through B.C. when he thought of her. He had only seen her twice in his life. The first time was when he was a small child. She had come out to L.A. to visit from some place far away . . . someplace down south his mama had told him.

Auntie Doreen was his daddy's sister. Her visit was a happy memory, for she and B.C. had taken a liking to each other from the start. She played with him and took him to the movies and bought him ice cream cones at Thrifty Drugs. It was also a happy time because, when she first arrived, his daddy had been on his best behavior.

Then one day it came to an end. It was as if his daddy could not hold his meanness back any longer, and he and Auntie Doreen got into a big fight. They yelled and screamed at each other and he threatened to beat her, but she yelled back that she would have him put in jail if he laid a hand on her. B.C.'s mama cowered in a corner, shaking and afraid to move. Fifteen minutes later Auntie Doreen was packed and walking out of the house. Before departing, she gave his mama and him a hug.

The next time B.C. saw his aunt was several years later when he was on trial for killing his daddy. Though it had been her own brother who had died, Doreen's sympathy had been with B.C., for she knew the kind of man her brother had been. B.C. had been comforted at seeing his Auntie Doreen sitting in the courtroom with his mama. She had visited him in the county jail during the court proceedings. Auntie Doreen had even given him her address and phone number and told him to call her if he ever needed anything.

A revelation struck Jones so suddenly he almost jumped. He reached into his back pocket and removed a worn leather wallet and searched the various compartments. Inside an opening between the photo folder and the currency section he found a piece of paper folded to a one inch square. He unfolded it and saw that it was sharply creased into four squares, with a tiny hole where the creases intersected.

The words on the paper had been written in pencil and were partially smeared. It was a struggle but Jones eventually deciphered the words and numbers. Under the name Doreen Brown was an address in Gulfport, Mississippi. Below the address was a phone number.

Jones looked all about the bus terminal until his eyes fell on that for which he was searching. Against the wall near the restrooms were two public phone booths, neither of which were in use.

He was filled with a rush of excitement, but he also experienced a sense of apprehension. These conflicting emotions caused him to hesitate. What if she doesn't remember me? He thought. What if she's mad at me now for what I did to Daddy? But as these questions occurred to him, he was also aware that there was no one else to whom he could turn. He was desperate, and the more he thought about it the more determined he became to call her. If she acted like she didn't want to see him, he would just hang up the phone.

B.C. had never made a long distance call in his life, but he did know that if he dropped a dime in the slot and dialed "O", an operator would come on the line and help him with the call.

He shifted the grocery bag from his lap to the cradle of his left arm and slowly stood up. The apprehension grew and he felt slightly sick to his stomach as he moved with deliberate steps toward the phone booths.

EIGHT

Pasadena, California
Sunday
August 3, 1969

GARLAND FLOWERS SAT beside his daughter, Danielle, on a cushioned bench inside Bob's Big Boy Restaurant and waited for their names to be called for a table. It was late afternoon and he was returning Danielle to her home after spending the day at his parents' house in Altadena, a residential community north of Pasadena. Garland's mother had tried to talk him into having dinner with them, but he had promised his daughter that they could eat at a restaurant.

Both of Garland's parents had been teachers for the L.A. City Schools. His father, Simon, had taught eighth grade math for several years, then became a school administrator. At the time of his retirement he was a junior high school principal. Garland's mother, Eunice, had been content to teach ninth grade English throughout her thirty-year tenure.

Garland's older sister, Laurel, and his younger brother, Oscar, had followed their parents into the teaching profession. But teaching never interested Garland. For as long as he could remember he wanted to be a peace officer. Even as a child his favorite game was cops and robbers, and his favorite radio programs were crime dramas. He especially liked *Dragnet* and *This Is Your F.B.I.*

While Danielle was busy scribbling with a green crayon across the faces of characters in a complimentary Big Boy comic book, Garland stared absently out the window toward the campus of Pasadena City College. Bob's Big Boy and P.C.C. both faced Colorado Boulevard. A small side street separated the restaurant from the school.

It had been a warm, clear Sunday, and he imagined most of the summer school students spending the day surfing or lying on the sand at Newport or Huntington Beach. One thing was certain; they were not wasting their day near the school, for the campus was almost completely deserted. The only person Garland could see was a young man sitting on the grass under a breadfruit tree, reading a book. His long hair was tied in a ponytail. Then a couple stepped into view on the near side of the mirrored pool that extended toward the street from the administration building. The couple appeared to be in their late teens or early twenties. He was black and she was white. As Garland watched them walk hand-in-hand beside the pool he was unpleasantly reminded of two other racially mixed couples who were now dead.

It had been two weeks to the day since the last murder, and Flowers dreaded having to call the duty detective that evening for fear of learning that B.C. Jones had struck again. There had been a two-week interval between the first and second murders, and each crime had been committed on a Sunday. Perhaps it was coincidence, perhaps not. Two events were not sufficiently conclusive to establish a pattern.

B.C. Jones seemed to have fallen off the face of the earth, and this caused mixed feelings within Flowers. In a way, it offered hope that he was no longer around to commit any more murders. On the other hand, an extremely dangerous suspect was still at large.

In the days and weeks following his failed attempt to arrest Jones at his apartment, Flowers had taken pains to learn everything he could about the suspect. He talked at length with the parole officer, Horace Blackburn, and obtained copies of every docu-

10250-MART

ment that the P.O. could provide, including reports from the Department of Corrections.

Flowers and Penner had driven to Bert's Disposal and interviewed various employees. One of them was Rafael Luna, the trash truck driver. It was apparent that Luna did not like Jones, and he was not reluctant to tell the investigators what he knew. He confirmed their suspicion that the house in Lawndale where the most recent murders took place was on their trash collection route. Luna seemed to take pleasure in relating Jones' strange behavior at that location two days before the crime occurred. Needless to say, Rafael Luna would be a valuable witness.

Flowers sent a teletype broadcast to every police agency in southern California. The broadcast included a full description of Jones and the charges against him. It also provided the arrest warrant number and the manner in which the crimes were committed. He sent a similar teletype to the National Crime Information Center (N.C.I.C.) in Washington, D.C. Virtually every police agency in the United States had access to N.C.I.C.

At first Flowers was optimistic that Jones would turn up somewhere. The Fugitive Detail had staked out his apartment for a week after he disappeared. Employees at Safeway and Thrifty Drugs, as well as several fast food establishments, recognized Jones from photos that Flowers and Penner passed around, and each one promised to call the Sheriff's Department if he showed up again. So far, no one had called.

The more Flowers studied Jones' lifestyle the more puzzled he became, for Jones lived in a very tiny world. His places of residence, employment and amusement were all within a mile of each other. There was no evidence of him venturing far beyond a five-mile radius of his apartment, unless his trash collection duties took him farther. All Flowers could do now was wait until Jones showed up somewhere. In the meantime he would pray that there would be no more murders committed by this strange, sick man.

Garland's thoughts were interrupted when he heard someone speak his name: "Flowers, party of two."

He looked up to see a pretty hostess standing nearby, holding two menus. She wore the familiar dark brown skirt and white blouse that was the uniform of Big Boy employees. A nametag identified the hostess as Jessica.

He got up slowly and nodded to her in acknowledgement that he was Flowers. The hostess returned his nod with a warm smile. He gently took the crayon and comic book from Danielle, then lifted her in his arms. Stealing a glance out the window in the direction of the mirrored pool he noticed that the mixed couple was no longer there. He felt a sense of relief as thoughts of murdered mulatto children and B.C. Jones and homicides in general faded from his consciousness. For the first time since stopping at the restaurant he realized that he did indeed have an appetite for a Big Boy Combo.

He looked at Danielle with an expression of feigned seriousness. "Are you sure you're hungry?"

"Yes sir. I'm real hungry," she replied with unfeigned seriousness.

"Me, too," he said, then father and daughter fell in behind Jessica as she escorted them to their table.

NINE

Gulfport, Mississippi
Monday
August 11, 1969

THE THUNDERSTORM THAT had passed over the Mississippi Gulf Coast the night before had done little to diminish the stifling heat, and by early afternoon the temperature had reached a very humid ninety degrees.

Doreen Brown dipped her fingers into a pan of water, then flicked them over a wrinkled blouse that lay atop an ironing board. A bead of perspiration rolled down the bridge of her nose, and her chocolate brown face glistened in the sweltering heat. The otherwise loose-fitting cotton-print dress that she wore clung to her ample body as if she had just stepped out of the bathtub and put on the dress without bothering to dry off.

After wiping her face with a damp cloth that she kept nearby for that purpose, she picked up the iron and began pressing the blouse. Doreen did not regard ironing as a chore. In fact, she found it relaxing. This was her thinking time.

The ironing board was strategically placed near the open front door. The closed screen kept most of the flies outside and allowed the air, as warm as it was, to circulate inside and lessen the heat created by the iron. To her right, facing south, an open window permitted a slight afternoon breeze to drift in from the Gulf, the shores of which were less than a mile away.

Doreen Brown had lived in the small wood-frame house since the 1930's. She and her husband had moved in shortly after they were married. They had been together two years when she became pregnant, but the child was stillborn. Several months later her husband ran off with another woman, and Doreen was left alone. She had lost her husband, but she did not lose the house. Though it had not seen a fresh coat of paint in over thirty years it was fully paid for, and she intended to live there for the rest of her life.

She had a small circle of friends, consisting primarily of fellow members of the local Baptist Church. The various activities of the church offered variety to an otherwise uneventful life. She found particular pleasure in teaching Sunday school.

The house was located in an all black area east of downtown Gulfport called Soria City. It was one of several residential communities found along the coast that, until recent years, were commonly referred to as the "nigger quarters." Since the mid-sixties, however, a more enlightened South was emerging, and such derogatory terms as "nigger quarters" were openly uttered by only the most die-hard bigots.

Soria City was an impoverished section of Gulfport. Most of the houses were poorly maintained. Some of the through streets were paved, but many of the side roads were nothing more than hard-packed dirt. Sidewalks were non-existent. Dilapidated cars parked on grassless yards were a common sight. Barefoot children played in the street, kicking up dust when the weather was dry and sloshing in the mud when it was wet. Some families kept chickens in their backyards, and it was not unusual to see an occasional goat or hog. Swatting flies and mosquitoes was a common pastime in Soria City.

Doreen glanced to her left, where her nephew sat in a large recliner watching "The Dating Game" on the T.V. She had picked up B.C. at the bus depot nine days earlier and he hardly left the house once she brought him home. Occasionally he would venture a block or so to the neighborhood grocery store on Railroad

Street to purchase chocolate cupcakes or ice cream. The rest of the time he spent sitting in front of the T.V.

She wondered at first if B.C. might be hiding something, but having nothing on which to base such a suspicion, she dismissed the thought from her mind.

Doreen experienced a feeling of sadness as she studied her nephew. God had certainly allowed nature to play a cruel joke on B.C. He was ugly and simple-minded, and almost grotesquely large. He did not fit into any group, and would surely be an outcast throughout his life. He would always be a loner.

Even as a child he had known very little love and a great deal of abuse and neglect. His very name, what there was of it, reflected an indifferent attitude toward him practically from the moment of his birth.

Doreen's thoughts drifted to the past. As images of B.C.'s mama and daddy–her own brother, came into focus, the feeling of sadness that had filled her a moment earlier turned to anger. A bitter gall crept toward her throat as she was reminded of the shameful manner in which they had treated their son. At first she resisted these thoughts, yet something tugged at her consciousness and urged the memories to flow.

DOREEN WAS BORN in Brookhaven, Mississippi, as were her older sister, Bertha and their baby brother, Lester. They were brought up in a three-room shanty on the outskirts of town. Their father, Herbert Jones, was a hard worker and a good provider, but he was also a cruel disciplinarian. He kept a razor strop handy for the sole purpose of beating his children, as well as his wife, when he felt that it was necessary, and that feeling arose often.

Soon after Bertha turned sixteen she married, as much out of a desire to escape her father's cruelty as for love of the groom, and they moved to her husband's home in Gulfport. Several months later Doreen went to visit her sister, and remained in Gulfport permanently. As soon as Lester was old enough he joined the Navy and was sent to San Diego for boot camp, and he never returned to Mississippi.

What Doreen knew of her brother's life after he left Brookhaven, she learned years later from B.C.'s mother, Marlene, as well as from her personal observations when she visited them in L.A.

Following boot camp Lester Jones was stationed in Long Beach, California. He was not quite nineteen when he met a twenty-three year-old woman in a bar and moved in with her and her four-year-old son. It wasn't long before Lester took up his father's methods of disciplining the child, especially after he had been drinking.

At first the girlfriend appreciated the heavy hand, for it appeared to give her son a father figure. But as time passed Lester became more violent. One Sunday morning he went too far and struck the child a blow severe enough to render him unconscious. The boy was rushed to the hospital. The girlfriend was so frightened and angry that she had Lester arrested. He was convicted of battery and sentenced to ninety days in county jail. He also received a bad conduct discharge from the Navy.

Following his release from jail, Lester remained in the Los Angeles area. He worked odd jobs for a year or so, then Pearl Harbor was bombed and most of the able-bodied men went off to war. His bad conduct discharge made him unfit for duty, which caused him no concern at all. In fact, it worked to his advantage, for numerous jobs were now available due to the departure of so many young men.

He soon landed a job as a steamfitter for a company located near Alameda Street in Los Angeles. It was there that he was working when he met Marlene.

Marlene Simmons was in her mid-teens when she ran away from her home in Omaha, Nebraska and made her way to Los Angeles. It was in the midst of the Depression and her departure resulted in one less mouth to feed, so a serious effort to find her was never undertaken by her family.

She had a rather plain face that was marred by acne. Her dishwater blonde hair was unkempt and stringy. Her teeth were fairly straight, but a few were blackened from decay, due to too many sweets and not enough brushing.

Soon after arriving in L.A. she got a job as a waitress in a greasy spoon restaurant near Broadway and First Street. She had been there several months when Lester Jones came in and sat down at the counter. He was fairly tall, lean and good-looking. She was attracted to him from the start. The fact that he was black and she was white, a combination that was taboo even in L.A., made the prospect of a relationship exciting.

As Lester drank his coffee he made flirtatious comments to Marlene and she responded in kind. He returned the following day as well as the next. Eventually he asked her out and she accepted, and soon they were together constantly. She moved into his apartment and, though they never married, he referred to her as his "old lady."

On April 24, 1943 eighteen-year-old Marlene gave birth to a son at Los Angeles General Hospital. From the very first day of his life the child began paying the price for his parents' union. He was treated as something less than human by the nursing staff, black and white alike. The white nurses regarded Marlene as white trash. The black nurses looked upon Lester as having betrayed his race. Everyone ignored the baby as much as possible.

When the hospital staff began to pressure Marlene for a name to be placed on the birth certificate, she was at a loss as to what name to give her son. Lester could not have cared less what she called him.

Marlene had a tendency to develop a headache whenever she was pressured or became anxious. She had learned that, if she took a dose of B.C. powder and swallowed it with Coca Cola, the headache would usually go away. She had experienced some headaches during her stay at the hospital and the flat blue packet of B.C. powder lay atop the table beside her bed.

She was beginning to feel one of her headaches coming on when a hospital staff member entered the room. She was a large woman with a stern, no-nonsense demeanor, and she demanded the paperwork on the baby. Marlene had been working on the form and everything was filled out but the child's name. She became flustered and automatically glanced toward the packet of B.C. powders. She had been holding a fountain pen in one had and the form in the other. She glimpsed once more at the intimidating staff member, then wrote the first thing that occurred to her. In the space calling for a first name she simply entered the letter B. For the middle name she placed a C. Having been admitted to the hospital under the name Marlene Jones, she wrote Jones in the space requesting a last name. From that moment forward the child would be known as B.C. Jones.

He grew up in a predominantly black neighborhood in south central Los Angeles. In school he was considered a slow student, and his mixed blood made him an outcast even at that early stage of his life.

At home Lester adopted the same disciplinary measures as his father. When B.C. was ten years old, Lester brought home a razor strop, just like the one his father had used on him. Most of the beatings occurred on Sunday. Lester got drunk once a week, on Saturday night, and an ugly hangover always followed on Sunday. B.C. was usually the victim of his daddy's foul moods, and he had to be punished. If the strop was not handy, a hard blow to the child's head would sometimes satisfy Lester's need to inflict pain. The few times that Marlene tried to intervene she was severely beaten by Lester. After a while she learned to cower in the corner and pray that her son would not be killed.

B.C. grew up to be quiet and sullen. He had no place to go to escape derision and rejection, and he had no one to whom he could turn for sympathy. On his sixteenth birthday he dropped out of school. He was still in the eighth grade and was failing. His ability to think clearly was becoming more and more difficult. No attempt was made to have him reinstated in school. He was already much larger than most of the faculty members, and there was something about him that wasn't quite right. The school administrators were glad to see him go.

B.C. got a job loading cinder blocks for a building material company. It was a job that relied on size and strength rather than intelligence, and it was not long before hard muscle began to develop on his huge bulk.

During the years that B.C. was growing up his mama became more withdrawn. The powders that had been her son's namesake no longer got rid of her headaches, so she turned to stronger painkillers. She became addicted to morphine and, eventually, heroine. Lester refused to give her money to buy narcotics, so Marlene went back to work as a waitress to support her habit.

The last time that Doreen saw her sister-in-law was the day that B.C. was sentenced to prison. She had gone to L.A. to offer Marlene and B.C. support during the court proceedings, and returned to Gulfport the same day the sentence was passed. She could tell at that time that Marlene was too far gone to be helped. But it was not until nine days ago, when B.C. arrived in Gulfport, that she learned that Marlene had died while B.C. was in prison.

DOREEN LIFTED THE freshly ironed blouse from the ironing board, placed it on a hanger, and hung it on a nearby rack. She then picked up a large cotton print dress, similar to the one she was wearing, and placed it on the ironing board. She liked the tedium of ironing, for it allowed her to lose herself in her thoughts. Usually the subjects were pleasant–her friends at church, or her Sunday school activities. But since the arrival of her nephew her thoughts tended to focus on sad memories.

She recalled the day, almost two weeks earlier, when her nephew phoned her from Phoenix. She was surprised and elated that he would remember his Auntie Doreen, and she happily agreed to have him come visit her. But he had now been a constant presence in her house for nine days. His enormous bulk seemed to remain fixed in her easy chair in front of the T.V. As much as she wanted to give him the love and support that he had been denied as a child, she realized that she also needed some time to herself. After all, she had lived alone for all these years. She was set in her ways, and any change in her daily routine would require some adjustment. She was not being selfish, she told herself. She just needed a few moments of privacy.

She dipped her fingers into the pan of water, then absently sprinkled the dress. Exhaling an audible sigh, she picked up the iron, held it for a moment, as if pondering a delicate thought, then set the instrument back on its end.

Turning toward her nephew she said, "B.C., honey. I really do think you need to get out of this house for a while."

He made no response for several seconds, then he turned from the T.V. and looked questioningly at his aunt. "Huh?"

"I said you really do need to get out of this house for a while. You been cooped up in here for over a week now."

"But I like it here," he said. "I ain't botherin' nobody"

Emotion began to swell inside Doreen. "No, honey. You aren't bothering anyone. I just thought it might make you feel good to go outside." She paused long enough for an idea to form, then said, "There won't be anything you'd like on T.V. for a few more hours. Why don't you take a ride downtown on the bus?"

B.C. stared at his aunt, but said nothing.

"Go on, now," she urged. "You can catch the bus in front of the store on Railroad Street. When you're ready to come home, just get on the same bus. It'll drop you off at the store."

He remained silent.

"I'll even give you the bus fare," she said. "Plus a couple dollars to buy something sweet. Maybe some chocolate pie at the lunch counter in Woolworth's."

Slowly B.C. pulled himself from the chair and stood erect. Doreen had still not gotten accustomed to how small he made the room appear when he stood in it.

"I don't need your money," he said as he moved to the door. "I got my own."

Doreen was beginning to feel guilty. "Honey, please don't be upset with me. I just think it'll be good for you to get out for a spell."

As he opened the screen door, he turned and looked at his aunt. "I ain't upset." He then crossed the porch and descended the steps.

Doreen followed him out the door. By the time she stepped onto the porch B.C. was already two doors down the street. Children who had been playing in their yard took a break in their game long enough to stare at the strange giant as he walked past them.

Doreen called after him. "I'll have a nice supper ready when you get back." He made no response, but continued walking toward the bus stop. She was not sure if he had heard her, but she concluded that he had. The sense of guilt remained. The last thing she had wanted to do was hurt his feelings. It was quite obvious that something was troubling him, but he was not willing to share it with her. A shiver suddenly came over her and she sensed that whatever had happened in L.A. was something very serious, perhaps something very bad . . . bad enough to send B.C. two thousand miles to get away from it.

TEN

THE DOWNTOWN SECTION of Gulfport had seen better days. During the 1940's and '50's it had been a thriving business center serving the needs of a surrounding population of fifty thousand. Like most medium-size towns across the nation, though, the downtown business section, in the sixties, was beginning to give way to malls and shopping centers on the outskirts of town.

But downtown Gulfport was far from dead. While most of the larger department stores had moved out, leaving vacant buildings here and there, many other smaller businesses stubbornly remained in the same locations that previous generations had patronized.

B.C. Jones stepped off the bus at 14th Street and 25th Avenue, and had no idea where to go or what to do. He was still sulking for having to come here in the first place.

As he looked about him, wondering what to do next, he felt uncomfortable, as if he did not belong here. This place was not like L.A. It was too quiet. There weren't many cars on the street, nor many people walking on the sidewalks, yet he appeared to be standing in the middle of town. He missed the heavy traffic and the crowded sidewalks and the noise of L.A.

Across the street from where he stood was what appeared to be the tallest building in town. Using his index finger as a pointer, he counted the floors. "Seven," he said aloud. "That ain't many." The Hancock Bank building towered above the surrounding structures, most of which were no more than two or three stories high.

He crossed 25th Avenue and stood in front of the bank. Standing six feet from the building, he looked up. "It sure looks like it's more than seven stories," he exclaimed. A woman carrying an A&P shopping bag gave him a strange look and a wide berth as she walked past. He shook his head, oblivious to the woman's reaction to him, and moved west along 14th Street.

When he had gone a block, he stopped again and looked about, but saw nothing that interested him. Half a block south, on 26th Avenue, was a movie theater. Having nothing better to do he moved in that direction. A moment later he was standing in front of the Paramount Theater studying the movie posters. "The Wild Bunch," he read aloud. "It kind of looks like a cowboy movie. Maybe I'll watch it."

He walked to the ticket booth and asked what time the movie would start and was told that the next feature would begin at 4:15 P.M. When he asked the woman in the booth what time it was now, she said that it was 2:45.

He stood near the ticket booth for a full minute, wondering what his next move would be. He did not want to be here. He wanted to be at his aunt's house watching cartoons on T.V. Then he thought how it would serve her right if he went to a movie and didn't return home until late at night. Maybe that would teach her to let him stay home when he wanted to.

As these thoughts were occurring to him he noticed, for the first time, that Woolworth was next door to the theater. It was one of a few chain stores that remained downtown. Just as the woman in the ticket booth was beginning to feel ill at ease at his reluctance to move along, B.C. sauntered in the direction of the "five-and dime." As he got closer he began to detect the aroma of the store's lunch counter and recalled Auntie Doreen's suggestion that he have something sweet at Woolworth's. Prompted by a sudden taste for chocolate, maybe a slice of pie, he walked into the nearest entrance.

B.C. had given no thought to the sultry heat outside until he stepped into the air-conditioned coolness of the store's interior.

Directly in front of him, adjacent to the north end of the store, was the lunch counter. Two husky men, each wearing a hard hat, sat on stools nearest the door. They were the only customers at the counter. They were talking to a middle-aged waitress who gave B.C. a sour look as he walked past. Moving to the far end of the counter, he straddled a stool, then dropped onto it. One of the men at the counter eyed B.C. for a moment, then turned to his companion and the waitress and shook his head.

B.C. looked in the direction of the waitress, but she made no move to wait on him. A full thirty seconds passed, then, in a surly, high-pitched tone, she said, "Frieda, you have a customer."

From an enclosed room adjacent to the counter a girl emerged wiping her hands on a towel. B.C. was immediately entranced with her. She appeared to be in her late teens and she was beautiful. She had large brown eyes and an olive complexion that was flawless.

Her smile revealed beautiful white teeth. "May I help you?" She asked.

At first B.C. was so taken with her appearance that he was unable to speak. But as he stared more deeply a frown appeared, as if a sudden revelation came upon him.

"Sir, may I help you?" Frieda asked again.

B.C. made a slight jerking motion, like someone coming out of a trance. "Uh, do you have any chocolate pie?"

"Let me check." Frieda turned her back to him and moved to the pie case that rested on a stand against the back wall.

She made a cursory search of the case, then turned to the other waitress. "Shirley, do we have any chocolate pie?"

"Do you see any in the case?" The older waitress responded sarcastically.

"No, ma'am," Frieda said.

"Then I guess we don't have any, do we."

Frieda gave Shirley a questioning look. "I guess not," she replied in a tone so soft as to be barely audible. The two customers sitting across the counter from Shirley stared into their coffee cups, embarrassed by the bad manners of the older waitress.

When Frieda turned back to her customer, B.C. was glaring coldly at Shirley. "I'm sorry, sir, but we don't seem to have any chocolate pie. We only have banana cream, coconut cream and cherry. Would you care for one of those?"

B.C. reluctantly turned his attention from Shirley to Frieda. "Uh, do you have chocolate ice cream?"

Her smile returned. "Yes. I know for sure that we have chocolate ice cream."

"Could I have two scoops in a dish?"

"Certainly," she said, then opened a lid to the ice cream freezer directly across the counter from where B.C. sat.

As he watched the young waitress struggle to scrape the hardened ice cream into the scoop he studied her face, for it reminded him of another pretty face that he could not get out of his mind. It was that of a younger girl in an apartment in L.A. Her skin had been darker than Frieda's, but it had the same smoothness. If he had not put the pillow over that sweet child's face, she would have grown up to be mistreated just like Frieda was being mistreated by that waitress named Shirley.

Just as the young waitress was placing the first scoop of ice cream into the dish, B.C. said, "I know why that woman is so mean to you."

Frieda looked up from her work. There was a questioning expression on her face. "I beg your pardon?"

"That woman over there," B.C. said, pointing to Shirley, "I know why she's so mean to you."

Shirley, who had been talking to the two men at the counter, abruptly stopped speaking mid-sentence, and the three of them turned their attention to B.C.

It was a slow time of day, and there were no more than a half dozen customers scattered throughout the store, and none were close enough to overhear what was being said. But a clerk working the notions counter two aisles away could easily hear the words of the big, strange-looking man, and she stopped what she was doing to listen more closely.

Frieda had become visibly uncomfortable. "I don't know what you mean. Shirley isn't mean to me."

"Yes she is. An' I know why. Other people might not know why, but I do." He paused, but no one spoke. He then added, "It's 'cause you got nigger blood in you."

Frieda's eyes widened, and she dropped the ice cream scoop onto the open freezer lid. It slid downward and fell into the ice cream container. Her mouth opened to speak but no words came out. She covered her mouth with her hands and backed away. Shirley stood as if frozen. It was an awkward moment and no one seemed to know how to react.

"Maybe you been tryin' to hide it . . . passin' yourself off as white," B.C. continued, "but I can tell, cause I got black and white blood in me too."

Shirley was the first to recover. "Now that's just about enough, Mister," she said as she started to move toward B.C. But a voice inside her told her not to get any closer to this strange man, for there was something dangerous about him. She held out her hands and motioned for Frieda to come to her. The young waitress moved quickly and Shirley put her arms around her.

The nearby sales clerk quietly stepped from behind the notions counter and moved hurriedly to the rear of the store. She went up a flight of stairs and entered the office of the store manager. The manager was not in, but sitting at his desk was one of the three or four senior employees who carried the euphemistic title of associate manager. After the clerk quickly explained what was happening at the lunch counter, the associate manager, a small, thin man with a mousy face and horn-rimmed glasses, got up from his desk and went to a small window that looked out onto the floor below. From here one could keep an eye on customers, as well as employees, in any part of the store.

At the lunch counter an awkward moment of silence passed. Then Shirley, who continued to embrace Frieda with an arm around the shoulder of the younger waitress, said, "Sir, I think it would be best if you left."

"Why?" B.C. protested. "I ain't done nothing."

"You got this girl upset by making insulting comments."

"I just told her the truth."

"That's ridiculous. Now, you're causing a disturbance and I think you should leave."

"I ain't had my ice cream yet."

"You haven't paid for it, either. Now, are you gonna leave or do I have to call the manager?"

During the exchange their voices had risen and could now be heard throughout the store. The associate manager, from his upstairs window, clearly heard Shirley's threat to summon him. He looked once more at the size of the recalcitrant customer, then went to the phone on his desk. He quickly dialed a number and, within seconds, was connected to the Gulfport Police Department.

"If it ain't because she's part nigger, why're you treatin' her so mean?" B.C. asked.

"First of all, she isn't part nig . . er . . .Negro. She's as white as I am," Shirley said. "And second, I haven't been mean to her . . . at least not intentionally." After a pause, she said, "I guess I just got up on the wrong side of the bed this morning. Frieda knows I don't mean anything by it." She glanced at the younger waitress. "Don't you, Frieda?"

Frieda nodded, but said nothing.

"Now, I'm asking you once more, sir," Shirley said. "Would you please leave?"

The look that B.C. gave Shirley sent a sudden wave of fear through her and she involuntarily stepped back, pulling Frieda with her. "I ain't leaving 'til I finish my ice cream," he said.

The two men at the counter, as if on cue, both got up from their stools and turned to face B.C. The larger of the two, a man in his mid-thirties, who stood a few inches over six feet and had a thick chest and beefy arms, addressed B.C. "Now, boy, the little lady here has tried to tell you nicely that it's time for you to leave."

B.C. paid no attention to the man. He continued to glare at Shirley.

The man was not accustomed to being ignored. He enjoyed a local reputation as a bar room brawler. He prided himself on being the toughest customer to frequent the Rebel Yell Bar up on Highway 49. He looked at his companion, who was only slightly smaller than himself, then returned his attention to B.C. "Are you gonna leave now, son, or do we have to throw you out?"

"I want my ice cream," B.C. said quietly, never taking his eyes from Shirley.

Shirley glanced nervously at the two men who were moving slowly toward B.C. "Now wait a minute," she said. "We don't want any trouble here." She looked at B.C. "We'll serve you your ice cream, but then you'll have to leave." She released her hold on Frieda and the younger waitress moved cautiously toward the ice cream freezer.

"No!" The larger of the two men exclaimed. "It's too late. He's insulted this girl, an' he shouldn't be allowed to get away with it."

For the first time B.C. slowly turned and faced the two men, but he said nothing.

"So what'll it be, boy? You gonna leave on your own or do we throw you out?"

"I ain't leavin' 'til I get my ice cream."

As the two men moved closer B.C. stood up, and they abruptly stopped. Only now did it occur to them how massive and fearsome he was. But it was too late. The champion of the Rebel Yell Bar had committed himself, and it was not in him to back down from a fight.

Shirley and Frieda, fearful of what was about to happen, moved hurriedly to the far end of the lunch counter and cowered close together against the back wall.

Without warning, the larger of the two men suddenly sent a right blow directly toward B.C.'s face, but he reached up with his left hand and caught the fist the way a catcher would catch a pitcher's fast ball. Then he instantly grabbed the man's neck with his right hand. The second man moved in and punched B.C. in the ribs with two chopping blows. B.C. let go of the first man's neck and used his right hand to push the second man's face back. The man lost his balance and fell backward onto a stool, then he rolled over onto the floor.

B.C. still held the first man's right fist in a bone-crushing grip. He grabbed the man's belt with his right hand, then let go of the man's fist and moved his left hand to the man's shirt collar. In a fluid motion that appeared to be effortless he lifted the construction worker up over his head, then he turned to his left and threw the man onto a nearby merchandise counter. The big man landed with a loud crash. There was the sound of glass breaking and small items of merchandise flew from their displays. The man's hard hat went sailing through the air and landed on the second man, who was still lying on the floor where he had fallen.

The second man rolled onto his hands and knees and started crawling toward the store entrance. He didn't mind getting involved in an old-fashioned fight, but this hulk of a man was too much. He seemed to have super-human strength.

The man stopped crawling when he saw two pairs of legs, each wearing blue trousers, walk hurriedly through the door. He sheepishly stood up as two police officers moved past him. Two other officers, having entered the store from the rear entrance, approached from another direction.

"What's going on here?" Asked the sergeant, a middle-aged man with gray hair and a slightly protruding stomach.

One of the officers had joined the second man, the one who had met them on his hands and knees, in assisting the first man off the merchandise counter. He groaned as they lifted him to a sitting position, then onto his feet.

The associate manager, upon seeing the police enter the store, quickly made his way down the stairs and walked swiftly to the lunch counter area. "Sergeant, please arrest that man!" He demanded. "I saw it all. This man attacked these two gentlemen."

"That ain't exactly so," said the first man as he rubbed his shoulders and back. "It's true he threw me onto that counter, but he didn't start the fight." He wasn't about to let someone else take the blame for a fight that he started.

"Would one of y'all please tell me what this is all about?" The sergeant asked.

Shirley and Frieda emerged from the corner where they had been cowering and moved to the far end of the counter, where the police, the construction workers and the store manager had congregated around B.C. The latter had taken his seat on the stool and quietly took in the exchange.

"It all started when I refused service to this man," Shirley said as she stopped on the opposite side of the counter from B.C.

The sergeant looked from B.C. to Shirley, then back to B.C. and back to Shirley. "And why did you refuse service to him?" He asked, praying silently that this was not going to turn into an ugly racial issue.

"Because he insulted Frieda here," she said, indicating the younger waitress, who stood a few feet from Shirley.

"And how did he happen to insult her?" The sergeant asked with declining interest in the entire affair.

"He said that she had . . . uh . . . that she had Negro blood in her."

The sergeant looked more closely at Frieda, then turned his attention to B.C. "Why would you say a thing like that?"

" 'Cause she has. I can just look at her and tell that."

"There, you see, sergeant," the associate manager began, "This brute is a trouble-maker. He insulted one of my employees, created a disturbance, battered these two men and . . ."

"Now hold on just a minute," the man who had been thrown onto the counter said. "Don't include me in any talk of battery. It was a fair fight and I come out on the short end. I don't care what y'all do to him for insultin' the little lady, but don't be throwin' in any charges of battery. Do you agree, Smitty?"

The second man silently nodded in agreement.

"Then I insist you arrest him for causing a disturbance!" The manager exclaimed. "You can see for yourself that he's chased all the customers out of the store. And just look at the damage he caused."

The sergeant closed his eyes, then opened them and breathed an audible sigh. Placing a hand on the officer standing nearest him, he said, "Hansen, why don't you take a statement from these ladies as well as any other witnesses, then meet us at the station for a report." He then looked at B.C. "Son, I'm afraid we're gonna have to take you in for disturbing the peace."

"But I didn't do nothin'!" B.C. protested. "I just come in for some chocolate pie. They didn't have any, so I said I'd have ice cream an'. . ."

"Be that as it may," the sergeant interrupted, "the fact is you did cause a disturbance. Just look at the mess here. Doesn't this place look a little different than it did when you first walked in here?"

B.C. stood up. There was a look of defiance on his face. "I didn't start it!"

"Yes, you did, son. You started it when you made that comment to this lady."

"I didn't mean it in a bad way."

The sergeant thought for a moment, then said, "You're not from around here, are you."

"No."

"Where are you from?"

"L.A."

"You're from Los Angeles?" The sergeant asked.

"Uh huh."

Under his breath the sergeant said, "That explains a lot." More audibly he said, "People around here react to certain words differently than they do out in California."

The sergeant took a step forward and B.C. stiffened. "Now hold on, son," the sergeant said as he held up his hands to indicate he wanted no trouble. "There's a whole lot more where we come from. You can't fight the entire Gulfport Police Department." He paused, then added, "Besides, all we want to do is take you over to the station. In a few hours you can pay your bail and go home."

B.C. seemed to relax somewhat.

"Are you staying with anyone while you're here in Gulfport?" The sergeant asked.

"I'm stayin' with my Auntie Doreen."

"That's fine. I'll tell you what, after we get you booked I'll let you call your aunt so she'll know where you are. After you pay your bail, we'll even give you a ride home." He paused, then asked, "Fair enough?"

B.C. thought for a moment, then said, "I guess so."

"Atta boy," the sergeant said, then motioned for one of the officers to place handcuffs on him.

The officer instructed B.C. to place his hands behind his back, but when he did so, his massive arms would not come together close enough for the cuffs to reach from one wrist to the other. At the sergeant's direction, the officer cuffed the prisoner with his arms in front of him.

Officer Hansen had taken out his notebook, sat on a stool and was taking down information from Frieda for his report. "What is your last name, Frieda?"

"Pinchon."

"Would you spell it, please?"

" P-I-N-C-H-O-N."

As the sergeant and the arresting officer were escorting B.C. past Hansen, the officer was asking, "And what is your address Miss Pinchon?"

As they stepped out of the store B.C. asked, "Would you be able to get me a copy of the report that's bein' written on me?"

The sergeant thought for a moment. "I don't see why not. So far as I know you're legally entitled to a copy."

B.C. then turned his head and looked back into the store. As Frieda was answering the officer's questions she happened to look out the door. A cold shiver of fear raced through her as she looked into the eyes of the strange ugly giant who stared back at her.

ELEVEN

FRIEDA PINCHON STOOD before the mirror atop the dresser in her bedroom and studied her features, as if for the first time. She was still a bit shaken from the incident at work, and had been relieved when the associate manager decided to close the lunch counter for the remainder of the day. The entire section had to be roped off in order to clean and repair the merchandise counter onto which that construction worker had been thrown.

Within fifteen minutes of being given the order to close the lunch counter, the two waitresses had cleaned the area, turned off appliances, locked the food cabinets, dimmed the lights and departed for home. Two minutes later she was backing her car out of the diagonal parking space in front of the store.

Frieda rolled the windows down in her '61 Volkswagen in order to take in the Gulf breeze as she drove west on Highway 90 to Pass Christian, a small, picturesque community eight miles west of Gulfport. On the outskirts of Pass Christian she turned onto a scenic tree-lined frontage road that paralleled the highway. Frieda loved this section of her drive home. There was something peaceful about the calm waters and white beach to her left and the large, stately mansions, manicured lawns and ancient oak trees off to her right. Many of the elegant homes, with their white columns, predated the Civil War.

At Menge Avenue Frieda turned right. She drove north for one mile before leaving the city limits of Pass Christian. Staying on Menge Avenue she drove another mile, through a rural countryside, and entered the sparsely populated village of Pineville. She then made another right turn, onto Briggs Street. Actually, it was not much more than a gravel-covered driveway, perhaps a hundred yards in length. She made a sharp turn to the left and parked the Volkswagen in a space beside the only structure on the short street. It was a small mom-and-pop grocery store with a modest residence attached to the rear of the store. The business was owned by her paternal grandfather, with whom she had lived for sixteen of her eighteen years.

Her grandfather was waiting on a customer when Frieda entered through the front door. She normally had a sweet, cheerful greeting for him, and when she walked past without a word he sensed that something was wrong.

Eugene Pinchon was a tall, slender man with thinning white hair and a prominent gray mustache that drooped at the ends. It gave one the impression that he was always frowning.

"Frieda? Are you OK?" He asked.

"I'm fine," she said without stopping.

"Isn't it a little early for you to be home from work?"

She was halfway through the store when she stopped and turned toward her grandfather. She felt badly about her rudeness in attempting to ignore him, but she was too upset to talk to anyone at the moment. "They closed the lunch counter to do some repair work, so they let us leave early."

"Oh," her grandfather replied as he watched her turn back and resume her walk to the rear of the store, then up three steps to a small landing that separated the business from their home.

Inside her bedroom she stared fixedly at her reflection in the mirror; at her dark brown wavy hair, then her mouth and, finally, her large brown doe eyes. What was it that the strange man in Woolworth saw that gave it away? It was true of course. She did have Negro blood in her. Not much, but enough to cause embarrassment if it ever got out. At least that is what had been driven into her all of her life.

AS THE STORY had been told to her, Frieda's mother was born to a Creole woman, whose blood was a mixture of Negro, French and Spanish. The father had been a sailor off a British merchant ship. It had been a weekend love affair that was spent in a tiny apartment above a bar in the heart of the New Orleans French Quarter. When the weekend was over the sailor shipped out and was never heard from again. Nine months later, in the spring of 1932, Frieda's mother was born. Her mother named her Monique. Having no idea what the father's last name was, the young mother gave Monique her own last name, which was Porier.

Eugene Pinchon, Jr. was born in 1930, in Bay St. Louis, Mississippi. In 1940 he moved with his parents to Pineville, where they opened a grocery store. When he was eighteen, Eugene went to work for a construction company in New Orleans. In 1949, while working on the construction of an office building on Canal Street, he met Monique. She was employed as a waitress in a nearby coffee shop.

For Eugene, it was love at first sight. He was captivated by the alluring beauty of the olive-skinned waitress with the full lips and large brown eyes. Her features were such that they gave one the impression that her origins were Italian, or, perhaps, middle-Eastern. By the time Eugene learned that Monique was one-quarter Negro he was so much in love that it did not matter to him.

It did, however, matter greatly to Eugene, Sr. He expressed his concerns to his son, to no avail. In 1950 Eugene and Monique were married. The following year Frieda was born. To the great relief of Eugene, Sr. her complexion and features were those of a white child.

The marriage between Eugene and Monique was not a happy one. Soon after her twenty-first birthday, Monique got a job serving cocktails in a bar on Bourbon Street. The tips were good and she enjoyed the attention that the male patrons gave her. It was not long before she began to feel the shackles of marriage. Eugene worked at the construction site during the day and stayed home with the baby at night, while Monique worked at the bar.

When Frieda was two years old, her mother left them. From what information Eugene could gather, Monique ran away with a barber supply salesman from New Jersey.

Eugene was devastated when Monique deserted him and their daughter, but he made no effort to go after her and bring her back. He had known for some time the kind of woman she was, and was well aware that he could not change her. He realized, however, that, if he was to ever get over her he would have to leave New Orleans. After serving out his notice to his employer he took Frieda to Pineville to stay with his parents while he looked for work.

He landed a job at the shipyard in Pascagoula, which was about forty miles east of Pass Christian. He commuted to work each day and worked several hours overtime each week. After four months on the job the fatigue began to show. His mother even commented on how tired and irritable he seemed.

One Friday morning, after a particularly long week, the fatigue caught up with him. He was driving to work, and was a few miles east of Ocean Springs when, according to the police report, he apparently fell asleep at the wheel and collided with a bridge abutment. He was killed instantly.

In grieving for their son, Eugene's parents grew closer to Frieda, the only grandchild they would ever have. In order to prevent a possible future attempt on Monique's part to take her away, Eugene, Sr. petitioned the court to grant him and his wife full custody of their grandchild. The petition was granted, though it was never challenged, for they never saw Monique again.

Frieda was only two years old when her father was killed, and she had no memory of him. Her Grandma and Grandpa were the only parents she ever knew, and no parent could have ever treated their child with any more love than her grandparents treated her.

If anything, her grandfather was overly protective of her. He had a nagging fear that someone would learn of the Negro blood that flowed through Frieda's veins. Though he loved her no less for it, he knew quite well the social barriers that would be created for her, not just in the Deep South, but in the hypocritical North as well.

As the years passed, though, Eugene, Sr.'s fears began to subside. She was enrolled in the all-white public school system and, at no time, was there the slightest suspicion of her mixed blood. She was always one of the prettiest and most popular girls in her class. In her senior year of high school she was chosen as the homecoming queen and was voted most popular girl. In May 1969 Frieda graduated from high school and, in September, she planned to enroll at Perkinston Junior College, which was located about thirty miles north of Gulfport. A week after graduation she went to work at Woolworth for the summer to help defray school expenses in the fall.

AFTER STUDYING HERSELF in the mirror for several minutes Frieda gave up and backed away. She sat on the edge of the bed and breathed a sigh. What should she do? Should she tell her grandfather what had happened? But then she knew the answer as soon as the thought occurred to her. Of course she could not tell him. There was nothing he could do about it, yet he would agonize over it for days or even weeks if he found out.

Then Frieda thought of her grandmother, and was momentarily filled with sadness. Her grandmother had passed away when Frieda was fourteen. They had been very close, and this was something that she would have shared with her. Grandma would have known what to do. And even if nothing could be done, she would at least have known what to say to make Frieda feel better.

Her thoughts drifted to the incident at the lunch counter and a troubling sensation came over her. What was going on in Shirley's mind now that she was away from work and had a chance to think about what that strange, ugly man had said about her? Was she wondering if it were true about Frieda having Negro blood? Then it occurred to her that she really did not care what Shirley thought. In a few weeks Frieda would no longer be working at Woolworth and would probably never see Shirley again.

No, it was not how Shirley felt that troubled her. It was the man himself. It was the way he looked back at her as he was being taken away by the police. Though he was now locked behind bars and, for all practical purposes she was safe, she experienced a sense of foreboding. She could not get out of her mind that scary look he gave her. From somewhere deep inside her Frieda knew that if that frightful man ever got out of jail, she would see him again.

TWELVE

DOREEN BROWN WAS beside herself with worry. She sat on the sofa and stared vacantly at the black and white image of Joey Bishop on the T.V. screen. For the hundredth time she chastised herself for insisting that B.C. go downtown. She had done it for selfish reasons, she told herself. She had sent him away because she wanted a few hours of solitude, and now he was sitting in jail.

She had received the call seven hours earlier, about 4:30 P.M. The caller identified himself as Sgt. Taylor, of the Gulfport Police Department, who said that he was calling at the request of her nephew. After confirming with Doreen that B.C. Jones was in fact his full name, the sergeant briefly explained that B.C. had been arrested for having created a disturbance at Woolworth. He told her that there had been some property damage and that someone had been slightly injured. He omitted any details as to how the incident came about, but he assured her that the only charge against her nephew was disturbing the peace. When Doreen asked if she should go to the police station to pay his bail, Sgt. Taylor said it was not necessary, since Mr. Jones had sufficient funds to pay his own bail. The sergeant added that it would take a few hours to run a routine record check on B.C. If everything checked out O.K., he should be home no later than nine-thirty, or ten at the latest. Before hanging up, Sgt. Taylor promised Doreen that he would have someone drive B.C. home after he was released.

Doreen glanced at the clock that sat atop the console television set. It was 11:40 P.M. He was two hours late. What could've gone wrong? On the coffee table in front of the sofa was the afternoon edition of the local newspaper. She had skimmed over it soon after it arrived, but that was before she learned of B.C.'s arrest. She looked again at the headlines, which read: TWO MORE MURDERS NEAR LOS ANGELES.

The uneasy feeling inside her increased to a sickening knot in the pit of her stomach. The thoughts that had occurred to her as B.C. walked out of her house earlier in the day rushed back to her. Why did he leave Los Angeles so suddenly? She picked up the paper and began to read the article. It related the discovery of two more victims, Leno and Rosemary LaBianca, who were murdered in the same manner as movie actress Sharon Tate and four others over the weekend. Doreen breathed a sigh of relief. This had nothing to do with B.C. He was in Gulfport with her when these crimes occurred.

Suddenly the impact of what she had been thinking struck her like a slap in the face. "What's wrong with me?" She asked aloud. "B.C. is my nephew! How could I even think that he might be involved in such a horrible thing as murder?" Then the image of her brother flashed through her mind and how B.C. had killed him with his bare hands. Though he had been provoked by Lester, the fact remained that B.C was certainly capable of taking a human life.

On the coffee table, next to the newspaper, was a worn copy of the Holy Bible. Its dog-eared pages attested to frequent use by its owner. Doreen had purchased the book a quarter of a century earlier and had twice read it from cover to cover, and a day did not pass that she didn't read a chapter or two. Leaning forward, she picked up the Bible. She thought of turning off the T.V. while she read, but decided against it. She needed the voice of someone else in the room to keep her company, and Joey Bishop had as pleasant a voice as anyone.

Just as Doreen was lifting the Bible from the table she heard the sound of a car pulling up and stopping in front of the house. A sense of relief came over her. Returning the Bible to the table, she slowly lifted her large bulk from the sofa, then stood for a moment to get the kinks out of her back.

She could hear the sound of footsteps on the porch as she made her way to the door. As she reached out to push the screen door open she said, "It's about time you got home, hon . . ." Doreen's greeting was cut short when she saw the white man facing her from the other side of the screen door. He appeared to be in his late thirties. He was of medium height with a husky build that might be regarded as slightly pudgy. He wore dark slacks, a white shirt, blue tie and a gray herring bone sport coat.

"Mrs. Brown?" He asked.

"I'm Mrs. Brown."

"Mrs. Brown, I'm Deputy Wojcik (pronounced wo-check) of the Harrison County Sheriff's Office."

Doreen's heart sunk and the sickening mass in the pit of her stomach felt as if it were rising toward her throat. She took in a deep breath, then let it out slowly. "What is it, deputy? Is this about B.C.?"

"I'm afraid it is," the deputy replied. There was a note of sympathy in his tone. "As you know, your nephew, Mr. Jones, was arrested this afternoon by the Gulfport Police Department."

"Yes?" Her response was in the form of a question, as if prompting him to continue.

"As a routine part of the booking process," Wojcik continued, "a nationwide record check is made. That is why it usually takes a few hours before an arrestee is able to make bail following his arrest." He paused briefly before continuing. "A few hours ago the Gulfport P.D. received a request from the Los Angeles County Sheriff's Department to hold Mr. Jones pending extradition proceedings."

"Why on earth would they do that?" Doreen asked, though she dreaded the answer.

"Because he is a named suspect in some very serious crimes."

The sickening mass had moved from Doreen's stomach to the base of her throat. "Can you tell me what those crimes are?"

"Yes, ma'am, I can."

Doreen mentally braced herself. "Well?"

This time it was the deputy's turn to take in a deep breath and blow it out in a sigh. "Murder."

Doreen's worst fears were realized. She put her hand to her mouth, then removed it long enough to ask, "You said crimes. How many were there?"

Deputy Wojcik shifted his stance. It was obvious that he took no pleasure in putting this woman through such an ordeal. "I don't know the details, but I understand there are multiple counts against him."

Doreen pressed her hand against her mouth and thought for a moment that she was going to be sick, but she made no sound. Her eyes filled with tears that began to flow down both cheeks.

"Once it was determined that Mr. Jones was going to remain in custody for an indeterminate amount of time, he was transferred to the county jail. He is now in the custody of the sheriff."

When Doreen made no reply, Deputy Wojcik took out a small sheet of paper and a pen and wrote something, then gently pulled the screen door open wide enough to hand the paper to her. "I've written down my name and phone number. I normally work during the day shift. If I can be of any help to you, please don't hesitate to call."

Unable to speak, she nodded in acknowledgement.

"Mrs. Brown," Wojcik began. "I am so sorry for having to be the bearer of such bad news." He paused again, then added, "Would you like for me to stay with you for a while? Keep you company?"

She looked into the deputy's eyes and knew that he was sincere. "No," she said softly, "I'll be all right. But you're very kind to ask."

Deputy Wojcik hesitated for a moment, then slowly turned. "Goodnight, Mrs. Brown."

Doreen remained in the doorway and absently watched him descend the porch steps and walk to his car. Only after he had driven away did she close the big wooden door. No sooner was it locked than she broke down and cried. She had not experienced such grief since her husband walked out on her thirty years earlier.

After a while she managed to collect herself long enough to turn off the T.V. and change into her nightclothes. But once she was in bed the emotion began to well up inside her once more, and she cried until there were no more tears to shed. An hour before dawn she finally drifted off to sleep.

THIRTEEN

Los Angeles, California
Wednesday
August 13, 1969

GARLAND FLOWERS COULD not conceal the expression of surprise and disappointment on his face as he sat in the coffee room adjacent to Homicide Bureau and stared across the table at Archie Penner.

"What do you mean you're not going with me on this extradition?" Flowers wanted to know.

"Just what I said," his partner replied.

"Why?"

"Because I've been pulled off the Jones case and assigned to a task force investigating the Tate-LaBianca murders."

"But that's L.A.P.D.'s case," Flowers protested. "Why are we involved in it?"

"I suppose it's because it's a high profile case. These murders have made international news." Penner paused long enough to take a sip from his coffee cup. "Like all highly publicized crimes people start crawling out of the woodwork with information. Each piece of information becomes a lead that has to be checked out. Several of these leads involve people and places in the sheriff's jurisdiction."

"Yeah," Flowers said, "but you and I both know that ninety-nine percent of the leads are bogus."

"Very true. But the fact remains that each one has to be checked out."

Flowers forced a smile. "So, while I'm way down south in redneck country trying to charm a two hundred eighty pound multiple murder suspect back to California, you'll be running down phony leads in a murder case that, by rights, belongs to L.A.P.D." He shook his head. "I don't know which one of us I feel sorry for the most."

Penner also smiled, but made no reply.

"Did they tell you who they were getting to replace you?" Flowers asked.

Penner's smile faded. "Yeah, they told me."

"From the look on your face I will assume it's not a homicide detective," Flowers said. "Probably one of the guys from Fugitive Detail, right?"

Penner shook his head.

"Then who is it?"

"Inspector Pierce."

"Inspector Pierce? You mean that pencil pusher from Admin Division? Why him?"

"He may be a pencil pusher," Penner said, "but he's also an executive member of the sheriff's department."

"You gotta be kidding!" Flowers exclaimed. His disappointment was turning to anger. "He's not a real cop. He's an admin pogue. The man's worked his way up through the ranks with one cushy admin job after another. From everything I've heard he wouldn't know a felon from a foot fungus!"

"All that may be true," Penner said. "I've even heard that he fancies himself some sort of a playboy . . . probably explains why he's been married and divorced four times. But the way it stands now, he's your new partner on this extradition."

"But why? Why did they select Pierce?" Flowers asked.

"My guess is he requested the assignment. You know, department executives do that a lot."

"Yeah, that's usually when the extradition is from somewhere glamorous, like Hawaii. Why would this playboy snob want to go to a place like Gulfport, Mississippi?"

"Because of its proximity to a glamour spot," Penner said. "Gulfport is only about seventy miles from New Orleans. In fact, New Orleans is the nearest international airport to where you're going. You'll probably fly in to New Orleans, then rent a car and drive to Gulfport."

"So what?" Flowers asked. "If I have my way, all we're going to do after we get off the plane is go straight to Gulfport, pick up our prisoner, return to the airport, and fly back to L.A."

Penner looked at his partner the way an older brother might regard an innocent sibling and smiled. "You're a great guy, Garland, and a smart cop. But you don't know didley squat about this sort of thing, do you."

"What do you mean?"

"I mean, whenever someone like Pierce goes on an extradition, bringing back the prisoner is only secondary to him. This is a junket to him. He doesn't give a rip about your prisoner. What he cares about is spending time in New Orleans . . . especially the French Quarter.

"The way it works is like this: Pierce will time it so that you won't arrive in Gulfport until Friday afternoon. It'll be too late to get the court to release the prisoner to your custody, so you'll have to wait until after the courts open on Monday morning. In the meantime our friend Mr. Pierce will have the entire weekend to enjoy himself in New Orleans, courtesy of the taxpayers of L.A. County."

Flowers was silent for almost a full minute, then he stood up and pushed his chair back.

"Where are you going?" Penner asked.

"To talk to Lieutenant Skinner. I've got to have a decent partner with me on this trip."

"Skinner's not in," Penner said. "But I think I saw the captain in his office."

"Then I'll go see the captain," Flowers said as he moved toward the door.

"Garland," Penner called after him. When Flowers turned, his partner said, "good luck."

"Thanks," Flowers said, then walked out of the coffee room.

CAPTAIN GILFORD LOOKED up from his work when he heard the light tap and saw Sgt. Flowers standing in the open doorway. Waving the sergeant into his office, Gilford took a final drag on his cigarette and crushed it in an ashtray on his desk.

"Garland," he greeted. "What can I do for you?" Before Flowers could answer, Gilford asked another question. "Have you got everything in order for your trip?"

"Not quite, Captain," Flowers replied.

"Well, now, don't you think you better get a move on? This is Wednesday, and the day is almost half over. You've got to get all the paper work over to the D.A.'s office so they can pick up the airline tickets, calculate your travel expenses and process the extradition papers."

"Yes, sir," Flowers said. "But I need to talk to you about something first."

Gilford studied Flowers for a moment, then asked, "Does this have anything to do with Inspector Pierce?"

"Yes, sir, it does."

Gilford breathed a deep sigh, then said, "Close the door and have a seat." When this was done he asked, "Now, just what is the problem you have with Pierce?"

"First of all," Flowers began, "I don't have a personal problem with Inspector Pierce. As a matter of fact, I don't even know the man."

"I do," Gilford interrupted. "And I can tell you that I don't like him. I've known Winston Pierce for close to twenty years, and as far as I'm concerned, he's a first class jerk."

"Yes, sir," Flowers said. "I've heard others say the same thing about him, but that's not what I'm concerned about. I don't really care how big a jerk he is. I'm concerned about my safety. This guy we're going after, B.C. Jones, is an extremely dangerous man. He's killed at least seven people with his bare hands, and one of those happened to be his own father.

"This suspect is no one to mess with. I guess what I'm getting at is that I need a partner I can depend on to back me up." Flowers paused and shook his head. "Frankly, Captain, I don't know that I can count on Inspector Pierce."

There was a moment of silence as Gilford lit a cigarette. He took a long drag, then exhaled it through his nose. He offered no comment as he reached for the phone receiver and dialed a number.

When the party on the other end answered, he said, "Hi, Cindy, this is John Gilford. Is the chief in?" Pause. "I see. Well, can you set up an appointment?" Pause. "No, not for me. It's for one of my investigators, Sergeant Flowers."

Flowers looked at Gilford questioningly.

"Two o'clock? That's the earliest?" Gilford asked. Following another pause, he said, "I see. Well, I guess that'll have to do." Pause. "It concerns the Mississippi extradition." Pause. "Thanks, Cindy. Talk to you later. Bye."

After hanging up the phone, Gilford addressed Flowers. "Chief Maxwell was the one who approved Pierce for this trip. The fact that both Pierce and Maxwell outrank me, I'm in no position to countermand the decision. However, I think you raise some legitimate concerns, and you have the right to be heard."

Flowers considered what Gilford said, then asked, "Will you go with me to the chief's office, to help me plead my case?"

Gilford winced and there was genuine disappointment in his tone when he said, "You know I would if I could. Unfortunately, though, I have to be in Pomona Superior Court for a meeting in the judge's chambers at one-thirty this afternoon. I'll probably be there the rest of the day." The captain then smiled and added, "Don't worry, Garland. I'm sure you'll do fine."

AT ONE-FIFTY P.M. Garland Flowers stepped into the outer office of the chief of Detective Division. He was greeted by the friendly smile of the secretary, Cindy Ramirez.

"Hi, Sergeant Flowers," she said. "You're a few minutes early."

Flowers returned the smile. "Well, I figured it best that I wait for the chief than have him wait for me."

"I'll let him know you're here," she said as she lifted the phone receiver. She spoke briefly, then hung up. "The chief said that he'll be with you in just a few minutes."

"Thanks."

Flowers walked to the office window. It provided a view to the south. Directly below was Temple Avenue, and across the street was a parking lot, and beyond that was the State Building. Due south was the building that was the home of the *Los Angeles Times*, surrounded by the hundreds of other structures that comprised the heart of downtown Los Angeles.

Slightly to the right, half a block away, was the old Hall of Records, which sat diagonally to all the other buildings in the Civic Center. Plans were underway to tear it down and construct a criminal courts building. Rumor had it that the new building would be several stories higher than the Hall of Justice and would take up the entire block. Flowers tried to envision a structure so large that it would block any other view of the city from where he now stood, but then dismissed the depressing thought.

His gaze then wandered to the left, and stopped at the southwest corner of Temple and Spring Street. On that very corner, forty years earlier, his grandfather, George Flowers, operated a shoeshine stand. Garland smiled to himself as he recalled the stories his father had told him of his Grandpa George.

It was in the mid-1920's when he first set up his stand. George worked nights as a janitor in a nearby office building so he could run the shoeshine business during the day. From the money he made as a janitor, he fed and clothed his family, and every dime he collected from shining shoes went into a college savings fund for his two sons.

The shoeshine stand was in an ideal location. During those days the space that now served as a parking lot was the site of the Los Angeles County Courthouse, a massive red stone structure of Victorian design. Grandpa George's stand sat adjacent to the northeast entrance to the courthouse, and his customers included the likes of Sheriff William Traeger, Undersheriff, and later Sheriff, Gene Biscailuz, as well as dozens of prominent lawyers, judges and newspaper reporters.

George Flowers worked his two jobs for over ten years, saving every penny he could scrape together for his sons' education. Sadly, he did not live long enough to see all the fruits of his labor, though he did see his two sons graduate from college. The older son, Simon–Garland's father, would enter the field of education, and eventually retire as a school principal. The younger son, Calvin, would go on to earn a Ph.D. and become an associate professor of sociology at Los Angeles State College.

As Garland stared out the window he tried to picture his grandfather working at his stand. From what his father had told him, Garland resembled Grandpa George. He was a fairly tall man, just over six feet, with a lean, muscular build. Garland had even been told that he got his good looks from his grandfather. He was a small child when Grandpa George passed away, and Garland regretted never having gotten to know him better.

"Sergeant Flowers?" It was Cindy's voice.

Like a person being awakened from a vivid dream, Flowers was slightly startled as his thoughts returned to the present. "Yes?" He said as he turned from the window.

"Chief Maxwell will see you now."

Cindy got up from behind her desk and went across the room, where she opened the inner office door. Flowers thanked her as he walked past.

He could hear laughter even before he entered the spacious office of the Chief of Detectives. Chief Maxwell was obviously enjoying a humorous comment made by the only other person in the room. As soon as Flowers stepped into view the man seated across the desk from the chief looked in his direction and stopped laughing. An expression of momentary surprise appeared on his face, then he immediately recovered and an unfeeling smile replaced the look of surprise.

Garland Flowers had never regarded himself as racially sensitive. He had been reared in a family that taught him that a man's worth is measured by his character and not by the color of his skin. Yet he knew that look, as did all black men and women whose skin color takes someone by surprise.

Flowers knew Inspector Winston Pierce by sight; his tailored Brooks Brothers suit, his bronze tan, immaculately styled dark brown hair with a touch of gray at the temples and, of course, his trademark–a cigarette protruding from a three-inch holder. He reminded Flowers of a poor impression of Franklin Roosevelt. Though Flowers knew the inspector, the reverse was not true. It was quite apparent that Pierce learned only just this minute that the man who would be accompanying him on the extradition was black.

Inwardly Flowers smiled. He took a degree of pleasure in Pierce's momentary discomfort. But the inner smile faded and he felt disheartened by the sudden realization that he was about to engage in a battle that was already lost, and he resented Chief Maxwell for placing him in this awkward position. He knew before he opened his mouth to state his case that it would do no good. No matter what he said, Inspector Winston Pierce would be his companion on the trip to Mississippi.

FOURTEEN

Mississippi Gulf Coast
Friday
August 15, 1969

IT WAS MID-AFTERNOON when the Greyhound bus crossed the Mississippi state line from Louisiana. Garland Flowers sat near the window. The bus was filled to only half capacity and he used the vacant seat next to him to place his briefcase, which contained the necessary extradition paperwork. Though it was not the way he had envisioned traveling to Gulfport, this was actually the first opportunity he had to relax since departing Los Angeles seven hours earlier.

As the bus proceeded east along Highway 90 Flowers noticed that the sunny sky that had greeted him in New Orleans was giving way to darkening clouds that appeared to be forming in the southeast. He was intrigued by the simultaneous presence of the sun, the dark clouds and the patches of blue sky. It was not a sight commonly seen in L.A., where the sky was usually a pale blue or slate gray. Often there would be a touch of yellowish-brown, the mixture of which depended upon the smog level on any given day. But here, Flowers thought, the bright sunlight and the deep blue of the sky and the dark, almost black, clouds offered a contrast that was refreshingly different.

He leaned his head back and closed his eyes. The anger that he had felt in New Orleans was beginning to subside, though his opinion of Inspector Winston Pierce remained extremely low. From the moment they boarded the plane in L.A. Pierce began demonstrating that he was as big a jerk as his reputation claimed.

Actually, the conflict between Flowers and Pierce began in Chief Maxwell's office two days before. After the chief had made it quite clear that Pierce would be accompanying Flowers on the extradition, Pierce insisted that the trip be put off until Friday. He explained that he had some pressing engagements on Thursday, so Friday would be the earliest that he could leave.

As Flowers sat on the bus with his head back and eyes closed he could not help but grin to himself. He recalled his conversation with Archie Penner in the coffee room, and how accurately his partner had predicted Pierce's efforts to delay the trip in order to stretch it out over the weekend.

As soon as the meeting with the chief had ended Flowers went directly to the district attorney's office to make travel arrangements. In doing so, he chose a flight that would depart L.A. at six A.M. and arrive in New Orleans shortly after noon Central Daylight Time. Flowers would have preferred an earlier flight, but this was the best he could get. It was good enough, though, for there was still time to rent a car and make the two-hour drive to Gulfport before the courts closed.

Throughout the flight Pierce made a nuisance of himself with the flight crew. He flirted with the stewardesses and made one request after another for special service. He made it known to everyone around him that he was a high ranking official of the Los Angeles County Sheriff's Department and he was on official business. Flowers could see the look of annoyance on the faces of the stewardesses and he felt embarrassed, not for Pierce, but for the sheriff's department, as well as for law enforcement in general.

As soon as the "No Smoking" light went out Pierce pulled out his cigarette holder and inserted a Pall Mall. The woman seated directly in front of him had reclined her seat, and Flowers was concerned for a moment that the extended cigarette might set fire to her hair.

The dark clouds had moved in a northeasterly direction and were directly overhead when the bus reached the west end of the Bay St. Louis Bridge. Large drops of rain hit the window and rolled erratically down the glass, blurring Flowers' view of the bay. By the time the bus had made the two-mile trip over the bridge it was pouring rain, and the sky was black overhead. Flowers was amused by the fact that, off to the north, he could still see rays of sunlight and patches of blue.

On the east side of the bay the bus turned right and proceeded south a short distance until it was parallel with the mouth of the bay, which was off to the right. This area was known as Henderson Point. The bus then rounded a curve to the left and headed east. The bay was behind them, and to the right Flowers was afforded his first good view of the Gulf of Mexico.

He was amazed at the calmness of the water. He was accustomed to looking out over the Pacific Ocean and seeing white foam as the heavy surf crashed onto the beach. Now, when he gazed out over the Gulf there was water as far as he could see, yet there were no big waves. The water seemed as calm as a lake.

Shortly after rounding Henderson Point the bus entered Pass Christian. Flowers took in the scenery on the opposite side of the highway from the Gulf. He was impressed by the stately white-pillared mansions that sat fifty yards off the road, on massive lawns that were populated by huge oak trees.

Farther east the large homes gave way to a string of motels, apartment complexes and small shopping centers. In a vacant lot between two buildings was a billboard sign that caught Flowers' eye. It was an advertisement for a seafood restaurant in New Orleans that boasted the best shrimp gumbo in Louisiana. As Flowers stared at the sign his thoughts returned to New Orleans . . . and Inspector Pierce.

The inspector did not reveal his plans to Flowers until after they had landed and were standing in front of the car rental counter inside the terminal. It had been Flowers who had obtained the extradition documents and made all of the travel arrangements in

Los Angeles. But as soon as they arrived in New Orleans Pierce took over. He made it a point to rent the car in his name, and ordered Flowers to give him all of the cash and travel vouchers. When Flowers started to protest, Pierce reminded him that an inspector far outranked a sergeant, and announced that he would make all of the decisions during the remainder of the trip. He allowed Flowers to retain only the extradition papers.

When they picked up the car at the rental lot Pierce obtained a street map of New Orleans, then asked one of the employees for directions to the Greyhound bus depot. It was only after they were driving out of the lot that Pierce told Flowers of his plan.

It was really quite simple. Pierce would drop Flowers off at the bus terminal, where he would purchase a one-way ticket to Gulfport. Upon arrival he could begin the extradition process. Flowers would, of course, be given sufficient cash and vouchers for meals and a hotel room. Pierce would remain in New Orleans. As soon as he was checked into a hotel he would call the Harrison County Sheriff's Office and leave a phone number where he could be reached. Whenever it was time for the prisoner to be transported, Flowers was to call Pierce, who would then drive to Gulfport and pick up Flowers and the prisoner. The three of them would then drive back to the New Orleans airport for the return flight to Los Angeles.

The downpour that had begun so dramatically when the bus passed over the Bay St. Louis bridge was now reduced to a moderate shower as the bus continued eastward on Highway 90 through the community of Long Beach and into the city limits of Gulfport.

Though most of the anger had left Flowers by now, he recalled how furious he had become when Pierce described his plan. Aside from the humiliation of having to travel by bus to pick up a prisoner, and Pierce's confiscation of most of the travel expenses, Flowers' anger was primarily aimed at the inspector's devious attempt to turn this potentially dangerous venture into a pleasure trip. He was doing everything he could to delay Flowers' arrival in Gulfport so that he would be unable to obtain a court order for the release of B.C. Jones before Monday.

Flowers looked at his watch. It was 3:50 P.M. If the courts in Harrison County functioned like those in L.A. County, Flowers thought, by the time he arrived at the courthouse it would be highly unlikely that he would find a judge still on the bench–especially on a Friday afternoon.

Oh, well, he thought. There's nothing I can do about it at the moment, so I might as well sit back and enjoy the ride. No sooner had this thought entered Flowers' mind than the rain stopped. The dark clouds were drifting away, on a north-by-northwest course. Then, as if on cue, the sun came out. The sudden change in weather fascinated Flowers. Everything around him seemed clean and bright, and it served to lift his spirits.

He chuckled to himself as he thought of how suddenly the blue sky opened up in front of him. All he needed was a chorus of angels singing in the background and he would have sworn that he was caught up in a Cecil B. DeMille movie.

Five minutes later the bus turned north onto a narrow street and entered the business district of Gulfport. It proceeded one block, then turned left, into the driveway of the bus terminal.

FIFTEEN

WHEN FLOWERS EMERGED from the comfort of the air-conditioned bus he felt as if he were stepping into a sauna. It seemed to be even hotter and more humid than when he first encountered this sticky southern climate outside the airport terminal in New Orleans.

After claiming his baggage he sought directions to the courthouse, and was relieved to learn that it was across the street from the bus depot. A minute later he had crossed the street and was moving toward the stately red brick structure that was the Harrison County Courthouse.

As he approached the steps of the building he noticed a tall statue in front. Atop a pedestal that appeared to be almost twenty feet in height was the bronze likeness of a Confederate soldier. It stood like a sentry, silently guarding the entrance to the courthouse. A plaque near the base of the pedestal proclaimed that it was a memorial to the soldiers who fought for the Southern cause and was dedicated by the United Daughters of the Confederacy. A sense of caution came over Flowers as he ascended the courthouse steps. The presence of the statue, coupled with the sultry heat, reminded him that he was in the Deep South. Moreover, he was a lone black man in a strange town, and he could not help wondering what kind of reception awaited him.

The interior of the courthouse had the same pungent and musty odor that Flowers had detected in other old government buildings. He decided that it was probably an accumulation of half a century of tobacco smoke absorbed into the walls of the building. He imagined Grandpa George experiencing similar odors in the old courthouse in Los Angeles, and he found a degree of comfort in the thought.

At the counter of the chancery clerk he was given some directions, and a moment later he entered the outer office of the Harrison County Sheriff. The only other person in the room was a middle-aged woman sitting behind an ancient oak desk, busily typing on an IBM Selectric typewriter. Flowers was setting his suitcase on the floor when she looked up and smiled.

"May I help you?" She asked in an accent that was right out of *Gone with the Wind.*

"I hope so. I'm Sergeant Flowers, with the Los Angeles County Sheriff's Department, and I'm supposed . . ."

"Oh, yes!" She cut him off. "You're here to pick up that prisoner."

"That's right."

"Pleased to meet you, Sergeant Flowers. My name is Gertie. Gertie Allgood. Won't you be seated and I'll get someone in here to assist you."

"Thank you," Flowers said as he found a chair behind him and sat down.

Gertie picked up the phone and dialed a number. "Frank?" She asked the person on the other end. "Hi, this is Gertie. A Sergeant Flowers is here from Los Angeles to pick up that prisoner. The sheriff said that you would be handling it." After a brief pause she said, "Thanks, Frank. See you in a bit."

She hung up the phone and turned to Flowers with the same warm smile that had greeted him. "Someone will be here shortly to assist you. In the meantime, could I get you a cup of coffee?"

"I'd love a cup," he replied.

"What do you take in it?"

"Just coffee."

Gertie excused herself and was about to step away from her desk when she stopped long enough to pick up a small piece of paper. "I almost forgot," she said. "I have a phone message for you. It's from an Inspector Pierce." She handed Flowers the paper then disappeared through one of the inner office doors.

Flowers glanced at the paper. It contained Pierce's hotel phone and room numbers. A note at the bottom of the message stated that Flowers was to call Pierce no later than seven P.M.

A moment later Gertie returned, holding a cup with steam rising from it. Flowers stuffed the note in his shirt pocket before taking the proffered cup from Gertie.

Flowers held it for a full minute to let it cool before taking a sip. After tasting it he pursed his lips and shook his head as if to clear it from an unpleasant experience. "Wow! This is strong stuff!"

"Why, thank you," Gertie said proudly. "I hope you like it."

"Well . . ."

"That's the way we Southerners drink our coffee."

Flowers forced himself to take another sip and was surprised to find that it was not as bad as the first. Though much stronger than he would have preferred, the coffee actually had a good, rich taste. "You know, this isn't half bad." He grinned and added, "Although I have an idea it's gonna keep me awake for a week."

Gertie beamed as if it were the best compliment Flowers could pay her.

Flowers had managed to drink half the contents of the cup when the outer door opened and a man in his late thirties entered. He was of medium height and stocky build. He waved a greeting to Gertie, then, as he closed the door he saw Flowers.

Extending his hand he said, "Sergeant Flowers? I'm Deputy Frank Wojcik. I'll be working with you on the extradition."

"How do you do? I'm Garland Flowers," he said as the two men shook hands.

"Garland," Wojcik repeated. "Do folks call you Gar for short?"

"No, I prefer Garland." When there was no response Flowers added with a grin, "To me, Gar is just as bad as Garland. So I might as well go for the whole name."

Wojcik smiled warmly. "O.K., Garland it is." He then noticed the suitcase. "From the looks of things you haven't even checked into a hotel yet."

"No, I just got off the bus a few minutes ago."

"The bus?" Wojcik asked. "You came by bus?"

"Well, yes," Flowers said with a hint of embarrassment. "At least from New Orleans. We flew to New Orleans from L.A."

"We?"

"My partner and me." Flowers suddenly experienced a sense of disgust at the thought of referring to Pierce as his partner. His partner was Archie Penner, who was back in L.A. working on the Tate-LaBianca murders. Pierce was a fraud, and was here only to have a good time. He breathed a deep sigh, then added, "Actually he's not really my partner. He just came along as a back-up."

Flowers briefly explained his professional relationship with Pierce, as well as Pierce's plan to stay in New Orleans until the last minute. Though he was careful not to speak ill of the inspector, he could tell from the expression on Wojcik's face that the deputy was perceptive enough to read between the lines.

"Sounds like this Inspector Pierce has an agenda of his own," Wojcik said.

Flowers shrugged his shoulders but offered no comment.

"But what about you, Garland?" Wojcik asked. "Are you anxious to get back home?"

Flowers thought for a moment, then said, "Let's put it this way. The sooner I get Jones safely locked inside the L.A. County Jail the better I will feel." He looked at Wojcik and asked, "I'm curious, have you had any personal contact with B.C. Jones?"

"I've seen him, if that's what you mean. He appears to be a little simple-minded." Wojcik grinned wryly and shook his head. "He's also one big son-of-a-gun."

"He's also a cold-blooded killer."

"That's what I've been told," Wojcik said as he was reminded of the unpleasant chore of having to break the news to Jones' aunt.

"He went to prison for killing his father. He was released last

March. Since then he's committed six murders that we know of." After a pause he added, "Needless to say, I want to get this business over as soon as possible."

Wojcik was silent for a full minute. It was obvious to Flowers that he was engrossed in deep thought. He then turned to the secretary.

"Gertie, would you do something for me?"

"Sure."

"Would you please call Gulfport Municipal Airport and find out if they have a commuter flight to New Orleans tomorrow?"

Gertie picked up the phone and began dialing. Wojcik turned his attention to Flowers. "As much as I hate to put a damper on Inspector Pierce's weekend plans, we can have you and your prisoner out of here tomorrow. Pierce can meet you at the New Orleans airport, and by tomorrow night you can be back in L.A."

"What about the extradition proceedings?" Flowers asked. "Don't we have to appear in court?"

"We have to get a judge to sign the extradition order. Since the prisoner, Mr. Jones, has already signed a waiver, there's no need for a formal hearing. The courts are closed now, but I have a friend who happens to be a judge. We can go by his house this evening and get him to sign the papers."

Gertie cupped her hand over the phone speaker and said, "Excuse me, Sergeant Flowers."

"Yes?"

"On what airline did you fly into New Orleans?"

"Delta."

"Is your ticket for the return flight open?"

"Yes. I can use it on any flight that has seats available."

"Thank you," she said, then resumed her phone conversation with the party on the other end of the line.

Wojcik continued, "Gulfport P.D. has a holding cell at the pistol range, which is near the airport. I'll arrange for some deputies to transport Jones to the holding cell first thing in the morning.

Then a few minutes before flight time we'll run him over to the airport."

Flowers and Wojcik both looked at Gertie when she hung up the phone.

"O.K.," she began. "There's a flight leaving Gulfport at 8:00 A.M. and another at 1:15 P.M. Delta has a nonstop from New Orleans to Los Angeles at 3:30 P.M."

Wojcik looked at Flowers. "I recommend that you take the 1:15 flight. That way you won't have a long layover in New Orleans."

"Sounds fine to me," Flowers said.

"Good," Gertie put in. "Because I've already booked you on that flight. You also have reservations for three on the Delta flight out of New Orleans."

Flowers was impressed by the business-like manner in which Wojcik had taken charge. There was a no-nonsense quality about him that Flowers liked. He was nothing like the stereotypical southern cop that was so frequently depicted in the movies. It was apparent that he was intelligent and decisive. Flowers also observed that, although Wojcik spoke with a slight southern accent, it was nothing like Gertie's heavy drawl.

"I hope you don't think we're anxious to get rid of you," Wojcik said. "But Camille is beginning to cause us some concern."

"Camille?" Flowers asked.

"Hurricane Camille. It made landfall in Cuba today, and it looks like it's making its way into the Gulf."

"I'm sorry," Flowers said. "I haven't watched the news or read a paper in the past few days. I wasn't even aware there was a hurricane."

"That's understandable," Wojcik said. "I doubt if hurricanes get much front page coverage out in California. But down here we try to track them pretty closely. Take Camille, for instance. If it enters the Gulf, it is highly probable that it will make landfall somewhere between Texas and Florida.

"No matter where it lands, though, we're definitely in for some rough weather . . . at least gale force winds. That could be enough to shut the airports down."

"When do you think it'll hit?" Flowers asked.

"That's hard to say. Depends on what its forward speed is. If it continues on its present course, my guess would be Sunday or Monday."

"I see," Flowers said. His respect for Wojcik was growing by leaps and bounds.

"This is why I'm rushing to get you out of here. If we can get you and Mr. Jones on the plane by tomorrow afternoon, you'll be back in California before so much as a stiff breeze kicks up back here."

"I want you to know," Flowers said, "that I really do appreciate your help as well as your concern." He looked past Wojcik and added, "I appreciate your help, too, Gertie."

She looked up from her work and drawled, "That's what we're here for."

"O.K. now," Wojcik began as he rubbed his hands together. "So much for extraditions and hurricanes. What we have to do now is find you a place to stay for the night."

"I'm open to suggestions."

"We won't have any trouble finding you a place to stay. There's a whole string of motels on the beach between here and Biloxi."

Wojcik glanced at his watch. "Tell you what. Why don't you wait here for a minute while I run back to my office and pick up my coat and make a few phone calls, then we can be on our way."

Taking note of the cup of half-consumed coffee in Flowers' hand, Wojcik turned to Gertie and said teasingly, "Whatever you do, Gertie, don't be serving him any more of that tar you call coffee while I'm gone. You'll have him wound tighter than a two dollar watch."

"Humph!" Gertie replied. "You don't know what good coffee is." She shook her head in mock disgust and added, "Once a Yankee always a Yankee."

SIXTEEN

IT WAS AFTER 5:00 P.M. by the time Flowers checked into a modest motel that faced the Gulf from the north side of Highway 90. Wojcik followed him into the room, carrying the suitcase. After the two of them looked over the accommodations and nodded their approval, Flowers went to the phone and sat on the edge of the bed. Removing the phone message from his pocket he dialed the number to Inspector Pierce's hotel. Half a minute later he was connected to the appropriate room and the familiar voice of the inspector answered on the second ring.

It was a brief but unpleasant conversation. In as respectful a tone as Flowers could muster he informed his superior of the sudden change of plans, and suggested that the inspector meet him at the New Orleans Airport at 2:30 P.M. on Saturday. Pierce was outraged that Flowers had approved the travel arrangements without consulting him. Wojcik, who was standing across the room, could hear Pierce's raised voice over the phone.

Flowers calmly explained the need for a timely departure from the Gulf Coast before the arrival of Hurricane Camille. Pierce at first was too angry to listen to reason. His weekend was ruined. He had been looking forward to a seafood dinner in a quaint restaurant in the French Quarter. But Flowers had gotten him out of the mood and he was quite certain that he would be unable to fully enjoy his meal.

Somewhere in the back of his mind, however, his sense of political survival told him that it was best not to countermand these new plans. After taking a moment to cool off, he grudgingly agreed to meet Flowers at the airport the following afternoon.

After Flowers hung up the phone he stared at the instrument for almost a full minute. Wojcik watched him as a slow grin appeared on the detective's face. It was an impish grin, filled with devilish satisfaction.

"Gotcha!" He finally exclaimed. "I finally got you, you pompous jerk."

Flowers looked up at Wojcik apologetically. Try as he may, though, he could not suppress his grin. "Sorry about that, Frank, but as you've probably gathered, that man and I just don't see eye-to-eye."

Wojcik returned the grin. "I did indeed gather as much. It also appears that you put the kabosh on his weekend plans."

Flowers' grin broadened. "It would certainly seem so, wouldn't it."

"Now that your absentee associate is on board," Wojcik said, "suppose we concentrate on matters of a more immediate nature."

"What did you have in mind?"

"Before leaving the courthouse, I made two phone calls. The first was to my wife, asking her if she minded if I brought a guest home for supper. Naturally, she was delighted." He looked at Flowers and added, "I hope you don't mind my being so presumptuous. I just figured, since you're alone in town, and only just arrived, you might enjoy a delicious home-cooked meal with some great company."

The invitation took Flowers by surprise. Wojcik's apparent disregard for the color barrier was nothing like he expected. He had envisioned a situation similar to Sidney Poitier's character in the movie *In the Heat of the Night*.

"Are you sure?" He asked.

"I wouldn't have asked if I weren't."

"In that case you have yourself a dinner guest. Excuse me . . . *supper* guest." After a pause Flowers added, "Uh, you said that you made two calls."

"Yes. The second call was to my friend, Judge Williams. He gave us the O.K. to stop by his house to go over the extradition. He pretty much assured me that, if everything is in order, he'll sign the papers."

"That's great," Flowers replied. He could not believe his good fortune.

"Then it's settled," Wojcik said. "Why don't we leave now? We'll stop by the judge's house on the way home."

Flowers picked up his briefcase, then hesitated. He had a sudden urge to call Rochelle, then remembered the two-hour time difference. She would not be home from work yet. Perhaps he would call her when he returned to his room later in the evening. With that thought he followed Wojcik out the door.

JUDGE WILLIAMS LIVED on East Beach, three miles west of the motel where Flowers was registered. As they drove along Highway 90 Flowers took in the wide sandy beach that separated the four-lane highway from the shoreline. The waves appeared to be less than a foot high, and they rolled with the gentlest of motion onto the beach.

"It's hard to imagine," he said as he shook his head.

"What's that?"

"That there's a hurricane out there somewhere. The only clouds in the sky are those white puffy ones, and the water is so calm."

Wojcik grinned. "If you want to see that water turn ugly, just stick around a few days."

"It'll get pretty rough, huh?"

"Rough? If we get nothing more than a tropical storm, the water will get rough. But if we get the brunt of the hurricane, those little ripples out there could turn into ten foot waves."

"Ten feet?" Flowers asked skeptically.

"Oh, yes. Maybe higher. The waves could easily come up over this highway." He paused, then added, "Water is the most destructive aspect of a hurricane."

"Oh? I would've guessed that the high winds would cause the most damage."

"Well, the winds certainly do a lot of damage. Come to think of it, it's actually the wind that indirectly causes the water damage."

"You've lost me."

"It's the force of the wind blowing over the water that determines how strong the tidal surge will be. The wind pushes the water in front of it. The stronger the wind the higher the seas. The higher the seas the greater the damage when the hurricane makes landfall. The rising of the water and the relentless pounding of the waves onto whatever is in its way is known as a storm surge. Anything that gets in the path of a storm surge is usually destroyed . . . trees . . . buildings . . . whatever."

"How long does the storm surge last?" Flowers asked.

Wojcik shrugged. "That depends upon the forward speed of the hurricane. The speeds inside the hurricane might be moving in excess of one hundred miles per hour. Those winds move in a wide circle . . . fifty, sixty, maybe even two hundred miles in diameter. The closer to the eye of the hurricane the faster the winds. At the same time there is a forward movement of the storm, which might be no more than ten miles per hour. That is what determines how long a hurricane remains in one place, and how long the storm surge will persist. The slower the forward progression the more destructive the hurricane."

"Let me see if I got this right," Flowers said. "A hurricane moves in a huge circle around a hole in its middle. Sounds to me like what you're describing is a gigantic tornado."

"I guess there are some similarities, though a tornado spins around at a much greater speed and is compacted in a smaller space." Wojcik thought for a moment, then added, "As a matter of fact, it's not uncommon for a hurricane to spawn several tornadoes inside it, which, of course, compounds the dangers in coping with a hurricane."

"Big waves, high winds, rain and tornadoes," Flowers said. "All wrapped up in one storm?"

"That's about it. Of course, it's the storm surge that causes the greatest loss of life." Wojcik breathed a deep sigh. "The sad part is that the loss of life is so unnecessary. People are given ample warning to get away, but every time we have a storm there are those who decide that saving their property is more important than saving their lives–as if being there could prevent the damage. They always underestimate the awesome power of the storm surge."

Wojcik slowed the car and negotiated a right turn, into the driveway of a beautiful single-story brick home. He stopped the car in front of the house. Flowers grabbed his briefcase and followed Wojcik up the steps to the door. As Wojcik rang the bell Flowers turned and looked out over the Gulf.

"How often does a hurricane hit the Gulf Coast?" He asked.

"Oh, we get at least a piece of one every few years. Occasionally, maybe every quarter century or so, an unusually big one comes along. Those are the killers."

Flowers looked to his left and right. "It amazes me that people would build these elegant homes so close to the beach. Aren't they afraid of losing them in a hurricane?"

"Well, as you can see, most of these houses have been here for quite some time. A few of them along the beach are over a hundred years old. They're built to withstand strong winds, and they sit pretty far back on the property, which protects them from high seas." After a pause he added, "Besides, I don't see much difference in building these homes near the Gulf and building homes in California within spitting distance of an earthquake fault."

"Good point," Flowers conceded, then turned again when he heard the door open.

A young man who appeared to be in his early twenties stood in the doorway. He was dressed in Bermuda shorts, white tennis shoes and an Ole Miss T-shirt. He had a crop of red hair that reminded Flowers of Archie Penner.

"Mr. Wojcik!" The young man greeted with a broad smile.

"Hello, Jack," Wojcik replied.

"What brings you over this way?"

"We just dropped by to see your dad. Is he home yet?"

"Yes he is," Jack said as he eyed Flowers questioningly. "Won't y'all come in?"

As they stepped into the foyer Wojcik said, "Jack, this is Sergeant Garland Flowers. He's with the Los Angeles County Sheriff's Department. Garland, this is Jack Williams, Jr."

Garland and Jack shook hands, then Jack ushered them into the living room and excused himself to go in search of his father. A moment later he returned and announced that the judge would be with them shortly.

"Have a seat," Jack invited. When Flowers and Wojcik were seated on the sofa, Jack asked, "Could I get y'all something to drink? Ice tea? Lemonade?"

Both men declined and an awkward moment of silence followed before Wojcik asked, "So Jack, how are things going at Ole Miss?"

Jack's face brightened at the opportunity to break the silence. "It's going great. I'll be starting my senior year in a few weeks."

"Still majoring in history?"

A look of disappointment came over Jack. "No. Dad talked me into changing to government. Said it would be more beneficial to my law career." Then, as if offering an apology, he said, "But I'm minoring in U.S. history." He regarded Wojcik for several seconds. "I guess you had too much of an influence on me for me to completely give up history."

Flowers gave Wojcik a puzzled look, but said nothing. Wojcik caught the detective's questioning expression and smiled. "What's wrong, Garland? You look confused."

Flowers shrugged. "I guess I am."

"Actually, I teach American history at Gulfport High School. Jack was one of my students a few years back."

"Heck, Mr. Wojcik is the best teacher that school ever had," Jack put in. "I used to hate history, but when he taught it he made it interesting. When I started college it was my intention to be a teacher just like him." He frowned. "But Dad is a third generation lawyer and, well, I didn't want to disappoint him by breaking tradition."

"Did you ever consider teaching full-time?" Flowers asked Wojcik.

"As a matter of fact I do teach full-time. During the regular school year I work part-time as a deputy sheriff. During the summer I forego teaching summer school so I can work full-time as a deputy."

"Interesting," Flowers said, having no idea what to make of this revelation.

"So. Jack," Wojcik began in an attempt to take the attention from himself. "How're the Rebels gonna do this year? Is Archie Manning gonna take them to the Sugar Bowl?"

"It's possible. I know many of the sports writers have predicted they'll take the Southeastern Conference title."

Their conversation was interrupted when Judge Williams entered the room. He was wearing slacks, loafers and a pullover sport shirt.

"Hello, Frank," he greeted with a warm smile. "Sorry you had to wait. I just got home and was changing clothes when you arrived." He then looked at Flowers. "And this must be your colleague from California."

"How do you do, your honor," Flowers said as he stood and extended his hand. "Garland Flowers."

"How do you do, Garland? Please call me Jack."

Flowers observed that the judge, who also had bushy red hair, was an older version of Jack, Jr. The son was the spitting image of the father.

"If y'all will excuse me," Jack, Jr. said. "I have to go finish packing." After shaking hands with Flowers and Wojcik, he left the room.

"Packing?" Wojcik asked.

"Yes," the judge replied. "In fact, we're all packing tonight. Eleanor and I are driving Jack, Jr. to Oxford tomorrow. Normally, he wouldn't leave for school for another week or so, but what with this storm coming in and all, we thought this might be a good weekend to get away."

"Not a bad idea," Wojcik said. "In fact Garland and I were just talking about the hurricane. We're trying to expedite the extradition so he can catch a plane tomorrow before the weather gets nasty."

"Well then, let's get on with it," Judge Williams said as he rubbed his hands together.

Flowers sat down again and placed the briefcase on his lap. He opened it and removed a large Manila envelope that contained the documents prepared by the L.A. County District Attorney's office. Wojcik produced the waiver that had been signed by B.C. Jones.

The judge spent the next several minutes studying all the papers. Then he took a pen that Wojcik offered him and signed the extradition order. "These documents are very well prepared," he said.

Flowers smiled wryly. "Practice makes perfect. And in L.A. they certainly get enough practice."

Judge Williams chuckled. "I suppose they do."

He stood up. Wojcik and Flowers did likewise. "Is there anything else I can do for you, Frank?"

"No, sir. I think that'll do it."

The judge escorted them through the foyer and opened the front door. Before stepping outside Flowers turned and offered his hand. "Thank you again, Judge. This has been a great help to me."

"I'm glad I could be of assistance." The judge frowned as he looked past the two detectives and out over the Gulf. "I'll tell you, son, you're absolutely right about leaving tomorrow. If Camille decides to turn and head this way, by Sunday you'll want to be as far away from here as you can get."

SEVENTEEN

WOJCIK AND FLOWERS resumed their drive west on Highway 90 for two miles before turning right onto 25th Avenue, which took them through the heart of Gulfport's business district. They passed the post office and, a block farther, crossed 14th Street. It was at this intersection, four days earlier, that B.C. Jones stepped off the bus and began his fateful walk to Woolworth.

They had traveled in silence for several minutes, then from out of the blue Flowers said, "You're not from around here, are you, Frank?"

Wojcik was mildly surprised by the question. "What makes you say that?"

"Oh, I don't know. Just a few observations, I guess."

"Like what?"

"For one thing, it's the way you talk. You have a slight accent, but you don't have that heavy drawl that Gertie has. Even Judge Williams and his son speak differently than you, like it's more deeply embedded in them.

"But more than that, it was a comment that Gertie made back at the courthouse. When you were teasing her about her coffee, she referred to you as a Yankee."

Wojcik smiled. "I must say, you're quite observant. As a matter of fact I was born and reared in Chicago."

"How did you wind up here?"

"By way of Korea."

"Come again?"

"When the Korean War broke out I joined the Air Force and spent the first two years of my enlistment in South Korea. Then I was transferred to Keesler Field. That's an Air Force base in Biloxi, about twelve miles east of here. I immediately fell in love with the Gulf Coast.

"After my discharge I decided to stick around. I attended Mississippi Southern on the G.I. Bill, got my teaching credential, picked up a Master's degree, met a lovely lady named Darla Necaise, got married, and I've been here ever since."

"I thought it might've been something like that."

"What do you mean?"

Flowers searched for the right words to say what was on his mind. "For as long as I can remember I've heard horror stories about the way blacks have been treated in the South, especially in Mississippi. Yet, ever since I stepped off the bus I've been given the red carpet treatment."

"Are you complaining?"

"No, of course not. I suppose I'm waiting for the other shoe to drop."

Wojcik grinned. "Sorry to disappointment you, but I couldn't arrange a lynching on such short notice."

"Very funny."

"So what you're saying," Wojcik began, "is that the reason I'm treating you well is because I'm not from around here. If that is the case, how do you explain the way others have treated you since your arrival? People like Gertie and Judge Williams, and Jack, Jr. Have any of them treated you badly?"

"No, they haven't."

"Yet they were all born and reared right here in Mississippi."

"Maybe so, but who among them would've invited me into their home for dinner . . . excuse me . . . *supper*?"

"What if the roles were reversed, and one of them had to go to California to pick up a prisoner? Would you have thought to invite them to your house for supper . . . excuse me . . . *dinner*?"

Flowers shook his head slowly, but made no effort to respond.

Wojcik dismissed any further attempt at levity. "Look, Garland. I don't mean to minimize your concerns. The sad fact is that most of the horror stories you grew up with are probably true. There's no denying that Mississippi has had a sordid history of racial injustice. But it's also a fact that there are many people in this state who are trying their best to bring Mississippi into the twentieth century.

"Now that's not to say there aren't an abundance of redneck bigots still running loose. And I can assure you that the Ku Klux Klan is alive and well in Mississippi, but unfortunately it's also alive and well in California, and just about every other state in the union. I'm not sure that we will ever completely get rid of hate groups like that.

"Of course, hate groups aren't restricted to white organizations. So far as I'm concerned, the Black Panther Party is filled with as much racial hatred as the Klan is."

Flowers breathed a deep sigh. "I can't argue with that."

"I don't know what else to say, Garland. Our races have been in conflict since before Mississippi became a state, and it's going to take some time for the wounds to heal. But I truly believe that we're on the right road."

"I hope so," Flowers said, then both men fell into another period of silence as they drove through North Gulfport, then past the city limits.

As they proceeded north, out of town, Flowers noticed that, somewhere along the way, 25th Avenue had turned into Highway 49. The landscape assumed a rural character. Small businesses and private residences were separated by wooded areas that were densely populated with pine trees.

They drove another ten minutes, then turned left, onto Landon Road, and headed west. Two minutes later they turned right and drove a quarter of a mile before making another left, onto a narrow gravel road. On their right was a pecan orchard several acres in size. Just beyond the orchard Wojcik slowed, then turned into a long gravel driveway. Flowers guessed that it was at least a hundred yards in length. At the end of the driveway, amidst an oak-shaded lawn, was a large two-story farmhouse.

Flowers stared at the house, then looked at Wojcik questioningly. "Is this where you live?

"This is it."

"Wow! I guess teachers and sheriff's deputies get paid a lot more in Mississippi than they do in California."

"Not hardly. Land is fairly cheap out here in the country. The house was in bad shape when we bought it, and I got it for a good price. Darla, her brothers and I did the remodeling ourselves."

Wojcik brought the vehicle to a stop near the front porch of the house. As they were getting out of the car a screen door opened then slammed shut after two small screaming girls ran out, excitedly announcing to the world that Daddy was home. They crossed the wide, open porch and met him at the steps, where he knelt down to hug them.

By the time Flowers had walked around the car, both girls were embracing their father. He was suddenly filled with thoughts of Danielle, and he had to fight back the emotional knot that was rising toward his throat. How he envied Frank Wojcik at this moment.

Wojcik gently removed the four small clinging hands from around his neck and stood up as Flowers approached. "Girls, I'd like for you to meet a friend of mine. His name is Mr. Flowers. He traveled all the way from California today and he's going to be our guest for supper tonight."

"Oh, goody!" Both girls exclaimed.

"Garland, these are two of my sweethearts. This is Kathy. She's eight. And this is Becky. She'll be six next month."

Flowers smiled. "I'm very pleased to meet you."

"I'm going into first grade!" Becky exclaimed proudly.

"Wow! That's great!" Flowers said. "I have a little girl, too. Her name is Danielle."

"How old is she?" Kathy wanted to know.

"She's only three."

"Can we meet her?"

"Well, not this trip. She's a long way from here. Way back in California."

"Oh."

At Wojcik's urging the girls led the way into the house. As they walked across the porch Flowers asked, "How many children do you have?"

"Just two. And if the energy level of these two is any gauge, two's about all I can handle."

"Hmm. When you introduced Kathy and Becky, you said they were *two* of your sweethearts. I got the impression there might be more."

Wojcik grinned. "I only have two daughters, but I have three sweethearts. The third one is probably in the kitchen fixing our supper."

They stepped into a large, spacious living room. Three of the walls were covered with richly embossed wallpaper. The fourth was painted off-white. The high ceiling bespoke of a house that was at least fifty years old. The furniture, Flowers guessed, was French Provencial. Its elegance seemed almost out of place in the renovated farmhouse.

Directly across from the front entrance was the dining room, separated from the living room by double French doors, both of which were open. A woman, who appeared to be in her early thirties, entered the dining room through a swinging door from a room that was presumably the kitchen. She had medium length brown hair and a pretty face. She had an attractive figure, if somewhat on the thin side.

As she walked through the double doors into the living room she smiled broadly, revealing white, even teeth. She went directly to Wojcik and they embraced and kissed.

They slowly pulled apart and Wojcik said, "Honey, I'd like you to meet our guest, Garland Flowers. Garland, this is my wife, Darla."

"I'm pleased to meet you, Garland," Darla said in a drawl that was almost as pronounced as Gertie's.

"How do you do, Darla?"

"I hope y'all are hungry," Darla said. "Supper will be ready in about twenty minutes."

"I'm famished," Flowers said.

"Do you like catfish?" She asked. "This is what we normally have on Friday night." Before Flowers could respond she added, "If not, I have a nice steak I could cook. It'd be no trouble."

Flowers smiled. "I've never eaten catfish, but I would like to give it a try."

"Then catfish it is."

"Garland," Wojcik began, "why don't you shed your coat and tie?" He then addressed Darla. "If you will take Garland into the den and keep him company for a few minutes, I'll run upstairs and get out of this monkey suit."

When Wojcik had gone, Darla led Flowers into a room adjoining the living room. The height of the ceiling was more conventional than in the living room, and Flowers decided that the den must have been added on at a later period. Two of the walls were covered from floor to ceiling with bookshelves, and most of the shelf space was filled with books. A glance at some of the titles revealed that those volumes related to history.

The other two walls were paneled in a dark walnut. On one of the walls numerous family photographs were displayed. On the other was a framed discharge from the Air Force, a few diplomas and a collection of plaques.

Garland moved closer so he could read the inscriptions. The first plaque that he read was awarded to Frank Wojcik from the Gulfport High School Class of '67 "with special gratitude and affection." Another was from the Superintendent of Schools proclaiming Noel Francis Wojcik the "Outstanding Teacher of 1965." There were other awards commemorating achievements in other years.

"Frank must be quite a teacher," Flowers said.

"He's the best," Darla replied in a tone that left no doubt that she was extremely proud of her husband.

"It takes a great deal of dedication to be a school teacher," Flowers said. "I know because I saw it first hand. Both of my parents were teachers."

"Were?" Darla asked. "They no longer teach?"

"Oh, no. They're both retired." Now it was Flowers' turn to feel proud. "My father was a jr. high principal when he retired."

"That's great," Darla said. A moment later she asked, "Are you named after your father?"

"No. Why do you ask?"

"Oh, I don't know. It's just that Garland somehow sounds like a family name."

Flowers grinned. "No. I'm the first in the family to be named Garland. It was my mother's idea. Having married into a family named Flowers, she must have felt obligated to give names to her children that, in some way, however remote, related to flowers. You know . . . garland . . . as in wreath . . . or lei."

Darla smiled but said nothing.

Flowers continued. "My sister's name is Laurel."

"That's a pretty name."

"Yes, it is." He shook his head. "Of course, it was our younger brother who got the worst of it."

"It's that bad?" Darla asked, still smiling.

"You be the judge. As I mentioned, my mother was a schoolteacher, and English literature was her favorite subject. So I suppose she thought it altogether fitting to name her youngest son Oscar Wilde Flowers."

Darla almost laughed but managed to stifle it. "It sounds like you have quite a family. Are you close?"

Flowers shrugged. "I suppose so. We try to see one another fairly regularly."

"Are you married, Garland?"

"Yes, I am." He then frowned. "Well, sort of. We're separated at present."

Darla's smile faded. "I'm sorry to hear that."

"I'm sorry, too." He breathed a deep sigh. "But I'm hopeful we can work things out."

"Do you have children?"

"A girl. She's three."

"Well, I hope things do work out for you. For all three of you."

Wojcik entered the den. He was wearing tan khaki trousers, white tennis shoes and a plaid sport shirt. In his hands were two cans of Jax beer. "Honey, do we have time for a beer before supper?"

"Yes, but the food will be ready in a few minutes."

"We'll be out at the gazebo. Just yell when it's ready."

As Darla walked past her husband on the way back to the kitchen he leaned toward her and kissed her on the cheek. Flowers watched but did not know what to make of it. He was not accustomed to such open displays of affection.

Wojcik handed Flowers one of the beers and said, "Let's go outside."

Flowers followed Wojcik out the front door and they walked diagonally across fifty feet of St. Augustine lawn to a white gazebo that rested under the limbs of a huge oak tree.

"This is really nice," Flowers said as they stepped into the round lattice enclosure. "Did you build this yourself?"

"Not hardly. When it comes to woodworking, I'm all thumbs. Actually, Darla's younger brother built it for us."

"Seems to me he could make a good living at building these things."

"He probably could have," Wojcik began. "Unfortunately, he was killed year before last."

"Killed? How did it happen?"

"Vietnam. Some place called the Mekong Delta."

"I'm sorry," Flowers said.

"Just one of the casualties of that miserable war." Wojcik sighed. "Darla and I make it a point not to dwell on the subject. So let's change it."

Flowers sat on a bench and took a swig of beer, then held the can out in front of him and examined the label. "Not bad," he said. "I don't think I've heard of Jax beer."

"I think it might only be sold in the South. It's brewed in New Orleans."

Another long moment of silence passed. Then Flowers said, "So your full name is Noel Francis Wojcik." When Wojcik looked at him questioningly, Flowers smiled. "I read it on one of your plaques."

Wojcik returned the smile. "I was named after my father. He was born on Christmas Day, so it seemed appropriate to name him Noel. My grandparents were devout Catholics, and the parish priest, Father Francis, was a close friend of theirs. So they named their son Noel Francis. When I came along my parents wanted to name me after my father. Since my father went by the name of Noel, and they didn't want to call me Junior, I got stuck with the name Francis." Wojcik shook his head and continued to smile as warm memories of his childhood came to mind. "I was raised in a pretty tough Polish neighborhood. By the time I got to high school I had been in about a hundred fistfights over kids making fun of me for having a girl's name. So I insisted on being called Frank."

"So now everyone calls you Frank?"

"Everyone but my mother. To this day she calls me Francis."

They both laughed and each took another sip of beer.

Wojcik took a seat on a bench opposite Flowers and regarded his guest for a moment. "Garland, if you have no objections, I'm going to loan you one of our cars to take back to the motel."

"I don't want to put you out any more than I have already."

"It's no trouble. Darla has her own car and I'm using a county car this weekend. Mine is just sitting in the garage taking up space."

Flowers looked doubtful. "I'm not sure I can find my way back to the motel."

"I'll draw you a map. The tricky part is getting back to the highway from here. Once you get to the highway all you have to do is go south on 49 through town. It ends at Highway 90. Turn left on 90 and it'll take you directly to the motel."

"Well . . . if you're sure you want to."

"I'm sure. In the morning you can drive back here. We'll have brunch, then I'll drive you to the airport."

"Thank you again." Flowers didn't know what else to say.

A full minute passed with neither of them speaking. They sat in silence and sipped their beer. It was almost dark. Off to the west, through a forest of trees, the final orange glow of sunset lingered above the horizon. It was a calm, peaceful evening and Flowers was suddenly filled with thoughts of his wife and daughter. He never imagined that he could miss them as much as he did at this moment. That emotional lump that he felt earlier was again swelling in his throat.

As if reading Flowers' mind, Wojcik asked, "Are you thinking about your family?"

"Yeah." Flowers was worried that his voice might crack if he spoke more than one word at a time.

"I overheard you telling Darla about you and your wife being separated. It must be hard on you."

"Yeah," Flowers said again. After a pause he managed to ask, "Tell me, Frank. What is Darla's and your secret? You seem to be so happy together."

"That's because we *are* happy."

"But don't you ever have disagreements?"

"Of course we do."

"I mean serious disagreements. About your job, for instance. What if Darla came to you and gave you an ultimatum? What if she said she couldn't live with you if you continued doing the job you loved?"

"But why would she say such a thing?"

"Because she's scared. She can't handle the phone calls in the middle of the night calling you out on homicide investigations. The constant fear of you getting shot."

"Those sound like some pretty legitimate concerns to me," Wojcik said. He grinned and added, "Especially if I worked in a place like L.A. County."

"Yeah, but what if it was what you were trained to do and what you wanted to do?"

Wojcik took a deep breath and blew it out in a sigh. "Garland, I know you won't like my answer, but you asked, so I'm going to tell you. I would try to find an assignment that my wife could deal with more easily."

"You would give up the job you loved?"

"First of all, I don't *love* my job. I *like* it. I like both my law enforcement and teaching jobs very much. But I would give up either or both of those occupations in a hot second if they posed a threat to my family's happiness. I would do that because I *love* my wife and daughters." Wojcik paused, then added, "When Darla and I married I made a vow to love, honor and cherish her all the days of our lives. I made no such vow to the Harrison County Sheriff's Department . . . or the Gulfport School District either, for that matter."

Flowers did not reply. Instead, he stood and moved slowly to the edge of the gazebo, his back to Wojcik, and stared into the wooded area beyond the property line. A gentle breeze rustled through the thick foliage, and his nostrils were filled with the sweet fragrance of honeysuckle.

A long moment passed before Wojcik asked, "What is your wife's name?"

"Rochelle." There was a husky quality to Flowers' voice.

Neither of them made any further attempt to speak. Each quietly drank his beer and communed with the darkening surroundings in his own way. A few more minutes passed before they heard Darla's voice calling them to supper.

Flowers turned slowly and saw Wojcik waiting for him at the entrance to the gazebo, and he moved toward him. When they were side by side Wojcik put an arm around Flowers' shoulder and gripped it firmly.

"Don't ask me to explain it, Garland. But I have a strong hunch that things are going to work out just fine for you and Rochelle."

Flowers could not explain it either, but he actually found some comfort in Wojcik's words. A sense of relief came over him and the knot in his throat began to fade.

Kathy and Becky came onto the porch and Flowers was amused at their playful antics. They held the screen door open and stood at attention like miniature soldiers as their daddy and his new friend made their way back to the house.

EIGHTEEN

Saturday
August 16, 1969

B.C. JONES lay on his bunk and studied, for the hundredth time, the police report that had been delivered to him on the evening following his arrest at Woolworth. He recalled that the deputy sheriff handed him the report only after he signed something they called a waiver. He had no objections to signing anything, as long as he got a copy of that arrest report.

When not studying the report, he kept it folded in his back pocket. After four days it had become creased and wrinkled, and in the early hours before dawn he found it difficult to make out the words on the first page. The cell lights were turned off every evening at ten o'clock, but there was partial illumination from a dim light in the cellblock corridor.

Jones had no interest in the narrative portion of the report. There were too many words that he could not understand. His interest was only on the few lines of the first page that provided the name and address of that poor girl at Woolworth who had the mixed blood. He vividly recalled her telling the policeman that her name was Frieda Pinchon and she lived in a place called Pineville. Once he found her name on the report he would stare at it the way one might regard the photo of a loved one. It was his only memento of her.

Since his incarceration every waking moment had, in one way or another, been devoted to thoughts of Frieda. As hours turned to days the image of her became more enhanced. Her skin assumed a darker shade, and her lips grew in fullness. The more she took on the appearance of a mulatto the more the anger and frustration swelled within him. Jones had never known happiness. There had never been a day in his life that he ever experienced real joy. He was treated differently because of his mixed blood. Frieda had mixed blood, therefore she would go through life suffering as he had suffered.

He could not get her out of his mind. After four days of incarceration he had become desperate to free himself and seek her out.

He had been informed the night before that he would be leaving the jail and be driven to the airport. From there he would be flown to Los Angeles. For days he had been visited by fantasies of delivering Frieda Pinchon from the countless cruelties that awaited her. When he was given the news of his return to L.A. Jones was almost overwhelmed with worry. What if he was denied any chance of seeing her again? But before the worry had a chance to consume him he was suddenly calmed by an inner voice. It described a plan that would set him free and allow him to satisfy the need that was surging within him.

The voice had kept him awake all night, reminding him of the sensuous gratification that had come following those two visits he had made in Los Angeles. Now he would experience it again by destroying the people who had brought Frieda into the world, and by gently sending her to a better place. She could be with that little baby and young girl who had gone before her. He even dared to hope that he might someday join all three of them.

Footsteps in the corridor caused him to sit up on his bunk. The jailer and two other men, both wearing suits, stopped in front of his cell. Jones stood up, then folded the papers and stuffed them into his back pocket.

As the jailer inserted the large key into the lock and turned it he said, "It's time to go, Jones. Step out of the cell."

When Jones complied with the order the jailer added, "These are the deputies who'll be taking you to the airport."

The two men escorted Jones down the corridor and into a room where he was instructed to change out of the jail uniform and into his personal clothing. After doing as he was told Jones made a point of transferring the folded police report to the back pocket of the trousers he was now wearing. The property clerk handed one of the deputies a clear plastic bag that contained Jones' wallet and a sealed envelope.

"Do I get my money and stuff?" He asked.

"No. We'll hold your personal property. It has to be turned over to the authorities you'll be traveling with."

When the deputies attempted to cuff Jones' wrists behind his back they discovered, like the officers at Woolworth had, that his arms were too massive to bring his hands close enough for the cuffs to reach from one wrist to the other. So they cuffed him with his arms in front of him.

It was several minutes before dawn when they walked out a door at the rear of the county jail. There had been a brief thunderstorm during the early morning and the wet pavement in the parking area glistened in the darkness. Jones was led to an unmarked car. One of the deputies opened the right rear door and told Jones to get in. When he did so the deputy leaned over him and buckled the seatbelt across the prisoner's lap. The same deputy then walked around the car and climbed into the back seat opposite Jones. The other deputy got behind the wheel of the car, started the engine, and backed out of the parking space.

THEY DROVE NORTH on 25th Avenue as far as the Pass Road, then turned east. The Pass Road was a two-lane thoroughfare that dated back to the 1800's. It had been a stagecoach route that connected the old settlements of Biloxi and Pass Christian. In those days Gulfport did not exist, and the area through which they now drove was nothing but a pine forest. But the old stage route had long since been paved, and now a continuous chain of commercial establishments occupied both sides of the road.

Ahead of them the dark sky was giving way to a gray dawn. Jones was beginning to feel anxious. Butterflies were swarming in his stomach. He had no idea where he was or how much farther they had to go before his chance of escape came to an end. Then the voice began to prod him, insisting that time was running out.

There had been no conversation since leaving the jail, then Jones broke the silence. "Are we almost there?"

The deputy who sat beside him looked at Jones and grinned. "You're not in a hurry to get back to California, are you?"

"Uh, no. It ain't that. It's just that I got to take a leak real bad."

"If you can hold it for five more minutes we'll be there."

The car slowed and turned north, onto a narrow street. They passed a few houses then entered a stretch of woods. Jones changed positions as if to ease the pressure on his bladder. As he did so he placed his cuffed hands over the seatbelt buckle and carefully lifted the release mechanism. He saw the railing of a short bridge a hundred yards ahead. At the same time a wave of adrenaline rushed through him.

Just as the car arrived at the bridge Jones lifted both arms and swung them hard to his left. It was a powerful blow that caught the deputy sitting next to him on the forehead. The edge of the handcuffs cut a deep gash just above the right eye. The deputy was out cold.

The driver glimpsed the movement through the rearview mirror, but before he could react Jones leaned over the front seat and grabbed the steering wheel. The car had passed over the bridge and, just past the railing, Jones turned the wheel sharply to the right. The driver, who was losing the battle over control of the vehicle, made no attempt to brake. The car rolled down the forty-five degree embankment and struck the trunk of a tree before coming to an abrupt stop. The impact caused the driver to be thrown forward and his chest smashed into the steering wheel. Jones was catapulted over the front seat.

He was stunned but unharmed. The inner voice urged him to move. The vehicle had come to rest nose downward and it was difficult for Jones to move about. He looked at the driver and noted that the deputy was not conscious. He reached over to the steering column, turned the key and pulled it from the ignition. He quickly looked over the other keys on the ring until he found the one for which he was searching. He had been cuffed too many times in his life not to be able to recognize a handcuff key.

With considerable effort he managed to turn his huge body so that his head faced the front passenger door. He reached over and lifted the handle. He gave it a slight push, then gravity took over and the door fell open. He slid over the seat on his stomach and out the door, then fell to the ground.

Jones slowly stood up on the sloping embankment. He was still shaken from the collision and his legs trembled. He leaned on the side of the car for support. The voice was becoming more persistent. *Get away from here! Leave before a car comes along!* This caused him to move.

He started up the side of the steep hill, then stopped as he remembered something. Leaning inside the car he searched around until he found the plastic bag that contained his wallet and retrieved it from the floorboard. Placing the bag and ring of keys in his trouser pocket, he made his way up the slope.

Before stepping onto the road he looked in both directions. It was not quite sunrise, but the light of dawn provided sufficient visibility for him to see that the road was deserted. He cautiously emerged from the embankment and ran across the road. Looking back, he saw that the car was completely hidden from view.

Turning his attention to his side of the road he ran beside the bridge railing until he reached the midpoint. Looking down he saw a small river. Yet it was not a river. It was a canal. The water did not flow like a river or creek. It sat motionless, a green scum covering its surface. The jungle-thick foliage on both sides of the canal covered the ground as far as the water's edge. The canal was the only opening through the woods, but Jones wanted no part of wading through the slime. What if there were snakes, or even alligators? No, he was a city boy and was not about to wade through the canal. He ran back to the end of the railing and after some hesitation, forced himself down the embankment and into the dense brush.

The progress was slow and the limbs of small trees slapped at his face as he reached the bottom of the slope and moved deeper into the woods. Behind him the sun had come up, producing a dull glow through an overcast sky.

He had gone two hundred yards before reaching a small clearing five feet in diameter. Removing the ring of keys he sat under a water oak and struggled to insert the key into the cuff. Once the first cuff was removed the second one was unlocked with little effort.

Jones then threw the handcuffs and the ring of keys into the canal. He rested another minute before the voice inside him urged him to stand. He was frightened and had no idea where he was. He knew only that he had to get far away from that wrecked sheriff's car. As was his practice when he worked for Bert's Disposal back in L.A., he had to focus on the chore at hand. At this moment that chore was to keep moving. The farther he ran the safer he would be. With that thought he left the clearing and trudged slowly westward along the bank of the mucky canal.

NINETEEN

FLOWERS AWOKE AT 7:15 A.M. fully rested. He lay in the bed for several minutes taking in the surroundings of the motel room. To his surprise he had slept soundly, something he normally did not do in a strange bed. But yesterday had been long and full, and he attributed his good night's rest to travel fatigue, a busy afternoon arranging the extradition, and Darla's excellent cooking.

She had stuffed him with two helpings of catfish, turnip greens, blackeyed peas and cornbread. For dessert he had devoured a large helping of peach cobbler. He smiled to himself when he recalled mentioning to her that, back in L.A., blacks referred to this kind of meal as soul food. Darla was quick to respond, "In the South this is a staple . . . for blacks *and* whites. We just call it food."

It had been a very pleasant evening with the Wojciks, but by ten P.M. Flowers was exhausted and decided to call it a day. As promised, Frank drew him a map and handed him the keys to his car, a '64 Chevy Nova. The directions were easy to follow and he had no trouble finding his way back to the motel.

As soon as he arrived in his room he called Rochelle. It was a short but pleasant conversation. He inquired about Danielle and said that he missed them both. He asked Rochelle if she would have dinner with him one day next week. Just the two of them. There were some things he wished to discuss with her. When she said yes he felt elated, like a schoolboy who had just made a date with the homecoming queen.

Flowers had given considerable thought to what Wojcik had told him in the gazebo. At first his ego had been bruised when Frank seemed to have taken Rochelle's side. But the more he thought about it the more he realized that his friend was not intentionally taking sides. He was simply giving Flowers his honest opinion. There was certainly nothing profound in what Frank had said. Flowers had heard the same argument from Rochelle. But hearing it from an unbiased third party caused him to take stock, for the first time, in their relationship from Rochelle's point of view. It boiled down to a simple but difficult question: was his job more important than his family's happiness? While the obvious answer would appear to be no, it involved a possible change in his career. The reality was that it was a deeper question than what appeared on the surface.

But today was not a good day to dwell on such thoughts. Today must be devoted to transporting a very dangerous man back to L.A. The fact that his so-called partner, Winston Pierce, could not be counted on if things got rough gave him no comfort at all. He thought of Archie Penner and wished that his real partner could be with him today.

Flowers took a deep breath and blew it out in a long sigh. "Oh, well," he said resignedly, then pulled the covers from him and got out of bed. He shaved, showered and got dressed. He then packed his suitcase and departed. After checking out of the motel, he climbed into the Nova and drove west on Highway 90.

B.C. JONES EMERGED from the woods at 28th Street near 19th Avenue. At this point the canal went under 28th Street at an angle and continued in a southwesterly direction. This was a commercial area with businesses claiming the property adjacent to the canal, thus denying him further concealment.

He felt a sense of relief to be on a street again. His face and hands were scratched from the limbs of saplings and thorny bushes. His shirt and trousers were damp from brushing against dew-covered bushes, and his shoes were muddy from having walked on the soft, wet ground.

Jones crossed the road and proceeded west along 28th Street. It was still fairly early and the Saturday morning traffic was light. The few vehicles that did pass caused him to tense, but the motorists drove by without giving him a second glance.

He had gone about six blocks when he came upon a wide street. It was 25th Avenue. He waited for the traffic signal to turn green then he hurriedly crossed the four-lane boulevard.

Continuing along 28th Street he walked past a car repair shop to his left. Behind the shop two young black men were squatting on the ground with a large pan filled with a black liquid between them. They were cleaning car parts. Jones hesitated a moment, then decided to ask them for directions.

As he moved toward them the younger of the two, a thin, wiry man in his early twenties looked up. "Say, blood! What's happnin'?" He asked in a high-pitched voice.

"I got to get to a place called Pineville. Can you tell me how to get there?"

"Pineville? What you wanna go to Pineville for?"

"I got to see somebody."

"Man, they ain't no bloods livin' in Pineville that I know of."

At first Jones did not reply. He silently stared down at the man. He could not understand why this person answered his question with another question.

Several seconds passed before Jones asked, "Can you just tell me how to get there?"

The second man, who appeared to be in his early thirties, had been studying Jones, and he saw something in the big man's eyes that made him uneasy. He lifted a grease-stained hand and pointed toward 28th Street. "Take that street in the direction you were going. It goes for five or six miles. When it ends go to the left. I don't know the name of that road, but it'll take you into Pineville." After a pause he asked, "You got wheels?"

"Huh?"

"You got wheels? You know . . . a car."

"Uh, No. I'm walking."

"Then you got a long walk. It must be eight miles or so to Pineville."

"I don't mind," Jones said. He gave the second man a slight nod, then turned and walked away.

He had gone several yards when he heard the younger man say, "Man, that is one strange blood."

"And you're one nosey blood," the second man replied. "I thought for a minute he was gonna wring your skinny neck like a chicken."

Just as Jones was walking out of the driveway of the repair shop he heard a siren and almost froze. Looking south, in the direction of the shrill sound, he saw a police car racing north on 25th Avenue. It was followed by a second police vehicle a moment later, and he knew they must be searching for him.

He resumed his walk up 28th Street at a quickened pace as fear stabbed at him like a hot poker. Butterflies flew about wildly in his stomach. He walked on the sidewalk until he came upon a railroad crossing. On the other side of the tracks the sidewalk disappeared and he was forced to walk on the narrow shoulder of the road. To the left of the shoulder a chain-link fence took away any chance of ducking for cover if a police car happened by. He was out in the open with no place to hide. He wanted to run, but the inner voice told him that running would arouse suspicion, so he forced himself to walk.

He had gone a few hundred yards when he came upon a large building. It looked like a factory. The glass panes of several windows had been shattered and bunch grass grew out of the cracks in the asphalt of the empty parking lot. The factory appeared to have been shut down for at least a year or more.

Jones cut across the vacant lot adjacent to the east side of the building. He stepped over broken glass and other debris as he made his way around to the rear of the old structure. He looked around until he found a window that had no glass panes. He picked up a nearby empty wooden crate and placed it under the window.

Standing on the box, he leaned forward until his head, shoulders and arms were inside the building. On the other side of the window was a large table. He placed his hands on the table and kept his arms stiff, as if he were about to do push-ups. Then he began walking forward on his hands, pulling his legs through the window.

Once inside he eased off the table onto the dusty floor, then slowly looked around, studying the huge open interior of the building. Several rows of long tables occupied most of the floor space, and numerous sewing machines were lined side by side atop the tables. He made his way through the maze of equipment to the front of the factory and looked out the window onto 28th Street.

Suddenly a police car went by and Jones ducked under the window. Its siren was not on, but the car sped past at a high rate of speed. Jones was now convinced that they were looking for him. As much as he wanted to get to Frieda, he decided that it would be best if he hid inside the factory until after dark.

10250-MART

TWENTY

THE DRIVE FROM the motel to the Wojcik residence took less time than Flowers had estimated. As he drove past the pecan orchard he mentally patted himself on the back for having made it all the way without once referring to the map. When he slowed for the turn into the long driveway it occurred to him that he might have arrived too early. He had anticipated that the trip from the motel would take longer, but traffic had been light and the drive had taken less than half an hour. After bringing the Nova to a stop in front of the detached garage at the rear of the house, he glanced at his watch. It was a few minutes before nine A.M.

Oh, well, he thought. I'm here now.

Getting out of the car, he removed his suitcase and briefcase from the back seat, walked to the front of the house, crossed the porch to the front door, and rang the bell. He waited a full minute before Darla opened the door.

"Morning, Darla," he greeted with a smile. "Hope I'm not too early."

"No. Please come in." She did not return the smile.

Entering the living room, he set his luggage down near the front door, then he saw Wojcik standing just inside the dining room with the phone receiver to his ear. He was frowning. When Wojcik saw Flowers he waved and motioned for Flowers to follow Darla into the den.

Flowers looked questioningly at Darla. "What's going on?"

"Something terrible has happened," she said. "The prisoner you were to take back to California has escaped."

"What?" Flowers could not believe what he heard.

Darla led him into the den. "It's on the news right now."

At the far end of the den against the wall, surrounded by bookcases, was a large console T.V. Filling the twenty-one inch screen was the face of B.C. Jones. It was a photo selected from a series of mug shots taken at the time of his arrest.

An off-camera commentator was saying, "The deputies were transported to Gulfport Memorial Hospital, where both men are listed in serious but stable condition. Sheriff's spokesman Dwight Cuevas urges everyone to use caution if you see the suspect. He is considered extremely dangerous. Do *not* attempt to apprehend him, but report any information you may have to the Harrison County Sheriff's Office at the number on your screen."

Flowers was stunned by the news. As Darla crossed the room to turn off the T.V., he asked, "How did it happen?"

The newsman had switched to another topic. "In other news, Hurricane Camille is continuing on its northwesterly path up the Gulf of Mexico with winds up to one hundred miles per hour . . ."

Darla pushed a button on the T.V. and the picture faded. "I'm not sure. Frank got a phone call a few minutes ago. A moment later he interrupted his conversation to tell me to turn on the T.V. to the Biloxi channel. I had just turned it on and learned of the escape when you rang the doorbell."

Just then Wojcik entered the den. "That was Deputy Cruthirds. He said they're mobilizing the Sheriff's Department. I'm to report immediately to the courthouse for a briefing." He looked at Flowers. "I was also asked to invite you to the briefing."

"I wouldn't miss it," Flowers said. "Did they tell you how it happened?"

"Yes. It seems Jones overpowered the two deputies who were transporting him to the holding cell near the airport, then fled on foot. It isn't known how he got the best of them. Neither deputy is in good enough condition to talk at the moment."

"Are the deputies going to be O.K?"

"They should be. The injuries weren't life-threatening."

"Well, at least that's something to be thankful for."

"Amen," Darla put in.

"Let me just run upstairs and grab a coat and tie," Wojcik said. "Then we can be on our way."

"What about your breakfast?" Darla asked. "There's no telling when you'll get another chance to eat."

"They'll probably have donuts and coffee at the courthouse."

"While you're getting your coat," Flowers began, "would you mind if I put in a call to New Orleans? I know it's long distance, but I do need to get in touch with Pierce before he checks out of the hotel. Let him know what's going on."

"Not at all," Wojcik said, then added apologetically, "Seems like that's the least we can do."

Darla looked at Flowers. "While you're making your call, could I fix you something to take with you?"

"No, thank you," he said. "To tell you the truth, I just lost my appetite."

DOREEN BROWN SAT on the edge of her sofa and stared vacantly at the T.V. The image on the screen was that of the weather forecaster. In the background was a large map of the Gulf of Mexico. It included Cuba and the states that made up the Gulf Coast. A large dot on the map, northwest of Cuba, depicted the current location of the eye of Hurricane Camille.

The forecaster was informing his viewers of wind velocities and headings of the storm, but for Doreen Brown, his words were falling on deaf ears. Ever since the preceding news story, which told of her nephew's escape, a numbed sensation had crept into her entire being.

For five days she had worried and fretted and cried until there were no more tears to shed. On the coffee table before her was the Holy Bible to which she had turned so often for solace. In the past week she had spent hours reading countless verses, seeking answers to the question of why this trial of her faith had befallen her. She had sought out the Psalms of David and the Wisdom of Solomon, and had read the book of Job at least twice. The seemingly endless search for an answer had eventually exhausted her, and it was only then that a sense of peace came over her. And when the face of her nephew appeared on the T.V. screen, it was as if God had intervened by shielding Doreen from the agony of more bad news. She had humbly submitted to His will, and He had responded by simply removing her capacity for further pain.

WHEN FRIEDA PINCHON saw the face of B.C. Jones on the T.V. screen she recognized him immediately. It was as if the big, ugly man had invaded her living room and was staring back at her. A shiver of fear ran through her and she involuntarily backed away from the television set.

She stood across the room and stared in shocked disbelief. The newsman was relating that Jones had been on his way to the airport where he was to be flown back to California to stand trial for several counts of murder. They were less than a mile from the airport when he overpowered the deputies and made his escape.

Less than a mile, Frieda thought, and he would have been gone forever. A mixture of fear and anger stirred within her, creating a sickening feeling in the pit of her stomach. She felt the urge to scream and cry at the same time. Instead, she emitted an audible sob. How could they have been so careless?

It was only after the face of Jones was removed from the screen that Frieda mustered the courage to go to the television and turn it off. She then went into her bedroom, closed the door and lay across her bed.

The day following the encounter at Woolworth Frieda had difficulty thinking of anything other than the possibility of confronting this strange man again. But as the days passed the details of Monday began to fade, and by Friday she thought that she had pushed him from her mind altogether. Then, as she gazed once more at his face on T.V., she realized that the look he had given her

10250-MART

as he was being taken away on Monday was indelibly planted in her mind, and it would take more than a few days to erase that frightening image.

She had refrained from relating the incident to her grandfather, fearing that he might overreact in some way, such as forcing her to quit her job. And now, just as she was beginning to feel that her secret was secure, this horrible man was on the loose again.

And he was wanted for several counts of murder!

Frieda breathed a deep sigh, then slowly sat up. The time had come for her to let her grandfather know what was going on. She sat with her shoulders slumped and her feet dangling from the bed as she rehearsed words that she hoped would have the least impact on the way he would receive the news.

Breathing another sigh, she straightened her shoulders and stood up. She walked out of her bedroom and moved with deliberate steps across the living room and through the door that separated their private residence from the grocery store. She stood at the top of the steps and waited while her grandfather, wearing his white bib apron, waited on an elderly woman who seemed unhappy with the price of Crab Boil. Five minutes passed before the woman finally paid for her groceries and left the store. During that time, Frieda remained on the steps, butterflies fluttering madly within her. She waited until after the screen door slammed closed following the departure of the unhappy customer before descending the steps.

As she approached, her grandfather looked up from his work. "Well, now. Finally decided to get up, heh?"

Frieda forced a half-smile. "I've been up for a while." She paused briefly, then said, "Grandpa, I need to talk to you about something that happened . . . several days ago."

Her grandfather frowned. "Several days ago? Since you made a point of not telling me about it, I can assume it's something I won't like."

"No, sir, you won't like it." She swallowed and bit her lip. "But I have to tell you anyway."

TWENTY-ONE

GARLAND FLOWERS SAT on the passenger side of the unmarked sheriff's vehicle as Wojcik drove them south on Highway 49 toward Gulfport. The air conditioner worked hard to cool the car's interior. Outside the air was hot and muggy. Even Wojcik had commented that it seemed more humid than normal. Overhead large patches of blue were fighting to overcome a gray and sullen sky.

They had traveled in silence for the first few miles, then Wojcik asked, "I'm curious, Garland, how did your friend Pierce receive the news of the escape?"

Flowers grinned and chuckled. "I could be wrong, but I do believe that I detected a note of relief at the news. Of course, he tried to sound serious in his response to the 'terrible turn of events.' And I regret to point out that he was not very complimentary of the Harrison County Sheriff's Department. As I recall he referred to you as a bunch of yokels." Flowers shook his head in mock seriousness. "Naturally, such a thing could *never* happen in L.A. County."

"So, how does he view the situation from his lofty perch in New Orleans?" Wojcik asked. "What does he want you to do? For that matter, what's *he* going to do?"

"Well, he wants me to stick around and work with you 'yokels' in trying to find the suspect. Of course, he will stay in New Orleans to await news of our search." Flowers paused, then added, "I suspect that Pierce is giddy with delight." He shook his head again.

"I'd be willing to bet a month's pay that he's already making plans for another eventful night on the town."

They continued south into downtown Gulfport. At 14th Street Wojcik turned left, drove one block, then turned right, onto 24th Avenue. As soon as they made the turn they saw a crowd of men standing in front of the courthouse. Some were wearing the uniform of the Gulfport Police Department, but most were in civilian attire with badges pinned to their sport shirts.

"Are all of the men in civvies deputy sheriffs?" Flowers asked.

"Some of them are," Wojcik replied. "They're actually reserves that we use in emergencies. The others are members of the auxiliary police. Gulfport P.D. uses them for traffic control, security at football games and the like. They're mostly businessmen who would secretly like to be cops but aren't willing to take the pay cut." After a brief pause he added, "That's not a fair statement. They actually perform a valuable service to the community."

The parking spaces on both sides of the street were filled, and Wojcik had to pull into the parking lot on the far side of the bus depot. When Flowers glimpsed the depot it occurred to him that less than twenty-four hours had passed since he stepped off the Greyhound bus. Though his visit had not been unpleasant, he felt as if he had been in Gulfport for several days.

They got out of the car and walked toward the group of police and deputies who milled about on the sidewalk. Wojcik was greeted by several of the men. He shook hands with those nearest him as he and Flowers made their way through the crowd.

Someone in the back yelled, "Hey, Frank! When are we gonna get some word on what's goin' on?"

"I'm going into the briefing right now," Wojcik replied. "A supervisor should be out shortly to give you your assignments."

"I hope they make up their minds about what to do with us before Camille gets here," another man shouted. "I got to go board up my house." This brought a round of laughter.

Flowers and Wojcik walked up the steps and entered the courthouse. Flowers noticed two large coffee urns on a table near the door. Next to the urns were several donut boxes, most of which were empty. Half a dozen men stood near the table, each holding a styrofoam cup in one hand and a donut in the other. As Flowers walked past he suddenly realized that his appetite had returned with a vengeance. He felt a gnawing emptiness in his stomach.

The first thing Flowers noticed when they passed through the double doors of the courtroom was the lack of air circulation in the crowded enclosure. Since the courts were closed on weekends it was decided to use one of the courtrooms to conduct the briefing of the command staff. Almost every seat was occupied in the spectator section as well as in the jury box. The small window air conditioning unit was noisily running at maximum capacity, but its effect was negligible. It seemed to Flowers to be almost as warm inside the courtroom as it was out on the sidewalk.

Some of the men present wore uniforms of different police agencies. Flowers observed that every one of them had either lieutenant's or captain's bars pinned to their collars. He also noticed that, of those dressed in civilian attire, he and Wojcik were the only two who still wore their coats. Wojcik must have made the same observation, for he took his coat off and hung it on a coat rack at the back of the room. Flowers was not hesitant to follow his lead.

The room was noisy. Everyone appeared to be engaged in conversation with the person next to him. Wojcik motioned for Flowers to follow him as he weaved his way around and between those who were standing in the aisle. Flowers followed him past the bar rail and counsel tables.

Standing in front of the judge's bench was a tall man with broad shoulders and a narrow waist, who appeared to be in his late forties. He had a distinguished bearing with a handsome face and a head full of dark hair that was graying at the temples. He was engaged in conversation with two other men as Wojcik approached.

When the man saw Wojcik he abruptly excused himself from the other two and said, "Frank, you finally made it." There was a deep, resonant quality to his voice.

"Morning, sir. We got here as soon as we could." Wojcik turned to Flowers and said, "I would like for you to meet Sergeant Garland Flowers. Garland, this is Dwight Cuevas, special assistant to the sheriff."

Cuevas displayed a friendly smile as he and Flowers shook hands. "Sergeant Flowers, I'm pleased to meet you. I just wish it could've been under less embarrassing circumstances."

"A pleasure to meet you, sir." Flowers started to make some dismissing comment about the escape, but decided against it.

"I've been waiting for y'all to arrive before starting the briefing," Cuevas said. He looked at Flowers and added, "If you have no objections, I would like to call upon you in a few minutes to give us some background information on the fugitive."

"I would be happy to."

"Why don't y'all have a seat at the counsel table and I'll get this meeting under way."

As Flowers and Wojcik took their seats Dwight Cuevas held up both hands and spoke in a voice loud enough to be heard at the back of the room. "Gentlemen, may I have your attention please?"

There was an instant response as everyone stopped talking at the same moment.

Cuevas continued. "I would like to begin by apologizing for the cramped space. Someone suggested earlier that we hold the briefing in the board of supervisors hearing room, but I thought a courtroom would be large enough to hold us." He gazed about the crowded room and grinned. "I guess I underestimated the turnout."

There were several chuckles in the audience.

"I realize that it's warm in here, but we'll keep this as short as possible. Then y'all can return to your respective departments and pass along the information to your personnel.

"Let me begin by giving y'all an update on the two deputies who were injured during the escape. When I left the hospital about an hour ago both men were awake and talking. Buddy Ladner has a nasty cut over his right eye and he's suffering from a mild concussion.

"From what Buddy told me our suspect has such huge arms that they had to cuff him with his hands in front of him. He was quite docile on the ride from the jail. Then, from out of the blue, he swung both arms over and caught Buddy on the head. The handcuffs put a nasty gash on the side of his forehead. A little lower and it would've put his eye out. The blow on the head was the last thing Buddy remembered.

"Alvin Dedeaux was the driver. According to Alvin, right after the prisoner attacked Buddy, he reached over the seat and grabbed the steering wheel then jerked it to the right, causing the car to go off the road and over an embankment. Alvin was thrown forward and hit the steering wheel. Next thing he remembers is being placed on a stretcher. He passed out again and didn't come to until after he was in the emergency room. He's got some nasty bruises on his head and chest, but the doctor says there are no indications of serious internal injuries. They'll both remain in the hospital overnight for observation, but the condition of each has been downgraded from serious to guarded."

Cuevas paused for a moment as several members of the audience expressed their relief at the news that the deputies would recover. He then held up his hands and the room fell silent once more. Flowers was impressed by Cuevas' ability to command an immediate response from these representatives of other police departments. He decided that it was a sign of the respect they had for the sheriff's special assistant, as well as for the sheriff himself.

Cuevas resumed. "For what it's worth, I need to point out that Deputy Dedeaux was not wearing his seat belt. Had he been wearing it, there is a chance that he would not have been injured in the car crash. If your officers are like our deputies, they don't like wearing seat belts. They feel that the belts slow them down when they have to get out of the car in a hurry to respond to an emergency. But this is one example where a seat belt might have prevented, not only the deputy's injury, but the escape of a suspect as well."

Flowers was tempted to raise his hand and point out the fact that, if the driver had not been knocked unconscious in the car crash, there was a better than even chance that Jones would have killed him to make good his escape. He thought back to the two male victims in Los Angeles. In both cases Jones had broken their necks in a matter of seconds. But Flowers decided that it was not his place to dispute an executive of another law enforcement agency.

"Now, before we get into specifics about our escapee, I'm going to change directions for a few minutes." Cuevas paused again as if carefully selecting the words he was about to say. "It seems that, in our line of work, it doesn't rain but it pours. It's either feast or famine. We can go for weeks, or even months at a time with nothing happening. Then all of a sudden everything falls on us at once. Needless to say, this weekend will be one of those busy times.

"In addition to having a dangerous fugitive running loose in the community, we also have a hurricane headed this way. Whether or not we get the full force of the storm is still not known. But at the very least we're in for some bad weather.

"Since we have command level representatives of most of the law enforcement agencies in the county here this morning, I thought this would be an excellent opportunity to get an update on the hurricane. So I've taken the liberty of inviting Mr. Robert Hamilton, of the county civil defense office, to give us an up-to-the-minute report on Camille." Cuevas gestured to a frail-looking man with a thin face who was seated at one of the counsel tables. He reminded Flowers of Barney Fife, from *The Andy Griffith Show.*

Robert Hamilton stood and walked to the front of the judge's bench. Cuevas moved to one side to give him the floor. The moment Hamilton began to speak, Flowers' image of Barney Fife faded, for the civil defense representative spoke eloquently and with authority.

"Good morning, gentlemen," he began. "As most of you are aware, Hurricane Camille struck the western end of Cuba yesterday afternoon. It passed over the island last night and is now in the Gulf of Mexico, moving on a north-northwesterly course. The National Hurricane Center in Miami reports that, as of nine o'clock this morning, Camille is about four hundred miles south of Panama City, Florida. Forecasters predict that she will turn northward some time today. If that happens the Florida Panhandle can expect to get hit pretty badly. At present, a hurricane watch remains in effect from Biloxi to St. Marks, Florida. I suspect that it will be upgraded to a hurricane warning by the end of the day.

"As hurricanes go, Camille is not very large. In fact, when compared to Betsy, back in '65, this one is rather small. By way of comparison, the eye of Hurricane Betsy was thirty-five miles in diameter. Some experts estimate the eye of Camille may be as small as five miles across." Hamilton held up a precautionary hand as murmurs of relief could be heard among members of the audience. "Let me make it quite clear, though. Camille has all the makings of a killer. Although she's small, she is developing into an extremely powerful storm, even more powerful than Betsy. She's tightly wound. That's why the eye is so small. The winds circling the eye are in excess of a hundred miles per hour. As she moves across the Gulf, those winds will probably grow stronger. Make no mistake, Camille has the potential of being one of the most devastating storms to ever hit the Gulf Coast.

"As Camille moves closer to the mainland she will push the water with her, causing high tides. By tonight the area east of Biloxi will experience gale force winds. It is expected that she will make landfall some time late tomorrow. Now, where that will be is anyone's guess at this time. It depends upon when she makes that turn to the north."

"What if the storm doesn't turn?" Someone in the audience asked. "What if she keeps moving on her present course?"

"The best that I can calculate," Hamilton replied, "is that she could make landfall somewhere between central Louisiana and east Texas." He paused, then added, "But as I indicated, the weather experts seem convinced that she *will* turn.

"The Board of Supervisors has ordered all county equipment moved off the beaches. All city and county emergency vehicles should be gassed up and ready to roll.

"The civil defense director has requested that grocery stores, hardware stores, lumber yards and other retail businesses be prepared to open on Sunday to accommodate those who are preparing for the worst.

"Needless to say, all public safety employees will be on standby throughout the weekend." He looked around the room and grinned. "Of course, it appears that y'all already have plans for the weekend."

There was half-hearted laughter among several members of the audience.

Hamilton continued. "There will be weather updates throughout the weekend on radio and television. I urge everyone to closely monitor those reports." He looked at Cuevas. "Dwight, that's all the information I have." He then turned back to the audience. "Are there any questions?"

When there was no response from the audience, Cuevas said, "Thank you very much, Bob, for the update. Please pass along to the director that our department stands ready to assist in any way we can."

Mr. Hamilton nodded, then returned to the counsel table, picked up his folder and quietly left the room. No sooner had he departed than Gertie Allgood entered carrying a stack of five-by-seven photographs. She walked directly to the counsel table and set the stack between Flowers and Wojcik. Flowers noticed that they were mug photos of B.C. Jones.

After placing the photos on the table Gertie addressed Cuevas. "Will that be all, sir?"

"Yes, Gertie, thank you," he replied.

Gertie then leaned toward Flowers and whispered loud enough for Wojcik to hear. "When you're through here, why don't you drop by my office? I just made a fresh pot of coffee." She looked at Wojcik and made a face, then walked away.

Flowers and Wojcik watched as she moved sassily through the courtroom. After she was out the door they glanced at each other and neither could refrain from grinning. Wojcik shook his head but made no comment. Both men then returned their attention to the front of the room as Cuevas began to speak.

"I believe it goes without saying," he began, "that we all hope that this hurricane passes us by. But we have to proceed on the assumption that we are going to get hit, in some way, with bad weather. As Mr. Hamilton pointed out, at the very least we will experience gale force winds.

"Now the first thing for us to do, as commanders, is to see to it that our personnel are taken care of. The best way to do that is to convince them that an emergency does in fact exist, and it is incumbent upon them to see that their families are safe. If they know their families are safe, they will be better equipped mentally to respond to the needs of the community. Each officer, and each deputy sheriff, has his own set of family circumstances, and they must be addressed individually. I think that is what we should work on now. It will better prepare us for the crisis that will come later.

"With that said, let's change direction once more and return to the original purpose of this briefing." Cuevas then addressed Wojcik. "Frank, would you please take that stack of pictures and pass them out?"

When Wojcik began doing as the special assistant requested, Cuevas resumed. "What Frank is passing out are copies of a mug photo of our suspect. We have plenty, so take as many as you think you'll need. It is the sheriff's intention to have the suspect's picture in every patrol car and detective unit in the county by the end of the day."

Cuevas looked at Flowers and motioned for him to come forward. As Flowers got up and moved toward the front Cuevas said, "And now I would like to introduce you to Sergeant Garland Flowers, of the Los Angeles County Sheriff's Department. Sergeant Flowers is the homicide investigator who came to Gulfport to take the prisoner back to California to stand trial for murder. Sergeant Flowers knows more about our suspect than anyone here, and he's kindly consented to give us some background information on this character. Sergeant Flowers?"

When Flowers looked over his audience it occurred to him that he was the only black person in the room. He wasn't surprised, though, for these were men in positions of command, and equal opportunity was in its infancy in Mississippi. Integration into the higher ranks would take time. At least the expressions on their faces were friendly, and most of them appeared eager to hear what he had to say.

"Good morning," he began. "I'll keep this as brief as I can, but I do want to fill you in on who our suspect is and why it is imperative that we use extreme caution when apprehending him."

For the next several minutes Flowers related in detail his investigation into the murders committed by B.C. Jones. Relying on information provided by Horace Blackburn, Jones' parole officer, Flowers described the suspect's background, including the fact that he was of racially mixed blood and was physically abused by his father, and he told of Jones' imprisonment for having killed his father.

"To the best of our knowledge," Flowers said, "all of his murder victims have been either partners in a racially mixed marriage or the children of mixed couples. However, he has also demonstrated that if he feels threatened, or if he is provoked, he will react violently."

A middle-aged man in the front row raised his hand. The shoulder patch on his uniform was that of the Biloxi Police Department.

"Yes, sir?" Flowers invited.

"Has he ever been known to use a gun or knife, or any other weapon?"

"There is no evidence that Jones has ever used any weapons in his attacks." Flowers smiled without humor. "Of course his bare hands have been all the weapons he has needed." He paused and the smile faded. "I cannot emphasize enough that we are dealing with a very dangerous man, and, again, I urge you to use extreme caution when confronting him. If there is an attempt to arrest Jones, make sure there is sufficient backup.

"There's one other fact about our suspect that should work to our advantage, and that is that he does not know how to drive. So we can all but eliminate the prospect of him stealing a car to make good his escape. I do recommend, however, that we alert all companies that provide public transportation."

Flowers looked around the room. "Are there any other questions?"

When no one spoke he said, "Thank you," then returned to his seat at the counsel table.

At the direction of the special assistant, a deputy carried an easel from a corner of the courtroom to the front of the judge's bench. On the easel was an enlarged street map of Harrison County. For the next ten minutes Cuevas outlined the sheriff's plan for the capture of B.C. Jones. He pointed out that the Gulfport Police Department was already heavily committed to the search. Roadblocks had been set up at the major arteries leading out of the city, and a saturation patrol was underway. He requested that the other agencies throughout the county do likewise.

Members of other departments came forward and studied the map, then identified various intersections where roadblocks would be established. Officers would be posted at all of the bus terminals, train depots and the airport. Local bus lines and taxi services would also be alerted. Frequent announcements would be made over the radio and television warning motorists not to pick up hitchhikers.

Time was a critical factor, for within a matter of hours the focus would, of necessity, move from the search for the escapee to possible evacuation of thousands of people in the event Hurricane Camille changed course and moved in on the Mississippi Gulf Coast.

As the briefing was about to end, Wojcik raised his hand. When Cuevas acknowledged him he said, "If you have no objection,

Sergeant Flowers and I would like to pay a call on Jones' aunt. She lives in Soria City. I met her a few days ago and she strikes me as being an honest, law-abiding person. If Jones has attempted to contact her, I believe she will tell us.

"We would also like to go by the police department and pick up a copy of Jones' arrest report and contact those witnesses. I know it's a long shot, but so far as we know those are the only people who have had any personal contact with him."

"That's a good idea," Cuevas said. "I would just ask that y'all keep us posted on your progress." After a pause Cuevas addressed everyone in the room. "For the time being this courtroom and the sheriff's office will serve as the command post. All communications must flow through us. If there is nothing more, this briefing is concluded."

The room was immediately filled with voices and the sounds of seats being folded upward as everyone seemed to stand at the same time to make their way to the exit. Flowers and Wojcik were among the last to leave.

As they slowly moved toward the door behind several stragglers Wojcik said, "Let's stop by Gertie's office and get her to call the airport. Maybe it's not too late to cancel your flights." He grinned slyly and added, "Besides, I'm sure you're just dying to have another cup of her delicious coffee."

Flowers returned the grin. "As a matter of fact I would like a cup, especially if she has a few donuts to go with it. I'm hungry."

TWENTY-TWO

IT WAS PAST noon by the time Wojcik and Flowers left the courthouse. Flowers' appetite had been satisfied for the time being by two glazed donuts and a cup of Gertie's coffee.

They drove east on 15th Street, past the high school, and turned north onto 20th Avenue. After crossing the railroad tracks Wojcik turned the Plymouth east onto Railroad Street. Three blocks farther he turned left and they entered Soria City.

As Flowers took in the surroundings he thought how they conformed to his previous image of what a town in Mississippi would look like. Most of the houses were in need of paint. Few of the yards had any grass or flowers. Shade trees covered areas strewn with cars in various states of disrepair.

On an unpaved side street two small boys, sporting cowboy hats and cap pistols, chased one another on broomstick horses. In front of one house a young pregnant woman held a toddler on her hip. She was talking to another woman who appeared to be a few years older. They interrupted their conversation long enough to stare at the unmarked sheriff's car as Wojcik and Flowers drove past. The expressions on the women's faces were not unlike those Flowers had seen on faces in the ghettos of Los Angeles. The looks were not hostile, but wary, revealing a general distrust of the police.

They drove another block, then Wojcik brought the car to a stop in front of a modest wood frame house on the left side of the street. "Well, this is it," he said as he turned off the ignition. He breathed a sigh then added, "I'm not looking forward to this. Mrs. Brown's a nice lady, and she certainly doesn't deserve being dragged into this mess."

"Unfortunately, we can't always choose our relatives," Flowers replied as he opened the car door. "And we do need to talk to her."

Wojcik led the way up the steps and onto the porch, then knocked on the door.

Half a minute later the door opened and Doreen Brown stood before them. It was apparent, even through the screen that separated them, that she had been distraught and had gone for a long period of time without sleep. In one hand she held a Bible clutched to her breast.

"May I help you?" She asked in a voice that was surprisingly calm and collected.

Wojcik stepped forward. "Mrs. Brown, I don't know if you remember me, but . . . "

"Oh, yes. You're Mr. Wojcik, from the sheriff's office."

"Yes, ma'am. And this is Sergeant Flowers. He's with the Los Angeles County Sheriff's Department. He's the one who came back here to pick up your nephew." After a pause, he added, "I suppose you've heard by now about his escape."

"Yes. I saw it on the T.V. a while ago."

Several awkward seconds passed in silence, then Wojcik asked, "Mrs. Brown, may we come in to speak with you?"

"Mr. Wojcik, if y'all have come here to see if I'm hiding B.C., then you're wasting you're time. I haven't seen him since the day he was arrested." After a heavy sigh, she added, "Let's see. When was that? Last Monday?" She closed her eyes and slowly shook her head. "Seems like a lifetime ago."

For a fleeting moment Flowers thought the woman was going to burst into tears, but then she opened her eyes and quickly regained her composure. He admired her strength, and was touched by the pain that she was enduring because of her nephew. Flowers wanted to tell her that her nephew was a cold-blooded murderer, and was not worth all the grief that he was causing her. But he knew that he could never tell her such a thing.

"Well, yes," Wojcik said. "We did come to see if you had heard from your nephew, and to see if you could provide us with any information that might help us find him." He then nodded in Flowers' direction. "I asked Sergeant Flowers to accompany me here because he knows everything there is to know about this case. He's agreed to answer any questions you might have about your nephew's involvement."

Doreen Brown was shaking her head before Wojcik finished speaking. "No. No, Mr. Wojcik. I understand that what B.C. did back in California was bad. Real bad. I don't need to know any details."

Flowers and Wojcik exchanged glances, then Flowers addressed Doreen. "Mrs. Brown, I fully understand you're not wanting to know the sordid details of your nephew's crimes. But there are a few things you need to know. It certainly won't make you feel any better, but it'll help you to understand the critical nature of the situation."

Flowers paused long enough to take a deep breath, then continued. "B.C. Jones has murdered six people that we know of, two of whom were small children." He could hear Doreen Brown's audible gasp, but he continued to speak. "Now, I don't know why he's killing people, but I suspect that he is a very sick man, and he needs help." Doreen clutched her Bible more firmly against her bosom. Flowers took no pleasure in what he was saying, but she was Jones' only known contact in Mississippi, and it was vital that she knew the extent of her nephew's propensity for violence. "Mrs. Brown, if your nephew is not found very soon and brought into custody, it is quite probable that he will kill again."

What followed was a period of silence that lasted the better part of a minute. Mrs. Brown closed her eyes once more. When she opened them Flowers was mildly surprised to see a smile appear on her face. It was a serene smile, born of deep faith. When she spoke, the words came softly but clearly. "Sergeant Flowers, I am a Christian woman. I place all my faith in the saving grace of Jesus Christ. And I give you my word, I have neither seen nor heard from B.C. since he left here Monday afternoon. As a Christian I cannot abide what he has done, so you also have my word that if I hear from him I will let you know."

"Thank you, Mrs. Brown." There was nothing more Flowers could say. He believed her, and he was coming to understand why Frank Wojcik liked this woman. He was convinced that, whatever situation Doreen Brown was confronted with, she would do the right thing.

They had started to leave, and Flowers was descending the steps from the porch, when Wojcik stopped and turned back to Mrs. Brown. "I supposed you've also heard about the hurricane out in the Gulf."

"Yes, I have."

"We still don't know if we're going to get the full brunt of the hurricane, but it's certain that we're in for some bad weather. Probably gale-force winds. Civil defense is setting up shelters at some of the schools. Soria City Elementary School is one of them. If you like, I can come by tomorrow and drive you over to the school."

"I appreciate it, Mr. Wojcik. But you needn't bother."

"It'll be no trouble."

"No," she said flatly. "I'll just ride it out here. This old house made it through the '47 hurricane with no trouble, and we rode out Betsy in '65. I'm sure we'll be just fine."

"O.K.," Wojcik said. "But if you change your mind, you have my number."

"Thank you," she said, then slowly turned her back to them and disappeared into the interior darkness of her home.

MORE THAN FIVE hours had passed since B.C. Jones sought refuge in the garment factory, and he was growing restless. He was alone in the huge room with nothing to look at but rows of large tables and sewing machines. The floor was covered with a layer of dust, as well as bits of broken glass that had fallen from shattered windows. When he stepped on the glass the noise seemed to echo throughout the cavernous building.

The fact that he was alone was of little concern to him, for he had spent most of his life alone. His greatest concern at the moment was his having to hide in this empty building, instead of having the freedom to make his way to Frieda's house.

Jones sat on the edge of a wide worktable that extended perpendicular from the front wall, near the south end of the building. He stared absently out a window. A moderate flow of Saturday afternoon traffic passed along the two lanes of 28th Street. It angered Jones to be trapped as he was, while others had the freedom to drive their cars and move about as they pleased. A frustration gnawed at him to the point that he was on the verge of taking a chance and continuing on his journey.

Suddenly he heard the sound of car tires rolling on gravel. He leaned forward on the table and craned his neck to the right, in an effort to look in the direction of the sound. As soon as the vehicle came into view from the eastern side of the building he jumped back.

It was a police car!

Jones slid off the table and crawled underneath it, and huddled motionless against the wall. He could hear the muffled sound of car doors open, then close. Several seconds passed, then he heard the front door of the building rattle, but it did not open. A moment later he heard voices. He could barely make out the words, though the officers seemed to be standing just on the other side of the wall, perhaps no more than four feet away.

"Door's locked," said one of the officers.

"And there's no sign of life inside," the second officer replied. He was apparently cupping his hands and peering through a window.

"Should we find an open window and search the interior?" Asked the first officer.

"No way! I just got this uniform back from the cleaners last night. I ain't about to go crawling through windows and rummaging through all that clutter."

"What should we do, then?"

"I say we state in our log that we made a cursory search of the garment factory, with negative results, and let it go at that."

"That's O.K. with me."

Jones remained still. He began to feel a cramp in the calf of his leg, but he dared not move until he heard the officers drive away. What was taking them so long to return to their car? Suddenly he was startled by a rustling sound behind him. With an effort he slowly turned his head far enough to see a small shadow emerge from a cardboard tube. The tube was four inches in diameter, and had once served as the center support for a bolt of cloth.

A gray, furry head appeared from the end of the tube and nervously looked around. A moment later it ventured all the way out. It was at least ten inches long from its head to the tip of its hairless tail. From somewhere in the back of his consciousness Jones heard the car doors shut, an engine start, and the police car pulling away from the abandoned factory. For the moment, though, he was not concerned about the police. The focus of his attention was now on the fact that he was not alone after all. His newly discovered companion gave B.C. Jones an uneasy feeling. In fact, his skin began to crawl as he stared into the pink eyes of a large gray rat.

GARLAND FLOWERS SAT on the passenger side of the unmarked sheriff's car and read, with great interest, the narrative describing the arrest of B.C. Jones. He and Wojcik had stopped off at the Gulfport Police Department after leaving Doreen Brown's house and obtained a copy of the report. They were now parked in front of a hamburger stand on 14th Street in downtown Gulfport.

The door on the driver's side opened and Wojcik got in. He was holding a bag, the contents of which filled the car's interior with the aroma of grilled onions. In his other hand he held a bottle of Coca Cola and a bottle of Barq's Root Beer.

Flowers smacked his lips. "If those burgers taste as good as they smell . . ."

"They do," Wojcik replied.

Flowers accepted the coke from Wojcik and set it on the open glove compartment door, which served as a makeshift tray. He then took a proffered hamburger and removed the wax paper wrapping. The temporary sustenance he had gained from Gertie's donuts had long since passed, and his stomach was growling from hunger. He took a bite and closed his eyes as he chewed, savoring the taste.

After swallowing he smiled and declared, "Now that's a good burger."

Wojcik nodded toward the hamburger stand. "That little greasy spoon operation isn't much to look at, but for my money, it makes the best hamburgers on the Gulf Coast."

For the next five minutes they ate in silence. After taking the last bite Flowers gathered the wrappings and napkins and placed them in the paper sack. He took a drink from his coke then picked up the police report.

"Have you had a chance to read this?" He asked.

"No," Wojcik replied. "It was Gulfport P.D.'s arrest, and a pretty lightweight one at that, from what I understand. There was never really any reason for me to read it . . . at least not before now."

"Without knowing the background on B.C. Jones it would probably be difficult for anyone to make the connection. But knowing what I know about the man, I'm now fairly confident of his destination."

"And where is that," Wojcik asked.

"A place called Pineville. Do you know where that is?"

"Yes. It's a little place about eight or ten miles from here. Just north of Pass Christian."

Flowers noted that Wojcik pronounced it Pass Crist-yan, with the accent on the last syllable. He started to ask about the pronunciation, but decided not to get sidetracked.

"So what does Pineville have to do with B.C. Jones?" Wojcik asked.

"Let me give you the gist of what's in the report, and see if it makes sense to you. On August 11, last Monday, Jones sat down at the lunch counter in Woolworth's. For some reason he accused the waitress, a Frieda Pinchon, age eighteen, of having Negro blood in her. Miss Pinchon lives in Pineville.

"When he accused her of having mixed blood, two construction workers decided to defend Miss Pinchon's honor, and Mr. Jones promptly kicked their butts. There was some minor damage done to the store and Jones was arrested for disturbing the peace."

"And?" Wojcik prompted.

"Like I said, without having some background information on Jones, it would be difficult to derive any significance from this report. But based upon what I know about our suspect, Frieda Pinchon is going to play a major role in our finding him.

"As I pointed out in the briefing this morning, every one of his murder victims had something to do with mixed blood, either as parents or as offspring. Jones himself is of mixed blood, and he hates the world because of it. As much as I hate to admit it, part of me feels sorry for him. I doubt if he has ever had a truly happy day in his life. And he apparently feels that everyone of mixed blood is as unhappy as he is. So it's his mission in life to punish mixed couples, and to send their innocent children to a happier place.

"That's where Frieda Pinchon comes in. Now, I don't know if she is of mixed blood or not. It really doesn't matter, as long as Jones thinks she is, and I have a strong hunch that he is going to try and find her."

"I don't know," Wojcik began. "Seems to me his only goal at this time would be to get as far away from here as he could. As simple minded as he is, he must have enough sense to realize what's at stake if he's sent back to California. At the very least, he would spend the rest of his life in prison." After a pause, he added, "Besides, how would he know how to locate this Frieda Pinchon?"

"Because he has a copy of the police report."

"He what?" Wojcik asked.

"B.C. Jones has a copy of this report I'm holding in my hands. Compliments of Sergeant Bernard Taylor, of the Gulfport Police Department. Taylor even attached a supplemental report describing his good deed. Apparently he was of the opinion that he was legally required to give the arrested party a copy if so requested. And Sergeant Taylor felt obliged to document that fact in a report.

"It's my opinion that the only reason Jones wanted a copy of the report was to obtain Miss Pinchon's address."

"Doesn't sound like the workings of a simple mind to me," Wojcik said.

"Oh, he's simple minded alright, but that doesn't mean he isn't cunning. I don't know what the I.Q. of a fox is, but we know that a fox is sly. I doubt if B.C. Jones could calculate long division. He may not know who George Washington was, or even that Richard Nixon is our current president. But he has an animal instinct for cunning.

"I suspect that he's hiding out at the moment, but eventually he's going to make his way to Pineville." Flowers looked at Wojcik, then added, "And if he finds Frieda Pinchon, he's going to kill her."

TWENTY-THREE

FIVE MINUTES AFTER leaving the hamburger stand Wojcik turned the car west onto Highway 90 from 30th Avenue. To their left was Gulfport Harbor. Flowers noticed a few large freighters tied to the docks.

It was late afternoon and most of the dark clouds that had threatened rain during the morning had given way to hazy sunshine. Flowers silently observed that the sky was not the bright blue that it had been the day before, nor was it like the slate-gray marine layer that so often hovered over Los Angeles for days at a time. This sky had an unusual cast to it. Something in the atmosphere had reduced the sun's radiance to a dull reddish-orange glow. He made no comment, but concluded that it probably had something to do with the approaching storm.

He looked out over the grayish-blue waters of the Gulf. "Looks a little choppy out there today. Is that because of the storm?"

Wojcik took his eyes from the road long enough to steal a glance at the water beyond the beach. "It's possible. Mr. Hamilton told us at the briefing that some areas could expect gale-force winds by this evening. Could be that the coming winds are stirring up the water." After a pause he added, "Then again, it's not unusual for the Sound to get a little choppy in the afternoon."

"What do you mean by 'the Sound'?" Flowers asked.

Wojcik gestured toward the Gulf. "All of that water that you see out there is known as the Mississippi Sound. There is a chain of islands running along the coast. They range anywhere from eight to twelve miles out. They're known as barrier islands. You can't see them very well because most of them are no more than a few feet above sea level with short scrub vegetation growing on them. Although you can usually see Cat Island because it's one of the closer ones, and it has trees growing on it.

"Anyway, these barrier islands create sort of a breakwater from the Gulf of Mexico. That's one of the reasons the water is so calm.

"Last year I took some of my students to Ship Island, which lies about twelve miles out. There's an old fort out there that was occupied by the North during the War Between the States. The fort was used to hold Confederate prisoners of war.

"Darla and the girls went with us on the field trip, and while we were waiting for the boat to take us back to the mainland, I took my family for a walk along the beach on the south side of the island. I was impressed by how different the water was from the north side. It was a rich greenish-blue, which, I understand, is indicative of deep water. There were big waves hitting the beach, and white caps farther out. I imagine it's much like the Pacific Ocean that you see out in California.

"The water south of Ship Island is the real Gulf of Mexico. The islands separate the Gulf from the mainland, and the water in between is called the Mississippi Sound.

"Another reason for the calm water is because the Sound is quite shallow." Wojcik pointed toward the Gulf. "You could sail five miles out from here and find places where the water is no more than ten feet deep."

"Ten feet?" Flowers asked skeptically. "How can that be?"

"Because of the Mississippi River."

"Come again?"

"The mouth of the river is less than a hundred miles from here, and the volume of sand and silt that it empties into the Gulf is incredible. Millions of tons a year. The silt is spread all along the Gulf Coast. These alluvial deposits extend out as far as the barrier islands. This has been an ongoing process for millions of years, and tends to keep the water shallow in the Sound."

Wojcik paused again, as if giving some thought to his next comment. Flowers could not help but smile inwardly. He was amused by his friend's tendency to lecture. Teaching was definitely Frank Wojcik's calling. It came so natural to him. What's more, he was good at it. Until a few days before, Flowers had never given any thought to the Gulf Coast, yet here he was listening to a lecture on Mississippi mud . . . and enjoying it.

"You see that white sandy beach out there?" Wojcik resumed. "Well, twenty years ago that beach did not exist."

"What?" Flowers asked.

"That entire beach, as far as you can see in both directions, is man-made. Fifty yards wide and twenty-some-odd miles long.

"In order to allow large ships to enter the Gulfport harbor, a deep water channel had to be dredged. The beach you see out there is the sand that was pumped out to form the shipping channel. Of course, the muddy Mississippi keeps trying to fill in the channel with more silt deposits, so every few years it has to be re-dredged." Wojcik smiled wryly. "Going against nature is a never-ending battle."

Both men fell silent for a moment, then Flowers said, "I have another question."

"Fire away."

"Why is the name Pass Christian pronounced with the accent on the last syllable?"

"Because the name has nothing directly to do with Christianity," Wojcik replied. "The town was named after an early settler of French heritage. His name, I believe, was Christian Ladnier. If I remember my high school French correctly, the name Christian is pronounced with a nasal accent on the last syllable. Apparently, some time during the past two hundred years the nasal sound was lost, but the accent remained."

"Two hundred years?" Flowers asked.

"Oh, yes. In fact, the town we now know as Pass Christian was settled as far back as 1699. The same is true of several of the towns along the coast: Pensacola, Mobile, Ocean Springs, Biloxi, Bay St.

Louis, just to name a few. They can all trace their roots back almost three hundred years."

"What about Gulfport?" Flowers asked.

Wojcik smiled. "No. Gulfport is the new kid on the block. It's strictly a product of the twentieth century."

Leaving Gulfport behind them, they entered Long Beach. A minute later Flowers noticed a wooden church, painted white, that rested serenely on a large green lawn amidst a grove of oak trees.

"That's a quaint looking church," he commented. "Looks old."

"That's St. Thomas Catholic Church," Wojcik said. "Actually, it's not as old as it looks. I believe it was built in the early 1900's." He thought for a moment, then added, "I agree with you, though. It does have a quaint look about it."

For the next few miles they rode in silence, then entered the city limits of Pass Christian. A moment later Wojcik turned off the highway onto a two-lane road that angled slightly to the right, but paralleled Highway 90. A sign proclaimed it as the Scenic Drive.

As they drove past Menge Avenue Wojcik said, "That's the street we'll take to get to Pineville, but I thought I'd take a slight detour to show you Pass Christian."

Just west of Menge Avenue Wojcik pointed to a large white mansion to their right. It was one of many such structures along the drive. On the front lawn was a historical marker, identifying it as "The Dixie White House."

"This house was built in 1851," Wojcik began. "Presidents Ulysses Grant and Teddy Roosevelt stayed here when they visited the Coast. And in 1913, President Woodrow Wilson spent his winter vacation here. Hence the name, Dixie White House."

"Sort of an early version of Nixon's Western White House in San Clemente," Flowers said.

Wojcik nodded in agreement. "That's a good comparison."

A few blocks farther they entered the town's business district. Except for the modern cars on the street, it gave Flowers the impression that he had been taken back to some previous generation. Off to his left he could see a picturesque small craft harbor, populated by numerous fishing boats, sailboats and small yachts.

"Pass Christian takes pride in its history, and tries to maintain a certain historic ambiance," Wojcik said. "In this regard, it's been compared to Newport, Rhode Island."

Wojcik glanced at Flowers, who had an amused grin on his face. "I suppose I sound like a tour guide."

"A little," Flowers said. "But I find it quite interesting."

"Guess we better head up to Pineville."

Flowers shrugged and said teasingly, "It's your tour."

Wojcik continued to drive through the business district. A block before the scenic drive merged once again with Highway 90 he turned right. At 2nd Street he made another right turn and proceeded east to Menge Avenue, where he turned north again. Shortly after crossing the L and N Railroad tracks they drove past the city limits of Pass Christian. A few minutes later they entered the rural community of Pineville.

At Briggs Street they turned right. No sooner had they made the turn than it occurred to Flowers that his friend had made a mistake, for there appeared to be no residences on either side of the short, gravel road. The only structure in sight was a food market on the left side of the street.

In front of the store was a tall, slender man with white hair and a gray mustache that drooped at the ends. He wore a white grocery apron and was working on a signpost that had been placed in the ground several feet east of the store's veranda.

Wojcik turned left and the unmarked sheriff's car pulled up in front of the store and stopped. Both men got out at the same time and moved as one toward the man working on the sign. As they approached the grocer, he looked in their direction but continued working on the sign.

"Afternoon, sir," Wojcik greeted. "We seem to be lost. We're looking for the Pinchon residence. It's supposed to be on this street, but..."

"You're not lost," the man said. "I'm Eugene Pinchon. We live behind the store."

"Mr. Pinchon, I'm Deputy Frank Wojcik, with the Harrison County Sheriff's Department. And this is Sergeant Garland Flowers. He's with the sheriff's department in Los Angeles, California."

Eugene Pinchon regarded both men for several seconds, but made no move to offer his hand. "I know why yall're here," he said at last. "It's because of that man that escaped from your jail. My granddaughter told me all about it." He stopped his work long enough to glare at Wojcik. "Because of yall's incompetence, Frieda's beside herself with worry. For some reason she thinks that man might come after her."

Flowers and Wojcik exchanged glances. Flowers took in a deep breath and blew it out in a sigh. On his face was an expression of genuine concern. "Mr. Pinchon, I'm afraid that you're granddaughter might be justified in her fears."

Pinchon shifted his glare from Wojcik to Flowers. "What do you mean?"

"I mean that the escapee might very well come looking for Frieda."

"And why would he do that?"

As Flowers gave the question some thought he glanced toward the store's entrance. On the other side of the screen door, behind a Colonial Bread logo that was embedded in the screen, stood a girl, or perhaps a young woman. He could not be sure because of the darkened background, but he suspected that it was Frieda Pinchon. It was obvious that she was listening to their conversation.

Flowers returned his attention to Eugene Pinchon. "Did your granddaughter tell you what happened at Woolworth?"

"Yeah, she told me."

"Did she also tell you about his claiming that she was of racially mixed blood?"

Pinchon stared at Flowers for a long moment as his glare turned into a scowl. When he spoke there was animosity in his tone. "Yeah, Sergeant. She told me that, too."

Flowers' regard for this man's feelings was beginning to fade, and it was an effort to refrain from sounding harsh when he spoke again. "Well, Mr. Pinchon, let me fill you in on some information about the escapee that you don't have."

For the next five minutes Flowers graphically related the crimes of B.C. Jones, intentionally giving details as to how each victim died. He made it a point to place emphasis on the suspect's propensity for targeting those of mixed blood. As he spoke he noticed a change come over Eugene Pinchon. The scowl was replaced by a look of concern. His eyes widened and he shifted his gaze from Flowers to the store, then back to Flowers.

A period of silence followed as Pinchon stared off in the distance. The two detectives offered no further comment, allowing the older man to absorb this new information. Flowers idly studied the signpost. It was nothing more than a four-by-four that rose seven feet above the ground. Another four-by-four extended two feet out from the top of the post at a right angle, supported by a large L-bracket. At the bottom of the extension were two metal hooks spaced one foot apart. Lying on the ground was a metal sign in the shape of an old-fashioned ice cream cone, three feet in length that tapered to a sharp point at the end. When Flowers and Wojcik first arrived, Pinchon was cutting two lengths of quarter-inch cotton rope, and while they conversed he tied one end of each length to a hook.

A full minute passed before Pinchon spoke, and when he did it was as if he was coming out of a trance. "Well, thanks for that cheerful bit news," he said. "But I believe I can take care of myself." He nodded in the direction of the store. "I keep a .357 magnum revolver behind the counter in there. I'm sure it'll stop this killer, no matter how big he is."

"I think you should let the sheriff's department handle this," Wojcik said.

Pinchon sneered. "It was the sheriff's department that caused this problem in the first place."

He turned his back to them and moved toward the ice cream sign. As he bent down to lift it Wojcik stepped forward. "Can I give you a hand with that?"

Pinchon straightened up. "Suit yourself."

"Why don't I lift the sign up to the post while you attach it," Wojcik suggested.

Pinchon said nothing, but backed away to give the younger man room. When Wojcik stooped and lifted the sign Flowers saw a look of surprise on his friend's face.

"Whew! This thing's heavy," he exclaimed.

Flowers walked over and assisted Wojcik with his burden. The sign was made of quarter-inch sheet metal and was much heavier that it appeared. Together they carried it to the post and lifted it up to the base of the extension. Pinchon stood between them and threaded the ends of the rope through a hole on each side of the metallic scoop of ice cream. This portion was painted a shade of brown to represent a chocolate flavor. When the sign was secured the two detectives stepped back and studied their handiwork.

Wojcik reached toward the sign and gave it a slight push. It swung back and forth under the four-by-four extension. "I don't know, Mr. Pinchon. Are you sure that cotton rope is going to hold the weight of the sign?"

"It'll hold 'til next week, when I get a chance to get some chain at the hardware store."

Wojcik shook his head. "I sure wouldn't want to be standing under it if the rope broke. That thing could sever a foot."

Flowers grinned. "That'd be hard to explain at cocktail parties. When asked how you lost your foot, you'd have to say it was cut off by an ice cream cone."

He glanced at Pinchon, who was frowning. Flowers concluded that the man simply had no sense of humor. The older man had gathered the excess rope and was walking toward the store, without so much as a 'thank you.' Flowers noticed that the young woman who had been standing inside the door was no longer there.

Wojcik called after the older man. "Mr. Pinchon."

Pinchon stopped and turned.

"Mr. Pinchon, I'm going to request that a surveillance be set up near the store, just in case the suspect shows up."

"Suit yourself."

"Do you have a phone I can use to call sheriff's headquarters? The sooner we set up the surveillance the better."

Pinchon pointed to a phone booth at the far end of the storefront. "There's a pay phone over there." He then resumed his walk to the store entrance, opened the screen door, and stepped inside.

Flowers looked at his friend. "Takes all kinds, I guess."

Wojcik shrugged and dug into his pocket for coins, then turned and began walking toward the phone booth.

TWENTY-FOUR

FRANK WOJCIK PARKED the unmarked sheriff's car on the south side of Briggs Street facing Menge Avenue. The store was thirty yards away, on the opposite side of the gravel road. The fact that they were parked on the wrong side of the street was of little concern to the detectives, for there was nothing on either side or behind them but woods. And from this angle they were afforded a better view of the front of the store.

It had been an hour and a half since Wojcik made the call to the sheriff's command post. He spoke to the watch commander, who at first was reluctant to dispatch a surveillance unit to Pineville, citing a shortage of manpower. After Wojcik explained the reason for fearing that Frieda Pinchon's life was in danger, however, the watch commander acquiesced, but said that it would be an hour or so before their relief would arrive.

Overhead a thundercloud moved toward them from the east, and from the west the late afternoon sun glowed faintly through a haze. The heat was stifling. For the first twenty minutes of the stakeout Wojcik had let the engine idle in order to run the air conditioner, but then he had to shut it off before the engine overheated. By the time they rolled the windows down the interior of the vehicle felt like a sauna. Both men had shed their coats hours earlier, and now their ties were loosened and their shirt sleeves were rolled up to the elbows. Their white dress shirts were stained with sweat. Flowers wondered if he could ever adjust to such a humid climate.

He watched with only half interest as a pickup truck pulled up to the front of the store and stopped. Just as the driver was getting out a car arrived and parked near the truck. At the same time another customer stepped out of the store carrying a sack of groceries and a large bag of ice.

"For such a sparsely populated area," Flowers commented, "that store sure does a good business."

Wojcik, who had been studying a county road map that was spread out across the steering wheel, looked up to observe the customer traffic in front of the store. "I doubt that it's normally this busy," he said. "My guess would be that folks are just stocking up supplies in case the hurricane decides to head this way." He paused and grinned. "And I'm sure that all this business is just breaking Mr. Pinchon's heart."

Wojcik expected his partner to chime in on the comment about the unfriendly storekeeper. Instead, Flowers said, "I had almost forgotten about the hurricane. I guess it's because I've been concentrating so much on catching our suspect before he has a chance to strike again."

"That's understandable." Wojcik looked at Flowers. "You know I do share your concern about B.C. Jones. And I think you make a good case about Frieda Pinchon being his next victim." He then shifted his gaze southward, in the direction of the Gulf. "But we can't forget the storm. The closer it gets to us the more of a factor it is going to become. If Camille makes landfall anywhere near the Mississippi Gulf Coast the search for Jones will have to be put on the back burner." He looked back at Flowers. "At least until after the storm passes."

Wojcik resumed his study of the map. Flowers watched him for several seconds, then inquired, "Mind if I ask what you're looking for?"

"I was just looking over the different routes between Gulfport and Pineville. The way I see it, there are only two practical ways to get here: either the way we came along the beach through Pass Christian, or by way of 28th Street."

Flowers craned his neck to get a better view of the map.

Wojcik turned the map to make it easier for Flowers to see. "Here, I'll show you." He put his index finger at the spot where 25th Avenue intersected 28th Street, then ran his finger to the left. This road here, 28th Street, runs west about six miles, then ends here, at Red Creek Road. As you can see, Red Creek Road goes in a southwesterly direction for about two miles. It runs into Menge Avenue, about a half a mile north of where we are now."

Wojcik then moved his finger back to the right and stopped at a spot east of 25th Avenue. "This is where Jones escaped. As you can see, it's close to 28th Street.

"Like I said, there are only two direct routes to Pineville. The beach route is too far out of the way for a man on foot. So that leaves the back way, along 28th Street."

Wojcik regarded the map in silence for a moment, then added, "I would estimate that the distance between where Jones escaped and the Pinchon store is between nine and ten miles.

"This raises a few questions in my mind about our friend, Mr. Jones." Wojcik shifted his attention from the map to Flowers. "Number one, is he smart enough to find his way here? Number two, is he willing to walk ten miles to get here? Since we've pretty well shut down all other means of transportation, walking is his only option. And number three, is he cunning enough to avoid detection?"

Flowers did not hesitate in his response. "The answer to all three questions is yes. He's con-wise enough to seek directions from someone who is not likely to volunteer information to the police. As for the distance he will have to walk, it didn't stop him the last time he committed murder."

Flowers had a vivid recollection of the night he was called away from his birthday celebration with Rochelle. It had been such a wonderful day . . . until he got the phone call.

"It was a triple homicide that took place in a community called Lawndale. Jones lived in an apartment in Watts, about seven miles away. The murders occurred some time between two and four A.M.

According to his landlady, Jones was home when she went to bed at eleven o'clock, and he was home when she got up the next morning." Flowers thought of Mrs. Thomas, and wondered what became of B.C. Jones' T.V.

"Taxi and bus service shuts down in the early morning hours in that part of L.A. So the only way he could have gotten to his victims' house was on foot. To the best of our knowledge, Jones walked seven miles, committed three murders with his bare hands, then walked back seven miles to his apartment without detection. So I would have to say yes, he is perfectly capable of covering that distance on foot.

"As for his cunning, B.C. Jones is like an animal that has located his prey. In this case, his prey happens to be Frieda Pinchon, and he's sly enough to overcome almost any obstacle to get to her."

Flowers stared vacantly toward the store as the owner of the pickup truck returned to his vehicle carrying an armload of groceries. He climbed into the cab of his truck, started the engine, and drove away. Flowers watched, but his mind was elsewhere. "I don't know what evil thing lives inside Jones that drives him to commit murder, and frankly I don't care. It apparently has something to do with his being a social outcast. And I suppose he blames his hateful black father and his cowardly white mother for his being so screwed up." Flowers breathed a deep sigh. "But that's for a psychiatrist to figure out. I'm more concerned about preventing him from murdering anyone else."

The thundercloud was now directly overhead. Flowers was disappointed that the darkening sky did not offer any relief from the sweltering heat. It remained hot and sticky. The cloud did, however, bring with it a refreshing scent of moisture in the air.

His thoughts turned to his wife and daughter. He then remembered telling Rochelle that he would be back in Los Angeles by late this evening. Tomorrow was Sunday. Perhaps he could drive to Hacienda Heights to see them. As he recalled his phone conversation with her the night before it suddenly seemed like ages ago. So much had happened since then.

Flowers made up his mind to call her when they returned to the command post to fill her in on the turn of events. He knew that it might further alienate her from his job as a homicide investigator, but she needed to know why he would not be back in L.A. this evening.

He looked at his watch. It was almost five P.M. Had things gone according to plan, he and his prisoner would have been on the plane by now. Instead, here he was on a stakeout in a village in Mississippi. Until a few hours ago he had never heard of Pineville.

Flowers' thoughts were interrupted when he saw a young woman step out of a side door near the rear of the store. It appeared to be an entrance to the residential part of the building. After descending the three steps from the landing, she ran across the gravel road and approached the sheriff's car. As she neared them Flowers recognized her as the one who had overheard their conversation with Mr. Pinchon from inside the store.

She slowed to a walk when she was ten feet away and moved to the passenger side of the vehicle. She bent forward slightly to be able to see inside the car. "Hello, officers. My name is Frieda Pinchon."

"Hello, Frieda. I'm Garland Flowers, and this is Frank Wojcik."

Wojcik smiled and waved a greeting, but said nothing.

"I overheard what you said to my grandpa," she said. "And I'd like to apologize for his rudeness." She glanced back at the store nervously, then returned her attention to the detectives. "He isn't normally like that. He's been upset all day, at least ever since I told him about what happened at Woolworth."

"You mean he didn't know about it until today?" Flowers asked.

"No. I saw no need to tell him before . . . before that horrible man escaped. It would have just upset him for no reason."

Flowers shrugged. "I suppose so." He was still not ready to believe that Eugene Pinchon was a particularly nice person.

"I also wanted to thank you for being here." She paused long enough to look at each man squarely in the eyes. Flowers looked back at a pair of eyes that were striking. There was little doubt that Frieda Pinchon would soon develop into a beautiful woman.

"Officers," she said, "this man scares me. Ever since I heard of his escape I've had a feeling that he would be coming after me. When you showed up, it just confirmed my fears."

"What gave you the idea that he would come after you?" Wojcik asked.

"It was the way he looked at me when the police were taking him away the other day." She stared into the distance, and Flowers knew that in her mind she was back behind the counter at Woolworth. "I've been haunted by that look since last Monday."

Wojcik looked at her reassuringly. "Well, don't you worry, Miss Pinchon. Someone will be parked here at least until tomorrow morning. After that, we'll see what else we can do."

It began to sprinkle. "I guess I should be getting back inside. It's been busy this afternoon, so I've been helping Grandpa. When it slowed up a bit I told him I had to take a break. I just wanted to sneak over here and let you know that I do appreciate what you're doing." She glanced again toward the store. Flowers wondered what Pinchon's reaction would be if he knew his granddaughter was out here talking to them.

"You best get inside before you get soaked," Wojcik said.

"Yes. You're right." She smiled and added. "Thank you again."

"You're welcome," both men said.

She turned and started running back across the road. Several large drops of rain splattered on the hood of the car. By the time Frieda Pinchon was opening the door to her residence behind the store, it was pouring rain. Both men quickly rolled up their windows, then Wojcik started the engine and turned on the air conditioner.

A moment later another unmarked sheriff's car turned onto Briggs Street from Menge Avenue and moved toward them. Their relief had finally arrived.

TWENTY-FIVE

AFTER THOROUGHLY BRIEFING the deputies who relieved them, Wojcik and Flowers departed. At Menge Avenue they turned right, having decided that it would be a good idea to return to Gulfport by way of the back road.

Half a mile north of Briggs Street they crossed a short bridge, beyond which the road curved to the right. After rounding the curve Flowers noticed that the name changed from Menge Avenue to Red Creek Road.

The countryside was decidedly rural. There were open fields on both sides of the road. To their left were several acres of dried corn stalks. Beyond the field was a large barn. The reddish-brown structure, which sat no more than fifty yards off the road, was a more imposing sight than the owner's modest residence. The small house could barely be seen at the end of a driveway that Flowers guessed was four times longer than Briggs Street.

The storm that began as a downpour fifteen minutes earlier had diminished and was now nothing more than light drizzle. Recalling the rain storm he had witnessed through the window of the Greyhound bus the day before, Flowers expected to see the sky suddenly clear up at any moment and the sun to come out. Yet there was no indication that it would happen any time soon.

As they continued on their northeasterly route, the open fields gave way to wooded areas, broken up occasionally by single-family homes on small lots. They had gone a short distance farther when Wojcik slowed the car and made a right turn, then proceeded east on 28th Street. The foliage on both sides of the road was as thick as a jungle. It reminded Flowers of the old Tarzan movies he saw as a youngster.

The dense woods continued for the better part of a mile, then, on the left side of the road, a large clearing opened up. Inside the clearing was, of all things, a housing project.

It was not what Flowers expected to see in such rural surroundings. Housing projects belonged in the city and were generally segregated. Yet, in this project, loitering between buildings in the light drizzle of rain, or sitting in chairs on covered porches, were a mixture of whites and blacks. Most of the residents were elderly. . .and most of them were white.

The houses were not unlike other government-owned dwellings. The exteriors were made of cinder blocks, painted in various pastel colors that were darkened by a film of dirt embedded in the pores of the concrete. There were several rows of buildings. The row that fronted 28th Street was three-tenths of a mile in length.

Flowers' expression betrayed his mild surprise, and Wojcik asked, "What's wrong, Garland? Surprised to find a housing project out here in the sticks?"

Flowers nodded. "Well, yes." He paused, then added, "But more than that, I'm somewhat surprised that it's racially integrated. I don't even see that in L.A."

"Needless to say," Wojcik began, "integration is a recent development in these parts. Until a year or so ago, this housing project was all white. But the property is owned by the government, and the tenants were given an option to either accept integration or move out. Most of them couldn't afford to move, so they accepted it."

"Have there been any problems?" Flowers asked.

"To my knowledge there haven't been any signs of racial tension, which is quite significant, considering the fact that this was one of the first racially integrated residential communities on the Gulf Coast. Of course, integration is now the law of the land, so the project doesn't stand out like it did at first."

Flowers chuckled. "I have to say, these past two days have been full of surprises. This is just the latest one."

"In what way?"

"Just what we're seeing here. Back in L.A. every housing project I've come across is either ninety-nine percent black or ninety-nine percent Hispanic or ninety-nine percent white. The races just don't seem to mix very well, especially in an impoverished community." He shook his head slowly. "It's ironic that I have to travel to the Deep South to find a housing project where two races live next to one another in harmony."

Wojcik breathed a long sigh. "It's like I told you yesterday. We've got a long way to go, here in Mississippi. But I do believe we're moving in the right direction."

Beyond the housing project they drove through another stretch of woods. On the right side of the road was a small forest of pine trees. Signs posted intermittently on the side of the road warned passersby that it was federal property. An eight foot chain link fence discouraged trespassing.

They came upon another clearing on the left side of the road. It was a residential community made up of lower income homes. Facing 28th Street was a small grocery market.

"Let's stop at this store," Flowers said.

Wojcik slowed and turned into the parking area in front of the market. "Did you see something?"

"No. But I think we ought to leave them one of the photos of Jones."

"Good idea," Wojcik replied as they both got out of the car.

There were no customers inside the market when the two detectives entered. A lone clerk sat on a stool behind the counter reading a Superman comic book. From a radio on a shelf behind the counter Bob Dylan was crooning the lyrics to *Lay Lady Lay.*

The clerk was an obese man who appeared to be in his early thirties. He had a pockmarked face and long, greasy hair. He glanced up long enough to determine that the two men were cops, then returned his attention to the comic book.

Wojcik approached the counter. "Sir, I'm Deputy Wojcik, and this is Sergeant Flowers. We'd like to ask a favor of you."

The clerk slowly looked up at Wojcik. He then shifted his gaze to Flowers and a smirk appeared on his homely face. "What kinda favor?"

Flowers produced a five-by-seven photograph of B.C. Jones and handed it to the clerk. "First, we'd like to ask if you've seen this man?"

The clerk reluctantly set the comic book aside and took the photo. He studied it for a moment, then said, "The city cops were here earlier showin' the picture around. I'll tell y'all like I told them. I ain't seen him."

"Are you sure?" Wojcik asked, beginning to get annoyed with the man's surliness.

"Yeah, I'm sure." He slapped the photo with the back of his free hand. "I know I'd recognize this nigger if I saw him. He'd be the only man around here uglier than me." He guffawed loudly at his own attempt at humor.

"The favor we'd like to ask," Wojcik said, ignoring the clerk's last comment, "is that you post this photo so your customers can see it. This man is extremely dangerous. If he comes in here, don't try to hold him. Just call the police as soon as you are able to."

The clerk stared at Wojcik, then at Flowers. "Sure, I'll put it somewhere." The sarcasm was not lost on either man.

"We'd appreciate it," Wojcik said. "There's a good chance he's somewhere in this area."

The clerk made no effort to respond. Flowers and Wojcik exchanged glances, then walked out of the store. When they were seated inside the car Wojcik looked at Flowers and grinned. "Like I said, we still have a ways to go."

THE CLERK WATCHED as the sheriff's car pulled out of the parking area and onto 28th Street. He did not like cops. In fact, he hated them. He had recently been released from the county jail, where he had spent ninety days for nothing more than beating his wife.

He could not care less about this Jones character. He was getting off work in a few minutes and would not return until Monday. So Jones meant nothing to him. Besides, why should he be doing the cops any favors? They never did anything but cause him grief.

Holding the photo between each thumb and forefinger, he tore it into two pieces, then dropped the pieces into a nearby trash can.

FLOWERS AND WOJCIK resumed their drive east on 28th Street. Shortly after leaving the market they came upon a cemetery. It stretched for half a mile on both sides of the road. A six-foot chain link fence protected the property.

"This is Evergreen Cemetery," Wojcik said. "It's by no means the only cemetery in Gulfport, but it's where most folks around here end up."

Just past the cemetery the surroundings took on an urban appearance. Small business establishments mingled with private residences, none of which reflected the slightest hint of affluence.

In the midst of the small businesses a large factory came into view on the south side of the street. It was quite apparent, from the numerous broken windowpanes and the bunch grass that flourished between the cracks of the paved parking lot, that the factory had not been operational for some time.

"That's the old MacSmith Garment Factory," Wojcik said. "From what I've been told, they made shirts there. I've heard it did quite well in the forties and fifties, but hasn't done much in the sixties. Once every few years a company will try to get it up and running, but it never seems to work out." After a pause he added, "I imagine the owners will tear it down some day to make room for a shopping center, or some such thing."

A block south of the factory they arrived at 25th Avenue. Wojcik made a right turn and they headed toward downtown Gulfport.

INSIDE THE FACTORY B.C. Jones lay on the dusty floor, sound asleep. His snores were muffled by the flattened cardboard boxes that covered him. It had taken him a few hours to relax following the appearance of the police, but during the thunderstorm he made himself a bed under the stack of cardboard and eventually drifted off to sleep.

His dreams were of a beautiful young girl who worked behind the lunch counter at Woolworth. Her name was Frieda, and she was being tormented because of her mixed blood by that other waitress named Shirley. Then the dream shifted to the man who attacked him. But the man was not a white construction worker. He was black, and had the face of B.C.'s daddy. And in the dream, instead of throwing the man onto the counter, he choked him to death. The scene then shifted back to Shirley . . . yet it was not Shirley. It was his mama, and she cowered in the corner behind the lunch counter while Frieda stood by helpless and frightened.

As Jones slept, his breathing became more labored, and he began to toss about restlessly under the stack of cardboard.

Several yards away a rat also lay on the dusty floor, never to move again. This is where it had landed after being tossed across the room by the same powerful hands that had crushed the life out of it.

IT WAS FIVE-THIRTY P.M. when they arrived at the courthouse. The rain had stopped, but the dark clouds maintained their ominous presence overhead. Flowers followed his partner up the steps, past the statue of the Confederate soldier, and into the main corridor of the old building.

Wojcik led the way to the courtroom that had been converted into a temporary command post. When he peered inside the door he found the room empty, except for one person. Morris Cruthirds, a heavyset man with a large head and drooping jowls, sat at one of the counsel tables facing the rear of the courtroom. At seventy years of age, Cruthirds was the oldest deputy sheriff in the county. Because of his advanced years, he seldom went into the field, so the sheriff normally allowed him to handle menial tasks around the office.

"Hello, Morris," Wojcik greeted.

Deputy Cruthirds looked up and waved. "Hey, Frank. 'Bout time y'all got back."

"Looks like everyone's deserted you," Wojcik said.

"Yep, they've all gone home. Everybody but Mr. Cuevas and Gertie and me. They got me answering the phones here at the C.P., and keeping the log up to date."

"You say Mr. Cuevas is still here?"

"Yep, he's in his office."

"Thanks, Morris. Be seeing you."

The old deputy grinned. "Not if I see you first."

GERTIE ALLGOOD LOOKED up from her typing when Wojcik and Flowers entered the sheriff's outer office. It had been a long day and she was tired, yet she managed to greet them with a warm smile.

"Well, look what the cat drug in," she said.

"What are you doing here so late?" Wojcik asked. "Especially on your day off."

"Well now, if y'all hadn't let that prisoner slip through your fingers," she teased, "I wouldn't have to be here on my day off."

Flowers was amused by the banter between Frank and Gertie. It was obvious they were quite fond of each other.

"I understand Mr. Cuevas is still here," Wojcik said. "What's chances of us seeing him?"

"The chances are excellent. In fact, I'm sure he'll want to see both of y'all as soon as he gets off the phone." She looked directly at Flowers and lowered her voice. "He's on the phone with your friend, Inspector Pierce."

"Why does everyone refer to him as my friend?" Flowers asked. "I don't even like the guy."

"Humph," Gertie exclaimed. "Sounds to me like you and your friend have a problem."

Before Flowers could reply, Gertie stood up. "Excuse me," she said, then disappeared into the special assistant's office, which was adjacent to the sheriff's office.

Wojcik looked at Flowers and grinned. "She's a character, isn't she."

A moment later Gertie returned to her desk. Instead of sitting down, though, she retrieved her purse from a desk drawer. "I'll be leaving now. Mr. Cuevas knows y'all are here." She pointed to an instrument on her desk. "When you hear that buzzer go off, just go on in."

She then turned her attention to Flowers, and the teasing twinkle in her eyes faded. "I'm taking a few days off and won't be back before the middle of the week. So I doubt if I will be seeing you again." Extending her hand, she added, "It's been a pleasure meeting you, Garland. If you're ever down this way again, please drop by."

Taking her hand, Flowers said, "And if you're ever out in Los Angeles, I'd love to show you around."

"You got yourself a date," she said, a touch of emotion in her voice.

"What are you going to be doing with all these days off?" Wojcik asked.

"I'm driving up to my sister's house in Laurel tomorrow morning. I want to be away from the Coast in case that hurricane heads this way."

"Laurel?" Flowers asked.

"Yes, it's a town about eighty miles north of here."

"Oh," Flowers said. "I have a sister named Laurel."

"That's a pretty name," Gertie said as she moved to the door.

As she was opening it, she stopped and turned toward Flowers. Her eyes widened as if a light had come on inside her head. "Laurel! Garland! Flowers!" She smiled broadly. "I get it! Whose idea was it to give you such clever names?"

"My mom's," Flowers said. He started to tell her about his brother, Oscar Wilde Flowers, but decided that it would be too much.

"Well, you tell your mom that I approve." With that last word, Gertie stepped through the door and closed it behind her.

Both men stared after her for several seconds. Neither of them seemed able to wipe the grins from their faces.

It was Wojcik who broke the silence. "Actually, I'm rather surprised that Gertie picked up on the name association so quickly."

"Not me," Flowers said. "I'm convinced that she and my mom both picked out their brains from the same novelty shop."

As if on cue, the buzzer on Gertie's desk sounded, and the two detectives crossed the room and entered the office of the sheriff's special assistant.

DWIGHT CUEVAS SAT behind a large oak desk and lit his pipe. He took a few quick puffs to stoke the bowl and soon the room was filled with the sweet aroma of tobacco smoke. The pipe seemed to enhance the appearance of distinction that his graying temples and handsome features already provided. Flowers decided that he looked more like the movie image of a college professor than the stereotypical southern law enforcement officer.

"Have a seat, gentlemen," he invited. When they did so, he addressed Flowers. "Before we discuss the day's events, Garland, you should know that I just got off the phone with your associate, Inspector Pierce."

Flowers was grateful that Cuevas had not referred to Pierce as either his partner or his friend.

"I must say," Cuevas continued, "that he did not sound like a happy man." He took a puff from his pipe. "Am I mistaken, or did I detect note of arrogance in his tone?"

"No, sir. You're not mistaken," Flowers said. "That's the way he comes across to everyone."

Despite the pipe stem clenched between his teeth, Cuevas managed a wry smile. "Inspector Pierce informed me that he is driving here from New Orleans tomorrow. Seems he wants to discuss the escape . . . and our inept handling of it."

A look appeared on Flowers' face that reflected a blend of surprise and embarrassment, but he made no comment.

Noting Flowers' expression, Cuevas hastened to add, "He didn't actually use the word 'inept.' I just read between the lines.

"We scheduled a meeting for ten A.M. tomorrow in this office. I would like for y'all to be here for that meeting."

"Yes sir," both men replied at the same time.

"Very well," Cuevas said. "So much for Mr. Pierce. Now I'd like to hear what y'all have been up to today."

Flowers politely deferred to Wojcik, who said, "We've been following a few leads that Flowers uncovered. Frankly, I'm convinced he has a handle on where Jones is heading."

"Yes," Cuevas said. "I'm aware of the stake-out. I just don't know the facts surrounding it."

Wojcik nodded toward his partner. "I think it would be best if Garland filled you in."

With the special assistant's concurrence, Flowers spent the next several minutes describing their activities since leaving the courthouse following the morning's briefing. He began with the visit to Doreen Brown's home, and how he was convinced that Mrs. Brown would notify them if her nephew attempted to get in touch with her. He related what he had learned from the arrest report, and why he was certain that Jones would be attempting to make his way to Frieda Pinchon. He concluded by telling of their return to Gulfport by way of 28th Street, and why he believed that Jones would be taking that route to Pineville.

When Flowers finished speaking, Cuevas looked at Wojcik. "Anything to add, Frank?"

"Only that I fully concur with everything that Garland has said."

"There's one thing that I would like to suggest, sir," Flowers said.

"Go right ahead."

"If we could saturate 28th Street and Red Creek Road with patrol cars, I'm quite sure that Jones will eventually be spotted."

"That may be true," Cuevas replied. He took another puff on his pipe and used the time to give some thought to his response. "Our only problem is that we don't have enough patrol units available to saturate the area.

"As a matter of fact the sheriff has sent two-thirds of the department home. He had to do it to keep from exhausting our resources." He paused long enough to breathe a deep sigh. "We anticipate having to place the entire department on twelve-hour shifts sometime tomorrow."

"Does that mean the hurricane is heading this way?" Wojcik asked.

"Well, at present it's heading north, toward western Florida. It also seems to be getting stronger by the hour. The weather bureau has informed us that we're definitely in for some rough weather. There's also the distinct possibility that Camille might turn in our direction, and we could get the full force of it."

Cuevas regarded Flowers with a look that revealed both sympathy and regret. "Garland, I truly wish we could give you whatever assistance you needed to catch this killer. Unfortunately, there is just so much we can do. The sheriff has the safety of the entire county to think of.

"I have a sneaking suspicion that most of tomorrow will be spent evacuating several thousand people from their homes. The safety of the community is where the focus of our attention must be, and at the moment Camille is a much greater threat to the community than B.C. Jones is."

"Yes sir, I understand," Flowers said.

"Tell you what I'll do, though," Cuevas resumed. "I'll see that the area patrol units spend as much time as they can along 28th Street and Red Creek Road. Mind you, it won't be much, but it's the best I can offer. I will also ask the sheriff to authorize the stakeout at the Pinchon residence to continue throughout the night. After that, I can't make any promises.

"In the meantime, I will assign Frank to continue to work with you on this case." He paused and a humorless smile appeared.

"Unless, of course, Inspector Pierce has other plans for you. He may decide to send you back to California tomorrow."

Flowers' brow furrowed and he frowned, but he offered no comment.

Cuevas set the bowl of his pipe in a large ceramic ashtray. "For now, I think y'all should call it a day. Get some rest, because we're all going to be busy tomorrow."

He looked at Flowers. "Garland, do you have a place to stay tonight?"

Before Flowers could offer a reply, Wojcik spoke up. "He's staying at my place, sir."

Cuevas shifted his gaze to Wojcik, then back to Flowers, and smiled. "Good."

He stood up and walked the detectives to the door and opened it. "Don't forget, I'll see y'all here at ten o'clock in the morning. In the meantime, Frank, see to the needs of your family. I recommend that you board up your windows before coming in tomorrow." He scratched his head, then smoothed down the area where the hair had become tousled. "I don't mind saying that I'm worried about this hurricane." After a brief pause, he added, "I just have a bad feeling about it."

TWENTY-SIX

WHEN B.C. JONES awoke it was pitch dark. The interior of the factory was not even afforded the partial illumination from the moon, for a thick blanket of dark clouds hid the lunar glow.

He remained under the flattened cardboard boxes for several minutes, refreshing his memory as to where he was and wondering what he should do now. He was anxious to move on. The persistent dreams of Frieda Pinchon had excited his senses, and the voice inside him was urging him to go to her.

Jones slowly arose, and the cardboard mound that covered him fell away like boulders during a volcanic eruption. He stood and stretched and tried to shake loose the stiffness caused by lying on the concrete floor for several hours. An audible growl emanating from his stomach lent emphasis to the hunger pangs that were gnawing at his insides. He had not eaten since the evening meal at the jail the night before.

He made up his mind to leave the factory the same way he had entered, and began moving slowly toward the rear of the building. It took several minutes, for he had to feel his way through the darkness. On more than one occasion he bumped into a table, or walked into one of the numerous concrete roof support columns that were located throughout the structure.

Eventually he made his way to the long table beneath the window through which he had crawled that morning. Without hesitating, Jones climbed onto the table and crawled to the window, then began exiting the building legs first. His feet found the wooden box that he had used to climb inside the building. He allowed his full weight to come to rest on the box, then he pulled the upper part of his body through the window.

Stepping off the box, he looked around and was relieved to find that it was not quite as dark as it had been inside the building. Jones made up his mind that he never wanted to be inside a place like that again. It was almost like being locked up in jail.

Although there was no moonlight, there was at least a small amount of visibility. Recalling the direction from which he had come upon the factory that morning, B.C. Jones resumed his journey. He made his way around the western side of the building and moved to the front. A moment later he was walking along 28th Street . . . ever closer to Frieda Pinchon.

IT HAD BEEN a busy day for Garland and Frank, and for Darla as well, so the entire Wojcik household decided to turn in early for the night. Darla had spent the day preparing for the coming storm, which included filling water containers, stocking up on canned goods and purchasing batteries for the flashlights and portable radio. When Frank called her from the courthouse and informed her that Garland would be spending the night at their house, she set about converting the sewing room into a guest bedroom. This chore consisted of nothing more than moving her sewing dummy and a few other items into a corner and laying out the rollaway bed.

Flowers lay on his back with his hands behind his head and stared into the darkness. He had certainly lain on softer surfaces than the thin mattress of the rollaway bed, but he was too grateful for the Wojciks' hospitality to dwell on such a minor discomfort.

Outside, a steady drizzle of rain pattered softly on the roof. Its rhythmic sound had a soothing effect and Garland could feel the day's tension slowly fading. From down the hall he could hear Frank saying something to Darla. He could not make out the words, but it must have been humorous, for she laughed. Then she made a reply and they both laughed.

He envied the closeness that Frank and Darla shared, and vowed to pursue a similar relationship with Rochelle. He would have told her so this evening had he been able to reach her. He had tried calling her before leaving the courthouse, but there was no answer. He made a second attempt after arriving at the Wojciks, and still there was no answer.

He then called Rochelle's mother, Mrs. Bullock. She informed him that Rochelle had taken their daughter and a friend to Disneyland and would not be home until late in the evening. Garland left a message that he had been delayed in Mississippi and would probably not be home until later in the week. Before hanging up, he had asked Mrs. Bullock to please let her daughter know that he loved her and wanted very much to see her as soon as he got back to L.A. Mrs. Bullock was quite fond of her son-in-law, and he was confident that she would give Rochelle the message.

The idea of being delayed a few days caused him to conjure up thoughts of Winston Pierce. He wondered how the meeting between the inspector and Dwight Cuevas would go tomorrow. He also wondered if Pierce would insist that they give up their part in the investigation and return to L.A. on the next flight. To do so would be to make Frieda Pinchon vulnerable to B.C. Jones. Cuevas had made it clear that he was leaving her fate in his and Wojcik's hands. With Flowers gone, would his friend be allowed to focus all of his attention on this one case, or would he be forced to take on other responsibilities?

All of these questions led to the one that nagged at him the most. If Pierce did, in fact, order Flowers to abandon his part in the investigation and return to Los Angeles, would he have the requisite fortitude to disobey that order?

B.C. JONES HAD walked less than three hundred yards when it began to rain. It was not like the heavy downpour that had fallen that afternoon, but more of a light shower.

A chain link fence ran along the south side of the street, and commercial buildings, closed for the weekend, occupied the north side up to the shoulder of the roadway. There was no place to go for shelter.

Like an animal caught in the open with no place to hide, Jones quickened his pace. If the police happened by, they would surely stop him. They were looking for him, and they knew what he looked like. Furthermore, he was the only person in the area who was out walking in the rain.

Somewhere within Jones' simple mental processes, these thoughts occurred to him. It was an instinct for survival. He realized that he would have to find a way to avoid walking on the side of the road as much as possible.

At the end of a long block Jones came upon a north-south street that ended at 28th Street, forming a T-intersection. On the other side was a cemetery. Without hesitation he ran across the street and began climbing the six-foot fence that marked the east border of Evergreen Cemetery.

Dropping down on the other side of the fence, he moved diagonally to the left until he came upon a lane that separated two rows of graves. Even in the darkness he could see that the narrow roadway probably ran the full length of the cemetery.

For the most part the grounds were open, with occasional growths of cedar and rows of shrubbery that separated family plots. Traditional tombstones marked most of the graves, but there were a sufficient number of above-the-ground tombs to offer concealment. Even without the burial vaults to hide behind, it was not likely that any passersby would see him. He found that, whenever a car's headlights came into view, all he had to do was squat down and he would not be seen.

The fact that Jones was alone in a cemetery at night, in the rain, caused him no discomfort at all. Though he was incapable of contemplating such thoughts, the graveyard, to him, was a sanctuary. It was a place that shielded him from detection. As for those who were at rest all around him, he was not ill at ease in their presence. Jones was not consciously aware of it, but he felt a certain envy of them, for they were now at peace. They had managed to escape the evil and the ugliness of the world.

Aside from the persistent hunger pangs, his only discomfort was from the rain, for the cemetery offered no overhead protection. So he continued along the grassy lane that paralleled 28th Street, which was fifty yards to his right. He had walked half a mile when he arrived at the north end of the cemetery property, and it was with some regret that he climbed over the fence and made his way to the roadside.

A sense of vulnerability caused him to be alert to any movement or sound. He was in the open again, and he constantly looked behind him for cars. To his left was another chain link fence, eight feet in height. Beyond it there were several structures, but he could not make out what they were. The fact that it was the northern section of the U.S. Naval Construction Battalion Center was of no interest to him. His only concern was that the fence blocked any chance of escape if the police happened by.

On the other side of 28th Street was a tract of homes. Two hundred yards farther was a grocery store. Thoughts of food began to flood his mind, and caused him to momentarily forget the dangers of being caught.

He ran across the road, then slowed to a fast walk. This side of the street was safer anyway. If a car happened by, he could duck between the houses until it passed. These were his thoughts as he moved eagerly toward the lights of the store.

MARVIN ROTH SAT on a stool behind the counter and surveyed the shelves of the store with satisfaction, for most of them were empty. It had been a busy evening, with customers purchasing virtually all of his canned goods and his entire supply of ice.

Thank God for hurricanes, he thought. They scare folks into buying things they would not normally buy.

He had already made up his mind not to open tomorrow. What would be the sense? Merchandise deliveries were not made on Sundays, and there was nothing left to sell, except for some stale pastry items and a rack half full of candy bars.

The thought of candy caused a sourness to swell within him as he was reminded of that fat, lazy Ersell, who worked the afternoon shift. A voice inside him had told Marvin two months ago not to hire that jailbird, but he didn't listen. The man was no good. Furthermore, he was eating up all the profits. Marvin had spent the first ten minutes of his shift picking up empty wrappers that Ersell had discarded after helping himself to the goodies on the candy rack. Marvin had also found a dog-eared Superman comic book stuffed behind the cash register, no longer in any condition to be sold.

It was late, and there hadn't been any customers for over an hour. Looking about the store once more, Marvin saw nothing that anyone would be likely to purchase, so he decided to close early. He would take the day off tomorrow. It would be a day of rest and relaxation. At sixty-seven years of age, he could certainly use it. After all, most folks were retired by the time they were his age.

Having made the decision to close, Marvin arose from the stool and stepped from behind the counter. He went to the window adjacent to the store entrance and removed the *OPEN* sign. On the reverse side was the word *CLOSED*. Turning it around, he placed the sign back in the window, then he moved to the door.

As he was closing it, the sudden opening of the screen startled him. Standing in the doorway, in clothes that were drenched, and with water dripping from his yellowish-brown hair, was the largest and scariest man Marvin Roth had ever seen.

A wariness came over the storekeeper. He envisioned himself being robbed, then beaten to death by this strange-looking man. There was no one around to help him. He had not seen another person in an hour or more. He knew most of his customers, at least by sight, but this man was a stranger to him.

"I . . . uh . . . I was just closing," he stammered.

"I won't be but a minute," the huge man replied. "I just need to get a bite to eat."

"We're all out of food. Canned goods, ice, almost everything is gone."

"No sweet rolls or cupcakes?" The stranger asked, suddenly disappointed.

A bell came on in Marvin's head. The wariness temporarily vanished as he thought of the prospect of getting rid of the leftover pastry that remained on the shelf.

"Well," he said with feigned reluctance. "There might be a few things left. I don't suppose it'd hurt to stay open a few more minutes."

He opened the door wider and allowed the stranger to enter the store, then showed him where the pastry could be found. Marvin then moved to his place at the cash register. He felt more secure behind the counter, as if it could serve as a protective barrier between him and this scary giant.

A minute later the customer approached the counter carrying three large packages of cinnamon rolls and a dozen chocolate moon pies. He set the items on the counter, then went to the cooler at the back of the store. A moment later he returned, holding two R.C. Colas and two cold sandwiches; a turkey salad and a ham and cheese. Marvin Roth could not hide the gleam in his eyes. He had forgotten all about those sandwiches. He could not believe his good luck.

"This is all," the customer said as he removed a wad of bills from his pocket.

Marvin calculated the figures on his adding machine, then informed his customer of the cost of the items. After he was paid, the storekeeper placed the items in a large paper sack and handed it to the customer.

As soon as the stranger with the enormous sweet tooth stepped out of the store, Marvin locked the door. Only then did he breathe a sigh of relief. What a great end to a very profitable day, he thought as he resumed his routine of closing the store.

As he was stepping behind the counter something on the floor caught his eye and he stopped. Bending down, he pulled a Hershey wrapper from underneath the counter, and he was filled with anger. This had not come from an ordinary Hershey Bar. This was the wrapper of a *giant size* Hershey. At that moment Marvin Roth made up his mind. On Monday he was going to fire that gluttonous thief Ersell.

Wadding up the wrapper, he dropped it into the trash can, atop other refuse that covered the torn remnants of a photograph. Marvin was not aware of the discarded photo. Had he seen it he would have been stricken with fear; for it was the mug shot of a murderer, and it bore a striking resemblance to his most recent customer.

THE RAIN HAD stopped by the time Jones left the store. Before he had gone five yards the gnawing pangs of hunger got the better of him and he reached into the paper sack. Pulling out a moon pie, he ripped open the cellophane wrapping and devoured the chocolate-covered cake and marshmallow in three bites. Before swallowing the last of it, he reached into the sack for a second moon pie.

He moved along at a steady pace on a sidewalk that paralleled 28th Street. It was with some relief that he came upon the housing project off to his right. He was not a stranger to housing projects, and he was fully aware that they offered safe haven from the cops. All he had to do was run between buildings if a police car happened by. That's what he had seen others do in L.A.

A surge of homesickness came over him as he thought of Los Angeles. How he wished he was back in his apartment watching cartoons on his new T.V. Then he wondered what had become of his T.V. Maybe, after he visited Frieda Pinchon, he would go back to L.A. and see if Mrs. Thomas had kept his apartment for him. If not, maybe she was at least holding his T.V. until he returned.

By the time Jones arrived at the western end of the projects he had eaten two more moon pies. Beyond the projects there were woods on both sides of the road. On the south side of 28th Street a tall fence separated the road from the woods, so he remained on the north side, where there was no fence.

He had walked beside the woods for a few hundred yards when a set of headlights came into view in front of him. As soon as Jones saw them he darted into the thick brush to his right. This was not an act resulting from conscious thought, but was a reaction to danger based on animal instinct. When he had gone twenty feet he squatted down behind a tree.

The car slowed when it approached the vicinity of where Jones had run into the woods. Then a spotlight came on and its beam danced all around the trees and bushes that surrounded him. The vehicle came to a complete stop and Jones crouched lower. He wanted to lie flat on his stomach, but was afraid to move. The light shined all around, but the jungle-like foliage concealed him.

The two occupants of the vehicle were sheriff's deputies. One of them thought he had glimpsed movement at the side of the road. It might have been a person, or an animal, or perhaps the deputy's imagination. The search with the spotlight had been done half-heartedly, for neither deputy was completely convinced that it was anything at all. Any thought of getting out of the car and investigating further by traipsing through the wet jungle growth was completely out of the question. After a minute of searching, the driver turned off the spotlight and the deputies slowly drove away.

B.C. Jones remained motionless for a full five minutes after the car had gone. Another car passed along the road at a normal rate of speed. As he sat behind the tree with his weight resting on the backs of his legs the inner voice began talking to him. It instructed him to stay off the road, or he would be seen. If he were seen he would be caught, and would be unable to rescue Frieda Pinchon from all the people in the world who wanted to cause her pain. At the voice's urging Jones stood and slowly made his way deeper into the woods.

When he had gone ten yards he came upon a footpath that ran east and west, parallel with the road. The path was barely as wide as Jones, but it did allow him to escape the constant slapping of wet branches against his face and body.

He had moved along the narrow path for only a few minutes when he came upon a clearing. It was twenty feet in diameter, and in the center of it was what appeared to be a small shed. It was about eight feet square and no more than five feet high. The sides were constructed of mismatched boards that were nailed vertically at uneven heights. The roof was covered with tarpaper.

The sudden appearance of the small building puzzled him and he approached it with caution. B.C. Jones had never had friends, and had never experienced the fun of being part of a group of boys who formed clubs and built clubhouses in wooded areas or vacant lots in communities across the country. This was one such clubhouse, and had been constructed by boys who lived in a neighborhood at the northern edge of the woods.

But this was not a night for kids to be out romping in the woods, and Jones had it all to himself. As he moved closer to the strange little house it began to rain again. He hunched forward to protect the contents of the paper sack that was clutched to his chest.

The door to the clubhouse was four feet high. Jones opened it carefully and peered into the darkness. He could see nothing, but neither was there any sound or movement. Convinced that it was empty, he dropped to his knees and, with one hand on the ground for support and one holding onto the sack of food, crawled inside.

On the floor of the clubhouse was a rug. Jones knew that it was a rug because it had ridges in it, like several ropes tied together side by side. Auntie Doreen had a rug like that in her bedroom. He felt a sense of security as he crawled on the rug that reminded him of his stay at Auntie Doreen's house.

It was dry inside the little house and B.C. Jones sat cross-legged in the middle of the room, the paper sack in his lap. He reached into the bag and pulled out both sandwiches and one of the R.C. Colas.

As he ate he began to relax. He was safely hidden from the cops, he had food in his stomach and he was dry. He was glad that he had listened to the voice inside him, for it had led him to this place. As B.C. Jones chewed his meal, he stared into the darkness and listened to the soft rain falling on the tarpaper roof . . . and waited for the voice to fill his head with thoughts of Frieda Pinchon.

TWENTY-SEVEN

Sunday
August 17, 1969

GARLAND FLOWERS AWOKE to the inviting aroma of fried bacon and freshly perked coffee. The soft drizzling rain that had lulled him to sleep the night before was gone. In its place was a soft breeze that rustled the leaves of the trees.

Looking at his watch, he saw that it was almost seven o'clock. He had slept for more than eight hours. The rollaway bed had obviously not been a deterrent to his getting a good night's sleep.

He removed the top sheet that covered him and sat up, swinging his legs onto the floor. He retrieved the slacks he had worn the day before from the foot of the bed and slipped into them, then sat back down on the bed. After yawning and scratching his head, he leaned forward and reached into the open suitcase that he had placed on the floor near the bed the night before and removed his shaving kit, toothbrush and a change of clothes. He held the items in his lap for several seconds while he shook the last vestiges of sleep from his head, then slowly stood, and made his way to the upstairs bathroom.

As he moved down the hallway he could hear Kathy and Becky playing in the living room. From the sounds of utensils being moved about, it was apparent that Darla was in the kitchen. Somewhere in the background he could hear the faint sound of either a radio or television. He could not tell if Frank was awake yet, but assumed that he was. The fact that he had the entire upstairs to himself gave him a sense of privacy, as well as the comforting feeling that he was not intruding into the Wojciks' routine.

Twenty minutes later, having shaved and showered, Flowers returned to his room and finished dressing, then went downstairs. As he passed through the living room he made a teasing comment to the girls, who both giggled, then resumed their game.

In the kitchen he found Darla in front of the stove scrambling eggs. On a nearby counter top was a portable radio, through which a weatherman was providing the latest update on Hurricane Camille.

"Morning, Darla," Flowers greeted.

"Good morning, Garland. Sleep well?" Darla asked as she reached over and turned off the radio.

"Like a log."

"I heard the shower running," she said. "Looks like you're all gussied up and ready for the day."

Flowers glanced down at the clothes he was wearing and grimaced. "I think I've got one more change of clothes, then I won't have anything left to get gussied up in."

"Bring all of your dirty things downstairs and I'll throw them in the wash with ours. I'm washing everything I can this morning." Darla paused and frowned. "I'm afraid we may not have water or electricity for the next several days."

Flowers looked at her questioningly. "How's that?"

She nodded toward the radio. "We've been following the weather reports this morning. Hurricane Camille changed direction sometime during the night." A somber tone came into her voice when she added, "It's heading straight for us."

Having never experienced a hurricane, Flowers was not quite sure how to respond. After a moment he asked, "When do they think it'll hit?"

"Late tonight." Darla breathed a sigh, then added, "According to the reports it's a very strong hurricane . . . stronger than any I've ever heard of. They're saying that, near its eye, the winds are over a hundred and eighty miles an hour."

"A hundred and eighty!" Flowers repeated. He could not fathom a wind that strong.

"They said that the waters in the Sound could rise twenty feet above normal, with ten foot waves on top of that."

Flowers tried to envision the calm waters of the Mississippi Sound in such violent upheaval, but found it difficult.

The back door opened and Frank Wojcik entered the kitchen. "Morning, Garland," he greeted with a smile.

"Morning, Frank."

"I suppose Darla has filled you in on the latest news."

"If you mean the hurricane, we were just talking about it."

"Y'all are just in time for breakfast," Darla said as she picked up a platter filled with scrambled eggs and carried them into the dining room.

After Frank washed his hands at the kitchen sink, he and Garland followed Darla and each took a seat at the table, where hot biscuits, butter, jam, orange juice and a platter of bacon and sausage patties had already been placed. Darla summoned the girls to breakfast, then took a seat next to Frank.

As platters of food were being passed around, Garland shook his head and declared, "I can't imagine the five of us eating all of this."

"Probably not," Darla said. "But I decided that I might as well cook it anyway. If we lose our electricity it's going to spoil."

"That reminds me," Frank said. "We need to turn the refrigerator up to maximum cold. That way, if we lose power, it'll take longer for the food to go bad."

"Oh yes," Darla said. "You also asked me to remind you to remove the attic crawl space door."

"I'll do that right after breakfast."

Garland looked questioningly at Frank. "What's the purpose of opening the attic?"

"It's important to allow air to flow under the roof. If we fail to do so, it's quite possible that the pressure created by hurricane-force winds could take the roof off." He paused for emphasis. "It would almost be like an explosion. To equalize air pressure we should also keep a window open on the leeward side of the house."

Frank then thought of something else. "By the way, Garland, could I get you to help me put the plywood over the windows?"

"Of Course," Garland replied.

"I know we have to be at that meeting at ten o'clock. But I have the window covering routine down to a science, so it shouldn't take long." Frank smiled and a gleam of pride showed in his eyes. "Right after Hurricane Betsy hit us in '65, I decided to tailor-make our window coverings. I cut each sheet of plywood to match a specific window. I then drilled a hole in each corner of the wood, as well as a matching hole in the corner of each window frame. In each window frame hole is a threaded sleeve. So, all we have to do is set the plywood in place and screw a wing bolt into each hole. I've already taken the plywood out of the shed and placed each sheet under its matching window."

Darla smiled admiringly at her husband. "Isn't he a genius? He even made little covers for the holes in the window frames so they can't be seen when not in use."

Frank nodded his head toward Darla and addressed Garland. "See this lady here?" He puffed out his chest and grinned. "I'm her hero."

"You're *one* of my heroes," she said.

"Oh? And who else might I be in competition with?"

She looked at him teasingly. "Well, now, let me think. There's John Wayne, Elvis . . . and Archie Manning, of course."

"Of course," Frank replied with mock jealousy.

Darla looked up at him and batted her eyes. "But you're the biggest hero of them all."

"Thanks," he said, pretending to mend his deflated spirits.

Garland was amused by their playful exchange.

For the next few minutes they all concentrated on their breakfast. Occasionally either Frank or Garland would make a complimentary remark to Darla on her cooking skills. Otherwise, the meal was enjoyed in silence.

Finishing the last bite from his plate, Garland set his fork down and took the first sip from his second cup of coffee.

"You're not quitting so soon, are you?" Frank teased.

Garland patted his stomach and shook his head. "I couldn't eat another bite." He looked at Darla. "Everything was delicious."

"Thank you," she replied.

Garland took another sip of coffee and set his cup down. "Just before you came into the house, Darla was telling me that the water out in the Sound could rise as high as twenty feet, with ten foot waves on top of that."

"That's right," Frank said. "That's the storm surge I was telling you about on Friday."

"But all those beautiful homes and businesses along the beach . . . they can't be more than eight or ten feet above sea level."

"Right again."

"Is there anything that can be done to protect them?" Garland asked.

Frank shook his head solemnly. "The owners can board them up as best they can, pray that the weather forecasters are wrong, and evacuate to higher ground." He took in a deep breath and blew it out in a long sigh. "I'm just glad this house is far enough away from the water not to be affected by the storm surge. Our biggest concerns up here are the strong winds, heavy rain . . . and tornadoes."

"That sounds bad enough," Garland said.

"That's true. But most of the damage, and ninety percent of the deaths, will occur within a mile of the water. In fact, most of the city and county emergency service agencies will be spending the day evacuating everyone from along the coast." He frowned, then added, "Of course, there will be that small percentage that think they can ride it out. They're the ones we'll be digging out of the rubble this time tomorrow."

Frank looked at his watch. "We'd better get busy. That meeting starts in less than two hours."

BECAUSE HE HAD slept much of the previous day, B.C. Jones spent most of the night lying on the rug in the clubhouse, staring into the darkness. Wadded up on the floor nearby was an empty paper sack. It lay amidst wrappers that had once covered cinnamon rolls, chocolate moon pies and sandwiches. Both R.C. bottles were also empty.

An hour before dawn he finally managed to fall asleep, but awoke as soon as it became light. He felt slightly nauseated, and his stomach was in turmoil. With an effort he sat up, and thought for a moment that he was going to vomit.

The air inside the clubhouse was stale, and the voice from within told him to go outside and breathe in some fresh air. Crawling on hands and knees he moved toward the door, then stopped. He reached back and retrieved the paper sack and stuffed it in his back pocket.

Jones was met by a gentle breeze as he stood outside the boys' clubhouse. He took in a deep breath and blew it out. Once again the voice inside him was right. The fresh air did cause the nausea to subside. His stomach, however, was another matter, and he was glad that he had the paper sack . . . just in case.

Finding the path at the opposite side of the clearing from which he had entered the night before, Jones continued on his quest to find Frieda Pinchon.

But he was on the trail for less than ten minutes when his stomach began to cramp, and he felt a desperate urge to answer a call of nature. Afterward, having relieved the nausea as well as the pain in his stomach, he felt much better, and moved along the path with a lighter step.

The breeze seemed to be growing in strength, and it caused the trees and foliage of the forest to come alive with movement and sound. The wind on his face felt good. He also liked the rattling of the leaves in the trees and the rustling of the bushes all around him.

Jones had walked another twenty minutes when he came upon a narrow dirt road that ran perpendicular to the footpath. He approached it cautiously. When he arrived at the side of the road he looked in both directions. It was clear. To his left, a hundred yards away, the dirt road ended at 28th Street.

Directly across the road the growth of woods continued. He studied the terrain in front of him until he found that for which he was searching. The path that he had followed resumed on the other side. Taking another look in both directions, he darted across the road and into the woods. He ran along the path until he felt the security of the dense forest all around him. Only then did he slow to a walk.

He moved along at a steady pace for half a mile before coming upon another road that cut through what he was beginning to consider his domain. Taking the same precautions as before, he crossed over and resumed his journey westward.

B.C. Jones gave no thought to the fact that there was little evidence of animal life on this particular windy morning, such as rabbits, squirrels and birds. To a naturalist, the absence of such critters would be significant, but it meant nothing to Jones. His only concern was to move ever closer to his destination without getting caught.

TWENTY-EIGHT

IT WAS THREE minutes before ten A.M. when Flowers and Wojcik ascended the steps of the courthouse and walked hurriedly toward the sheriff's office. Wojcik had not intended to arrive quite this late, but the drive into town took longer than he had anticipated. The roads were already becoming congested with vehicles containing coast residents who had heard the news of the coming hurricane and were leaving town. Fortunately for the two detectives, the southbound lanes of Highway 49, though busier than normal, were not as bad as the northbound lanes, heading out of Gulfport.

Later in the day it would get worse, when those who had put off their departure until the last minute finally decided to leave. The stress of leaving their homes to the mercy of the storm would be compounded as they all converged on the roads at once in a desperate attempt to evacuate before it was too late.

Flowers followed his friend into the sheriff's outer office. Seated at Gertie's desk was Deputy Morris Cruthirds.

"Why, Gertie," Wojcik teased. "I hate to say this, but you're getting uglier by the day."

The old deputy grinned. "Mornin', Frank." He pointed to a clock on the wall. "Cuttin' it a little close, ain't you?"

"Traffic was a bit heavy this morning."

"Yeah. The smart ones are leavin' early."

Wojcik nodded toward the door to Dwight Cuevas' office. "Has Inspector Pierce arrived yet?"

"Yeah. Got here about twenty minutes ago." Cruthirds made a face. "Not what you'd call a friendly cuss." He then looked at Flowers apologetically. "No offense, Sergeant Flowers."

Flowers smiled. "None taken."

Cruthirds arose and moved to the office door. He tapped lightly, then stuck his head in. A moment later he turned back to Wojcik and Flowers. "Mr. Cuevas says to come on in."

Cuevas, who was seated behind his desk, smiled and motioned for the two detectives to step inside. Seated on the opposite side of the desk, with his back to the door, was Inspector Winston Pierce. He made no attempt to turn in their direction as they entered.

Flowers sat in the chair next to Pierce. He would have preferred to sit much farther away, but decided that this was the appropriate place for him to be. Wojcik took a seat in the only other chair in the room, which was to the left of the large desk. He adjusted its position so that he was able to see Cuevas, Pierce and Flowers equally. He did not want to appear intrusive. So far as he could tell, his role was that of a spectator.

Pierce sat with one leg crossed over the other at the knee. A Pall Mall cigarette extended from a three-inch holder. When Flowers introduced Frank Wojcik, Pierce merely nodded in Wojcik's direction and offered a condescending smile.

Cuevas removed his pipe and a pouch of tobacco from a desk drawer and began filling the bowl of the pipe. "I was just giving Inspector Pierce an update on the events of the past two days," he began. "It seems that he only this morning learned of the hurricane, and that it is due to hit us tonight."

Flowers and Wojcik exchanged glances. They were both recalling Flowers' phone conversation with Pierce from the motel room on Friday afternoon, when Pierce was informed that Camille was heading in the general direction of the Gulf Coast.

Pierce took a long drag from his cigarette, then held it between two fingers as his elbow rested on the arm of his chair, his forearm extending upward. After slowly blowing the smoke from his mouth he said, "Well, now, I could hardly be expected to sit in front of the T.V. all day watching the local news, could I?" His patronizing smile had moved from Wojcik to Cuevas. "Especially with all the activity going on a few blocks away, in the French Quarter."

Cuevas forced a humorless smile. "Of course not."

"However," Pierce continued, "considering the fact that no progress has been made in the capture of our suspect, I've decided to step in and take over the investigation."

Flowers stared at Pierce in disbelief. He was both astounded and embarrassed by what his superior had just said. A silence fell over the office for several seconds. Flowers stole a glance at Cuevas and he could see the anger in the man's face.

Dwight Cuevas slowly set the bowl of his pipe in the large ceramic ashtray. His jaw muscles tightened as he stared directly into the eyes of Winston Pierce. In a deep, commanding voice he said, "Let's get something straight right now, Inspector. I am quite confident that I speak for our sheriff when I say that, not you, nor your department, nor any other local authority is going to come into this county and 'take over' anything."

Pierce found himself unable to meet the penetrating stare of Cuevas, and he shifted his eyeballs to left and right, then downward. A sheepish expression appeared on his face. "Well, now, uh . . . I didn't mean to infer that..."

"Yes, you did, Inspector. You did mean to infer that we're just a bunch of incompetent buffoons down here in Mississippi. You've looked down your nose at us ever since arriving in New Orleans."

Pierce looked angrily at Flowers.

"No, Inspector," Cuevas continued, "Sergeant Flowers has not been bad mouthing you. I came to this conclusion after talking to you on the phone last night, and your attitude this morning merely confirmed it."

"I assure you, Mr. Cuevas..."

Cuevas ignored Pierce's attempt at rebuttal. "You say you've decided to come here and take over the investigation. I don't know what your background is, Inspector. As for myself, I came to work for Harrison County after spending twenty years in the F.B.I., and I'm willing to pit my investigative skills against yours any day of the week."

Pierce made no further attempt to respond. He stared out the window behind Cuevas, and focused on a view of the Markham Hotel a block away. This was not at all what he expected. Perhaps he had come on too strongly. The fact was, he had no desire whatsoever to be involved in this case. But how could he let them know that it was not his idea to be here? He was here because he had called Chief Maxwell in Los Angeles the previous night to give him an update on the status of the extradition. To his surprise the chief had ordered him, in no uncertain terms, to make himself available to the Harrison County Sheriff. He was directed to offer his assistance in putting closure on this case. If it appeared that the escapee would not be apprehended within a day or so, he and Flowers were to return to Los Angeles until the suspect was found.

Flowers was relieved to see the jaw muscles of Cuevas begin to relax, and when the sheriff's special assistant spoke again, it was in a softer tone.

"I apologize for blowing up like I did, but you happened to hit a sensitive nerve. I'm sure that your department would react the same way if another department tried to come in and take command of an investigation that rightfully belonged to your sheriff.

"The escape that occurred yesterday morning was clearly a blunder on our part, but the fact is that it could have happened with any agency, even the L.A. County Sheriff's Department.

"Now, if you wish to offer your assistance in trying to find the suspect, we would be pleased to have you. Lord knows we need all the help we can get.

"As we were discussing earlier, Sergeant Flowers and Deputy Wojcik have worked diligently on this case. Sergeant Flowers has convinced me that he has a lead on where the escapee is heading. Frankly, I think that he should be allowed to follow that lead." Cuevas paused long enough to breathe a sigh. "The biggest concern the rest of us have right now is the hurricane. We'll be spending most of the day evacuating thousands of people from their homes."

He looked at Wojcik. "Frank, the sheriff has authorized you to continue to work with Garland on the escape." He then addressed Flowers. "Garland, you'll be relieved to know that the surveillance at the Pinchon residence has been extended for a few more hours." He frowned and added, "Eventually, though, as the storm gets closer, we'll have to pull them off."

Cuevas then returned his attention to Pierce. "So what do you think, Inspector? Can we count on you to assist in the capture of the escapee?"

Winston Pierce was slow to reply. At the moment he hated Cuevas for humiliating him in front of a subordinate. The softened tone of the special assistant caused Pierce's arrogance to resurface. He placed the cigarette holder between his lips and took a long drag from the Pall Mall. After removing the holder from his mouth and holding it between his fingers with his upturned arm resting on the arm of the chair, he blew the smoke from his nostrils.

"I think not, Mr. Cuevas," he said at last. "It has been over twenty-four hours since our suspect flew the coop. As I understand, there has been no trace of him since his escape. In all probability he is hundreds of miles away by now.

"As for Sergeant Flowers and me, we'll be returning to New Orleans, then on to Los Angeles on the next available flight. If the suspect ever shows up around here again and you manage to hold onto him, by all means give us a call."

Pierce arose from his chair and turned toward Flowers. "Shall we go, Sergeant Flowers?"

Flowers remained seated. He exchanged glances with Wojcik and Cuevas, then he turned and looked up at Pierce. "I can't leave now, Inspector."

"I beg your pardon?"

"I said I can't leave now, sir."

"Then let me put it another way. I'm giving you a direct order. You are to accompany me back to Los Angeles now!"

Flowers swallowed, then slowly stood up and faced Pierce. "Inspector, you heard what Mr. Cuevas said. His whole department is going to be tied up on this hurricane. In the meantime, there is a young lady whose life is in danger. I'm convinced that B.C. Jones is still in the area, and he is going to try to find her and kill her." After swallowing again, he added, "I can't abandon her now, sir."

"Did it occur to you, Sergeant, that this is no longer your concern? If the woman dies, the fault will lie with them," he nodded toward Cuevas and Wojcik, "not you."

Flowers could feel the anger rising inside him. "I'm not concerned about whose fault it will be if she's killed. I'm concerned with saving her life."

Pierce stared coldly at Flowers. In almost a whisper he said, "Suit yourself."

Suit yourself. For a fleeting moment Flowers thought of Eugene Pinchon. Those had also been his words. *Suit yourself.* What kind of cold-blooded arrogance caused Winston Pierce and Frieda Pinchon's own grandfather to have such similar reactions concerning her fate?

Pierce reached into a pocket of his coat and removed an airline ticket. Handing it to Flowers, he said, "Here. Take this. It's for your return flight. From this moment forward you're on your own time, therefore I don't feel that it would be appropriate to give you any more expense money. You'll just have to make do as best you can."

Flowers accepted the ticket. "I don't need any money."

Pierce turned and walked to the door. As he was opening it, he looked back at Flowers. "We'll discuss this further when you return to Los Angeles."

"Yes, sir," Flowers replied as he watched Pierce walk out the door.

No one spoke for the better part of a minute. Just as the three men were beginning to feel uneasy with the silence, Flowers said, "I hope you don't judge our department by Inspector Pierce."

"Not to worry," Cuevas replied. "Every organization has its share of pompous jerks who are filled with an overblown sense of self-importance." He smiled warmly and added, "Besides, if I was inclined to judge your department, I would judge it by you, Garland. Not by him."

Flowers assumed he was being paid a compliment, but made no reply.

Wojcik spoke up for the first time. "I imagine Inspector Pierce could make it rough on you when you get back."

"I suppose so," Flowers said.

"Maybe there's something we can do," Cuevas said. "Last year our two sheriffs had occasion to meet at the National Sheriff's Conference. Tomorrow, after this hurricane blows over, I'm sure our sheriff would be willing to call yours and fill him in on what's been going on here. I'll write a nice follow-up letter from the sheriff. That should help to smooth things over for you."

Flowers managed a half-smile. "I would appreciate it."

"I wouldn't worry, Garland," Wojcik put in. "After your sheriff gets the phone call and the letter, I have a hunch that Inspector Pierce will be the one called on the carpet."

TWENTY-NINE

B.C. JONES CAME upon the structure quite unexpectedly. One moment he was walking along the narrow path amidst a thick growth of bushes and pine trees, and the next moment he was in the backyard of a ramshackle old house. The clearing that surrounded the place was cluttered with the remains of washing machines, refrigerators and stoves. Automobile tires and other discarded items were also scattered about the yard, partially hidden by a growth of tall grass and weeds.

Near the back porch a pipe extended four feet above the ground, with a faucet attached to the top. Jones had been longing for a drink of water all morning. The sweets that he had devoured throughout the night had caused him to awaken with a terrible thirst. If there was no one around, perhaps he could get a drink.

Though the house appeared to be abandoned, Jones was wary. He moved along the southern edge of the property line, as if continuing his trek through the woods, until he was adjacent to the front yard. He then noticed that the house fronted a paved road. Across the road the woods continued westward.

The breeze that had been blowing all morning, entertaining Jones with a constant rustling of leaves and branches as he moved along the path, had grown in intensity, and was now more of a wind than a breeze. Though it was not quite as noisy after he stepped out of the woods and into the clearing, the wind felt stronger in the open area. Jones could feel its slight force against his back as he moved cautiously across the yard and up the steps of the front porch.

The torn screen door had been detached from its hinges and tossed aside, where it rested against the porch railing. The wooden door was slightly ajar. Jones pushed his head into the opening and peered inside. The front room was void of furniture. On the dusty floor was glass from a broken windowpane.

The door creaked when he pushed it open and stepped inside, and there was an echo as he moved throughout the four-room house. In the bedroom Jones found a mattress on the floor. Scattered about were several food wrappers and cigarette butts. The walls were filled with graffiti depicting various slogans denouncing the war in Vietnam. In the midst of the slogans was the peace sign. Its circle was three feet in diameter.

Jones made no attempt to decipher the writings on the wall, for their messages held no significance to him. He had no opinion about the war whatsoever. Politics in any form were beyond the boundaries of his thought process.

Jones went out the back door. Crossing the open porch, he descended the steps and proceeded to the hydrant. He turned the faucet handle and water flowed out with more pressure than he had anticipated. Before he could turn it down part of his shirt, having only recently dried from the previous night's rain, became drenched. After adjusting the pressure, he put his head under the faucet and drank. The water was cool and refreshing.

After drinking his fill he walked around the side of the house and sat on the steps of the front porch. Jones was at a loss as to what he should do next. He wondered about the road that passed in front of the house, and whether or not it was the one that would take him to Pineville. He was aware that the road that he had taken from the factory was off to his left somewhere. The road in front of the house probably met the other road a short distance from where he sat.

Jones recalled what those two men told him yesterday morning. He was to take the first road for about six miles, then turn left.

Was this where he was supposed to turn left? It sure seemed like he had gone six miles.

Or should he continue through the woods?

Across the road and slightly to the left Jones could see where the path resumed. Without further contemplation he arose from the steps and walked to the edge of the road, then crossed it at an angle toward the path.

MILDRED WATSON DIPPED her fingers into the holy water, then made the sign of the cross as she moved toward the exit of St. Thomas Catholic Church in Long Beach. At the door she was met by a strong wind blowing in off the Gulf. She descended the steps, then stopped and looked out over the water, oblivious of the other members of the congregation who had also come out of the church and were milling about all around her.

Mildred overheard several comments about the hurricane that was heading their way. Observations were made concerning the rising water level and the three-foot surf that was crashing onto the beach. Two teenage boys announced that they were going home and change into their swimming trunks, then go down to the beach and try a little body surfing.

For the most part the mood was jovial, but not for Mildred Watson. There was nothing jovial about the way she felt, for she was frightened. She had lived all of her fifty-two years on the Mississippi Gulf Coast, and she had weathered many storms. She had gone through the '47 hurricane in the same house she lived in now. They had lost some shingles off the roof, and two large oak trees had blown down, but that was the extent of the damage. She had also gone through Hurricane Betsy and numerous tropical storms with no trouble.

But there was something about this new storm that gave her a sense of foreboding. According to the latest news bulletins Hurricane Camille was growing stronger by the hour, and Long Beach was directly in its path. The rising seas and the wind in her face were like a message from Camille, telling Mildred it was out there, and was headed her way.

She wanted very much to be away from here. If she had had her way, she and her husband, Earl, would have boarded up their house early this morning and driven up north. They could have stayed at a motel in Jackson, or Meridian.

But Earl would not hear of it. He reminded her that he was in the lumber business, and, because of the hurricane, this weekend would probably generate more sales than any other two days of the year. He had even sent two large trucks up to the northern part of the state on Saturday morning to pick up a load of plywood in anticipation of the demand that was sure to come. He had remained at the lumberyard until ten o'clock Saturday night, and was back at work at six o'clock Sunday morning. Normally he attended Sunday Mass with his wife, but not this morning, for today there was money to be made.

Mildred had offered a mild protest as Earl was walking out the door, and he shot back an impatient response. He invited her to look around at the luxuries that surrounded her. They lived in a beautiful beachfront home in Long Beach. It was a large, two-story house with white columns in front, reminiscent of the antebellum era in the South. Each of them drove their own late model Cadillac. She wore fine jewelry and had a generous allowance. She had all these things because of her husband's ability to make money.

In the 1940's he had opened a small lumber outlet on the Pass Road in Handsboro. After years of long hours and hard work his business developed into one of the most successful building supply companies on the Coast. Earl Watson had learned, over the years, to take advantage of moneymaking opportunities, and this weekend offered a great opportunity.

Mildred breathed a deep sigh, then slowly made her way to the parking lot. Occasionally she would nod a half-hearted greeting to an acquaintance. She felt a little guilty at her lack of social presence, for these were nice people, and they were her neighbors. Furthermore, Camille was coming for them, as well as for her.

Though she was quite aware of all this, the sense of foreboding denied her the ability to manage any semblance of a genuine smile.

As she was opening the door to her car, Mildred glanced up at the church. There was a quaint charm about St. Thomas that, for many years, had endeared it to the community. The beauty of the white, wooden structure could be found in the simplicity of its design. The building would have blended in naturally in any New England town a hundred years earlier. It might have been a place of worship in New Bedford, Massachusetts during the days of whaling ships called *Pequod* and sea captains named Ahab. It had that look about it.

Mildred Watson lingered longer than she had intended, as if reluctant to leave an old friend. And she would have been even more reluctant to depart had she known that the Mass that she had just attended would be the last that would ever be conducted within the walls of that beautiful old church.

THIRTY

THE SKY BECAME sullen and the wind grew stronger as B.C. Jones made his way through the woods. Though the path was wider than it had been on the other side of the paved road, he did not like this section of woods. There was a downward slope to the terrain, and a dampness on the ground that reminded him of the banks of that smelly canal where he made his escape the day before.

Jones wanted to turn back, but was not sure where he would go if he did so. Besides, there was a sense of progress in forward motion. This was not a thought that he was capable of contemplating, but was more a feeling that he had inside of him. B.C. Jones was a person who lived by instinct, and was guided by voices in his head. For the past hour the voices had not spoken. It was his instinct, therefore, that pushed him forward.

He had been on the path for no more than fifteen minutes when he noticed an opening in the woods. It was downhill from where he was, and at first he thought it was a wide road, with trees and bushes growing on either side of it. Then he heard the sound of running water. It was loud enough to be heard even above the noises created by the wind.

He had come upon a river.

BILLY RAY LOVE knelt on one knee on the grassy bank of Wolf River and pulled in his trout line. It was one of several lines that he had placed along the river's edge the night before. He could tell, even before they were near the surface, that the hooks were empty. It had been the same all along the river. It was the first time in his memory that he would go home without so much as a single fish.

No fish in the stream, he thought, and no game in the woods. Must have somethin' to do with this danged herrycan. He curled his upper lip against his gums and spat a stream of snuff through a gap that had once been occupied by a front tooth. He thought again of his bad luck and loudly issued a string of profanities. The strong wind coming from the south was blowing against the flow of the river, causing a turbulence that was certainly the reason for the fish not biting. If nothing else, it was stirring up the mud in the river bottom.

He was gathering the string of fishhooks when he heard the sound coming from upwind. Still kneeling, he looked over his shoulder and to his left, and was startled to see someone lumbering down the path. Billy Ray stood up just as the huge man emerged from the woods.

He was at a loss as to how to react to the sudden appearance of this odd-looking stranger. His size alone was enough to intimidate the average man. At five feet nine inches and weighing one hundred forty pounds in his Payday overalls, Billy Ray counted himself among those who could easily be intimidated by the man's enormous bulk. But there was something else about him—something frightening in his face. It was not just the man's ugly features. It was more of a look in his eyes. They were cold and expressionless.

There was also something familiar about this person, yet Billy Ray knew everyone hereabouts, and he knew that this man, who was part black and part white, did not belong around here. Yet he had seen that face somewhere quite recently.

When the stranger saw Billy Ray he stopped, a look of surprise on his face.

Billy Ray summoned the courage to smile, revealing an empty space surrounded by a mouthful of teeth stained brown by frequent use of snuff and chewing tobacco. "Howdy!" He greeted.

The stranger nodded slightly, but said nothing.

"Ain't seen you around here before."

The big man stared at Billy Ray for several seconds before replying. "I ain't from around here."

"Where you from?" Billy Ray asked.

"L.A."

"L.A.?" Billy Ray looked questioningly at the stranger. Then it came to him. "Oh! You mean Los Angeles. Hot Dang! That's a long ways from here."

The stranger made no attempt to reply to this observation.

"Where you headin'?" Billy Ray asked.

"Pineville."

"Pineville?" Billy Ray grinned and shook his head. "Man, you're headin' in the wrong direction."

A sudden look of concern appeared on the stranger's face. "Which way do I go?"

"You got to go back up the way you came . . . back up the path to Red Creek Road. That's that paved road you just came down from. When you get up there, turn right and stay on it for two or three miles. It'll take you right into Pineville."

The strange man nodded again and turned back toward the path. As he did so, it suddenly occurred to Billy Ray where he had seen this man. It was in a picture that was thumb tacked to a bulletin board at the Jitney Jungle in Gulfport. This was that man who escaped from the Harrison County Jail.

A sudden thrill, born of a combination of fear and greed, raced through Billy Ray Love. The origin of his fear was obvious. This giant was wanted for murder, and he was alone in the woods with him. The man could snap him in two like a toothpick, and his body might not be found for several days. Folks would just think he was killed in the storm.

The origin of Billy Ray's greed was less apparent. There was almost certainly a reward for the capture of this escaped murderer, and the good Lord knew how much he and Missy could use the money. He dared not give the matter much thought. If he did so he would be unable to go through with it. So he decided on the spot to take a chance on collecting whatever reward there might be.

"Hold on a second, Mister," Billy Ray said.

The stranger stopped and turned to face Billy Ray.

"You mind if I ask who you're goin' to see in Pineville?"

"A girl," was the man's simple reply.

"What's her name?"

"Why do you wanna know?"

"Well, 'cause I know most folks around here. Maybe I could show you where she lives."

The stranger gave this some thought for several seconds. Then he said, "Her name's Frieda."

"Frieda what?"

"Frieda Pinchon."

Billy Ray frowned. "Frieda Pinchon? I don't think I know a Frieda Pin . . . oh, wait. Pinchon. That must be ol' man Pinchon's granddaughter. He owns a grocery store there in Pineville. They live right there at the store. Or at least they live in a house that's connected to the store."

The stranger turned once more toward the path, and Billy Ray knew that he had to think fast. "Say, Mister. How would you like a ride into Pineville?"

Again the man stopped and turned. Billy Ray slowly approached him. "Are you interested?"

The man nodded.

"O.K., then here's what we'll do. When you get up to the road there's an old house on the other side. You remember seein' it?"

"Yeah. I stopped there and got a drink of water."

Those were the most words Billy Ray had heard the stranger speak. He knew he was making progress.

"Then you know nobody lives there. So, what you need to do is go back to that house and wait for me, an' I'll be along directly. I live about a mile from here and I have to bring in a few more trout lines. After that I'll go home, get my truck and head over to that house to pick you up. We're startin' to get a little rain, so you better wait inside. If you wanna crash, go ahead. I'll come in an' get you." Billy Ray smiled. "How's that sound?"

"Why?"

"Why what?"

"Why're you doin' this?"

Billy Ray managed a hurt look on his face. "Cause that's how we are down in this part of the country. I'm doin' it cause it's the neighborly thing to do." His smile broadened and he added, "Another thing we do is introduce ourselves to strangers. My name's Billy Ray. Billy Ray Love. What's yours?"

The slightest hint of a smile appeared on the stranger's face. "B.C. Jones."

"What's B.C. stand for?"

"It don't stand for nothin'. That's my name."

Billy Ray decided not to push his luck. "Well, B.C. It's nice to meet you."

B.C. nodded silently and Billy Ray decided that his new acquaintance was just not much on social graces.

"So, what d'ya say? You want me to drive you to Pineville or not?"

"O.K.," B.C. replied.

"Then it's settled. Now, like I said, I'll be along directly. We don't have a lot of time to kill cause of the herrycan."

"What's a herrycan?" B.C. asked.

"It's a big storm. It's gonna hit sometime tonight." An incredulous expression came over Billy Ray. "You mean you don't know about the herrycan?"

"Uh uh," B.C. replied as he shook his head.

"Well, anyway," Billy Ray resumed, "it's a big one and it's headin' this way, so we don't have a lotta time to kill.

"I'll be bringin' my wife along with me, so me an' her can head over to the shelter after we drop you off." Billy Ray paused, then asked, "Is that O.K. with you?"

"Yeah."

Billy Ray smiled. "Good. Then I'll see you up at that ol' house in a little while."

B.C. turned and moved toward the path. This time Billy Ray did not stop him.

Billy Ray waited until B.C. Jones was out of sight before breathing a sigh of relief. A moment later he was formulating his plan.

THIRTY-ONE

FRANK WOJCIK DROVE the car into a turnout adjacent to the seawall along East Beach and stopped. There were a series of parking alcoves along the twenty-six miles of beach that were used for buses and other vehicles to pull out of the traffic lanes on Highway 90 and park without impeding the flow of traffic.

Wojcik turned the engine off but neither he nor Flowers were in any rush to get out of the car. The skies had darkened and rain was falling steadily. The high winds blowing in from the Gulf were causing the raindrops to fall to earth almost horizontally.

But it was neither the wind nor rain that prompted Wojcik to stop the car. It was the group of swimmers out in the surf that caught his attention. The tide had already risen several feet. The water had crossed most of the fifty yards of sandy beach and was approaching the seawall. The seas needed to rise only four more feet and the waves would be crossing the highway.

It had been three hours since the meeting with Inspector Pierce ended, but this was their first opportunity to leave the courthouse. After Pierce departed, Cuevas asked Wojcik and Flowers to man the phones in the command post until additional manpower arrived. Evacuation efforts were in full operation, with the National Guard called in to assist. Sheriff's deputies and civil defense workers were attached to guardsmen and were going from house to house in the most threatened areas to urge residents to lock up their houses and leave. Even Morris Cruthirds had been assured by Cuevas that he would be given an opportunity to take part in the evacuation effort. This delighted the old deputy. He would jump at any chance to go into the field.

At first Wojcik protested the command post assignment, citing a need to go to Pineville as soon as possible. But after Cuevas explained that several calls had to be made to some very important places, such as the governor's office and the Red Cross national headquarters, and that he wanted someone with Frank's verbal skills to make the calls, the school teacher who worked part-time as a deputy sheriff reluctantly acquiesced.

As it turned out, working the phones had its advantages. While Wojcik was making his calls, and responding to inquiries from a variety of sources, Flowers took the opportunity to make a few calls himself. The first was to Frieda Pinchon. He was relieved to learn that she was helping her grandfather in the store. It had been busy all morning. They intended to remain open for as long as there was merchandise to be sold. At least she would be safe for the time being, for Jones would surely not make a move with customers going in and out of the store.

After obtaining permission, Flowers placed a long distance call to Rochelle. Hearing her voice seemed to take a heavy weight from his shoulders. From her tone, she sounded excited to hear from him. Garland wondered if Rochelle's mom had talked to her since his conversation with his mother-in-law the night before. He was tempted to ask Rochelle, but decided against it.

He filled her in on events that had taken place since he last spoke to her on Friday: of B.C. Jones' escape, the concern for Frieda Pinchon's safety, the blow-up with Pierce . . . and the approaching hurricane. She said that she had heard some brief mention of a hurricane on the local news, but hadn't given it much thought until now. There was emotion in her voice when she asked Garland to please be careful. She then let Danielle speak for a moment. When Rochelle retrieved the phone they talked for a few more minutes, assuring one another of how much they loved and missed the other. Then they said their good byes and hung up.

Rochelle had lifted his spirits like no one else could. He realized at that moment that he would do whatever was necessary to make their marriage work.

While Wojcik fielded calls, Flowers kept himself busy making entries in the operations log and monitoring the weather updates on the radio. He learned that hurricane hunters had just returned from their latest flight into the eye of Camille, and had recorded winds near the center of the storm in excess of two hundred miles per hour. Flowers found that to be incredible. The hurricane was slowly closing in on the Gulf Coast, and was expected to make landfall between ten P.M. and midnight.

Eventually Wojcik and Flowers were replaced by a full crew of command post personnel, and they were free to go. Before leaving the courthouse, Wojcik found two clear plastic raincoats in a supply closet and they put them on, for the rain had already begun to fall.

Since there was no great rush to get to Pineville, they decided to take a drive along the beach. Wojcik wanted to show Flowers the effect the early stages of the hurricane was having on the normally calm waters of the Mississippi Sound. They had gotten as far as Mississippi City, an unincorporated community that separated Gulfport from Biloxi, when they spotted the small group of bathers playing in the water.

As Flowers sat on the passenger side of the parked car he watched two bikini-clad girls who appeared to be in their late teens. They were standing side by side, holding hands, at the water's edge. Each time a wave came in it would strike them with enough force to cause them to lose their balance. After regaining their footing they would wait for the next wave to hit so they could repeat the ritual of struggling to remain in an upright position.

At first he was amused by the silly game, but soon grew bored with watching them, and he gazed farther out into the Gulf. "I find it difficult to believe that I'm looking at the same body of water that I first saw on Friday."

"You haven't seen anything yet," Wojcik said. "The real storm is still several hours away. This is just a small preview. It'll get steadily worse between now and the time the full force of the hurricane hits."

They watched a young man venture out into the water about twenty yards. As a large swell approached he began swimming frantically toward shore. The wave broke just as it reached him and the would-be body surfer was tumbled helplessly inside the churning water until the wave tossed him onto shore like so much flotsam. The young man slowly stood up, a bit shaken, but wearing a big grin. A moment later he returned to the water for another ride.

Wojcik shook his head disapprovingly. "The thing that disturbs me at the moment, aside from those idiots playing in the surf, is how high the water has risen so far. According to the latest reports it'll be another eight or ten hours before Camille makes landfall. The closer it gets the faster the water will rise." After a brief pause he added, "And it's almost up to the seawall now."

Wojcik inhaled deeply and blew it out in a long sigh, then opened the car door. "Well, here goes."

When Flowers started to open his door Wojcik stopped him. "You might as well wait in the car. No need for both of us to get wet. I'm just going to try to talk some sense into to these folks. Be right back." With that, he got out of the car. He put his hands in the pockets of the transparent raincoat, hunched his shoulders against the wind, and walked over to a middle-aged couple who was sitting on the top step of the seawall, watching the younger ones playing in the surf.

Flowers watched his partner through the car window. His view was blurred by the driving rain, but he could make out what was being said by Wojcik's hand gestures. He was describing the rising tide and how the water would soon be over the seawall. He assumed that they were being warned of the dangers of being killed by the tidal surge. Instead of playing in the water, they should all be using this time to get as far away from the beach as possible. Time was a factor that was slipping away rapidly.

As Wojcik turned and walked back toward the car, Flowers saw the man and woman stand up and shout something to the young trio in the water. By the time Wojcik was opening the car door, the bathers had joined the couple on the seawall and were preparing to cross the road, presumably to return to one of the motels that occupied the north side of the highway.

"Tourists," Wojcik commented as he slid behind the steering wheel and closed the car door. His hair and the lower part of his pant legs were drenched.

"Well, they're leaving," Flowers said. "Whatever you told them must have gotten their attention."

"I hope so."

"They're headed for one of those motels across the road," Flowers said, "So I assume they're not from around here."

"You assume correctly. They're from Little Rock. Down here on vacation. I suggested they check out of the motel immediately and head back to Arkansas." Wojcik grinned. "I think they took it more as a command than a suggestion." He chuckled. "When I told them that their motel probably wouldn't be there this time tomorrow, it seemed to get their attention."

Flowers looked questioningly at his partner. "Do you really think it'll get that bad?"

Wojcik's grin faded and was replaced by a frown as he looked out over the turbulent water moving ever closer to the seawall. "I'm not sure," he replied somberly. "But I think it might."

WINSTON PIERCE HAD to drive almost to Henderson Point before finding a bar that was open. It was called the Sea Foam Lounge, and it overlooked the Gulf of Mexico from a slight rise on the north side of the highway just west of Pass Christian. The lounge, with its flat roof and jutting corners, revealed a half-hearted attempt at modern architecture. The walls were painted a sickening shade of aquamarine. A stand of palm trees adorned each of the buildings front corners. The most attractive feature of the lounge was a huge plate glass window that slanted outward from floor to ceiling, providing a panoramic view of the Sound.

Pierce sat on a stool at the bar and nursed what would be the first of several martinis before day's end. Since it was still early, he decided to pace himself, perhaps averaging no more than one drink per hour.

He had been seething with anger when he left the Harrison County Courthouse and got in his car to drive back to New Orleans. It had been his intention to drop in at a bar for a few drinks to settle his nerves, and the Sea Foam Lounge appeared to be the only drinking establishment open along the Coast. All other businesses had closed for the day and boarded up their windows.

It occurred to Pierce that the local residents might be making too big a fuss over this storm. Surely they had gone through hurricanes before. He decided that bad weather was probably the only excitement these people had, and if they wanted to make a big deal over it, that was their business. As far as he was concerned, he couldn't get away from here soon enough.

As he sipped his drink his mood began to mellow. Aside from Pierce, the only other patrons in the lounge were three couples sitting as a group at a table between the bar and the large window. From their laughter and the tone of their conversation they seemed to share his lack of concern about any danger that might accompany the encroaching storm.

By the time the martini was two-thirds consumed the mellowness began to fade and his mood became darker. Recollections of the previous twenty-four hours filled his head with a deep regret, for he was forced to admit that he had made some errors in judgement that could negatively impact his career.

It began yesterday afternoon when he decided to touch bases with his friend, Chief Maxwell. He had thought it best to fill the chief in on everything he knew of the escape. So, from his room just off the French Quarter in New Orleans, Pierce made a call to his friend. Because it was Saturday, he placed the call to Chief Maxwell's home.

At first the conversation was friendly, but as Pierce related the events of that morning, Chief Maxwell's tone grew more distant.

His first question was why Pierce was still in New Orleans instead of in Gulfport offering his assistance to the Harrison County Sheriff. This had caught Pierce off guard. Surely his old friend Maxwell knew why he was in New Orleans–for the same reason any other executive would go on such an extradition. He was there to enjoy himself. It was an understanding that was shared by others of similar rank. Since it was impossible to deliver a wink and a nod over the phone, Pierce said as much to his friend.

That was his first serious error in judgement, and any semblance of friendship evaporated in Chief Maxwell's explosion. He began his tirade by reminding Pierce that his first obligation was the safe delivery of the prisoner to the Los Angeles County Jail–not whoring around in New Orleans. It appeared that Sgt. Flowers was the only one of the two of them who understood this. The chief finished by ordering Pierce to get in touch with the Harrison County Sheriff immediately and lend his support in apprehending the escaped prisoner. If it appeared that apprehension was not imminent, he and Flowers were to return to Los Angeles.

After the phone conversation ended Pierce lit up a Pall Mall. He took a long drag, then grinned smugly as he slowly exhaled the smoke through his nostrils, for he had found a loophole in the orders that Chief Maxwell had given him.

His orders had been to get in touch with the Harrison County Sheriff immediately. But he wasn't ordered to get in touch *in person*, and that was his loophole. If he simply made a phone call he would be in compliance with Maxwell's order. Of course, he would eventually have to show up in Gulfport in person, but he could do that in the morning. This was Saturday night, and he wanted so badly to spend Saturday night on Bourbon Street. So he would call and set up a meeting with that yokel sheriff for Sunday morning, then he would go out and have some fun.

As Pierce sat at the bar in the Sea Foam Lounge he recalled the previous evening in the French Quarter. It had been an interesting experience, but nothing spectacular. The music and the laughter and the gaiety had certainly been present, but a nagging feeling within him had taken away his ability to just let himself go. It was a feeling that he should not be there. Over the years he had enjoyed an upwardly mobile career, and Chief Maxwell had been his mentor. Now Maxwell had turned on him. Was he now risking his career by indulging in a night on the town in New Orleans?

By midnight he had returned to his room. After lying awake for several hours an idea came to him. He would go to Gulfport with an assertive attitude. He would simply take charge. That shouldn't be difficult for a person of his status. If they happened to find the escaped prisoner, he would get credit for it, and he could return to L.A. with a big feather in his cap. He would turn defeat into victory. If, on the other hand, the prisoner could not be captured, he would simply blame it on the incompetence of the local sheriff.

Pierce sipped his martini and frowned as he recalled his meeting with that special assistant to the sheriff. Of all his errors in judgement, the most serious was underestimating Dwight Cuevas. He had gone to Gulfport expecting to find a fat, ignorant sheriff with a name like Bubba, who wouldn't know a corpus from a delicti. As it turned out, he never got the chance to even get an audience with the sheriff. Instead, he had the misfortune of meeting a special assistant who happened to have twenty years experience with the F.B.I. The Harrison County Sheriff's Department was much more sophisticated than he had anticipated.

Winston Pierce cringed with hatred as he thought of how Cuevas had humiliated him at that meeting. The worst part was that Sgt. Flowers had witnessed it. Pierce was convinced that, within days of their return to L.A., news of his humiliation would be all over the department. This thought caused him to despise Garland Flowers as much as he did Dwight Cuevas.

Pierce swiveled the barstool so that he could look out the large window. It was raining steadily. Though he could not hear the wind, the way the palm trees were bending away from the Gulf he knew that it was blowing hard. As he looked at the white-capped waves he got the impression that they were hitting shore closer than when he first entered the bar.

He took a last swallow from his glass and set it on the counter, then signaled the bartender. Pacing himself was ludicrous. It was time for his second martini.

THIRTY-TWO

BILLY RAY LOVE reached into the cramped bedroom closet of the house trailer and pulled out the rifle that was leaning against the wall. It was a bolt action .22 that had been owned by his grandpa. When the old man died Billy Ray inherited an acre of land and the rifle.

The rifle was a keepsake more than anything, and he seldom fired it. Once he used it to kill an owl that was roosting in a tree behind the chicken yard. But he did not like using a gun to hunt the meat that he put on the table for Missy and himself. He preferred using traps to catch the opossums, rabbits and other varmints that provided much of their daily sustenance.

Financially, it had not been a good year for the Loves. An automobile upholsterer by trade, Billy Ray was laid off six months earlier and his unemployment benefits had run their course.

When he and Missy married in 1967 he purchased a used house trailer and parked it on the property that he had inherited. Fortunately the trailer was paid for, so they had no fear of being evicted. An artesian well in the back yard provided all the fresh water they needed for free. Missy raised chickens and maintained a small vegetable garden. In addition to the wild game Billy Ray trapped in the woods, at least once a week he and his young wife would have fresh trout or catfish caught on his fishing lines in Wolf River. Once in a while they would go down to Moses Pier at the small craft harbor in Gulfport and catch a mess of crabs. Missy had a knack for cooking crab gumbo.

Twice a month they would go to Gulfport to be issued commodities. It was a welfare program that provided food staples for impoverished families. For Billy Ray it was a humiliating experience and he hated it, but they could not afford to purchase the provisions that the county relief office offered free of charge. So every two weeks he and Missy would pick up their allotment of flour, corn meal, powdered milk and the inevitable block of government cheese.

Though they had a roof over their heads and they certainly would not starve, the Loves were desperate for cash. They needed money to purchase such things as cleaning supplies, gasoline for the truck and propane for cooking. Their only utility expense was electricity. The phone had been disconnected months ago.

Billy Ray spent a good part of each day trying to think of ways to raise money. These had been the thoughts occupying his mind two hours earlier, when B.C. Jones stepped out of the woods, onto the banks of Wolf River, and into Billy Ray's life. It was as if the Good Lord had sent him deliverance. The capture of this murderer would surely fetch a generous reward.

From a closet shelf he found a small box of .22 short cartridges. He opened it and removed one, then placed the box in a front pocket of his overalls. Sliding the rifle bolt back, he inserted the small round, then slid the bolt forward again. At one time the weapon had a clip that held five or six rounds, but his grandpa had misplaced it years ago. It never occurred to Billy Ray to purchase another clip. He simply used the rifle as a single-shot.

After confirming that the safety was engaged, he breathed a long sigh and walked out of the room, holding the rifle down at his side.

A light rain had been falling for over an hour. Ordinarily the sound of the rain falling on the metal skin of the house trailer was soothing, and had a calming effect on Billy Ray. But today it did not calm him. Today he regarded the rain as a nuisance.

It would be more accurate to say that the rain was not *falling* onto the trailer, but was being *blown* onto it by a wind that was growing stronger with each passing hour. Every few minutes a sudden gust would cause the trailer to rock like a boat in choppy water.

In the front room Billy Ray found his wife standing before a table placing items into a cardboard box. "You about ready, Honey?" He asked.

Missy was not a pretty woman, but there was a sweet innocence about her that caused Billy Ray to melt every time he looked at her. She was twenty years old but did not look her age. The numerous freckles surrounding the bridge of her nose, and her auburn hair that was always tied in a ponytail, gave her the appearance of a girl in her mid-teens.

"Just about. I was just gathering a few things to take with us to the shelter."

"Like what?"

"Family pictures, keepsakes and what-not." She raised her head toward the ceiling and listened to the wind. "The way it's rocking us now causes me to wonder how this trailer's gonna hold up when the herrycan gets here."

"I think it'll ride it out just fine," Billy Ray said, but there was no conviction in his voice.

"There," Missy said as she closed the top flaps on the box. "We're all set." She then turned and faced her husband for the first time since he entered the room. A look that was a mixture of disappointment and concern came over her when she saw the rifle.

"Billy Ray, are you sure you want to go through with this?" She asked.

Billy Ray did not answer right away. Instead, he stared at his wife and thought of how he must surely be a disappointment to her. He was out of work and on county relief. At twenty-two years of age, he was a failure. Yet this opportunity for a possible windfall had dropped into his lap. All he had to do was capture B.C. Jones and turn him over to the sheriff and they should be on easy street for a while. Hopefully, before the reward money ran out, he could find a decent job.

He forced a smile and nodded. "Yeah, I'm sure."

"But I'm scared," she said. "This man's a murderer, and from what they say on the news, he's huge and he kills with his bare hands."

Billy Ray held the rifle up. "That's why I'm takin' this." He hoped that he sounded sure of himself. The fact was, though, he knew he was taking a big chance. The rifle was a single-shot, and it carried a short round at that. He was depending on using it to bluff his captive. He was well aware that, if he was forced to shoot Jones, it would probably only serve to make him mad. Inwardly he shivered at the thought.

"Now, before we leave," he said, "I want to make durn sure you know what you're supposed to do."

Missy breathed a long sigh. "I'm to drive the truck to that old vacant house down the road. You'll ride in the back of the truck so you can jump out real quick when we get there. I'm to back the truck in the driveway and keep the motor runnin'."

"That's right. You gotta remember, the most important thing you do is keep that motor runnin'. Our lives may depend on it. Cause if it dies an' I got Jones at gunpoint I won't be able to push the truck to get it started. An' if, by some chance he gets the drop on us, we could be in real trouble."

"But that's what scares me. What if I panic and stall the motor?"

Billy Ray looked her in the eye. "I'm depending on you not to do that." He then shook off the stare and added, "When I bring him out to the truck, him an' me'll get in the back. When I yell, you pull out of the driveway, turn left, go to 28th Street and make another left, then get us to the county jail as quick as you can." He moved closer and put an arm around her. "You think you can remember all that?"

Her only reply was a reluctant nod.

"Good. Now let's go get this over with."

AT ONE HUNDRED ten pounds, Missy had to struggle to keep the gale force winds from blowing her over as she made her way to the truck. It was a dark blue 1956 Ford short-bed pick-up. Billy Ray was in the habit of backing the vehicle into the yard so that it was always facing the street. He would park it on a slight rise, which made it easy to push off to start. As he followed his wife to the truck he silently made a vow that the first thing he bought with the reward money would be a starter switch, so he could start his truck like normal folks did.

The driver's door was on the leeward side of the vehicle, so Missy had little difficulty opening the door and climbing into the cab. Because the door latch on the right side was broken, the passenger door had to be secured with a rope. A passenger, therefore, would have to enter the cab from the driver's side. In the event that he had to get out of the truck in a hurry, Billy Ray decided to ride to the vacant house in the back of the truck. It was only a mile down the road, and he had already made up his mind that he was going to get soaked from the rain anyway.

Prior to leaving the trailer, Billy Ray wrapped the rifle in an old checkered oilcloth that had once covered their table. The waterproof cloth would keep it dry, at least until they arrived at the vacant house. As he passed the rear of the truck he placed the rifle in the bed.

After Missy was seated behind the wheel, Billy Ray handed her the box of mementos, which she set on the seat beside her. Although Missy had started the truck by having it pushed off dozens of times she listened patiently as Billy Ray went over the procedures with her once more. After confirming that the emergency brake was released, the ignition was on, the hand throttle on the dash was pulled out a quarter of an inch, the clutch pedal was pushed down and the vehicle was in gear, he moved to the rear of the truck. Leaning against the tailgate, he found a foothold in the wet ground and pushed. It took little effort to get the old truck rolling down the hill. It had moved less than ten feet when Missy popped the clutch and the engine started. She quickly reapplied the clutch and brake. The engaged throttle caused the engine to idle loudly. Billy Ray climbed into the bed of the truck and Missy slowly drove it out of the driveway. She turned right and proceeded south on Red Creek Road.

Before seating himself with his back against the cab, he removed a flat circular box of Copenhagen Snuff from his back pocket. Hunching forward to protect the contents from the rain, he opened the lid and withdrew a pinch between his thumb and forefinger, then quickly replaced the lid. He placed the pinch of snuff between his lower gums and lip, producing a half-inch bulge between his lower lip and chin. After returning the snuffbox to his back pocket, he sat back and thought about what lay ahead.

Butterflies swarmed furiously in the pit of his stomach. He was well aware of the risk he was taking. What was worse, he was placing Missy in harm's way. The smart thing to do would be to drive past the old house and go directly to the shelter. A bad storm was coming and this was no time to be messing around with a dangerous killer who had arms that were larger than Billy Ray's thighs.

But he was desperate for cash, and desperate times called for desperate measures. Sure, there was a risk. But as his daddy always told him, anything worth having usually involved risk. The bigger the risk the bigger the reward.

Missy slowed the truck as they approached their destination. By this time Billy Ray had convinced himself to go through with his plan, so he made no effort to have Missy drive past the house and proceed to the shelter. Instead, she brought the truck to a stop in front of the old structure. At Billy Ray's direction, she backed into two muddy ruts that had once served as a driveway.

As he removed the oilcloth from the rifle, Billy Ray carefully surveyed the surroundings. There was no sign of B.C. Jones, but this was not surprising. Because of the wind and rain, as well as a desire to avoid detection, Jones would certainly be keeping dry inside the house.

With rifle in hand Billy Ray jumped from the bed of the truck. He swore aloud when his feet landed in a puddle of water. Tapping lightly on the driver's window, he motioned for Missy to roll it down. When she did so he could see the fear in her eyes.

"Don't worry, honey," he said. "It's almost over. Just keep the motor runnin'. I'll be right back."

Missy watched him as he turned and moved toward the front of the house. The wind blew rain in her face, so she rolled the window up, but continued to keep her eyes on her husband.

SOON AFTER RETURNING to the house following his meeting with that man down by the river, B.C. Jones went into the bedroom and lay down on the mattress. Having gone the previous night with almost no sleep, and walking a few miles in the wind and rain, fatigue had caught up with him. He had intended to just rest his eyes for a few minutes until that man who called himself Billy Ray Love came by to take him to Pineville. But within two minutes of putting his head on the stained and odorous mattress, he was fast asleep.

His last conscious thoughts before drifting into slumber were of Frieda Pinchon. And as he slept her image dominated his dreams. She had become his only reason for living.

Before leaving Los Angeles, the world of B.C. Jones had been extremely small, for there was no one with whom he could share his life. Since his arrival in Mississippi his existence had shrunk even more. Because he was now a fugitive, even his Auntie Doreen was cut off from him, for he dared not attempt to make contact with her. His entire world now consisted of the narrow path that separated him from Frieda. His only destination was Pineville, and his only mission in life was to find Frieda and deliver her to that safe haven where she might wait in peace for his arrival. She would be in the company of those two children that he had delivered a month ago. Eventually the four of them would be together, forever free from the hatefulness of people like his daddy—and that white trash in Lawndale.

B.C. Jones was incapable of articulating such thoughts while awake. But as he slept they persisted with a visual eloquence that filled his dreams with images of tranquil pleasures. He experienced a subconscious titillation that teased the senses. And at the center of it all was Frieda Pinchon.

HOLDING THE RIFLE at the ready, Billy Ray Love approached the house with the caution of a hunter stalking his prey. The broken screen door that had been leaning against the porch railing a few hours earlier was now lying on the floor at the top of the steps, having been blown over by the wind. After ascending the steps, Billy Ray stepped between the aluminum frames of the screen and moved across the porch.

Using the muzzle of the rifle barrel, he cautiously pushed the front door open. He had made up his mind that he would keep the rifle pointed in front of him at all times, or at least until his prisoner was safely behind bars at the Harrison County Jail.

The door creaked as it opened and Billy Ray immediately determined that there was no one in the room. To his right, an open door led into what he assumed was a bedroom. The absence of interior furnishings amplified the sound of his footsteps as he moved in that direction.

On the floor in the far corner of the bedroom was a mattress, barely visible under the behemoth that lay on top of it. Billy Ray's throat had become so dry that the snuff between his lip and gum felt like dust in his mouth. He tried to swallow but could not. With all the strength he could muster he moved across the room. As he nudged the shoulder of Jones with the rifle muzzle the thought came to Billy Ray that he had taken leave of his senses in attempting to awaken this sleeping giant. Yet, even as this thought occurred to him he nudged his quarry again.

Jones suddenly moved with a jerk and his eyes opened wide. Startled, Billy Ray jumped back, but kept the rifle pointed at Jones.

Jones looked at him questioningly and grunted, "Huh?"

"Come on, B.C. It's time to go." As Billy Ray spoke, it felt as if snuff dust was flying from the dry interior of his mouth.

10250-MART

Jones sat up on the mattress. "What you doin' with that gun pointin' at me?"

"Cause I'm turnin' you in to the sheriff."

"But why? I ain't done nothin' to you."

Billy Ray had to fight back a surge of sympathy for his prisoner. "I'm sorry, B.C. Real sorry. It ain't nothin' personal. I just need the money."

"What money?"

"The reward money, of course. You know. The reward for bringin' you in."

Jones shook his head. "I don't know about no reward."

"There's gotta be one," Billy Ray replied. "Now come on and stand up so we can get this over with."

B.C. Jones slowly moved to one knee then pushed up on the other leg. As he stood at full height atop the mattress Billy Ray was momentarily awed by his prisoner's enormous size. For a full ten seconds the two men stared at each other, and a cold chill ran down Billy Ray's spine.

Suddenly, without the slightest warning, Jones lunged forward and grabbed the barrel of the rifle. Billy Ray involuntarily backed away. He continued to grip the gun tightly, with his right index finger in the trigger housing.

Jones held onto the barrel with both hands and pulled hard. Billy Ray was jerked forward and almost lost his balance, but he remained on his feet. Jones then began swinging the barrel from left to right. Billy Ray held fast to the opposite end of the rifle and moved helplessly from side to side, like a dog that refuses to give up the stick that it has just fetched for its master.

Jones stopped swinging and suddenly pushed the rifle toward Billy Ray, then quickly pulled it back in an attempt to jerk it free. As he did so Billy Ray's index finger pressed against the trigger and the gun fired. A look of shock appeared on the face of B.C. Jones and both men dropped the rifle at the same time. A crimson stain appeared on the left side of Jones' shirt, just above the waist.

His eyes widened as he stepped back and raised his shirt to expose the wound.

Billy Ray decided not to wait around to assess the damage. He turned and ran from the bedroom. As he ran out of the house and onto the porch he almost tripped over the screen door, but he jumped just in time to clear the screen as well as the steps. Both feet came down hard into three inches of mud, which splattered his arms and face. Recovering quickly he raced toward the truck.

INSIDE THE HOUSE B.C. Jones learned that his injury was nothing more than a flesh wound. After tearing through his shirt, the bullet barely skimmed along his side. It was enough to draw blood, but no damage was done.

His fear was then replaced by anger. His breathing became stronger, the air exhaling audibly through his nose. After emitting a loud grunt Jones charged through the bedroom, across the living room and out the front door.

MISSY BECAME STARTLED when she heard the report from the rifle. And when her husband came flying out of the house she was almost frozen with fear. Only when he leaped into the bed of the truck and yelled for her to get them out of there did she snap out of her fear-stricken trance.

Through the rearview mirror she saw a gargantuan figure run out the front door of the house. She suddenly felt as if she was in the midst of a nightmare, but she forced herself to concentrate on shifting the truck into first gear. As her foot was easing up on the clutch, the huge man on the porch let out with a growl that could be heard above the wind and the rain and the rolled-up window. The sound startled her and her foot came up too fast from the clutch, causing the truck to lurch forward and kill the engine.

Billy Ray jumped from the bed of the truck and frantically opened the driver's door. He pulled Missy from the cab and, for reasons he could not later fathom, he slammed the door closed

10250-MART

after she got out. Taking her hand, he pulled her along as they both ran to the road.

B.C. JONES WAS not aware that the screen door was lying on the floor in front of him as he moved across the porch. By the time he saw it blocking his way it was too late. As he moved toward the steps one of his feet got caught under the aluminum frame. His forward motion caused the frame to push against the porch railing, and he was moving too fast to avoid being tripped. There being nothing to break his fall, the momentum carried him over the steps and he crashed onto the muddy ground below. His massive outstretched arms prevented him from landing on his head.

Though shaken from the fall, Jones recovered instantly. He jumped to his feet and began chasing them.

BILLY RAY AND MISSY sprinted toward 28th Street as fast as their legs would carry them. He had no doubt that if Jones caught them he would rip both their heads off. As they struggled to put distance between themselves and their pursuer, Billy Ray was strangely amused by the weird things that can go through a person's mind when he is running for his life. It occurred to him that this was the first time he had ever seen Missy run. And as she easily moved ahead of him he also became aware that she was a much faster sprinter than he was.

When they turned onto 28th Street they both glanced back and were greatly relieved to see that Jones had given up the pursuit. They had run another hundred yards when Missy heard a strange sound coming from Billy Ray. She looked back and saw that he had stopped and was doubled over and gagging. As she ran back to him he straightened up. They were both breathing heavily after their recent exertion. But with Billy Ray, something else was wrong. His face had turned a sickening green.

"Billy Ray!" She screamed. "What is it? What's wrong?"

Between pants he said, "I'm OK. I just . . . swallowed . . . my wad of snuff."

BY THE TIME Jones arrived at the road in front of the house the Loves were turning south onto 28th Street, and he realized that he would never catch them. As he turned back toward the house he was fuming with anger. From somewhere deep within him the inner voice had been awakened and it spoke to him of the betrayal that he had just experienced. In the past five minutes he had been shot and had taken a serious fall. But what was worse, he had once again been mistreated by someone in whom he had placed his trust. At the moment B.C. Jones hated the world and everything in it. At the urging of the voice he was determined more than ever to find Frieda and take her away from the sort of pain that he was now feeling.

When his eyes fell on Billy Ray's truck it was as if that scrawny white fool with the missing front tooth were standing before him. He moved toward it until he was leaning against the left fender. Raising both fists over his head he let out a growl and began pounding the hood of the truck with hammer-like blows. He beat it until the anger within him began to subside.

The voice then told him it was time to move on.

THIRTY-THREE

FOLLOWING THEIR ENCOUNTER with the tourists from Arkansas, Wojcik and Flowers resumed their drive eastward along the coast. For the most part the Gulf side of the highway was abandoned. The sand beach was now completely under water, and white-capped waves crashed against the concrete seawall three feet below the level of the highway. Traffic was light along Highway 90, and it seemed to Flowers that every third car on the road was a city or county emergency vehicle. There was also a large contingent of National Guard troops. Their primary duty was the evacuation of beachfront residents.

A block east of the lighthouse in Biloxi, Wojcik made a u-turn and they headed back toward Gulfport. The force of the wind had increased, and rain blew in from the Gulf in heavy sheets. The few vehicles on the road had their headlights on and windshield wipers running at maximum speed.

Flowers was fascinated by what he was seeing. Aside from the winds and the rain and the rapidly rising tides, there was something in the atmosphere that he could only describe as eerie. Beyond the dark overcast, off to the southwest, a reddish-orange sky glowed faintly through the clouds like a dull light through a thin layer of dirty cotton.

He recalled how pleasant the weather had been only two days ago, when he first arrived in Gulfport. The waters of the Sound, beyond the white sandy beach, had been as calm as a lake. And now the beach was gone, submerged beneath a sea that was as turbulent as water boiling in a caldron. A three-foot surf crashed against the seawall only a few yards from the highway, shooting a foamy spray skyward.

Wojcik glanced at his partner. "You seem lost in thought."

Flowers smiled. "I was just thinking about our conversation Friday afternoon, when we were driving along here from the motel." He gestured toward the Gulf. "It's just like you said it would be."

"As I recall, I also said that it would get much worse."

Flowers sighed. "Yeah. I'm afraid I do recall you saying something to that effect."

In addition to monitoring the police radio, Wojcik had also turned on the car radio to a local A.M. station to get the latest news on the hurricane. What he and Flowers heard was the newscaster's constant plea for Coast residents to evacuate the area. Hurricane Camille was just a few hours away, and there was no doubt that it would be a killer.

It was as if the newscaster was a preacher trying desperately to reach anyone who would listen. He repeatedly emphasized the fact that Camille could not be compared with any previous hurricane, for she was far more dangerous. Though smaller in size than other hurricanes, her energy force was much greater, as was her potential for death and destruction. Just to play it safe, anyone who lived south of the L.and N. Railroad tracks should evacuate immediately. There was no telling how far inland the storm surge would push the water. Time was running out!

Wojcik nodded toward the radio. "I wonder if that poor newscaster feels like a voice crying in the wilderness."

Flowers shrugged. "Maybe. Then again, there could be thousands of people who've decided to evacuate after hearing what he has to say." He paused, then added, "If I were in their shoes, I think he would have convinced me."

"I hope you're right," Wojcik said. "If so, when this is all over he should be given a medal."

Wojcik reached for the blower knob and turned it up a notch and air rushed out loudly from the defogger vents beneath the windshield. Visibility seemed to be getting worse by the minute. The noise inside the car had reached such a level that he turned off the car radio and reduced the volume on the police radio.

"Guess we better head over to Pineville while we're still able to drive," he said.

"Probably a good idea." Though he did not want to say anything, Flowers was becoming concerned about Frieda, and was relieved by his partner's announcement.

"Now that I think about it," Wojcik said, "I wish we had taken the time to go by Doreen Brown's house to see if we could talk her into going to a shelter."

Flowers made a facial expression that was a cross between a wince and a grin. "If you want my opinion, I would say that Mrs. Brown is a very self-reliant woman. She's been around a lot longer than either of us, and there's no doubt in my mind that she can take good care of herself."

Wojcik breathed a deep sigh. "You're right." There was a pause as he searched for the words to express his thoughts. "It's just that she's been through so much lately because of that nephew of hers. I'm concerned that she may not be thinking as clearly as she might under different circumstances."

Flowers looked at his partner and smiled warmly. "You're a good man, Frank. But I wouldn't worry about Mrs. Brown. Her church friends will look in on her. And if that's not enough," Flowers rolled his eyes heavenward, "I have an idea she's in pretty tight with the Man upstairs."

DOREEN BROWN SAT on a metal folding chair in a corner of the school cafeteria. Soria City Elementary School was the nearest designated shelter to her house, and Doreen had been driven there by three of her church friends an hour earlier. At first she had protested, but when her friends informed her that they intended to ride out the storm in Bible study, she finally acquiesced.

The four women formed a small circle, and each of them had a large Bible in her lap. The room had almost reached maximum capacity, and they considered themselves fortunate to have found four empty chairs and sufficient space to sit together. They all agreed that the Lord had blessed them.

The large room was a din of talking, laughing, singing and babies crying. Children chased one another between the tables, chairs and cots. The members of the Bible study group had to raise their voices to be heard.

"What passage should we begin with tonight?" Asked one of the women.

"This would be a good night for the twenty-third Psalm," offered a second member of the group.

"I agree," said the third member. "Then we can move into the New Testament and study the eighth chapter of Luke."

The first and second member exchanged glances. "And what passage is that?" They both asked.

"That's the one about Jesus and His disciples on the Sea of Galilee during a storm. The disciples are frightened and they ask Jesus to protect them. Then He stands up in the boat and raises his arms toward heaven, and tells the winds to be still, and it suddenly becomes calm." The third member looked at each of her friends. "After we study the passage, we should all hold hands and ask our Lord to protect us during this storm."

Doreen Brown nodded in agreement, though it was apparent to the others that she was not fully attentive to the discussion. Ordinarily, Doreen was an enthusiastic participant in the study group, but tonight she had to force herself to pay attention. Her thoughts were on B.C. She could not help but wonder where her nephew was, and how he would manage to find shelter from the approaching storm.

CONTINUING WEST ON Highway 90, Wojcik and Flowers entered the city of Long Beach. Due to the driving rain and poor visibility, their speed was no more than thirty miles per hour. Half a mile past St. Thomas Church, Wojcik touched the brake with his foot and the car slowed almost to a stop.

Flowers, who was lost in thoughts of Frieda Pinchon and her grandfather, straightened up in his seat as the car slowed. "Did you see something?"

"Yeah," Wojcik said as he turned the car into a driveway in front of a large residence. "That man and woman on the front porch. Why are they still here?"

It was a circular driveway, with entrances at each end of the property. They had driven past the first entrance when Wojcik spotted the couple on the porch, but he managed to slow the vehicle in time to negotiate the turn into the west entrance.

The driveway formed a concrete semi-circle around an expanse of lawn that separated the highway from a stately white two-story house. Round columns, two feet thick at the base, tapered slightly as they rose upward, supporting the roof of a wide wrap-around porch. Its architectural design was strictly nineteenth century.

On the porch was a man who appeared to be in his late fifties. He was attempting to nail a sheet of plywood to a window as the wind fought to tear it away from him. Standing nearby was a woman, small in stature and a few years younger than the man. Her arms were folded across her chest and she squinted against the wind and rain as she watched the car approach the front of the house. Wojcik stopped the car and turned off the engine, then the two detectives got out and made their way up the steps and across the porch.

Flowers felt uncomfortable. In spite of a slight drop in temperature brought on by the wind and rain, the plastic raincoat was trapping his body heat. He felt as if he were inside a portable steam bath. He made up his mind that, when they returned to the car, he was going to remove the raincoat. He decided that he would rather be drenched from the rain than from perspiration.

Without so much as a word of greeting, Flowers and Wojcik crossed the porch and each grabbed a side of the plywood and held it up to the window. The older man was startled at first, but said nothing. Instead, he picked up a hammer and several nails, then proceeded to attach the sheet of plywood to the window frame.

After hammering in the final nail, he stepped back, as if to admire his work. "There," he said. "That's the last one." He then looked at the two men who had come to his aid. "Thank you, gentlemen, for the help. The wind was giving me fits with that last sheet. The wife here tried to help, but she's so tiny the wind was whipping her around along with the plywood."

Extending his hand, he said, "My name's Watson. Earl Watson. And this is my wife, Mildred."

As they shook hands, Wojcik introduced Flowers and himself. "I believe we met before…a few years ago. You own the lumber yard in Handsboro, don't you?"

"That's right." Watson studied Wojcik more closely. "I'm sorry, but I don't seem to recall…"

"That's O.K.," Wojcik said. "I wouldn't expect you to remember me. My brother-in-law used to work for you during his summer breaks from college, and he introduced us once when I was in the store."

"What's your brother-in-law's name?"

"Paul Necaise. My wife's younger brother."

"Oh, yes. I remember Paul. He was one of my best workers." He hesitated a moment as the memory of Paul Necaise became clearer, then added somberly, "I heard that he was killed in Vietnam."

"Yes sir," Wojcik replied.

"I was really sorry to hear it. He was a good kid."

"Yes sir, he was."

For the first time, Mildred spoke up. "It must be a terrible thing your family has had to endure. I light a candle each week for all the boys fighting that awful war."

"Yes ma'am," Wojcik said.

"So, tell me," Watson said, abruptly changing the subject. "Who are you boys with? Police, fire or civil defense?"

"The sheriff's department," Wojcik replied.

"And you've come to talk us into leaving?"

"Well, yes. We saw the two of you on your porch and wondered if you might be stranded. We thought we'd see if you needed anything, such as a ride to the nearest shelter. It's getting late, and just about everyone who lives near the beach has left by now."

As Wojcik spoke, Flowers glanced at Mildred and thought he saw a change in her eyes…as if they were suddenly awakened by a ray of hope.

"We aren't leaving," Watson said flatly.

"What?"

"I said we're not leaving."

Wojcik was incredulous. "But, Mr. Watson, you can't stay here."

"Oh, yes I can. This house has been standing here for almost a hundred years. It has withstood a lot of hurricanes over the past century, and it's still here. I've been in a few storms inside this house myself, from that big one in '47 right up through Betsy a few years ago. And as you can plainly see, both the house and me are still standing."

"But this house hasn't stood up to anything like Camille. There's never been a storm as powerful as Camille…at least not in these parts." Wojcik looked from Earl Watson to Mildred, then back to Earl. "Mr. Watson, if you've been following the weather reports, then you know that the winds have already reached two hundred miles per hour. It's creating swells of up to twenty feet. We can expect ten foot waves on top of that."

"Earl, please listen to him!" Mildred intoned.

Watson gave his wife an impatient glance and ignored her plea. "We'll be O.K."

Wojcik breathed a frustrated sigh. "Mr. Watson, this place can't be more than eight feet above sea level. Your house could be engulfed with water."

"If the water comes in, we'll go upstairs."

"But when the storm surge hits, it's not going to just seep into your house. It's going to hit it like a giant battering ram, one wave after another. And when your bottom floor collapses, the second story is coming down."

Flowers stole a glimpse at Mildred. What he saw in her eyes this time was terror.

"I'm begging you, Earl. Let's go to a shelter."

Watson had become angry. "Look what you've done to my wife. You've gotten her scared half out of her mind."

"I apologize, Mrs. Watson. But I felt duty-bound to let you know what you're in for."

"Thank you, deputies," Earl said. "Y'all can go back to the sheriff and tell him you did your best." He stared hard at the two younger men, then added with a note of finality, "I hate to sound rude, especially to a relative of Paul Necaise. But I'll have to ask y'all to leave."

Flowers and Wojcik exchanged glances, then Wojcik reached into a pocket and removed a sheet of paper. Handing it to Mildred, he said, "This is a list of shelters you can go to if you change your mind." He paused for emphasis, then added, "If you decide to go, you'll have to do it soon. You're running out of time."

The two detectives then turned and descended the steps. Before getting into the passenger side of the car, Flowers removed his raincoat and immediately felt a chill brought on by the wind and rain. After the initial shock, he began to feel refreshed by the cooler air. He placed the raincoat on the rear floorboard to keep it from dripping on his and Wojcik's jackets that were lying across the rear seat.

Wojcik started the engine and the vehicle proceeded around the circular driveway toward the exit at the eastern edge of the property. Flowers glanced back and noticed that the Watsons had apparently gone inside the house, for they were no longer standing on the front porch. "I can't help but feel sorry for Mrs. Watson. Makes me wonder if we should have insisted that she come with us. I'm sure she would have."

"I disagree," Wojcik said. "I think she would stay with her husband . . . no matter what." He paused before adding, "I'm just

10250-MART

afraid that that man's stubbornness is going to get them both killed."

Wojcik was about to turn right, onto the highway, to continue their ride to Pineville, when a voice came over the police radio requesting the attention of Sgt. Flowers. Flowers looked questioningly at Wojcik, who nodded toward the radio microphone.

As he took the microphone from its dashboard clip and placed it in front of his mouth, it occurred to Flowers that he did not know the radio code utilized by the Harrison County Sheriff's Department. He decided, therefore, to speak in everyday English. Depressing the button, he said, "This is Flowers."

"Sergeant Flowers," the dispatcher began, "you are requested to meet with Officer Reynolds, of the Gulfport Police Department, at the intersection of 25th Avenue and 28th Street, re: possible encounter with suspect Jones."

Flowers looked again at his partner, who said, "Just say 'ten-four, e.t.a. fifteen minutes.'"

Directly across from the driveway exit was a break in the median that separated the east and west lanes of Highway 90. As Flowers acknowledged the call and hung up the microphone, Wojcik made a left turn and they headed back to Gulfport.

THIRTY-FOUR

WORD HAD GOTTEN out locally that the Sea Foam Lounge was hosting a hurricane party, and drinks would be sold at happy hour prices. The lounge would be a gathering place for those who refused to get caught up in the frenzy of escaping this so-called killer hurricane. After all, it was just a big storm . . . a lot of wind and rain and much ado about nothing.

Twenty patrons had drifted into the bar during the past three hours, and most of them decided to stick around. It would be fun. And with the huge plate glass window they had an excellent view of the hurricane.

The owner of the lounge showed up in the late afternoon with his bride. She had been a cocktail waitress in his employ three months earlier. They introduced themselves to the partygoers as Buzz and Irma. They both set about assisting the bartender in seeing to the needs of the customers.

When one of the patrons asked Buzz why he had not covered his windows with plywood like all the other businesses along the beach, he proudly explained that this window was specially made to withstand hurricane force winds. It had a reinforcing laminate between two extra thick layers of glass, much like the windshield of a car, only stronger.

When the patron gave Buzz a skeptical look, the owner, whose physical appearance was not unlike that of Dick Butkus, did something completely unexpected. He smiled at the customer and said, "Watch this," then suddenly broke into a run across the floor of the lounge. When he was five feet from the window he jumped and turned his body horizontally and slammed a body block into the windowpane four feet above the floor. The impact made a loud *thwump* and Buzz slid to the floor. There was not so much as a scratch on the window.

His actions caught the customers off guard. Several of them gasped and a few of the women screamed. But their shock was short lived, and when Buzz picked himself up off the floor he was met with enthusiastic applause. He smiled, took a bow, then asked his audience, "Does anyone else question whether or not this window can withstand the force of a hurricane?" No one spoke up, for they were all convinced that the Sea Foam Lounge could withstand anything that Camille could dish out.

Winston Pierce sat at the same barstool he had claimed hours earlier and watched the window demonstration with only passive interest. He wondered how many times Buzz had put on that show for his customers. Frankly, it had not occurred to Pierce that the window would fail to keep out the storm. He had given it no thought whatsoever.

He had no particular desire to spend the evening among these strangers, but he had been informed that Highway 90, between Bay St. Louis and New Orleans, was unsafe for travel due to the storm. He had waited too long. With nothing better to do he decided to ride out the storm at the Sea Foam Lounge. At least, as far as Camille was concerned, he was of like mind with the other patrons. For the first time since arriving on the Coast, he felt a kinship with those around him.

With a Pall Mall placed firmly in the cigarette holder, Pierce took a long drag, then took it from his mouth and flicked the ashes into a nearby ashtray, while exhaling the smoke through his nostrils. Before returning the holder to his lips he picked up his drink and took a sip. He was intoxicated, but was not fully aware of it until he had finished off his third Martini. By the time he downed his fourth, he was unable to make it to the men's room without stumbling into chairs and tables. So he made no effort to move about. He chose to sit alone at the counter and savor his release from rational thought. His inebriated state gave him a temporary respite from the humility that lay ahead of him when he returned to Los Angeles. At the moment he simply did not care about tomorrow. He wanted only to bask in his intoxication.

His only complaint was his fellow patrons' seemingly singular selection on the jukebox. He felt that if he heard *Raindrops Keep Falling On My Head* one more time he was going to take it upon himself to unplug that overgrown record player. He then exhibited a drunken grin as he noticed the floor space that separated him from the jukebox and realized that he could not make it that far in his condition. He would just have to tolerate these yokels' monotonous taste in music. Besides, after his next Martini he probably would no longer hear anything coming out of the jukebox anyway. The thought caused Pierce to laugh out loud.

The bartender, who stood behind the counter wiping glasses at the opposite end of the bar, looked at the man sitting alone and laughing. There was something creepy about someone laughing out loud when there was no one else around, even if he was drunk. As he set the dry glass on the counter, the bartender picked up a wet glass and began wiping it with the towel. As he did so, he thought of the laughing man at the end of the bar, and decided that the time had come to start watering down the drinks.

TRAFFIC WAS STILL heavy in the northbound lanes of 25th Avenue as last minute evacuees rushed to escape Camille. Highway 49, which was called 25th Avenue within the city limits of Gulfport, was one of only a few major arteries that connected the Gulf Coast with towns in the central and northern parts of the state. Tens of thousands of people lived along the Coast between Bay St. Louis and the Bay of Biloxi, and a large percentage of those lived close enough to the Gulf to be affected by the storm surge. There were also those residents who lived farther inland in mobile homes and other dwellings susceptible to the hurricane's high winds that decided to abandon their homes and head north.

Virtually every driver on the road at this time was under some type of emotional stress. They were in the midst of a crisis and were uncertain about the future. Many of them would return home in a few days only to discover that they had no home. What had been their residence would be nothing more than a pile of rubble. Family mementos and other possessions would be gone forever. It was a wonder that fights did not erupt among the drivers.

Despite the high volume of vehicles, and the tension that the drivers were experiencing, the traffic was flowing smoothly. This was due in large part to the efficiency of the Gulfport Police Department and the National Guard, who had personnel assigned to every major intersection along the highway. Ignoring the traffic signals, they waved the vehicles through in a continuous northward flow.

Frank Wojcik had considered taking side streets to get to their rendezvous with the Gulfport police officer, but decided that it would be quicker to just move along with the flow on 25th Avenue. It took a few minutes longer than the estimated fifteen minutes to make it to 28th Street, but no one seemed to notice. He pulled the sheriff's vehicle into the driveway of a closed gas station and parked behind the city police car.

In the middle of the intersection a National Guardsman was directing traffic. Officer Bob Reynolds stood beside the right rear door of the police car and watched Wojcik and Flowers get out of their vehicle and walk toward him. He was tall and thin, but the bright yellow raincoat that he wore, which was oversized to fit over his Sam Browne and other equipment, gave him the appearance of being much larger than he was.

"Hello, Bob," Wojcik greeted as he and Flowers got nearer.

"Hi, Frank," Reynolds said. "Busy day, huh?"

Wojcik grinned. "That's what I would call an understatement." He then gestured toward Flowers. "Bob, this is Sergeant Garland Flowers. He's with the Los Angeles County Sheriff's Department."

As Reynolds and Flowers shook hands, Wojcik said, "I understand you have some information on our suspect."

"I have a young couple inside my car who had a run-in with him a while ago."

For the first time Flowers noticed two figures in the back seat of the patrol car. Condensation had covered the window glass and it was difficult to see the interior clearly. Reynolds opened the back door and both detectives peered inside. A thin man in his early twenties, and a girl who appeared to be in her teens, looked back at them. They were both drenched from the rain and each was wrapped in an army blanket to stay warm.

Officer Reynolds leaned forward so that his head was inside the car and addressed the young man. "Billy Ray, why don't you come on out and tell these deputies what you told me. Your wife can stay in the car."

As Billy Ray opened the door on the left side of the vehicle and was getting out, Reynolds straightened up. He looked from Wojcik to Flowers and grinned. "Y'all ain't gonna believe this."

When Billy Ray walked around to the passenger side of the car, with the army blanket still draped over his shoulders, Reynolds introduced him to the two deputies.

"Go ahead, Billy Ray," Reynolds urged. "Tell'em what you told me."

"Well, it all started when I was haulin' in my trout lines down at Wolf River. This huge colored man . . . well, he was part colored and part white . . . he come barrelin' out of the woods. Scared the tar out of me. I knew right off who he was, 'cause I saw a picture of him on the bulletin board at the Jitney Jungle.

"Naturally, I was afraid at first. I knew he was a murderer an' I didn't know if he was gonna kill me or not. But after a minute I realized he wasn't, and that's when I got the idea of capturing him and turnin' him in for the reward." He hung his head sheepishly and added, "I know now there weren't no reward."

Billy Ray spent the next few minutes relating his and Missy's experience in their failed attempt to capture B.C. Jones. When he mentioned that Jones was attempting to get to Pineville, Flowers and Wojcik exchanged glances, but neither of them spoke. They did not want to interrupt the story, for Billy Ray might provide them with another bit of vital information. At the same time they were both anxious to leave. Flowers had been right all along. B.C. Jones was making his way to Pineville so that he could kill Frieda Pinchon. Time was of the essence.

After describing the comedy of errors that took place at the abandoned house and his and Missy's narrow escape, Billy Ray added, "We walked a half a mile or so, then a man and woman in a pick-up truck came by. They give us a ride in the back of their truck as far as here, and we reported what happened to Officer Reynolds."

When Billy Ray finished his story, Wojcik thanked him and told him he could return to his seat in the car. The detective then turned to Reynolds. "Do you have all the information on Mr. and Mrs. Love?"

"It's in my notebook," Reynolds replied. "Just a minute, I'll get it for you."

"That's ok," Wojcik said. "We'll get it from you later. Can't stick around."

"What's the rush?"

"We have to get to Pineville before Mr. Jones does," Wojcik said as he and Flowers moved toward their car. As he was about to get into the driver's seat, Wojcik looked back at Reynolds. "What do you plan to do with the Loves?"

"I'll run them over to the nearest shelter. It's only about five minutes from here."

Wojcik then shifted his gaze to the intersection, where the National Guardsman was waving the northbound traffic forward. "What's chances of you holding up traffic long enough for us to get across 25th Avenue? We have to head out 28th Street."

"No problem," Reynolds said. He then turned and shouted instructions to the National Guardsman.

Wojcik got into the car and started the engine. By the time they pulled out of the driveway onto 28th Street the north and southbound lanes of 25th Avenue were stopped, and they proceeded across the boulevard. There was no other traffic on the road and Wojcik increased their speed.

From the moment Billy Ray Love mentioned that Pineville was Jones' destination, Flowers and Wojcik both experienced a strong sense of urgency. But now that they were speeding toward Pineville, and knowing there was nothing more they could do for the time being, they began to relax.

Flowers was silent for the first few minutes of the drive, then he shook his head and chuckled.

Wojcik looked his way questioningly. "What are you thinking?"

"I was just picturing the fiasco at that abandoned house between Jones and the Loves." He smiled and shook his head again. "It sounds like something out of a Three Stooges comedy." Then the smile faded and Flowers added, "I wonder if Billy Ray realizes how close he came to getting his wife and himself killed."

THIRTY-FIVE

MORRIS CRUTHIRDS FINALLY got his reprieve from the courthouse in the mid-afternoon. The old deputy was elated when Dwight Cuevas assigned him to accompany a squad of National Guardsmen in the evacuation effort. Their area included the southwestern corner of the county. They began at Henderson Point, where the Bay of St. Louis met the Mississippi Sound, and moved eastward along Highway 90. It was their task to go from house to house and from business to business and use all their powers of persuasion to convince stragglers to find shelter away from the Gulf.

By late afternoon the squad had moved eastward as far as the western boundaries of Pass Christian. For the most part the buildings along the beachfront were deserted. With a few exceptions, the stragglers were talked into leaving. Cruthirds obtained the names and next of kin of those who decided to remain, and he was not hesitant to bluntly inform them that, if they did not leave, they would probably perish.

Though it would not normally be dark for a few more hours, the charcoal gray clouds blotted out most of the sun's light. Even the ominous reddish-orange glow was barely visible. The surroundings were neither fully dark nor fully light. It was as if a suspended twilight had fallen on the Gulf Coast.

The evacuation squad's last stop was the Sea Foam Lounge. On the north side of the lounge was the parking lot. Cruthirds and the squad sergeant exchanged questioning glances when they found several cars in the lot. From the jukebox speakers inside the lounge they could hear B. J. Thomas crooning the lyrics to *Raindrops Keep Falling On My Head.*

Deputy Cruthirds led the entire squad through the double doors and into the foyer. Inside the main room of the lounge they found over two dozen patrons laughing and drinking. In their merriment no one seemed to take notice of the soldiers' presence. The sergeant instructed one of his men to go to the jukebox and unplug it. When the music stopped every head in the room turned in their direction, as if startled by the silence.

Taking advantage of the moment, Cruthirds spoke with a voice loud enough to be heard throughout the room. "May I have y'all's attention, please?"

A man of medium height and stocky build stepped forward. "I'm Buzz Beeman. I own this place. What can I do for you?"

"I'm Deputy Cruthirds, with the sheriff's department." He gestured to the sergeant, who stood beside him. "And this is Sergeant Montgomery, of the Mississippi National Guard. We've been assigned to evacuate the area."

Buzz Beeman gave Cruthirds a patronizing smile. "Now, Deputy, are you telling us that you and those soldier boys are going to force my customers and me to leave?"

Cruthirds took a moment to scratch his head before answering. "Well, no sir. We ain't got that kind of authority." He looked around the room. "About all we can do is to let y'all know what you're in for if y'all decide to stick around."

"We'll be quite safe if we stay here," Buzz said.

"No sir, I don't think you will." The old deputy's voice dropped an octave and the volume was raised a notch. "You haven't taken any precautions against the storm. Hell, you ain't even bothered to cover that window."

Buzz Beeman's patronizing smile turned into a self-assured grin. "As I've demonstrated to my customers, there's no need to cover that window. It's hurricane proof."

"And would you be so kind as to tell me how you performed that demonstration?"

Before Buzz could reply, one of the customers spoke up. "He threw a body block into it and it didn't even faze the window."

Cruthirds looked past Buzz and addressed the customer who had just spoken. "And you're willing to risk your life on Mr. Beeman's demonstration?" Before the man could respond, Cruthirds continued, "I'd like for y'all to turn and look out that window at the Gulf."

When everyone had turned, he said, "Y'all see that blackness out there?" Along the horizon was a strip of darkness the color of tar. It stood out like a wall of coal between the bullet-gray waters of the Gulf and a sky that was the color of slate. "That's the hurricane out there. Inside that ugly darkness is a force so powerful y'all can't begin to imagine it. My guess is that it's movin' toward us at about ten miles an hour . . . maybe a bit faster, maybe slower. At any rate, it'll be here in a few more hours.

"What y'all need to be aware of is what's goin' on inside that darkness. From what the hurricane hunters have reported, there are winds movin' around in a giant circle at about two hundred miles an hour. That's stronger than any storm I ever heard of. When it hits land there'll probably be a bunch of tornadoes formed.

"But what y'all need to be mostly concerned about is the water. That wall out there is pushin' the Gulf of Mexico in front of it. As y'all can see, the water's already sloshin' up onto the highway. And the closer the hurricane gets, the faster the water's gonna rise.

"Now I can't tell you how high the water's gonna get, but if it reaches the bottom of this window, y'all are gonna be in a world of trouble, 'cause it's gonna throw some big waves right through that window."

Sgt. Montgomery nudged Cruthirds. "Excuse me, Morris. Would you mind if I said something?"

"Not at all."

The sergeant cleared his throat, then began, "Folks, I don't pretend to be an expert on hurricanes, but I have had some training in disaster response. In that training they taught us that there is no force on earth more powerful than moving water. The greater the volume and the faster the water moves the more powerful it is.

"One cubic yard of water weighs about seventeen hundred pounds. And, believe it or not, it's just about as solid as a block of concrete.

"Now, one of you just mentioned that Mr. Beeman showed you how strong his window was by throwing his body into it. On the face of it, that seems like an impressive demonstration. But believe me, it doesn't begin to give you a picture of the force that will be thrown against that window." He paused long enough to visually scan the window from one end to the other, as if measuring it. "My guess would be that, if you placed six Volkswagens side by side, they would probably fit inside that window. Would everyone agree?"

"Easily," Buzz Beeman replied proudly.

"Ok, now picture this. Picture those VW's, moving side by side, barreling down on this building at fifty miles per hour, and they all crash into the window at the same time. Is there anyone in this room who believes that the window would remain in place after such an impact?" When no one spoke, he added, "That, ladies and gentlemen, more accurately describes what you're up against. A single ten-foot wave would crash through this window like a rock through wax paper. But it won't stop with just one wave. The storm surge will send wave after wave into the building until there's nothing left. I don't care how much concrete and steel and Plexiglas went into constructing this building. As far as the storm surge is concerned, this place might as well be made of balsa wood."

Sgt. Montgomery looked at Cruthirds, then at the customers. "That's about all I have to say."

For half a minute no one spoke. Then two couples stepped from the crowd and moved toward the door. Others began shuffling about, as if undecided as to whether they should go or stay.

Buzz Beeman held up both arms and shouted. "Now, hold on, folks. These men are just trying to scare y'all. They're exaggerating so that y'all will leave. That's what they get paid to do. They know they can't legally make us go, so they try to scare us into leaving."

"But what about the water?" Someone asked.

"What about it?" Buzz said. "Can you actually imagine the water rising this high?" Another couple moved toward the door and he could feel his party beginning to end. "Come on, now, folks. Think about it! The water is not going to get this high! If it did it would wipe out the entire Gulf Coast. If hurricanes were that powerful, places like Pass Christian and Gulfport and Biloxi wouldn't even be here. I'm telling you these men are exaggerating."

The fourth couple to walk toward the door stopped. After a moment of hesitation the man and woman turned back and rejoined the group. "OK, Buzz," the man said. "But if it turns out that these boys are right and we all get killed, I'm gonna sue you."

His comment at first caused some nervous chuckles. Then others caught on and soon all the partygoers were laughing heartily. The humor seemed to break the tension.

"Great!" Buzz exclaimed. His quick thinking had saved his party. Only six people had walked out. That still left almost twenty to enjoy the hurricane party. After the storm had passed and word got out that he and his customers had partied through it, and the Sea Foam Lounge had stood up to everything God could throw at it, the place would be famous. It would be *the* place to go to have fun.

He shouted to the bartender. "Eddy! The next round of drinks is on me!" The announcement brought a round of applause from the partygoers.

Buzz Beeman then faced Cruthirds and sneered. "Well, Deputy? Is there anything else?"

"Yes sir, there is one more thing." Cruthirds looked at Montgomery, who was still standing beside the deputy. "Sergeant, why don't you have your men circulate among these nice folks and get their names and the names and addresses of their next of kin?" He then looked back at Buzz and returned the sneer. "Why don't we start with you, Mr. Beeman? This time tomorrow your relatives will begin to wonder what happened to you."

Buzz Beeman began to seethe with anger. He put his back to the old deputy and walked away.

As the National Guardsmen circulated among the patrons, obtaining the names of their next of kin, a fear of God's wrath returned to several of the customers. By the time the soldiers were finished, five more would-be partygoers had walked out of the Sea Foam Lounge in search of a safer haven from the storm.

While the Guardsmen did their work, Cruthirds scanned the room, studying the faces of each of the customers. He was filled with a sadness that must be felt by anyone whose job it is to sound an alarm, and watching those who choose to ignore it. If only they understood the hell that was about to descend upon them.

When his gaze reached the bar he stopped and took a double take at the man seated on the stool nearest him. The man sat with his side to the bar, taking in the activity with seemingly passive interest. His elbow rested on the counter and his forearm was upraised. Between two fingers a cigarette protruded from a plastic holder. If Cruthirds had not been positive otherwise, the cigarette holder convinced him. The man sitting at the bar was none other than Inspector Winston Pierce, of the Los Angeles County Sheriff's Department.

Cruthirds crossed the room to the bar and stopped when he was next to Pierce. The inspector sucked in a supply of smoke through the cigarette holder and turned his head toward the deputy. He then exhaled through his mouth and nose. Cruthirds could not be certain if the smoke had been intentionally blown in his face or not. He waved a hand in front of him to ward it off but made no comment. He decided to chalk up the rude behavior to the inspector's obvious state of intoxication.

"Inspector Pierce," Cruthirds began, "you probably don't remember me, but I . . . "

"Oh, I remember you." Pierce's words were slightly slurred. "You're that old dinosaur I saw in the sheriff's office this morning." He produced a silly, intoxicated grin, and added, "I remember you because you are the oldest looking deputy sheriff I have ever seen. Tell me something. Isn't there a mandatory retirement age for peace officers in this state? If so, what is it? Eighty?"

Cruthirds fought to refrain from just turning around and walking out, and leaving this idiot to fend for himself. He thought back to when he first saw Pierce earlier in the day. This visitor from California had marched into the office like he was the sheriff himself. There was an air of pompous superiority about Pierce, and Deputy Cruthirds disliked him from the start. As he looked at the drunk on the barstool he saw nothing that would change his mind. But he also realized that he had to make an effort to save the man's life.

"I figured you'd be on your way back to California by now," he said.

"You figured wrong."

"Yes, sir, I did. Unfortunately for you I did figure wrong."

"Unfortunately?"

"Yes, sir. You heard what I told these folks a few minutes ago. And in spite of what Mr. Beeman says, I meant every word of it."

Pierce's silly grin faded. "I suppose they told you what happened this morning."

Cruthirds looked puzzled. "Come again?"

"Oh, come now! My meeting with your Mr. Cuevas this morning. I'm sure they told you about the meeting. How they purposely made me look like a fool."

"Inspector, they didn't tell me nothing. Why should they? It was none of my business." Cruthirds breathed a deep sigh and continued. "Besides, what's that got to do with anything now? Sir, I'm tellin' you for your own good. You've got to come with us so we can get you to a shelter. We're runnin' out of time."

The silly grin returned. "I'm among friends here. I'll take my chances with them."

For almost a full minute the two men stared at each other in silence. Cruthirds could think of nothing else to say, and he was not allowed to forcibly carry Pierce to safety if he didn't want to be saved.

"Please, Inspector, come with us. This is a very dangerous place to be right now."

"Get this clear in your oversized head once and for all. I am not going with you."

Cruthirds shrugged. "Suit yourself, Inspector." He breathed another sigh. "Lord knows I tried." He then turned and began walking away.

Pierce called after him. "There is something I would like to thank you for, Deputy."

Cruthirds stopped and turned to face Pierce. "Thank me? For what?"

"I want to thank you for unplugging the jukebox. I do believe if I hear that raindrops song one more time I'm going to pull my hair out."

FIVE MINUTES LATER Deputy Morris Cruthirds, Sgt. Montgomery and the squad of National Guardsmen stood in the parking lot of the Sea Foam Lounge. The wind seemed to have increased dramatically in the short time they had spent inside the lounge. The driving rain assaulted them and they had to cover their faces and hands. But their thoughts were not on the rain. They were thinking of the people inside the building. Each man felt a sense of disappointment at having failed to convince the partygoers to evacuate to a safer place. It was true that some of them did heed the warning and decided to leave, but the majority of customers had elected to remain . . . and there was nothing more they could do other than report their actions to the office of civil defense.

Deputy Cruthirds saw the look of disappointment on the faces of the Guardsmen and knew he had to say something. "Well, boys, we've done everything we possibly can to get these stragglers to safety. Some folks listened to us and some didn't. That's just the way it goes. We all did our best." He then addressed Sgt. Montgomery, who was standing beside him. "Sergeant, I think it's time we called it a day. We put in a good afternoon and we saved some lives. But it's gettin' late and we got to get these boys to their own shelters."

He looked out over the Gulf and studied the wide ribbon of blackness that was heading their way.

"You know, Sergeant," Cruthirds said, "I've lived in these parts all my life, an' I've seen every kind of storm there is." He shook his head slowly. "But I gotta tell you. Weatherwise, I ain't never seen anything as scary as that thing from Hell that's movin' toward us right now."

THIRTY-SIX

B.C. JONES MOVED along Red Creek Road at a slow pace. He was walking against the wind, which had grown steadily stronger throughout the afternoon. Raindrops were shooting into his face like pellets from a rapid-fire air rifle. He was becoming increasingly discouraged, ever since his confrontation with that lying Billy Ray back at the abandoned house. But the inner voice urged him on, reminding him that he was getting closer to Frieda with each step he took.

Jones had no idea what time it was, nor would it have mattered to him if he did know. He only knew that an hour earlier it looked like it was getting dark, yet full darkness did not come. And now it still appeared to be almost dark—the same as it looked an hour ago. He was confused by the strange weather.

On both sides of the road were open fields where dead corn stalks were being beaten into the ground by the wind and rain. Jones felt uncomfortable in the open, where there were no woods to offer refuge. Only twice had he seen any vehicles since leaving the house, and on both occasions he was able to duck into nearby brush before being spotted.

In one of the cornfields, off to his right about fifty yards, was a large barn. As he was walking past the reddish-brown structure something told him to turn around and look behind him. When he did so he saw the beams of headlights appear from around a curve. The vehicle itself was not yet in sight.

Reacting with the instincts of a hunted animal, Jones dashed across the field toward the barn. The front of the barn, where the large double doors would be found, was on the side opposite the road. There was, however, a narrow door attached to the rear of the building. Upon arriving at the door, Jones pulled the handle and was relieved when the door creaked open. He hurriedly stepped inside and closed the door behind him. The exterior twilight shown through several cracks in the wall, offering a feeble illumination of the barn's otherwise dark interior.

Jones peered through one of the cracks in the wall just in time to see a Plymouth sedan pass. He knew, just as any ghetto child in L.A. would know, that it was a police car.

There was little doubt in Jones' mind that he was still being protected by the voice inside him, for it was the voice that had told him to turn around when the car's light beams appeared. The voice had saved him once again.

Jones put his back to the wall, then slid down to a sitting position on the dirt floor. It felt good to be out of the wind and rain. Though the wind blew relentlessly against loose window shutters, creating a constant banging noise, the barn had a good roof and it was dry inside. He decided to stay where he was and rest for a while.

GARLAND FLOWERS GAVE little thought to the barn off to his right as he and Wojcik drove past the cornfields on Red Creek Road. His mind was on the Pinchons, and how he might protect them from B.C. Jones.

As if reading his partner's mind, Wojcik said, "We'll be at the Pinchons in about five or six minutes. Have you given any thought as to how you're going to deal with old man Pinchon?"

"What do you mean?"

"I mean you can't exactly stake his place out in a car during a hurricane. You've got to actually be inside the house with them." He grinned wryly. "And as I recall from our last meeting with him, he wasn't exactly thrilled with our company."

"Yeah, you're right." Flowers breathed a deep sigh. "You have any suggestions?"

"The best suggestion I can offer is that we load the Pinchons into the car and drive them up to my place. We can all ride out the storm together. Darla has enough food, water and other supplies stored up to last us a month. After Camille is behind us we can concentrate on our suspect."

Flowers shrugged. "I agree. That's the most logical thing to do. But you and I both know that Pinchon isn't going to budge." He thought for a moment, then added, "He probably believes that a customer might show up in the middle of the hurricane to buy a penny box of matches, and he wants to be sure he's there to sell it to him."

"Sounds like you just might have Pinchon's character nailed down." Wojcik paused, then a smile appeared. "I wonder if Mr. Pinchon has given any thought to the fact that he is sandwiched between two killer storms."

"Two storms?" Flowers asked.

"That's the way I see it. He's got Hurricane Camille coming in from the south. And closing in rapidly from the north is . . . Cyclone Jones."

SHORTLY AFTER FLOWERS and Wojcik departed from their meeting with Billy Ray and Missy Love, Officer Reynolds drove the couple to a shelter at North Central Elementary School on Pass Road.

They were met at the entrance to the school cafeteria by a heavy set middle-aged woman who wore the insignia of a Red Cross volunteer. When her eyes first fell on the disheveled couple, their drenched and forlorn appearance reminded her of two cats that had just fallen into a rain barrel. But she greeted them warmly and, after recording their names on a roster, issued them new blankets and assigned them adjoining cots.

A minute later Billy Ray and Missy arrived at their assigned area. They dropped the bedding on their respective cots and sat down, facing each other. The space that separated the two cots was so narrow that Billy Ray's knees touched the side of Missy's cot.

Missy rested her elbows on her knees and put her face in her hands, then began to weep. Billy Ray immediately got up and moved to Missy's cot and sat down beside her. He placed an arm around her shoulders and squeezed gently.

"There, there, now, Honey. Everything's gonna work out just fine."

She took her hands from her face and stared at him. Her sudden movement caused Billy Ray to take his arm from around her shoulder. Beyond the moistness in her eyes was a flash of anger.

"How can you say that? We're gonna lose everything, Billy Ray. It'll be a miracle if the trailer holds up against this awful herrycan. And the picture albums. I . . . I left them in the truck. They'll be ruined." She put her hands back to her face and began sobbing aloud.

Billy Ray looked around to see if anyone was watching. Though there were several other families nearby, no one seemed to be paying any attention. They all had worries of their own.

He had to fight the urge to sink into a pit of self-derision. There was no doubt about it; he was a certified failure. He was out of work and had no money whatsoever. And if that were not enough, his house was about to become a storm-versus-mobile home statistic. They would probably have to sponge off relatives for the next several months. The thought of it made him feel even more like a failure.

But it was not in Billy Ray's nature to feel sorry for himself, and he forced himself to think more positively. He had to do it for Missy's sake.

"You know, Honey," he said, "I have an idea them pictures are gonna be safe and dry during this storm."

She looked at him again. Her eyes were red but the anger had passed and she spoke softly. "Oh, no, Billy Ray. They're gonna get soaked and ruined."

"They'll stay dry in the truck."

"No. You don't understand. When I jumped out of the truck I left the door open. It'll be flooded in no time."

Suddenly Billy Ray remembered something that caused him to smile. He recalled being chased by B.C. Jones. And though he was in a panic and was hurrying to get Missy and himself as far from Jones as he could, he had still taken the time to close the door to the truck. He could not explain why he did it at the time, nor could he explain it now. Maybe he did it purely out of habit, or maybe God told him to do it in order to protect their mementos. He could not be sure. Billy Ray was not particularly religious and had never been known as a churchgoer, so he was more inclined to believe that he had closed the door out of habit. But whatever the reason, he had in fact closed the door.

As he thought of this he was suddenly filled with a sense of well being. Somehow he and Missy were going to make it through this crisis. Once again he placed his arm around her shoulder and gently pulled her to him.

"Believe me, Honey, things are gonna work out fine. The picture albums are as safe as can be." He turned her face toward his and gave her a loving smile. "Let me tell you how I know."

THIRTY-SEVEN

FRANK WOJCIK TURNED left onto Briggs Street from Menge Avenue, then made another sharp left and parked directly in front of the entrance to Pinchon's Grocery. There were no other vehicles to be seen, and the store's windows were covered with plywood. On the door was a closed sign.

The two detectives got out of the car and moved hurriedly to the door. The overhang that extended seven feet out from the front of the building offered no more relief from the driving rain than it did from the wind. Flowers, with elbows tucked against his sides, hunched forward to make as small a target as possible, and began to wonder if he had made a mistake in removing his raincoat.

Wojcik banged on the door with the side of his fist. They waited a full minute before he banged again, more loudly this time. Another several seconds passed, then he looked at his partner. "You think they might have gone to a shelter?"

Flowers offered a wincing smile. "That would be too good to be true."

Wojcik raised his fist to hammer on the door once more, but stopped when he heard a gruff voice from within. "We're closed."

"Mr. Pinchon, this is Deputy Wojcik, from the sheriff's department. Would you please let us in?"

"What for?"

"Sir, we have information that the suspect is on his way here!"

"Let him come! I got my .357 magnum."

"Mr. Pinchon, please let us in so we can talk to you. You're putting your granddaughter's life in danger!"

There was no response at first and the detectives knew that Pinchon was giving some thought to Wojcik's last statement. No more than a few seconds passed, but in the driving rain each second seemed like a full minute.

"Go around to the east side of the building," Pinchon grudgingly replied. "There's a door back there. I'll open it for you."

Flowers and Wojcik did as Pinchon said. As they rounded the corner they passed between the building and the ice cream cone sign they had helped Pinchon put up the day before. Flowers studied the heavy sheet metal sign and frowned. Due to the changing speed of the wind the huge chocolate ice cream cone swung erratically, causing the wooden signpost to creak. He also noticed that the cotton rope that attached the sign to the post was already beginning to fray.

There were actually two doors on the east side of the building. The first was at ground level and was probably a rear entrance to the store. The second door was at the top of three steps and was the main entrance into the living quarters. It was the door through which Frieda had come the day before, when she had run across the street and talked to them during their stakeout.

Just as they arrived at the first door they heard the sound of a latch being turned, then the door opened inward. Flowers pulled the screen door open and motioned for his partner to precede him. Wojcik led the way into the semi-darkened interior of the store. It was the section where canned goods had been stocked, but most of the shelf space was bare, as were other display racks throughout the store. The Pinchons had apparently had a busy day selling their merchandise.

Eugene Pinchon stood before them, his drooping mustache accentuating the frown on his face. He wore dark blue cotton slacks and a plaid shirt. He had probably shed the grocery apron as soon as the store closed.

Behind him Frieda stood on the steps of the inside entrance to the living quarters. She wore black pants that flared at the bottom. Her flower-print blouse was loose fitting and was not tucked in.

"Well, you're inside now," the elder Pinchon said. "What did you have to say that you couldn't say from outside?"

Wojcik confronted Pinchon's suriliness with an attitude of his own. "I suppose Sergeant Flowers and I could have continued to stand out in the rain and shout at you through the door, but neither of us were inclined to do so."

If Wojcik's response caused Pinchon to soften, he didn't show it. "Well, you're inside now. What'd you want to tell me?"

"We have a witness who talked to Suspect Jones a few hours ago. Jones told him he was looking for Frieda Pinchon and needed directions to Pineville. The witness not only told him how to get here, but also told Jones that Frieda lived with her grandfather behind a grocery store."

Pinchon was incredulous. "Who was this witness? And why would he be giving this Jones character information on where we lived?"

"It's a long story, Mr. Pinchon, and it doesn't really matter who the witness is. Suffice it to say the person didn't know what he was doing. What we have to concentrate on now is how we're going to respond to the situation as it stands now.

"Even though our suspect is not exactly the brightest individual around, he won't have any trouble finding this place. Pineville is small. How many grocery stores can there be? He'll find the place all right.

"This store is surrounded by woods on three sides. So far as we know he could be out there somewhere right now, waiting to make his move."

"Then why don't you get some more men and search the woods?"

"Because we don't have any more men. In case you haven't noticed, there's a major hurricane heading this way. Every emergency service agency in the county is tied up right now."

"There's no need to be sarcastic, deputy," Pinchon said.

Wojcik looked at Flowers, who rolled his eyes toward the ceiling but said nothing. Wojcik returned his attention to the storekeeper. "You're right, Mr. Pinchon, there's no need to be sarcastic."

"What do you think we should do, deputy?"

"The best thing for you and Frieda to do would be to go with us to my place. My wife and I have two girls. We live in a big house up in Orange Grove. You're welcome to stay with us for the night. After this storm passes over we can concentrate on finding the suspect."

Eugene Pinchon folded his arms across his chest as if to demonstrate that he was standing firm. "I'm not leaving. This is my house and my business, and I'll be hanged if I will let some two-bit criminal chase me out."

"What about the hurricane, Mr. Pinchon?"

"What about it? I'm not afraid of it either. I've been through hurricanes before."

"And what about your granddaughter?" Flowers asked, speaking for the first time since entering the store.

Pinchon's gaze shifted from Wojcik to Flowers. It was clear that he did not like this black intruder from California. "I'll protect her. Like I said before, I've got a .357…"

"I know," Flowers said, cutting him off. "You've got a .357 magnum. And I have no doubt that you are perfectly willing to use it to protect your home and family."

"You can bet your last dime I'll use it."

"But you won't be dealing with an ordinary person. B.C. Jones is more like an animal. Oh, I'm sure you'll be able to get a couple shots into him, and it may even be enough to kill him. But unless you're extremely lucky, before he falls dead he will still have time to rip the gun away and choke the life out of you, then go after your granddaughter."

Pinchon stared at Flowers but said nothing.

"You see, Mr. Pinchon," Flowers continued, "The way I see it, B.C. Jones doesn't value his life the way most of us value ours. He has one thing to live for right now, and that is to send Frieda to a better place. And he will willingly sacrifice his own life to carry out his mission."

"That's crazy!" Pinchon exclaimed.

Flowers shrugged. "I don't know what label a psychiatrist would put on his behavior. But like I said, you won't be dealing with a normal person with normal reactions." He stared into Pinchon's eyes. "And Jones won't be scared away by your .357 magnum."

"What do you say, Mr. Pinchon?" Wojcik asked. "Why don't you let us take you and Frieda out of here?"

Pinchon did not respond at first. He looked back at his granddaughter, who was still standing on the steps behind him. Her eyes were wide as she continued to absorb what Flowers had just said.

"Frieda is free to go with y'all if she wishes," Pinchon said at last. "But I'm staying." With one hand he gestured toward the store. With the other he gestured toward the residence. "This is my home as well as my business, and I won't be driven away from either."

Flowers and Wojcik both looked at Frieda. Pinchon also turned around and faced his granddaughter.

She reacted immediately to the stares of the three men who stood before her. "Oh, no! I'm not leaving my grandpa. If he stays, I stay!"

Frieda descended the steps and moved to her grandfather. Placing an arm around his waist, she said, "I'm not leaving you, Grandpa."

Pinchon looked from one detective to the other. "Well, there you have it, deputies. Now, if y'all don't have anything else, maybe y'all should get on back to your own families."

The detectives exchanged glances, then Flowers addressed Pinchon. "I'm going to stay with you."

Pinchon glared at Flowers. "Oh, no you're not!"

"Mr. Pinchon, you can't handle Jones by yourself. If there are two of us, maybe we'll have a chance against him."

Pinchon addressed Wojcik but motioned toward Flowers. "I don't want him spending the night in my house."

Wojcik's face suddenly reddened with anger. "Why not, Pinchon? Is it because he's black?"

"I didn't say that!"

"You didn't have to. It's pretty obvious."

"It's not that! It's just that . . . that . . . I don't like him. And he doesn't like me."

"You're not an easy man to like, Mr. Pinchon." Wojcik glared at the storekeeper. "I also think you're a bigot."

Pinchon returned the glare. "Think what you like."

"What if I keep out of the living quarters?" Flowers put in. "I can stay out here in the store." As he stared coldly at the storekeeper, Pinchon could not avoid looking away. "You see, Mr. Pinchon, I don't really care if you're a bigot or not, and I certainly wouldn't want to taint the inside of your house with my presence. What I do care about is keeping your granddaughter alive. So I'll just stay out here in the store. If you need me for anything, all you have to do is yell."

A silence fell on the group. Frieda slowly removed her arm from around her grandfather's waist. It was not an act of rebellion against him as much as it was a reaction to an awkward moment. She was embarrassed and could not bring herself to look at Flowers, for fear of his returning the look. She moved away from the three men in an attempt to fade into the background.

The long moment of silence seemed to pass interminably. Then at last Eugene Pinchon spoke. "Very well, Sergeant. You want to stay out here in the store? Then suit yourself." Saying nothing more, he moved to the steps and ascended them. Without so much as a glance back, he opened the door and stepped into the living quarters.

Frieda followed her grandfather up the steps. When she reached the landing she turned in the general direction of the detectives, careful not to look directly at them. "Excuse me," she said softly, then she, too, disappeared into her private sanctuary.

When they were alone in the store Wojcik turned to his partner. "You sure you want to go through with this, Garland?"

Flowers grinned. "You mean do I want to go through a hurricane in a building owned by a racist, standing between him and a crazed killer? Hell no, I don't want to do it." He shrugged and added. "But I don't see any alternative."

"Maybe I could call Darla and . . . "

"Don't even think about it, Frank. You have to be with your family during this storm. If anything happened to them while you were here you'd never forgive yourself."

"But I don't feel right leaving you here alone."

"I'm a big boy, Frank. I'll be O.K."

"What kind of firepower are you carrying?"

Flowers lifted his right trouser leg, revealing a holster strapped to the side of his leg, between the calf and ankle. Inside the holster was a snub-nosed revolver. "It's a Smith and Wesson .38 Chief. Holds five rounds."

"What kind of ammo does it have?"

"The most powerful our department will authorize; 158 grain hollow point."

Wojcik shook his head. "That still isn't much firepower. Unfortunately, what I have isn't any better." He forced a smile and added, "Maybe you could trade your weapon to Pinchon for his .357."

"Are you kidding?" Flowers said. "I don't want to let him know that I'm protecting him and his granddaughter with nothing more than a glorified peashooter. If he found out he'd probably chase me off his property."

The two friends returned to the car, where Flowers removed his jacket and raincoat from the back seat. He quickly put on the raincoat and tucked the folded jacket under the plastic in an effort to keep it dry.

They shook hands, then Wojcik got behind the wheel of the car and started the engine. He rolled down the window and regarded his friend for a long moment. "Be careful Garland. And I promise you, I'll get back here as soon as possible."

"I know you will, Frank. Give my best to Darla and the girls."

"Will do," Wojcik said as the car backed slowly toward the street.

Flowers watched Wojcik drive away. He then turned and, despite the wind and rain, took his time walking back to the store.

TWENTY-FIVE MINUTES after leaving Pineville, Frank Wojcik pulled into the long driveway of his home. Avoiding the heavy traffic of Highway 49, he had taken a series of back roads. There were very few vehicles on the rural thoroughfares and he made good time.

The first thing he noticed was the pick-up truck belonging to Darla's parents parked near the garage. He was glad to see it, for it meant that her parents would ride out the storm with them. The fact that they would all be together would ease Darla's mind.

He parked the county car several feet behind the truck and got out. As he moved up the steps and along the porch he glanced out over the huge lawn. The pine trees were already bending in the wind. Fortunately, none of them were close enough to the house to hit it if they fell. The oaks, with their heftier trunks, were not bending, but the smaller limbs in the upper reaches slapped one another, and their leaves rattled loudly against the gale.

Just as he was opening the screen, the main door also opened and Darla stood before him. He quickly stepped inside and she closed the door behind him.

"Honey, I've been so worried about you," she said as they embraced. "I haven't heard a thing from you all afternoon."

"I'm sorry, sweetheart," he said. "But these past few hours have been hectic."

Darla then pulled back from him and looked about. "Where's Garland?"

Wojcik sighed. "He won't be with us tonight." He then briefly explained the situation with the Pinchons.

"Poor Garland," Darla said. "Having to go through this dreadful storm with someone like that Mr. Pinchon."

Wojcik looked away, and when he spoke there was emotion in his voice. "I feel bad about this, Darla. On one hand I feel I had a duty to stay with him. But on the other hand I knew I had to be here with you and the girls."

Darla looked at her husband through squinted eyes, and she reached up and turned his head so that he faced her. "Now you listen to me, Noel Francis Wojcik. I understand how you must feel, having to leave Garland to handle this mess alone. But you've always said that your family comes first. The weathermen are telling us that Camille will be the worst hurricane to ever hit the Coast. If we had to go through it without you I would simply die. And to think of you out there somewhere, not knowing if you were safe or not…"

Her voice trailed off and she was unable to finish the sentence. Neither of them spoke for a long moment. Outside, the howling winds hurled sheets of rain against the walls and the plywood-covered windows. The only sounds inside the house came from the dining room, where Mr. and Mrs. Necaise were entertaining the girls with a game of Chutes and Ladders.

Darla pulled Frank to her and they embraced again. "I'm just so thankful that you're here with us." After a pause she added, "And I will pray for Garland."

THIRTY-EIGHT

IT WAS DARK when B.C. Jones emerged from the barn. The moon was not visible and the sky was pitch black. He made his way across the field and to the road more by memory than by visual reference. Once on the road, though, he was able to follow its vague outline as he trudged against the wind and driving rain in the direction of Pineville.

The bullet crease in his side was aching. It was actually more of an abrasion than a crease. As the bullet had flown past it had barely broken the skin. But sometime during the journey along Red Creek Road Jones' shirt had become stuck to the bloody surface of the wound and had since been pulled loose, taking the dried blood with it. Exposure to the damp air was now causing the open wound to throb. The voice told Jones to ignore the pain and concentrate on the chore at hand. With each step he was getting ever closer to Frieda.

He had been walking for twenty minutes when the road made a sharp curve to the left. After rounding the curve Jones crossed over a short bridge and found himself on the northern edge of Pineville. A thrill of excitement raced through him as it occurred to him that Frieda Pinchon lived around here somewhere. He struggled to recall what that Billy Ray had told him down by the river. He had said that Frieda lived with her grandpa behind a grocery store. So all he had to do now was find a grocery store.

But the storm was growing fiercer by the minute. It was impossible for him to walk straight, for the wind kept pushing him to the left. As big as he was he was no match for the gusts that moved him about like a feather in front of a fan.

Thoughts of Frieda filled him with the urge to trudge along until he found her. But the voice inside of him, the voice that had led him to where he was at this moment, spoke to him of caution. There would be plenty of time to search for Frieda, but for now he must seek shelter from the wind and rain. After the storm blew over he could find Frieda. And when he found her he could satisfy the passions that were erupting within him.

Pineville was a sparsely populated community. There were no sidewalks, and the few businesses and private residences that occupied both sides of the road were separated by vacant lots and small wooded areas.

A building on the left side of the road caught Jones' attention. It had an arched roof, like a large Quonset hut, and walls that were made of cinder blocks. The darkness prevented Jones from reading the sign on the front of the building, but it looked like an automobile garage.

There were no lights anywhere near the structure, and Jones had to feel his way along the side of the building as he made his way to the rear. Twice he stumbled over pieces of machinery, and once he slipped on grease and almost fell. His intention was to break into the back door where there would be less chance of him being seen. But when he arrived at the rear of the garage he discovered that the only entry was a large chain-driven sliding door, and he knew that he would be unable to force it open.

Several feet behind the garage, however, Jones saw a smaller building. It was also made of cinder blocks, and appeared to be a storage shed. It took little effort for him to move toward the shed because the wind pushed him in that direction.

On the east side of the building was a wooden door secured by a padlock. Without the slightest hesitation, Jones lifted a foot and kicked the door. Though the door was designed to open outward, the force of the kick broke it from the hasp that contained the padlock. The impact ripped the molding from the doorjamb. The hinges also pulled from the frame as the door was forced inward. But once the door was free of the lock Jones managed to pull it open.

When he stepped inside the small enclosure, he felt around until he found a clear space on the floor. He then pulled the broken door closed as best he could. The shed was not as comfortable as the barn, but at least he was out of the wind and rain. But best of all, he was in Pineville, and could not be more than a few minutes away from Frieda.

THE WALL OF pitch blackness out in the Gulf that Morris Cruthirds had contemplated earlier could no longer be distinguished from the black sea beneath it or the black sky above, yet it was out there . . . and moving ever closer to the mainland.

The ferocious winds of Camille blew across the Channel Islands. The hurricane struck Ship Island with such force that it cut a swath across the sand dunes so deep that the island was split in two.

When the tidal surge coming in from the deep waters of the Gulf hit the shallow waters of the Mississippi Sound it caused an immediate rise in the water level. The powerful winds of Camille pushed the immense volume of water ahead of it. The slow but steady rise of the tide that the Coast experienced throughout the afternoon shifted into a higher gear, and the water began to elevate much more rapidly. By the time Camille would make landfall the seas would have risen twenty feet, and above the seas would be waves ten feet high.

On the mainland almost everyone had taken shelter. The streets of Biloxi, Gulfport, Long Beach and Pass Christian were deserted. The business districts were like ghost towns. Even Highway 49, where evacuees had been rushing to get out of town a few hours earlier, was now as empty as every other thoroughfare. Those who had chosen to stay behind were now inside their homes or other places of refuge. Evacuation was no longer an option.

At a fire station in Pass Christian a huge siren began to wail, and could be heard even above the howling wind. It was a last minute warning to take shelter.

Camille was almost here.

GARLAND FLOWERS SAT on the stair landing with his back to the door that led into the living quarters. He listened to the persistent howl of the wind as he absently gazed about the interior of the store. There was ample illumination, for he had found the light switches shortly after returning from seeing Wojcik off.

In the two hours since he had been left alone, Flowers had gone over virtually every inch of the store in an attempt to gain all the knowledge he could about the place. Most of it was useless information, but one never knew. For instance, he had discovered that the store actually had four separate doors.

There was, of course, the front entrance, which was boarded up at present. And on the east side of the building was the entrance through which he and Wojcik had been admitted. There was the door to the living quarters behind him. And to the left of where he sat was the fourth door, attached to the store's back wall behind the stair landing. It was only about four feet high and was locked. That it led to a space under the living quarters was quite obvious, and Flowers concluded that it was probably a storage area of some sort.

In addition to the doors directly connected to the business section of the building, there was the side entrance to the living quarters that Frieda had used the day before, when he and Wojcik first met her during the stakeout. He recalled that the door opened onto a stair landing, and there were three steps to the ground level. It was identical to the landing on which he was now sitting.

Flowers' thoughts were interrupted by the sound of the door opening behind him. He looked over his shoulder and saw that it had opened only about a foot, then he saw Frieda's head appear from behind the door. He stood up to give her room on the landing and she pushed the door with her shoulder so that it opened wider. In one hand she held a paper plate containing two sandwiches. In the other she held a soft drink.

"I thought you might be hungry," she said as she stepped onto the landing and offered the food to him.

"Thanks, I'm famished."

He had not eaten since leaving the command post in the early afternoon. Morris Cruthirds had delivered box lunches to him and Wojcik that contained two dried sandwiches, an apple and a carton of milk. He ate part of one sandwich and washed it down with a swallow of the milk. But that was seven or eight hours ago and he was beginning to wish that he had that box lunch with him now. A few minutes before Frieda entered he had thought of looking around the store for something to snack on, but most of the food items had been sold.

He sat back down on the landing, placing the plate and soft drink beside him. Frieda also sat, squeezing between the railing and the food. Flowers moved the plate to the first step down from the landing to give her more room. His feet were on the second step, and he was able to pick up the sandwiches and soft drink from between his legs.

They sat in silence for a few minutes as Flowers ate his sandwiches. One was made of bologna and the other pressed ham. They both had mayonnaise, lettuce and tomato between slices of fresh white bread. He decided immediately after the first bite that they were far superior to the offerings in the box lunch.

Frieda gave him a chance to finish the first sandwich before asking, "Sergeant Flowers, why is he doing this?"

At first he thought she was referring to her grandfather. "Why is he doing what?"

"Why is he trying to kill me?"

Flowers felt a little foolish. Who else would be weighing more heavily on her mind than B.C. Jones?

"Because he's a homicidal mental case."

"That's pretty obvious, Sergeant, but why me?"

Flowers looked at her and shrugged. "For some reason he's become convinced that you have racially mixed blood in you."

"But why would that make him want to kill me?"

As Flowers studied Frieda he wondered why his last comment did not spark a stronger reaction from her. Then he recalled the police report and decided that Jones' opinion of her racial origins was not news to her. After all, that is what caused the disturbance in Woolworth in the first place.

"It would probably take a whole team of psychiatrists to sort it all out," Flowers said. "But I'm fairly certain they would conclude that his messed up thinking stems from his childhood.

"As you know, Jones is a mulatto. His mother was white and his father was black. And from what I understand his father began physically abusing B.C. when he was very young. I suspect that there was some brain damage, as well as emotional damage, during the course of that abuse."

"What about his mother?" Frieda asked. "Where was she all this time?"

"From what I understand, the mother was present during these abusive encounters. And while she didn't actually take part in the beatings, she never lifted a finger to stop them, either.

"When he was old enough to go to school he was treated badly by other kids because of his mixed blood. And because of his size, even his teachers treated him differently than the other students. I guess they considered him a threat to their safety. Needless to say, Jones grew up nursing one heck of a grudge.

"Somehow Jones, over the years, came to the conclusion that all of the mistreatment that he had endured was the result of his racially mixed blood. And somewhere along the line he decided that everyone of mixed blood was suffering just as badly as he was, and it fell upon him to correct the problem. His only solution has been to murder the parents as well as the children."

Frieda stared toward the front of the store, though her thoughts were somewhere beyond the interior of the building. "I can understand why he would want to hurt the parents—out of anger and revenge. But why murder the children?"

"The only thing I can come up with is that he figures there is no hope for them in this world. They'll suffer as badly as he has suffered." Flowers shrugged again and added, "I imagine he has a strong belief in an after life–a place that is far better than what we can offer here on earth—a place where these innocent children won't be persecuted. And the only way he can send them to that better place is by ending their lives here on earth."

Frieda turned and faced Flowers. "And I'm one of those children he wants to send to a better place."

Flowers nodded. "I'm afraid so."

She turned back and stared into space. Flowers took advantage of the silence that followed by picking up the second sandwich. He was about to take his first bite when Frieda spoke.

"There are two images of that awful man that I can't get out of my mind. The first was the scary look he gave me at Woolworth when the police were taking him away. And the second was yesterday when they showed his picture on T.V."

She shook her head and half-grinned, as if she had thought of something ironically amusing. "It's funny, but I almost never turn on the T.V. on Saturday morning–at least not since I stopped watching cartoons as a kid. But yesterday I was curious to see if they had any news reports on the Woodstock festival."

"The what?" Flowers asked.

"Woodstock. You know. That rock concert somewhere up in New York. Every rock group in the country was there."

"Oh, *that* concert," Flowers said. He did not care for rock music and had no idea what she was talking about.

"Anyway, it ended this weekend, and I wanted to see if, by some chance, they were showing any of it on T.V." She frowned and added, "But when I turned on the T.V., the screen was filled with a picture of that awful man. I was so shocked I thought I was going to die."

"I can imagine," Flowers said, then after what he hoped was a respectful interlude he took a bite from his sandwich.

"I want you to know one thing, Frieda," he said after washing down the sandwich with a swallow of soda. "And that is that my reason for being here is to protect you from B.C. Jones. Naturally,

I would like to capture him and take him back to Los Angeles if I can. But my primary duty is to keep you safe." He looked squarely into her eyes before adding, "I give you my solemn word; the only way he will get to you is through me. I will use every means available to stop him."

Her eyes moistened. "Thank you," she said in a soft voice that was filled with emotion.

An awkward moment of silence followed and Flowers was anxious to change the subject. "Tell me, Frieda," he said as he motioned to his left, "where does that little door go?"

She craned her neck to see where he was indicating. "Oh, that's just a small storeroom. As you can see, it's under the house. Grandpa dug out an area about eight feet square and put walls around it then put in that little door. He used it at one time to store empty soda pop bottles. He used to keep the bottles out back, but boys would steal them to collect the two-cent deposits. So Grandpa built the room to hide the bottles." She thought for a moment and added, "There are also a bunch of pipes down there."

"Pipes?"

"Yeah. You know, plumbing pipes."

"Is there any way to get into the storeroom from outside?"

"Oh, no. The room has a wall around it between the ground and the floor of the house. The only way in or out is through that door."

"I see," Flowers said. "What's chances of you getting the key that unlocks the door?"

Frieda shrugged. "I guess I could. But why do you want to unlock it? I told you there's nothing in there but some plumbing fixtures."

"Oh, I don't know. It just gives us another option, I guess. If worse comes to worse, it might offer a hiding place from Jones." He paused and added, "I would just like for it to be unlocked."

Frieda nodded. "I'll see what I can do."

They were both startled by the sudden opening of the door to the living quarters. Standing in the doorway with a scowl on his face was Eugene Pinchon.

"What are you doing out here, young lady?"

"I just brought Sergeant Flowers some food."

"That was ten minutes ago. Why didn't you come right back in?"

"We were just talking."

Pinchon looked from Frieda to Flowers, then back at Frieda. "Yeah, well . . . it ain't decent, being out here alone with him."

Flowers seethed with anger. "What's not decent about it, Mr. Pinchon?" He glared at the older man. "What did you think we were doing out here?"

Pinchon returned the glare but made no attempt to respond. When he spoke it was to his granddaughter. "I want you inside now." When she hesitated he spoke more firmly. "I said now, young lady!"

Frieda hurried through the door without so much as a "goodnight" to Flowers. After she had gone through the door Pinchon closed it behind them.

For the next several minutes Flowers sat on the landing, listening to the howling winds and sipping his soft drink. Then he heard a sound behind him. He looked back in time to see the door open a few inches and a hand appear through the crack. The hand belonged to Frieda and it held a flashlight. She set the light on the landing, then placed a smaller object beside it, after which she withdrew her hand and quietly closed the door.

He leaned back to retrieve the flashlight as well as the smaller object. As he held it in the palm of his hand he smiled. It was the key to the storeroom.

THIRTY-NINE

CAMILLE MADE LANDFALL on the Mississippi Gulf Coast late Sunday evening. The apex of the raging juggernaut struck just east of Bay St. Louis, which placed Pass Christian directly in the path of the hurricane's fiercest point. The gale-force winds that had blown throughout the evening were nothing more than light breezes compared to the massive force that ushered in the behemoth storm.

Among the first casualties of the hurricane were the power lines. Shortly after the advance winds struck the Coast everything between Bay St. Louis and Ocean Springs was thrown into darkness. Until hurricane lamps could be lit, the only illumination came from the constant flashes of lightening, hundreds of bolts streaking overhead at the same time. The lightning struck power transformers, causing loud explosions and outbursts of sparks that resembled fireworks displays. As loud as the explosions were, they could barely be heard over the deafening roar of the wind.

The tremendous winds, with gusts exceeding two hundred miles per hour, pushed the waters of the Gulf over Highway 90 and beyond. The water level rose rapidly. With each gigantic incoming wave the sea moved farther inland.

Tied up alongside the west pier in Gulfport Harbor the cargo ship *Alamo Victory* pitched violently in the churning water. It had been secured to the pier with line that would have held it fast in any ordinary hurricane, but the fury of this storm was more than anyone could have anticipated. The lines strained as the seas rose, and it would have been suicide for any crewman to venture on deck and attempt to loosen them.

The waves carried the huge vessel up ten feet and pushed it against the side of the pier. When the waves passed, the ship dropped and pulled away, stretching the line taught. This went on repeatedly, wave after wave. The ominous creaking of the cleats that held the lines on the pier would surely have been a warning that something was about to give, but there was no one around to hear it. And had there been ears to hear, the sounds of strain would have been lost in the wind that howled like the chorus of a thousand banshees.

There were two other ships tied up nearby, the *Hulda* and the *Silver Hawk.* Like the *Alamo Victory*, they were being bobbed up and down and relentlessly thrown against the pier. It was only a matter of time before they would slip their moorings.

WITHIN A HALF-HOUR after Camille's arrival waves were breaking on the north side of the highway and rolling against the foundation blocks of the Sea Foam Lounge. Partygoers stood at the large picture window and quietly watched the incoming tide. They were awestruck by the rapidly rising water and the enormous size of the waves. Few comments were made, though some were still in denial that they were in danger. Others began to pray silently, for it was becoming clear to them that the disaster the old deputy sheriff had warned them about was about to come to pass . . . and it was too late to do anything about it.

The interior of the lounge was in semi-darkness, the illumination coming from a half-dozen lanterns mounted on the walls seven feet above the floor. When the power had gone out the room was thrown into darkness for less than a minute before the lanterns came on.

Buzz Beeman, in his gregarious fashion, explained that the lights were battle lanterns that had once been used on Navy ships. He had purchased them at a salvage yard and rigged them to come on automatically when the power failed. Each lantern contained its own power source.

After providing his guests with this bit of information he added with a smug grin, “If, by some chance, the window does break and we get flooded, you’ll be happy to know that these battle lanterns are completely waterproof.” His feeble attempt at humor fell flat, and he tried to recover by announcing another round of drinks on the house, but only three or four of the partygoers took him up on the offer. It was becoming quite apparent to Buzz that the party mood was evaporating rapidly.

Among those who refused the free drink was Winston Pierce. Though he had not moved from the barstool, except to go to the restroom, he had abstained from drinking for the past two hours. Since the departure of Deputy Cruthirds, Pierce had allowed himself to slip into a depressed mood. At first his thoughts were of the failed extradition, which led to his reluctant admission to himself that he might have handled the situation in a more positive manner. He shuddered at the thought of how his own sheriff would respond to his behavior.

But when the hurricane struck with its full force, thoughts of his career took a back seat to more immediate concerns. Never in his life had he heard winds roar so loudly. He felt like he was trapped between two railroad tracks with locomotives racing along both sides of him. Unlike trains, however, this did not pass. The roar went on and on, without letting up.

Watching the walls of the building move in and out, as if the Sea Foam Lounge were breathing, was also disconcerting to Pierce. But it was the large plate glass window that had the most sobering effect on him. Forget the storm surge, the wind itself must be placing a tremendous strain on the glass. How much more could it take before shattering, and bringing the wrath of Camille in on them?

An icy chill made its way down Pierce’s spine as the realization finally hit him that he might very well die inside this bar.

LIKE ALL OF the small craft harbors along the coast, the yacht harbor in Gulfport had been cleared of most of its boats on Saturday. The owners, all too familiar with the destructive force of a hurricane, had moved their shrimp boats, small yachts and other craft into the inland waterways north of Biloxi Bay or the Bay of St. Louis. The few that remained would surely be destroyed.

Between the north side of the small craft harbor and the south side of Highway 90 was a stretch of lowland that the city of Gulfport had designated as a recreational area. In addition to the newly constructed Gulfport Recreation Center, the Teen Center, the Gulfport Little Theater and the Chamber of Commerce, the area was also home to the district substation of the Mississippi Highway Patrol.

By the time the rising water reached the highway these buildings were half-submerged. And when the waves of the storm surge began pounding the walls and roofs like massive wrecking balls it did not take long for the structures to collapse. Several hours later, after the water receded, only piles of rubble would remain.

INSIDE THEIR BEACHFRONT home in Long Beach, Earl and Mildred Watson stood in their living room and fearfully watched the water seeping under the front door. The hardwood floor of the entryway was already covered by seawater an inch deep. They knew it was seawater because Earl had dipped his finger in it and tasted the salt.

It was at that moment that he realized for certain that he had made a terrible mistake by insisting that he and Mildred ride out the storm in their house. In all probability his stubbornness would be the death of both of them.

He looked down at his frightened wife, who stood next to him. At five feet two inches, Mildred was ten inches shorter than her husband. She looked up at him and for a moment their eyes met. But Earl could not meet her gaze, for in her eyes he thought he saw something accusing in them. Then again, he could be wrong.

Perhaps it was simply a look of resignation; perhaps she was already resigned to her fate.

He closed his eyes and felt the moistness of a tear dampen his lashes. "I am so sorry, Mildred." He paused to fight back a sob. "I just couldn't imagine this storm being any worse than the one in '47." He tried to force a smile but failed. "Remember how we rode that one out? In this very same house. We were younger then and it was exciting. It was an adventure that you and I shared, and I look back on it with fond memories. I guess I thought we could relive that experience tonight."

He opened his eyes and Mildred saw fear in them. "I was a fool, Mildred. This hurricane tonight is nothing like the one in '47." He looked upward, as if searching for something on the ceiling. "Just listen to that howling wind. I've never heard a wind so loud in my life." He then shifted his gaze to the entryway and the water on the floor. "And what's worse, the Gulf of Mexico is right at our front door."

GARLAND FLOWERS WAS inside the small storage room when the hurricane struck Pineville. The sudden change in the sound of the wind was dramatic. At first he thought it was a loud machine of some sort, but as he listened he realized that the sustained roar was actually the wind. Camille had finally arrived in all her fearsome glory.

Suddenly he felt claustrophobic in the tiny enclosure. He had only been inside the room for a minute, but it was long enough to determine that it would make a fairly decent hiding place for Frieda if the need arose.

Upon entering the room he had had to bend over to go through the small door. He then descended two steps to a concrete slab that was the floor. But once inside the room he was able to stand up. It was like a shallow basement.

Illuminating the interior with his flashlight, Flowers saw several soft drink cases stacked in one corner. In the center of the room two thick pipes emerged from the concrete floor and extended upward, then ran along the floor joists of the living quarters, disappearing beyond the wall of the storage room. Otherwise, the room was empty.

Accompanying the storm's loud roar was an eerie whistling sound as the wind passed beneath the floor of the living quarters. It would have made excellent sound effects for a corny haunted house movie. Flowers smiled at the thought, but the noise was too loud and too close to be genuinely amusing. Instead, it served to increase the closed-in feeling that he had experienced since entering the small room, so he decided not to remain.

As he stepped out of the storage room he discovered that the store's interior was in darkness. There had obviously been a power failure. Using the flashlight, he made his way back to the steps that led to the living quarters and sat on the landing. In order to save the batteries he turned off the flashlight, and the surroundings were thrown into an inky blackness. There was not the slightest hint of light from any source. It was the most complete darkness that Garland Flowers had ever experienced.

FORTY

OF THE THREE freighters tied up alongside West Pier in Gulfport, the *Alamo Victory* was the first to break its moorings. The constant pulling and stretching of the lines as the ship bobbed up and down like a cork eventually caused the mooring lines to break. Within a matter of minutes the lines on the other two freighters also gave way and the three vessels drifted aimlessly away from the pier.

The sea had risen far above the breakwater and the normally still waters of the harbor had become part of the angry Gulf that was pushing itself farther onto land with each relentless wave.

The wind and seas carried the huge cargo ships ever closer to shore. The three freighters had no more control over their fate than toy boats would have in a bathtub. On the bridge of one of the vessels the gauge of the anemometer had frozen at 175 knots, or 201.5 miles per hour. This was the last wind speed recorded before the instrument's small spinning globes were ripped from atop the ship's mast.

The three freighters ran aground just south of Highway 90. Only one of them would ever again be seaworthy. In the months that followed, the ship's owners would manage to have it pulled back into the harbor and towed away for repairs. The two remaining vessels would eventually be dismantled and sold for scrap.

WINSTON PIERCE WAS now cold sober, as was every other occupant of the Sea Foam Lounge. The water had risen to the base of the plate glass window. The roar of the wind was deafening. The building groaned from the strain of first being pushed by an enormous gust of wind, then seemingly pulled as the force of the wind let up and the building settled back on its foundation. A moment later another gust would push the building and the groaning would return. It was the storm's unyielding and merciless attempt to tear the structure from its foundation. There was also seepage entering the lounge through the walls, and the patrons were ankle-deep in seawater.

From his stool at the bar Pierce stole a glimpse at Eddy, the bartender. He was leaning against the beer cooler behind the bar. The expression on his face was one of fear, and his eyes darted nervously from left to right.

As Pierce studied the bartender he noticed that the man's eyes were not moving from side to side without purpose. They were looking at specific objects. To his right, Eddy was worriedly observing the large window, as if expecting it to give way at any moment. Then his eyes shifted to the left, in the direction of a storeroom adjacent to the men's restroom. It was quite obvious to Pierce that Eddy was planning an escape from this death trap.

Suddenly Eddy made his move. Stepping from behind the bar, he walked hurriedly across the floor and disappeared into the storeroom. Pierce glanced to his left, toward the main part of the lounge. None of the other patrons had noticed the bartender's departure. They were preoccupied with the storm outside.

Pierce hesitated a moment, then got up and walked toward the door through which Eddy had vanished. Though his head was clear, a large volume of alcohol was still in his bloodstream and his balance was hampered. He moved with a decidedly unsteady gait.

When Pierce arrived at the door to the storeroom he noticed that the interior was much smaller than he had pictured it. It was about the same size as a large closet. To his right, bolted to the wall, was a metal ladder. At the top of the ladder was a trap door that opened onto the roof. Pierce glanced up in time to see the bottom of Eddy's shoes as the bartender stepped from the top rung of the ladder onto the roof of the building.

Smartest person in the bar, Pierce thought as he stood in the doorway and stared after Eddy. The only one with sense enough to get out before it's too late.

His thoughts were interrupted by the sound of glass exploding. The entire building shook violently as an enormous wave crashed through the plate glass window. The group of patrons who had been standing near the window were picked up like so many matchsticks and carried across the room. Among them was Buzz Beeman, who was pinned to the opposite wall by the rushing water.

With two quick steps Pierce reached the ladder. As he grabbed a rung he was thrown to his left. The entire building seemed to have been pushed from its foundation. Regaining his balance, Pierce began his climb up the ladder just as a river of seawater rushed into the storeroom. Then there was a shift to the right as the water receded. He ignored it and continued his climb up the ladder and through the trap door.

The assaulting wind made it difficult for him to breathe. Only when he managed to put his back to it was he allowed to inhale and exhale in a fairly normal manner.

With a great deal of effort he scanned the roof of the building in search of Eddy, but could not locate him. Pierce decided that the bartender must have taken refuge behind one of the numerous air conditioning units or turbo vents that cluttered the top of the Sea Foam Lounge.

Once again he put his back to the wind, and it was then that he saw Eddy. The sight caused him to gag. In the last huge wave the bartender must have been hurled backward from the roof of the building. The tremendous force of the storm surge drove him against a large oak tree that stood in the parking lot behind the lounge. He was helplessly attached to the trunk of the tree. Protruding from his midsection was the jagged end of a broken tree limb.

In the glow provided by a series of lightning flashes, Pierce looked into the eyes of Eddy and was shocked when the man blinked. Pierce wanted to look away but could not. The impaled bartender's lips were moving as if he were trying to speak.

The building shifted again and Pierce was almost grateful for the distraction. A moment later he heard a roar that was even louder than the howling wind. With an effort, he glanced back in time to see another gigantic wave coming his way. He had to look up to see the top of it, for the massive wave was higher than the roof of the building. The white foam at its crest had a bluish phosphorescent glow, and it moved toward him with incredible speed.

Instinctively he wrapped his arms around a nearby turbo vent in order to anchor himself to the roof. A second later several hundred tons of water crashed over the Sea Foam Lounge, causing it to completely dislodge from its foundation. After the wave had passed, the water began to recede. In doing so, it pulled the entire building along with it, until the structure was fully submerged beneath the churning water.

From his vantage point Eddy the bartender spent his final moments of life witnessing the tragic end of the Sea Foam Lounge. That arrogant customer who smoked cigarettes from a plastic holder and who had followed him onto the roof of the building was nowhere to be seen. He had been washed away with everyone else.

In the few seconds that remained to him Eddy thought not of his eternal fate, nor of any loved ones. As he stared at the building that lay submerged beneath the turbulent waters he thought of Buzz Beeman, and how proud Buzz would be if he knew that the battle lanterns were indeed waterproof. In the end, it was the faint glow of the lanterns from beneath the surface of the water that gave him his only comfort.

WHEN THE STORM surge of Camille hit the Gulf Coast, virtually every waterfront structure between Bay St. Louis and Ocean Springs suffered damage of one sort or another. Many homes and businesses experienced the same fate as the Sea Foam Lounge.

10250-MART

Others remained standing but were later declared unsafe and had to be demolished. And there were still others that were damaged but could be repaired.

Among those buildings totally destroyed was St. Thomas Catholic Church in Long Beach. The storm surge completely crushed the entire vestibule, thus exposing the interior of the church to the ravages of the storm. In Pass Christian, the Dixie White House, where Ulysses Grant and Theodore Roosevelt had visited, and where Woodrow Wilson spent his first winter as President, was beaten into a pile of wood and concrete rubble.

AT APPROXIMATELY THE same moment that Pierce was watching Eddy disappear into the storeroom, Earl Watson, standing in the living room with his wife, decided that it was best if they went upstairs. The water seeping in from under the door was already above their ankles.

Mildred led the way and was halfway up the stairs when Earl began to follow. But at the bottom step he paused and looked around. A bitter gall filled his throat as he realized that he was about to lose everything that he had worked for.

He deeply regretted that he had spent all day at the lumberyard trying to squeeze out a few extra dollars from desperate customers. Why had he not gone to Mass with his wife like he usually did? Why had he not foreseen the disaster that was coming, as Mildred had seen it? They would have had plenty of time to pack their belongings and go to a shelter.

He had always regarded himself as a good Catholic, yet in the end Earl Watson would leave this world without having the opportunity to confess to his priest his most recent sins of greed and pride.

Taking in a deep breath, he exhaled a long sigh, then began walking up the stairs. But he had taken no more than two steps when the roar of the wind was suddenly accompanied by the sound of glass being shattered. The front door burst open and a huge wave rushed in, flooding the foyer and living room.

Mildred was now at the top of the stairs. She let out a terrified scream as Earl ran up the stairs to join her. From the landing they gazed down at the rising water and were sickened by the sight. Mildred had spent her entire married life collecting antique furniture for her home, and now most of her collection was being destroyed by Camille. Cushions from the large sofa had dislodged themselves and were floating on the surface of the water, bumping into small wooden tables that were buoyant enough to stay afloat.

The entire house let out a groan as it moved several inches. Mildred reached for her husband. He put one arm around her, and with the other he grabbed the banister at the stair landing to keep both of them from falling. The staircase twisted but remained intact as the receding water pulled it back into its original position.

"Will we be safe up here?" Mildred asked, her voice shaking. "Will the water get up this high?"

Earl did not reply at first. He was thinking of that deputy . . . Wojcik was his name . . . and what he had said about the destructive force of the storm surge.

The calmness in his voice surprised even him when he said, "We have to get out of this house."

"Will the water get up this high?" Mildred asked again.

"I don't know. I doubt it. But the waves are battering the downstairs so badly I'm afraid it'll give way and the upstairs will collapse on top of it."

"But how can we possibly go out in that storm?" She looked up at her husband and her eyes revealed the terror that she felt. "We'll drown for sure."

"We've got to find something that floats. We can take it out with us and hang on to it." After a pause he added, "It's our only chance."

Suddenly a second wave struck and the house shuttered violently. The staircase twisted again. Its loud groans were then replaced by the sound of wood splintering. A moment later the bottom half of the staircase broke loose and fell into the small lake that had once been a living room. The top half of the stairs remained suspended from the upper level.

Pulling his wife with him, Earl moved hurriedly down the corridor toward the bedrooms. "You check our bedroom and I'll search the guest room," he said. "Look for anything we can hold on to that will float. We'll meet back here."

They separated and both frantically searched for a floatation device. A minute later Mildred returned empty-handed. She waited in the corridor and listened to the terrible sounds of the storm.

She was in a near state of panic when her husband emerged from the guest bedroom pulling a vinyl-covered foam mattress with him. It was the type sometimes used in chaise lounges.

Holding it up for his wife's inspection, he said, "I found this in the closet. I don't know how long it will stay afloat, but it's the best we have at the moment."

"How are we going to get out of the house?" Mildred asked.

"I've been thinking about that. Judging from the way it looks downstairs I'd say that the water level is nearly midway up the bottom floor. The bedroom windows open to the north, which is the leeward side. If we tie something to the bed we can lower ourselves down to the water. Hopefully the house will give us a little protection from the wind."

Less than a minute later Earl was tying a bed sheet to the heavy wooden bedpost in the master bedroom. He had insisted on being the one to tie the sheets since he was familiar with the types of knots that had to be applied. If anyone had suggested to him a few hours earlier that he and his wife would be using sheets tied to a bedpost to lower themselves out their bedroom window he would have laughed in their face. This was a stunt that happened only in corny movies, usually comedies. Yet here he was, doing that very thing. The fact was that there was nothing else available. All of his ropes were in the garage, which was detached from the house and, by this time, was probably destroyed by the storm surge.

Mildred held an armload of linen and watched her husband work. Earl Watson was a doer, and he was at his best when things had to be done. She was well aware that he was being eaten up inside with guilt and self-incrimination. Now he was working with all his might to save their lives.

Fortunately the upstairs windows had shutters, so it had not been necessary to cover them with plywood. With an effort he pulled up the large window. The water had swollen the wood and the window did not submit easily to being raised.

When it was open he unlatched the shutters and pushed them out. No sooner had he done this before the right shutter was snatched away by the force of the wind and ripped from its hinges. The same forces that tore away one shutter, caused the left one to slam back against the window. With a sudden strength that was born of accumulated anger and remorse Earl grabbed the shutter and pulled. He let out a growl that could be heard even above the howling wind as he ripped the shutter from its hinges and let it fly away into the night.

Wind and rain rushed in, throwing objects about as if a small tornado had been unleashed inside the bedroom. Dropping the makeshift rope of sheets out the window he turned to his wife. He had to shout to be heard above the shrieking wind. "I'll go first. As soon as I'm in the water, drop the mattress down to me, then start climbing down the rope."

He was about to lift his leg over the windowsill when he paused. "Wait. This isn't going to work." He then began pulling in the string of sheets.

"What's wrong, Earl?" Mildred asked.

"The wind is much too strong for you to hold on to the mattress once it's out the window. It'll fly away like the shutters did."

After pulling in the last sheet, which was soaking wet, he tied the end around the mattress, pulling it so tight that the mattress folded in two. He secured it with two half hitches. These knots would allow him to easily untie the mattress after he was in the water.

He then carried the mattress to the window and dropped it into the darkness. Rather than falling straight down, the powerful wind suspended the rope and mattress in an almost horizontal position.

Holding onto the rope, Earl climbed over the windowsill and slowly worked his way down to the water. Shielding her eyes from the onslaught of wind and water, Mildred stood at the window and watched her husband. Fortunately he was wearing a light-colored shirt, which made it easier for her to see him in the inky blackness.

Closing her eyes, she quickly said a prayer, then started to lift herself onto the sill. Suddenly she was jolted backward against the bed as another gigantic wave struck the house. Above the roar of the wind were the sounds of crashing as furniture slammed against walls and other objects. Lumber creaked and boards cracked. Popping noises could also be heard as bolts snapped from concrete footings.

Pushing herself from the bed she moved toward the window. The house shifted back as the water receded and she was thrown forward. Had she not fallen to the floor she would have been hurled through the window.

Mildred fought back the panic that was building up within her. She took a few quick breaths, then pulled herself up. In a single fluid movement she grabbed the sheet rope and climbed over the windowsill. It was awkward, but she managed to get her torso, then both legs, through the opening. With a strength that she never knew she had, Mildred lowered herself toward the churning water below.

By the time she reached the water, Earl had untied the makeshift raft. He was clinging to it with one hand as he held the rope with the other. At Earl's direction, Mildred grabbed him around the neck and let go of the rope. The sense of panic began to fade as she clung to her husband.

Shouting into his wife's ear in order to be heard, he said, "We have to get as far away from the house as we can! It's broken loose from the foundation. If it stays afloat long enough it might be pushed on top of us! If it collapses or sinks, it could pull us under with it!"

Mildred worked her way around her husband and onto the mattress. Earl grasped the rear corners of the mattress with both hands and began kicking his feet, pushing it in front of him. Mildred, lying on her stomach, paddled with her hands. Slowly the flimsy life raft carried them away from their house and into the blackness of the storm.

Once beyond the relative protection of the house all paddling became futile. They were completely at the mercy of the wind and water. This fact was made apparent to Earl when the next receding wave began pulling them back. He suddenly became alarmed at the thought that he and Mildred could very well be carried out into the Gulf.

His fears, however, were somewhat alleviated when the next wave carried them forward again. They were far enough inland that the waves were not as fierce as they were near the house. Also, the relentless wind helped to carry them away from the Gulf.

Nevertheless, he knew very well that they could not continue to drift around on a mattress that, despite the vinyl covering, was gradually becoming waterlogged.

They continued to drift, first in one direction, then another. Mildred's arms ached to the point of cramping, and eventually she ceased paddling and let her arms hang loosely in the water. As she lay on the raft she prayed. She prayed the *Our Father*. She prayed the *Apostle's Creed*. And she prayed at least a dozen *Hail Mary's*. She prayed for her husband and she prayed for herself. It was clear to her that they were absolutely, totally in the hands of the Lord. If it was His will that they survive, then no force on earth, not even this storm from Hell, could kill them. As she thought of this a sense of peace came over her. Though still terrified, she was comforted in knowing that she and Earl were not in this alone.

Earl had no concept of time. In the darkness minutes seemed like hours. It was impossible to determine how long they had been floating in the inky black water beneath a sky the color of tar.

Then there was the wind. The howling and shrieking was interminable, never letting up. At first it took his breath away, but after a while he found that he could adjust his breathing pattern to allow himself to inhale and exhale with relative ease.

Like Mildred, Earl was near the point of exhaustion. He feared that he might lose his hold on the mattress and slip into the turbulent water and drown. The thought that he might drown did not concern him so much as the thought of leaving Mildred to fend for herself in a situation that he had so foolishly placed her.

He was thinking of this when Mildred suddenly jerked her body, almost flipping the raft on its side. She let out a cry of pain just as Earl felt something slap him on the side of his face. He, too, screamed in pain as he raised his left arm to ward off whatever was assaulting them.

It took but a second for him to realize that it was a tree branch. Continuing to hold onto the mattress with one hand, he felt around in the darkness until he found a larger limb. He shouted to Mildred to cover her face to protect her from further slaps, then he pulled the raft into a thickness of limbs and branches that had been completely stripped of leaves.

Maneuvering amidst the branches while fighting the wind and the sea was a struggle, but eventually Earl found his way to a tree trunk. It was a large oak, and it appeared to still be firmly attached to the ground. Earl felt around in the darkness until he found that for which he was searching. Two feet above them was a limb that was about a foot in diameter at the trunk. With a newfound strength he assisted Mildred in reaching up and grabbing the limb, then he did the same. Wrapping one arm around the limb he used the other to boost one of Mildred's legs over it. This allowed her to roll her entire body onto the limb. Earl was well aware that his energy was almost completely spent. But with one final effort he managed to get a leg over the limb and pull himself up.

Without taking time to rest, he shinnied backward, toward the trunk. When he reached it he put his back against the tree with his legs hanging over each side. He then shouted to Mildred to do likewise. When she reached him, he put his arms around her and held her tightly. It was only then that he realized that they were both almost completely naked. The torrential waters had pulled their shoes from their feet and ripped their clothes to shreds. The rough tree bark cut into Earl's naked back, but he could not care less. As long as the tree remained standing he was confident that they could ride out the storm.

Though he was well aware that he had lost all of his material possessions, his most precious treasure was there with him. He gave his wife an affectionate squeeze, then said a silent prayer of thanks.

Earl and Mildred would remain in the tree throughout the rest of the storm. At eight o'clock in the morning, after the water had receded, they would be found by a rescue team, sitting at the base of the tree, embracing one another, and clothed only in their underwear. Though marred with several scrapes and bruises, all things considered, they would be none the worse for wear. Most of all they would be grateful just to be alive.

A quarter of a mile south of the tree that had been their refuge a hundred year-old brick and mortar foundation would be the only evidence that the Watsons' stately home had once stood on that site.

FORTY-ONE

THE EYE OF CAMILLE was small as hurricanes go—a circle of wind five miles in diameter moving at speeds in excess of 200 miles per hour. Its western edge passed over Waveland, just west of Bay St. Louis. The eastern side passed over the western part of Pass Christian. The right front quadrant of the eye, which many believe was the fiercest part of the storm, moved directly through the main part of that town. In the days that followed it would be discovered that Pass Christian suffered the greatest damage of all the communities along the coast.

Waters from the storm surge caused flood damage as far inland as the L and N Railroad tracks, several blocks north of Highway 90. Most of the damage north of the tracks was caused by the powerful winds and heavy rainfall. Camille also spawned as many as eighty tornadoes along the coast between Bay St. Louis and Ocean Springs.

ALTHOUGH GARLAND FLOWERS was not familiar with the patterns of a hurricane, and he had no way of knowing that the eye of the storm had made landfall, he was quite aware of a shift in the wind. As the direction changed so did the intensity. A few minutes earlier he would not have thought it possible that the screeching howl of the wind could get any louder, but it did.

For the next half-hour he sat in the darkness and listened to the terrible sounds of the storm. Occasionally a tremendous cracking sound could be heard above the wind as a tree would become uprooted and fall nearby. At one point he was startled when pine limbs struck the side of the store as a tree came crashing to the ground less than ten feet from the building.

After the eye had passed, the winds that had blown so fiercely along its wall decreased their intensity. Though the winds continued to blow in excess of 175 miles per hour, the decline from more than 200 miles per hour seemed significant to Flowers. Of course he had no way of knowing the actual speed of the wind. He could only judge it by the volume level of its howl. He knew the storm was far from over, but he sensed that perhaps the worst was behind him.

AS HE SAT inside the cinder block shed behind the automobile garage, B.C. Jones was also aware of a let-up in the storm's intensity. For what seemed like an eternity he had been trapped within the small confines of this cell and had been terrified by the sounds of the storm. The wind had blown the broken door in and caused objects inside the shed to be thrown around like shrapnel inside a bunker. Jones had covered his head to avoid being struck by flying debris, and suffered several cuts and bruises on his arms.

Never had he experienced anything like it. As soon as he took care of Frieda he was going to leave this place forever.

These were his thoughts when he detected a decrease in the force of the wind. He was ready to pounce upon any excuse to escape his cinder block prison, and the change in the wind's velocity provided him that excuse.

Unknown to B.C. Jones, the storm into which he ventured, though slightly weakened, was still more powerful than the vast majority of hurricanes in recorded history. The first thing he discovered was a force that seemed intent on blowing him away from his path of travel. The next revelation was the effort that he had to put forth in order to breathe. But he found that if he put his head down and his face away from the suffocating wind, he was able to breathe in and out in a reasonably normal manner. And if he walked with his right shoulder pointed in the direction of travel, he was able to move forward, however slowly, in what he believed was the direction of Frieda's house.

Feeling his way through the blackness he eventually arrived at the road. Recalling his previous direction of travel, Jones turned left and began the final leg of his journey.

The force of the wind was stronger than any other force he had ever experienced. Normally he could overpower anything with which he was confronted, but in this storm he felt as helpless as a child. Frequently the wind would blow him off the pavement and onto the shoulder of the road. With dogged determination he would point his shoulder into the wind and return to the pavement, then resume his travel.

Jones had gone fifty yards when he suddenly tripped over a large object and fell to the ground on the other side of it. After overcoming his shock and surprise, he slowly struggled to his feet. In the darkness he reached out and felt the barricade that he had tripped over. It was the trunk of a tree. The powerful wind had snapped it from its base and thrown the tree across the road like it was nothing more than a matchstick.

Despite his limited intellect, B.C. Jones was beginning to understand the destructive might of this storm. "That no-good Billy Ray called this a herrycan," he said aloud. "I never want to be in a herrycan again. Not ever." That said, he wiped away the pebbles that had become embedded in his hands when he fell onto the pavement, and continued into the night.

Jones trudged through the wind and driving rain for several more minutes before coming upon a small gravel road to his left. In the darkness he barely made out the outline of a building. It had the look of a grocery store. Without taking the time to even consider the matter, Jones turned onto the gravel road.

Upon arrival at the front of the structure he was immediately convinced that it was a grocery store. The front of it was boarded up with plywood, so he moved around to the side of the building. Off to his right he heard a banging sound, like metal striking a board. Squinting his eyes to ward off some of the driving rain, he looked in the direction of the sound. He strained to see in the darkness and was able to make out what looked like a huge ice cream cone hanging from a post. It had cut through one of the ropes and was now hanging to the side. The powerful wind caused the ice cream cone to extend horizontally, attached only by the few remaining strands of rope. Only when the gusts of wind let up momentarily would it fall back and slap against the post.

Jones shrugged and resumed his walk around the side of the building. He remained close to the wall as he felt his way toward the rear. After passing a side door that was tightly secured, he bumped into something. A quick inspection revealed that he had walked into the side of a step. It was a set of steps that led to a door four feet above the ground. There were two narrow panes of glass in the top portion of the door. Behind the glass was a dim light.

B.C. Jones' heart seemed to skip a beat as he recalled Billy Ray Love telling him that Frieda lived behind the store. He was filled with excitement as he made his way around to the front of the steps and ascended them. Had it not been for a side railing the assaulting wind would have pushed him off the far side of the steps. But the railing caught him and he quickly regained his footing.

FRIEDA PINCHON SAT on the sofa in the living room and stared absently into the flame of a candle that had been placed on the coffee table in front of her. Beside the candle was a flashlight, readily available if the candle went out. There was only one hurricane lamp in the house, and her grandfather was using it in the bedroom. He always liked to read before going to bed. There being no electrical power, the hurricane lamp provided the best light for reading.

Frieda was upset with her grandfather because of his attitude toward Sergeant Flowers. Just before turning in for the night he had locked the door that separated the living quarters from the store, then forbade his granddaughter from unlocking it. She became angry and wanted to shout at him and tell him that his racial prejudice was a hateful thing. But she did not. She could not, for he was her grandfather, and she loved him dearly. Besides, a girl simply did not talk to her grandfather disrespectfully.

So she sat on the sofa, her arms folded defiantly, and quietly sulked. Because the candle was the only illumination in the room, her eyes drifted toward the flame. As she sat there and watched it flicker her anger began to slowly fade.

THERE WAS A small landing at the top of the steps, and when Jones reached it he moved to the door and looked through one of the panes of glass. He was gazing into the living room. Though the interior was dimly lighted he immediately identified the only occupant of the room. Seated on a sofa against the opposite wall from the door was Frieda Pinchon. Her arms were folded and she seemed to be staring at something. Maybe it was that candle on the table in front of her.

Jones could not contain himself. He grabbed the doorknob and tried to turn it. When it would not move he attempted to twist it. His violent actions caused the door to rattle loudly.

Frieda suddenly looked up and glanced toward the door. She reached for the flashlight and turned it on, then pointed it at the glass panes. When the beam hit Jones' face Frieda let out a scream. Though he could barely hear the scream amidst the howling wind, the terrified expression on her face startled Jones and he stumbled back against the railing. His instincts told him to run down the stairs and hide, but the urge to get another look at Frieda caused him to pause. He waited for the voice inside him to speak, to tell him what he should do, but it said nothing. It had been the voice and his instincts that had gotten him this far, yet the temptation to gaze upon Frieda's face was more than he could resist.

EUGENE PINCHON'S BEDROOM door flew open and he darted through it. He met his granddaughter as she ran from the living room and into his arms.

"What is it, child?" He asked.

She was trembling with fear and was having difficulty speaking. After a moment she calmed herself enough to exclaim, "It's him! I saw him! He was standing at the door!"

"Who did you see?"

"That man! That horrible man that wants to kill me!"

"But that's impossible. No one would be out in a storm like . . ." His words froze in mid-sentence as he stared open-mouthed at the door. Staring back at him in the eerie light was the face of Frieda's monster. He was real . . . and he was out there.

As soon as Pinchon made eye contact with it the face vanished. But it was out there. He pushed Frieda away from him and ran into his bedroom. A moment later he returned, carrying his .357 magnum and a flashlight.

Frieda looked at the pistol and her eyes widened. "Grandpa! What are you going to do?"

"I'm gonna put an end to this mess right now."

"But you can't go out there!"

"Oh, yes I can! If he can survive in that storm, so can I."

"But he's a killer, Grandpa! Please don't go out there!"

"Let's see how bad he is with a magnum slug in his chest."

Without saying another word, Eugene Pinchon went to the door, unlocked it and turned the knob. When he did so a massive rush of wind and rain pushed the door open, snatching it from his hand. The living room was suddenly filled with the storm's wrath. The candle went out and the room was filled with darkness.

Eugene turned on his flashlight and stepped over the threshold. It took all of his strength, but he managed to pull the door closed as he ventured out into the storm.

Frieda stood in the darkness for several seconds and stared after her grandfather. Then, realizing that she was still holding her flashlight, she turned it on. At the same moment she thought of Sergeant Flowers. Frantically she ran to unlock the door.

GARLAND FLOWERS WAS at the far side of the building when he heard Frieda's scream. A minute earlier he had thought he detected the sound of someone attempting to open the door that was the rear entrance to the store. He realized that it was probably his imagination, but having nothing better to do, he decided to check it out.

It was a solid door, and there were no windows nearby, so it was impossible to visibly search for anything. But he inspected the lock and found that it was secure, then he put his ear to the door. The only sound was the persistent roar of the wind.

He shined his flashlight toward the front of the store and began walking along the aisle nearest the wall. He was not looking for anything in particular. It was merely a way of killing time until the storm passed.

It was then that he heard the scream. The high pitch penetrated the walls and pierced through the sounds of the hurricane. Flowers turned immediately and ran to the steps that led into the living quarters.

At the top of the landing he grabbed the doorknob and tried to turn it, but the door was locked. He swore angrily, then reached down and pulled up his right trouser leg and removed his .38 snub-nosed revolver from his leg holster.

Standing upright, he stepped back and was about to kick the door in when it suddenly opened. Standing in the middle of the doorway was Frieda. The first thing that Flowers saw was the terror-stricken expression on her face.

"Frieda! What is it?"

"That . . . that . . . man! He's here!"

"Where?"

"Outside! Grandpa went out to find him!"

"He did what?" Flowers was incredulous. "He went out after Jones?"

"Yes! Oh, sergeant, please go help my grandpa!"

"Idiot!" Flowers mumbled to himself.

Frieda showed no indication that she heard the comment, though at the moment Flowers did not care. He moved past her and into the living room. As he was about to open the door he turned back.

"Frieda. Listen to me." He spoke slowly and distinctly. "This is very important. I want you to go down to the storeroom. The door is unlocked. Get inside there and close the door behind you then put your back against it. I'm going to try to find your grandpa. As soon as I do we'll come back here. But just in case Jones gets past us and slips into the house, you should be safe for a while in the storeroom. When we return, I'll go get you. Do you understand?"

Frieda nodded her head but did not speak.

Flowers attempted a smile and said, "Good. Now get on down there."

As Frieda turned to go Flowers called after her. "And don't open the door unless you recognize your grandpa's or my voice."

Flowers could not tell if she had heard him, but assumed that she had. He turned back to the door, breathed a deep sigh, then opened it. With an effort similar to that of Eugene Pinchon he managed to close the door behind him.

After spending the better part of the next minute overcoming the shock of the hurricane's persistent attempt to rob him of oxygen and throw him from the landing, he was able to regulate his breathing and move cautiously down the steps. Once on the ground he made his way to the side of the building and proceeded slowly toward the front of the store.

By hugging the building he was afforded better concealment. The wall also gave him a backstop against the storm and prevented him from being tossed around helplessly. The downside was that he felt like he was pinned to the side of the building by the force of the wind. It was a struggle for him to move.

Holding his .38 at his right side and his flashlight in his left hand, he crouched slightly and inched forward. He noticed that the wind was blowing in gusts. It screamed in his ears like the sustained cry of a panther, while it pushed against his face and body in an attempt to suffocate him. Then there would be a slight let-up, followed by another tremendous gust.

The darkness was a black shroud that wrapped tightly around him, and he had to fight back the temptation to turn on the light to illuminate the surroundings. But he could not turn on the light. Not yet. There was a killer out there somewhere, a fearful giant whose physical strength was enough to crush a man with his bare hands. For Flowers to turn on the flashlight now would be to make a target of himself. He had to wait until he had some idea where the killer was.

Of equal concern to Flowers was the whereabouts of Eugene Pinchon. The old man seemed trigger-happy, and was as likely to shoot at him as to shoot at the suspect.

The thought of Pinchon filled Flowers with a sense of disgust. Why was he out in this God-forsaken storm trying to rescue that bigoted fool? Flowers would have been much better off remaining inside the house, where it would have been easier to protect Frieda. But he knew the answer even before he asked himself the question. He did it for her. Pinchon was stubborn and thoughtless, but he was also Frieda's only known relative. And despite his hateful intolerance toward Flowers, there was a loving bond between him and Frieda that only a grandfather and granddaughter could share. She would love her grandfather forever, despite his shortcomings.

As Flowers arrived at the front corner of the building he heard a loud banging off to his left. He started to turn on the flashlight, but paused to listen more closely. Then he remembered the ice cream cone sign. Apparently one of the cotton ropes had broken loose and the metal sign was banging against the post between gusts of wind. He decided to ignore it.

His next step took him beyond the side of the building. As soon as he had gotten past the structure he heard a muffled noise that was slightly different from the din of the storm, and it was coming from the front of the store. Apart from the howling wind and driving rain he was able to detect what sounded like a moan.

Without hesitating, Flowers turned on the flashlight and shined it in the direction of the sound.

Lying on the floor of the store's veranda, a few feet from the door, was Eugene Pinchon. The back of his head was resting in a pool of blood. Flowers also observed a smear of blood on the side of the door. It appeared that he had been thrown against the front of the store, where the back of his head struck the wooden doorframe, then he had fallen. The .357 magnum was not in sight.

Moving toward the fallen man was the massive bulk of B.C. Jones. Flowers shined the light in Jones' face and for a fleeting instant Jones looked in his direction. What Flowers saw staring back at him was as much animal as it was human. The face was contorted, as if filled with uncontrollable anguish. But it was the eyes that were most unnerving. It was as if the person in whose sockets they rested had abandoned all hope of being a part of the human race. The eyes were vacant, completely void of spirit.

Jones then abruptly returned his attention to Pinchon. He knelt on one knee beside the old man and reached down to place a hand behind Pinchon's neck.

In a flashback that lasted no longer than a fraction of a second, Flowers was taken back to the two crime scenes in Los Angeles. In each of them a man lay dead with a broken neck. In the autopsy the medical examiner had concluded that the killer had placed one hand behind the victim's neck, and with the other hand, pushed hard against the forehead, causing the neck to snap. There was no doubt in Flowers' mind that Eugene Pinchon was about to suffer the same fate.

"B.C.!" Flowers shouted in an attempt to distract him.

Jones made no indication that he even heard the shout.

Flowers moved closer and shouted again. Jones paused long enough to look his way, then returned his attention to the chore at hand. By now one of his hands was under Pinchon's neck. Flowers was desperate. Within a few seconds Frieda's grandfather would be dead.

Suddenly an idea came to Flowers and he shouted again. "Jones! I was in your apartment in L.A. while you were gone!"

Jones seemed to freeze. Then he slowly looked up at the detective.

"I sat in your chair and watched your T.V."

Jones removed his hand from behind Pinchon's neck and glared into the flashlight's beam. Somewhere in the dark, behind that light was the cop that caused him to leave L.A.

Flowers was relieved that he had found something that would get Jones' mind off Pinchon. But he could not stop now. He had to think of something else to say . . . something that would draw him away from the old man.

"Remember your landlady, Mrs. Thomas? Well, I gave her your television set. She yanked it from the wall and took it down to her apartment. I tried to give her your chair, but it was so worn and ugly that she wouldn't take it. So, you know what I did with it? I hauled it down to the alley and threw it in the Dumpster." It was a long speech, especially for one delivered in a hurricane, but it was quite apparent that Jones heard it, or at least most of it.

Slowly the huge assailant stood up, with his feet spread apart to steady himself against the torrent of wind. He was drenched from the rain and his face glistened in the light. Flowers studied his eyes once again. This time there was life in them, and suddenly Flowers wished for the detached look that Jones had a moment earlier. The eyes that stared back at him now were filled with hate.

Stepping over the fallen man who lay at his feet Jones moved toward Flowers. The detective backed up a few steps. He had noticed that Pinchon was no longer moaning. He wanted to shine his light on the old man to see if he was still alive, but he dared not take the light off Jones. To do so could get him killed. Once out of the beam of light Jones could disappear into the darkness and move about without being heard above the sounds of the storm.

As Jones moved forward Flowers stepped back in an effort to keep Jones from closing the gap. Flowers had backed up several feet before he realized that he was moving at an angle away from the building. Everything outside the ray of light was pitch black. He turned obliquely so that he was facing the wind. According to his calculations, this put him roughly parallel to the building. He did not want to drift too far from his safe haven.

The detective was at a loss as to what he should do now. It had not been his intention to kill Jones, but to take him into custody. But now he was in a predicament. His first priority was to protect Frieda from this giant. If Jones got past him, it was only a matter of minutes before he found Frieda and killed her.

The cold hard fact struck him that he had to shoot B.C. Jones. Once the decision was made Flowers did not hesitate. He lifted the .38 and fired. The flash from the muzzle startled him. How could such a small weapon create such a blinding flash? In that instant Jones disappeared into the darkness.

Flowers did not know if he had hit Jones or not, but at such close range, how could he have missed. He quickly searched the ground in front of him, hoping that Jones had fallen after being shot, but he was nowhere to be found.

The predicament suddenly turned into a crisis. Though he had the gun and the flashlight, it was quite obvious that Jones was the hunter and he was the prey. Flowers quickly turned off the light and moved to his right, toward the building. In the darkness he was somewhat on equal terms with his suspect. Though Jones had the physical strength, Flowers had the firepower; that is, as much firepower as a little pistol with a two-inch barrel could offer.

He was suddenly filled with a desperate urge to get back to Frieda. If he could make it to the storeroom before Jones found her he could make a stand there. His weapon was a Smith and Wesson .38 Chief Special, with a five-shot cylinder. There were four rounds left. He would empty all four into Jones and hope that it would stop him. As he thought of this he found himself longing for Pinchon's .357 magnum. But it was lying out there in the darkness somewhere, having done its foolish owner no good whatsoever.

If he could just find his way to the wall of the building he could be inside within a minute. He was about to move in that direction when he was struck a massive blow in his midsection. It came out of the darkness and he was completely unprepared for it. He landed hard on his back and began gasping for air. The fall had knocked his breath out. Though his weapon had flown from his grasp when he hit the ground, the flashlight had remained clenched in his left hand. As he struggled to breathe he managed to switch on the light. Standing over him was B.C. Jones. From where Flowers lay, the assailant looked like a giant hovering over his kill.

Jones let out a savage grunt then bent over and grabbed Flowers by the neck with both hands, then lifted him up as if he were a rag doll. Flowers continued to gasp for air, but now it was because he was being choked to death. He struggled to free himself, but he was no match for Jones' massive strength.

As a wave of blackness began to envelop him he expected at any moment to see his life flash before him. Instead, the thought occurred to him that, after all of his investigative efforts it came down to this. He had studied Jones for almost a month and knew everything there was to know about him, yet this was the first time he had actually seen him in the flesh. It was not a profound thought, and it seemed odd that it would be the last thing on a dying man's mind. But there it was. It was as if he were detached from it all. It was happening to someone else. Now the blackness was all he saw. He could no longer feel the thumbs being pressed into his throat.

Then there was a jolt, followed by a loud gasp. He fell back. He was lying on the ground. Something heavy was on top of him. Slowly he moved from one form of blackness to another. His head slowly began to clear and the only darkness was from the night and the storm.

He suddenly realized that Jones was lying on top of him, totally motionless. Off to his left, within arm's length, was the flashlight. He had dropped it during the struggle, but it was still shining. The batteries must be getting weak, he thought, because it doesn't seem as bright as before. But it's a light from heaven . . . a beautiful thing to see.

With an effort, he managed to slide out from under the hulk that lay on top of him. Once free he picked up the flashlight and shined its beam on Jones' lifeless body. What he saw startled him at first. Then he began to giggle, then the giggle caused him to laugh out loud. He laughed partly out of overwhelming relief from having been given a last second reprieve from certain death. But his giddiness was partly triggered by the sight before him.

Jones lay on his stomach. Protruding from his back was a huge chocolate ice cream cone. Its sharp point was deeply embedded in Jones' spine. The flimsy cotton cord that held the heavy sheet metal sign had finally given way. The wind gust had sent it flying through the air like a guided missile, aimed at the back of B.C. Jones.

Flowers recalled that Wojcik had warned Pinchon about the dangers of the sign breaking through the cord, but Pinchon had used it anyway. In an odd sort of way, Eugene Pinchon, who had no love for Flowers or his race, had actually saved his life.

The thought of Pinchon was like a slap that brought Flowers back to the situation at hand. His giddiness gone, he shined the light toward the store and moved in its direction, fighting the wind and driving rain every step of the way.

Arriving at the side of the building he quickly worked his way to the front. Pinchon was still lying where he had fallen. Flowers searched for signs of life, though he knew from having gazed upon hundreds of corpses that the old man was dead.

He was about to lift the body in an attempt to carry it inside the house when he heard what sounded like a freight train off in the distance. It was loud enough to be heard above the wind. He shined his light to the south, in the direction from which the noise was coming. In the woods on the far side of Menge Avenue he saw trees being lifted up by their roots and sucked into a gray swirling wind. It had the hue of slate, somewhat lighter than its surroundings. The funnel stood out in the darkness as it made its way toward the store.

"My God!" Flowers exclaimed aloud. "What next?"

Leaving Pinchon's body where it lay, he ran to the stairs at the rear of the building. He was not aware of struggling against the wind, for he moved with a power he never knew he had. Arriving at the steps he bounded up them so fast that the wind did not have time to slam him against the rail. He pushed the door open and left it that way. He darted through the darkened house and into the store. Only one foot touched the steps as he descended them.

With the side of his fist he banged on the door to the storeroom and yelled Frieda's name. A second later she opened it. Flowers pushed her farther inside and onto the floor. He then lay on top of her and wedged both of them under a web of plumbing pipes. Then he wrapped one arm around the largest water pipe he could find.

"Sergeant! What . . . ?"

"Tornado! It's coming this way!"

No sooner had he uttered the words than the sounds of the storm were suddenly broken by an explosion as the swirling demon churned into the front of the store like a router bit on soft wood. The walls were turned into splinters of timber that were sucked into the eye of the massive funnel.

Flowers felt as if he were under a railroad trestle with a locomotive passing a few feet above him. He gripped the pipe tighter and covered Frieda's face with his free arm. And like the proverbial soldier in a foxhole, he prayed desperately that God would get them through this.

FORTY-TWO

Monday
August 18, 1969

IT WAS MIDWAY between midnight and dawn when the last of Camille passed over the Mississippi Gulf Coast. It continued inland on a generally northward course through Mississippi and Tennessee. Because it did not have the Gulf waters to feed upon, it rapidly lost power with each mile that it traveled over land, until it was downgraded to a tropical storm. Though its winds were reduced significantly, the storm still contained a massive volume of moisture. In the days that followed Tropical Storm Camille would eventually change her course and move on a deadly heading toward Virginia.

SHORTLY BEFORE DAYBREAK Frank Wojcik backed the county car out of the driveway and onto the gravel road in front of his house. All of the other occupants of the Wojcik household were still asleep. Kathy and Becky had been unable to keep their eyes open past midnight, but the four adults remained awake throughout the storm. By the time the last of the high winds had passed, however, exhaustion caught up with Darla and her parents and they went to bed.

But Frank had not been the least bit sleepy. He still felt badly about leaving Flowers to face B.C. Jones alone. Though he knew that his place was with his family during the hurricane, a feeling of guilt remained with him.

For two hours he paced alone in the darkness of his living room. He tried calling the command post but was not surprised when there was no dial tone. When he could stand it no longer he wrote Darla a note explaining that he had to go check on Garland, then went outside. Before getting into his car, he made a cursory inspection of the exterior of the house and found that it had ridden out the storm fairly well.

Aside from an uprooted oak in the front yard there was no other damage that he was able to discern in the darkness. He was especially relieved to see that the gazebo appeared to be intact. It was Darla's most tangible memento of her brother, and Frank could only imagine her reaction if it had been destroyed.

When he arrived at Landon Road he turned right. It was his intention to retrace the route he had taken the night before. It was the shortest way to Pineville.

But he had gone no more than three-quarters of a mile when he came upon a roadblock. A large pine tree had fallen across the road, and there was no way to get past it. Wojcik turned the car around and headed toward Highway 49. He would just have to take a slightly longer route.

By the time he reached the highway it was fully light. The mostly clear sky gave every indication that it was going to be a nice day. If one could ignore the tons of debris and wreckage left in its wake, it was hard to believe that a hurricane had passed through a few hours earlier.

Before leaving home Wojcik had turned on the sheriff's two-way radio to monitor emergency vehicle traffic, but all that he could pick up was static. He concluded that a transmitter must have been blown over. Now, as he headed south on Highway 49 he turned on the commercial radio in an attempt to pick up news of the storm's aftermath. He rotated the dial until he found a prominent station broadcasting the latest hurricane reports out of New Orleans.

The newscaster sounded tired, as if he had been at the microphone most of the night. In a forlorn monotone he described the devastation along the Gulf Coast. Pass Christian was the hardest hit, he said, and the entire town was all but completely gone. Long Beach was not much better off. The downtown sections of Gulfport and Biloxi also suffered extensive damage. Reports were in that hundreds of homes and businesses along the beachfront on Highway 90 were completely destroyed. The Bay St. Louis Bridge and the Biloxi Bay Bridge were severely damaged and could not be crossed. This meant that the primary east-west routes connecting the Mississippi Gulf Coast with the rest of the world were cut off.

Wojcik was stunned by what he heard. He was expecting the Coast to be hard hit, but the devastation described by the news commentator was shocking. It was much worse than he had imagined it would be. He uttered a prayer of thanks for the protection of his family during the night's ordeal, then he prayed for Garland Flowers and the Pinchons. How had they fared in the storm? Wojcik was suddenly filled with an even greater urge to get to Pineville. He somehow felt responsible for his new friend. Flowers knew nothing about hurricanes and Wojcik felt that he should have been more assertive in warning him of its dangers. But he had lived on the Gulf Coast for more than fifteen years, and even he did not foresee the destructive might of Camille.

Wojcik turned off the newscast and switched the sheriff's radio to a car-to-car frequency. It was filled with the voices of several deputies, all seemingly trying to talk at the same time. That was the chaotic nature of radio traffic during an emergency. As his ears adjusted to the noise he began to identify specific conversations between units.

Picking up the microphone and depressing the transmit button, Frank joined in the chaos. After several attempts he finally received an acknowledgement from a unit less than a mile from his location.

In his brief conversation with the other deputy, which was frequently interrupted by overflow radio traffic, he learned that

Highway 90 was all but impassible. Only emergency vehicles were allowed on the beach route at this time. Though he might eventually get through, it would take at least three hours to drive the eight miles to Pass Christian. It was still unknown what the roads were like from there to Pineville. The 28th Street route was temporarily closed due to fallen trees and other debris blocking the road. There was even a report of a metal utility shed in the middle of the street just east of the cemetery.

"So far as I can see," the other deputy said, "the only way to Pineville is by helicopter."

"You're probably right," Wojcik said. "But how am I going to get a helicopter? I guess I'll just have to take the three-hour trip on Highway 90."

"Maybe not," the other deputy offered. "Dwight Cuevas is on his way out to Gulfport Airfield right now. He's accompanying some bigwig from the office of civil defense, who wants to view the damage first-hand."

There was only a very slight chance that he could hitch a ride with a civil defense worker, but with Cuevas along his chances improved greatly.

"Where are they taking off from?" He asked.

"I believe it's near those old World War Two hangars, across from the Air National Guard barracks. They're going up in one of those big Coast Guard rescue choppers. Should be easy to spot."

"Thanks," Wojcik said, then signed off and hung up the microphone.

The traffic was still light on Highway 49. Several pieces of heavy construction equipment had already removed fallen trees, disabled vehicles and other large items from the highway. Highway 49 was apparently the only major artery in reasonably good shape, and it was imperative that the road department work to keep it clear.

Wojcik was able to make good time. In a matter of minutes he would be at Gulfport Field. As he drove he rehearsed what he would say to Dwight Cuevas. If he could convince the special assistant to the sheriff, Wojcik was confident that Cuevas could easily talk the civil defense representative into taking him along.

He turned onto the road that separated the Air National Guard barracks from the airfield. As the old hangars came into view he was relieved to see that the Coast Guard helicopter had not taken off yet. It was a large craft, capable of carrying several passengers. Two men were standing beside it. One of them was Dwight Cuevas. Wojcik recognized the other as Mr. Robert Hamilton, the civil defense worker who had addressed the law enforcement brass at the briefing in the courthouse on Saturday.

He slowed, then turned and drove through a gate between the two hangars. He parked the car beside one of the old buildings and got out. As he did so Dwight Cuevas looked in his direction. It took a moment, but once he recognized the deputy he smiled and waved. Frank Wojcik also smiled and waved. He now knew for certain that he would get his ride on the helicopter.

THE FIRST RAYS of light were finding their way through the pile of lumber that covered Garland Flowers and Frieda Pinchon. They were two feet under a stack of kindling that had once been the store's back wall. The debris that covered them offered the only protection from the storm, for the tornado had completely destroyed the building. There being no other place of refuge, Flowers had decided to remain where they were until the hurricane passed.

In the silence that followed the storm the two of them lay quietly in the darkness. Flowers had managed to move things around enough that he could lie beside Frieda rather than on top of her.

The better part of an hour passed before Frieda spoke. "My grandpa's dead, isn't he." It was more of a statement than a question.

Flowers' response was slow in coming. He searched for words that would soften the blow, but decided that the best thing to say was the simple truth. "I'm afraid so," was his only reply.

Another long period of silence ensued, broken by an occasional sob. Eventually Flowers detected a change in Frieda's breathing, and he knew that she had fallen asleep.

He lay in the darkness and thought of his wife and daughter. It seemed like ages since he last saw them, and he missed them more than he ever thought possible. He knew now that he would do whatever it took to salvage his marriage.

Frank was right. No job in the world was important enough to come between him and Rochelle. He did not know what the future held for him career-wise, and frankly he did not care. All he wanted now was to tell his wife what was in his heart at this moment.

These were his thoughts as daylight began to appear through the stack of broken boards that covered them. Flowers gently nudged Frieda to awaken her and let her know that it was time for them to start digging out of the rubble.

He worked his knees under his body until he was able to position himself on all fours. He then managed to get his feet under his mid-section and push upward, using the strength in his legs rather than his back. The debris on top of them consisted mostly of broken bits of lumber, and it offered little resistance as Flowers pushed himself upward. Using his hands, he removed loose boards that might otherwise have fallen on top of Frieda.

In less than a minute Flowers was free. Kneeling on top of the lumber pile, he reached down and took Frieda's hand, then lifted her out of the hole that had been their shelter from the storm. They looked about them and were shocked by what they saw. The road and the yard were where they were supposed to be, but the store was gone. In its place was a cement foundation that was partly covered by broken bits of lumber and other pieces of material that had, a few hours earlier, been Frieda's home.

Flowers turned his attention to Frieda and examined her more closely. What he saw saddened him. She was dirty and her clothes were torn and disheveled. Of course he realized that he did not look any better. Fortunately there appeared to be no physical injuries.

But it was the expression of pain and despair on her face that caused him concern. Though Frieda was grown in size and legally grown in age, she now had the appearance of a little girl whose world had been violently snatched from her, as indeed it had. She reminded Flowers of photographs he had seen in various magazines. They were of children in a war-torn country who suddenly become orphaned refugees. The world they had known no longer existed. The vacant look in Frieda's eyes was the same look he saw on the faces of those children in the photographs.

As if in a trance Frieda slowly gazed about her, taking in the surroundings. Flowers could only imagine what was going on in her mind. Suddenly she gave a startled gasp as her gaze fell upon something behind Flowers. When he turned around he saw the body of B.C. Jones. It was lying on the ground where it had fallen. The tornado had apparently moved within a few feet of the body without even disturbing it. He was relieved to see that the ice cream cone sign was no longer protruding from Jones' back. The winds of the hurricane had obviously blown it away sometime during the night.

Flowers then thought of Eugene Pinchon and he quickly looked in the direction where the front of the store had stood. He was relieved to discover that the body was not in sight, at least from this vantage point. Looking upon the remains of her would-be killer was one thing. In fact, as gruesome as it might be, seeing B.C. Jones dead might have a positive effect on her recovery from this traumatic experience. But seeing her grandfather lying dead in a pool of blood would do her no good at all.

Taking Frieda's hand, Flowers led her across the pile of rubble and onto solid ground. He took her to the rear of the building and asked her to stay there while he looked for something to cover Jones' body. He had intentionally escorted her to the opposite side of the building from where her grandfather had been killed. In attending to the covering of one body he would have an opportunity to search for the other.

He was gone no more than ten minutes, during which time he found a sheet of corrugated tin, three feet wide and eight feet long, that he used as a makeshift shroud to place over Jones' body. As he moved about the yard he searched in vain for Eugene Pinchon, but there was no sign of him. As it turned out, Pinchon's body would be discovered two days later by workers from the Mississippi Power Company. They would find it lodged in the branches of a magnolia tree, several hundred yards north of where the tornado first picked it up.

As Flowers walked back to where Frieda was waiting he was at a loss as to what to do now. They had no transportation and no means of communication with the outside world. They were in an isolated part of a village, the residents of which were probably no better off than they were. For reasons known only to its first owner, the store had been constructed in a wooded area on the outskirts of town. Perhaps the builder had been anticipating a population boom that never took place. It was hard to say. The fact was that there were no houses in view, nor were there any other signs of life.

Of one thing he was certain, however. As soon as Frank Wojcik was able, he would do everything in his power to get back to Pineville. It might very well be that the only thing to do would be to wait for him to show up.

Flowers was about to share his thoughts with Frieda when the stillness was suddenly broken by the whirring sounds of rotor blades. He looked up and saw a large white helicopter coming in from the south. It had red and blue markings and the unmistakable insignia of the U.S. Coast Guard.

Flowers ran into the yard and began waving both arms. Then he realized that his efforts were not necessary, for the craft was already descending. It landed in what had been the parking area in front of the store. The blades were still rotating when a side door slid open. He immediately recognized the first person to step out. It was Frank Wojcik. The deputy was followed by Dwight

Cuevas. Flowers grinned and shook his head. Did his new friend have pull or what?

The homicide detective ran to meet them. After shaking hands and exchanging greetings, Flowers briefed Cuevas and Wojcik on the events of the previous night. He then showed them Jones' body and advised them that Pinchon's body was nowhere to be found.

At Flowers' beckoning, Frieda got up from where she had been sitting and moved slowly toward the three men. As she walked past the tin shroud, she gave the remains of B.C. Jones a wide berth, as if he might reach out and grab her if she got too close.

It was quite apparent to all of them that she was deeply traumatized by the violence and destruction of the past several hours. Without saying a word Wojcik removed his coat and placed it around Frieda. She was showing signs of going into shock and she needed warmth. Flowers had seen it coming and would have placed his own coat around her, but it was buried somewhere beneath several feet of rubble at the moment, along with Frieda's entire wardrobe.

Cuevas announced that he would notify the coroner to respond and take charge of the body. But he wasn't sure when the coroner would arrive. At present he was tied up with reports of bodies showing up all over the Gulf Coast. Cuevas was well aware that it was not normal practice to leave a crime scene unattended, but there was nothing normal about any part of this day. After he said as much, the four of them walked to the helicopter and climbed inside. For now, B.C. Jones was just another hurricane statistic.

Garland and Frieda were introduced to Mr. Hamilton, who shook hands with them, then turned toward the cockpit and asked the pilot to take them back to Gulfport Field.

The large craft ascended above the trees and headed south by southeast. As they approached the Gulf, Flowers looked out the window to his right and was stunned by what he saw. What had been the town of Pass Christian was now a gigantic mass of rubble. It was a view of Pinchon's store multiplied a thousand times. Only a few buildings remained to remind others that this was where a proud and beautiful community once stood.

No one spoke as the chopper moved eastward above the beach. The waters beyond the white sand appeared as calm and placid as when Flowers first caught sight of the Gulf three days ago.

Taking in the view to his left, it appeared to Flowers that the structures that were destroyed outnumbered those that remained standing. There was devastation everywhere. Occasionally he saw men and women moving about in the rubble, obviously trying to salvage something from the wreckage; some small memento that had been part of a world that was gone . . . perhaps forever.

As they flew over Long Beach he barely recognized what had been the beautiful white wooden church that Wojcik had pointed out to him on Saturday. The entire front of the building was missing.

Several boats the size of cabin cruisers could be seen on front lawns, where they had been deposited by the storm surge. There was even a tugboat that had come to rest on the north side of the highway. And in the median between the east-west lanes of Highway 90 was a seagoing barge, large enough to block traffic in both directions. Flowers had to take a second look when he saw a small sports car resting in the thick limbs of an oak tree.

As the aircraft flew over Gulfport Harbor the first things that caught Flowers' eye were three large freighters that had run aground. The harbor itself was littered with huge rolls of paper and thousands of tin cans. The paper was the type used by newspaper publishers, each roll weighing as much as a ton. The cans, Flowers would learn later, had been washed out of a nearby cat food plant. They were strewn over several acres.

All along the Coast the devastation continued for as far as the eye could see. Massive broken blocks of concrete, with bars of steel protruding from them like fingers, dotted the shoreline. Stately homes lay on their sides as if some behemoth of incredible strength had picked them up, then carelessly cast them aside. Millions of board feet of lumber covered the landscape in every direction. The trees that remained standing were without foliage, and appeared lifeless. It reminded Flowers of how he imagined a community might look following a nuclear attack.

The damage in Biloxi and Ocean Springs was as extensive as it was in Gulfport.

Two miles past the harbor the helicopter turned north and headed for Gulfport Field. As they approached the landing site Cuevas turned to Wojcik. "What are y'all's plans after we land?"

Wojcik nodded toward Frieda. "I thought we might take Frieda over to the hospital for a check-up."

Robert Hamilton said, "It'd probably be a waste of time." He smiled sympathetically and added, "I don't mean to sound insensitive, but the reality is that all of the hospitals are overwhelmed right now with patients who have serious physical injuries. I know that the young lady has been traumatized, but so have hundreds of other people along the Coast.

"My suggestion would be to take her some place where she can lie down and be kept warm. I imagine a good rest, and perhaps a hot meal, will work wonders for her."

"We'll take her to my house," Wojcik said. "She and Garland both need a good rest."

"Good," Cuevas said. "We expect to have plenty of volunteer workers out there today. So, Frank, I'm ordering you to take the day off. You're needed at home more than anyplace else."

The helicopter landed at the same spot from which it had taken off less than an hour earlier. Wojcik opened the sliding door and he and Flowers stepped out, then they both assisted Frieda to the ground. Cuevas and Hamilton remained inside the craft to resume their aerial surveillance of the hurricane damage. Wojcik waved farewell to the two men before sliding the door closed. By the time Frank, Garland and Frieda arrived at the car the helicopter was already aloft.

With Frank behind the wheel, the car backed out of its parking space. Garland, seated in the front passenger seat, glanced over his shoulder and smiled reassuringly at Frieda. Her eyes were reddened and swollen. She tried to return the smile, but at the moment she was too grief-stricken to exchange pleasantries.

"I know it's hard to believe it now," he said softly, "but the pain will go away. It just takes time." The words sounded hollow, but he could think of nothing else to say.

They were heading north on Highway 49 before the next person spoke. "I know you're anxious to get back home, Garland," Frank said as they approached Landon Road. "But from the looks of things I have an idea that it will be several days before you'll be able to leave here."

Garland let out a sigh and grinned. "Oh, well. I'm sure you'll find ways to keep me busy in the meantime."

"My guess would be that every public safety employee that has a pulse will be working some long hours for the next week or so," Frank said. He paused briefly, then added, "But for now I think we need to take advantage of the time off that Cuevas has given us and get some rest."

"O.K. by me," Garland said. "The way I feel now I could sleep for a week."

EPILOGUE

Friday
August 22, 1969

GARLAND FLOWERS HAD a window seat in coach class on his non-stop Delta flight from New Orleans to Los Angeles. He would be landing at 6:50 P.M. Pacific Daylight Savings Time, and his wife would pick him up at the airport. Her parents had promised to watch Danielle in order that Garland and Rochelle could have the evening to themselves. Of course, the first order of business would be for them to go by his apartment for a fresh change of clothes.

Though he had only been gone for eight days, it seemed more like a month. So much had happened in that short period of time. It was as if he had been snatched from one world and thrown into another, and the experience would forever change a part of him. Depressing the recliner button, he leaned back in his seat, closed his eyes and recalled the events of the past week.

When he first arrived in Gulfport he had a preconceived idea of what it would be like. He was in the heart of redneck country where racism abounded, yet he saw little evidence of it, and none at all among his small circle of acquaintances. In the days following the storm, as he accompanied Frank Wojcik in his law enforcement duties, he saw whites and blacks openly embracing, offering one another comfort in their hour of sorrow.

And there was much sorrow. The beautiful Gulf Coast that he had only briefly gotten to know had suddenly vanished . . . wiped away by the brutal storm surge. A total of sixty-eight square miles had been all but devastated. Hurricane Camille had affected virtually every one of the Coast's 160,000 residents, in one way or another.

Perhaps the most extreme case was that of a middle-aged man who had sought refuge with his large family inside a church in Pass Christian. Constructed in 1849, the old church had withstood eighteen hurricanes, and there was no apparent reason to doubt that it would easily stand up to Camille.

After obtaining permission from the pastor, he moved his wife and children into the church auditorium. Located only a few blocks from the Gulf, the church was in an almost unobstructed path of the storm surge. When the giant waves struck the building it collapsed like a house of cards, and the man's wife, eleven children and three grandchildren perished.

Flowers then thought of Frieda Pinchon. When her grandfather was killed, she, like the man at the church, lost her entire family. Had it not been for Frank and Darla Wojcik, she would have been left destitute. But they offered to take her into their home as a permanent guest, or at least until she could establish herself on her own. The sewing room, the one Garland had slept in, would be converted into a bedroom. Frieda could go through with her plans to attend Perkinston Jr. College. The Wojciks also offered to assist her with the cost of tuition and books, and she could save money by commuting to school.

Frieda was still grief-stricken by the death of her grandfather, but she was slowly coming around. Kathy and Becky did their part to cheer her up, and she seemed to genuinely enjoy their company. By the time the fall semester began she would probably be ready to attend classes. The change, Flowers thought, would do her good.

By Monday evening the phones had been restored at the Wojcik home. A few minutes after supper Flowers received a call from

Dwight Cuevas. He said that he had learned from Deputy Cruthirds that Inspector Winston Pierce had apparently been killed in the hurricane. Cuevas briefly related the old deputy's account of his encounter with Pierce at the Sea Foam Lounge. To the best of his knowledge, everyone who had chosen to ride out the storm from inside the lounge had perished. Pierce had definitely been one of those who had elected to stay. Cuevas assured Flowers that the sheriff would personally be in touch with Flowers' superiors to fill them in on everything that had taken place.

On Tuesday afternoon Flowers and Wojcik drove to Soria City to pay Doreen Brown a visit. They found her at home mopping water from her kitchen floor. The wind had blown part of her roof away and much of the interior of the house had become flooded. She had spent all day Monday trying to salvage her wet clothing and bedding before it became mildewed, and was only now getting around to removing water from the floor. During their short visit they informed her that B.C. Jones had been one of the casualties of the hurricane. Wojcik offered to assist her with the funeral arrangements, as well as any other way he could be of help to her. She thanked him and said that she might very well have to take him up on his offer.

Mrs. Brown took the news with very little display of emotion. She did, however, express relief that her nephew's life had ended by an act of God rather than an act of man. Neither Flowers nor Wojcik saw any need to tell her that B.C. Jones was attempting to commit another murder at the time of his death.

On Wednesday Garland was finally able to get through to Rochelle. She had been beside herself with worry. According to news reports in Los Angeles the entire Mississippi Gulf Coast had been washed away. The photos that were shown on TV of the storm damage seemed to verify the reports of total destruction. Garland assured her that he was fine, but that he would be unable to travel to New Orleans to make his flight home before Friday. He felt elated when she insisted on picking him up at the airport.

On Friday morning Garland, Frank, Darla, Frieda and the two girls crowded into the unmarked sheriff's car and drove to Gulfport Municipal Airport, where Garland would take a commuter flight to New Orleans. From there he would fly Delta to Los Angeles.

It was an emotional send-off. He had touched the lives of each of them, and none of them wanted to see him go. They had also touched Garland's life more than anyone could possibly know. He promised to return soon, and bring Rochelle and Danielle with him. He also extended an invitation to each of them to visit him in Los Angeles. Frank and Darla assured him that they would. Frieda said nothing. She was so filled with emotion that she could not speak without falling apart. She did manage to smile, however, but was unable to hold back the tears.

Garland was suddenly brought back to the present when a voice over the speaker announced that the plane was making its approach to LAX. A rush of excitement came over him as he returned his seat to an upright position and fastened his seatbelt.

Just a few more minutes, he thought. Just a few more minutes.

AUTHOR'S NOTE

A FEW DAYS after making landfall, Camille, now downgraded to tropical storm status, arrived on the East Coast. Though in a weakened state, she still contained enough moisture to drop 27 inches of rain on Nelson County, Virginia in less than eight hours, causing torrential floods. The rainfall was so intense that birds literally drowned while perched on the branches of trees. The death toll in Virginia nearly matched that of Mississippi.

Tropical Storm Camille then moved into the colder waters of the Atlantic, where she soon died. But as Virginians will attest, Camille was a killer almost to the very end.

IN THE 1970's the Saffir-Simpson Scale was developed to measure the intensity of hurricanes. The scale breaks hurricanes down into categories. A Category One is the weakest, with winds of 74 to 95 miles per hour and a storm surge of up to five feet. The scale progresses in intensity up to Category Five, which is the strongest. In order to be a Category Five, the storm must have winds in excess of 155 miles per hour and a storm surge greater than 18 feet.

Throughout the 20th Century there were only two Category Five hurricanes to make landfall on a U.S. coast. The first one hit the Florida Keys in 1935. The second one was Camille in 1969. Even Hurricane Andrew in 1992, by far the costliest natural disaster in U.S. history, never exceeded the level of Category Four.

HURRICANE CAMILLE HAD a lasting impact on the residents of the Gulf Coast. Many of those who were around in 1969 refer to the Coast in terms of *Before Camille* and *After Camille*, for it is certainly a different place now than it was before the killer storm struck.

No sooner had the hurricane passed than aid began pouring in from all over the United States, as well as from other countries. A cleaning and rebuilding effort started immediately. Rescue teams from the National Guard, Keesler Air Force Base, the Coast Guard, as well as from police and fire departments, searched feverishly for survivors. Civilian volunteers aided in the searches, as well as in the grisly task of recovering bodies. Doctors, nurses and medical technicians worked day and night in every hospital emergency room on the Coast to save the lives of those injured in the storm. Seabees from the Navy Base in Gulfport operated bulldozers and other heavy equipment in a massive clean-up effort.

President Richard Nixon declared the Gulf Coast a disaster area. Low-interest federal loans became available, and the rebuilding began in earnest.

Today the Gulf Coast, between Bay St. Louis and Ocean Springs, is one continuous chain of enterprises. Large gambling casinos are now a major attraction along the 26-mile stretch of beaches, and elegant hotels have been erected on property that had once been graced by southern mansions.

The social climate has also changed along the Coast. To the surprise of many outsiders, racial integration was embraced with little or no resistance.

Since the introduction of legalized gambling there have been many newcomers to the area. Those who were residents of the Gulf Coast prior to Camille are rapidly becoming the minority population. Except for an occasional historic landmark, reminders of the Old South are fading with each passing year. Without a doubt, the Mississippi Gulf Coast is rapidly becoming a modern Mecca for tourists, and is often referred to as the American Riviera.

While progress is both inevitable and welcome, I must confess that there is still a part of me that misses the way it was before a violent and destructive lady named Camille paid the Gulf Coast a memorable visit.